Section of the Hemel Hempstead Tithe Map

W0027714

The village of Hemel Hempstead

The natural landscape consists basically of part of the gently-tilted Chiltern Chalk plateau which forms wide flat-topped areas from 400 feet - 500 feet high, crossed by two steep sided valleys whose floors lie at about 300 feet. The Bulbourne valley forms a gap through the Chiltern Hills which now carries the London to Birmingham A.41 road, the old L.M.S. railway and the Grand Union Canal. It separated the territories of the medieval parish of Hemel Hempstead into two major upland blocks. On the south side were the hills of Bovingdon and Flaunden, for the early boundaries stretched over to the floor of the Chess valley, making it the largest parish in the district and unique in west Hertfordshire in the way in which it crossed the watersheds of three valleys. The northern block was subdivided by the Gade river into a west and east section, usually separately named in manorial documents from at least the Tudor period, as Boxhamsteadside and Eastbrookside. These two valleys have been the focus of life in the area since the Romans entered and settled in them. However, there is nothing in the present landscape to indicate the site of their large and wealthy villas at Boxmoor and in Gadebridge Park, but the roads along the north side of the Bulbourne through Chaulden and across Highstreet Green are thought to preserve the lines of Roman routeways. They again naturally formed the entry routes of the Saxon colonists in the sixth century and it is their settlements, lying on gravel terraces above the lowest parts of the valley floors, which formed the nuclei of the present towns and villages. From these earliest permanent sites other small units of habitation, vills, sub-manors or hamlets, hived off in the Middle Ages. It is not known exactly when this colonisation took place, but it seems to have been particularly active in the twelfth and early thirteenth centuries. The colonists occupied the intervening uplands or side valleys, creating islands of habitation in the forests which lay thickly over western Hertfordshire, and many of their settlements are still represented today by hamlets and farms like those of Felden or St. Agnels.

Hemel Hempstead itself first enters the written records in the eighth century when lands in the district of Hamele ('Haemele' is probably a personal name) were granted by Offa, King of Essex, to the Bishop of London in A.D.705. It occupied, as a village, a site in the Gade valley one and a half miles from its confluence with the Bulbourne. At this point a small dry valley entering from the east gave access to St. Albans across the uplands just at the place where the heavy clay-with-flints deposits which cover the Chiltern plateau are narrowest (Fig 1).In human terms this meant that the dense forest which normally clothed the clays would be less impenetrable over this section of the plateau. The track (which may even have been Roman in origin) following this routeway from St. Albans to Berkhamsted, crossed the Gade at a point which was suitable for the construction of a mill, and probably the earliest buildings were aligned along the track on either side of the crossing. Southwards below the village was the very flat floor of the Gade valley, frequently flooded and too marshy mear the junction with the Bulbourne even for use as meadows. The water level was much higher than it is now after so much has been pumped out of the chalk for water supplies, and at times of flood the area now occupied by Marlowes and the Water Gardens must have looked very much as it had done in Bronze Age times when large meres formed a watery expanse across the valley. Their sites are betrayed by the thick layers of peat which come to light whenever foundations are dug. The names Boxmoor and Gadebridge moor (the latter now lost) embody the Old English 'mor' meaning 'marshland'. With more water frontage than any other vill in the area it is strange to find in Domesday Book that Hemel Hempstead is recorded as having only sufficient meadow to feed four plough-teams, while Berkhamsted had enough for eight and Kings Langley enough for five. It may be that 'mor' or watery wastes were more extensive in the Two Waters area than higher up or down the river. There is reference to the valley floor meadows in the thirteenth century, some of them being large ones, sub-divided in ownership. Even as late as 1523, Lynkethorn mead near Bourne End, was held between thirteen men, mostly in half acre pieces. Near Two Waters was Mugglesmead (O.E. mycel = big) which between 1200 and 1229 was given to Missenden Abbey with three acres of pasture on its eastern side. Nearby was Apsley mead (O.E. aespe = aspen trees and leah = clearing) which first appears in some Ministers Accounts of 1269, when twelve shillings are entered as receipts to Berkhamsted Honour for sale of herbage there. There are still quite extensive areas of pasture on either side of the canal and railway in the Bulbourne valley but from Moor End to Gadebridge Park the Gade Valley is almost entirely built over and the former Cowlese and other meadows have not been visible since the early nineteenth century.

It has already been mentioned that at the centre of the early village of Hemel Hempstead was a suitable mill site, It seems highly likely that it had been utilised by 1066, for in the Domesday Book four mills (worth 37/4d) are recorded, the highest number possessed by any vill in the district. When the monastery of Ashridge was founded, part of its endowment was land in Hemel Hempstead and the charter of 1289 names five mills there. The sites of them can be identified and some are still occupied by mill buildings, (Fig 2). The five Ashridge mills were Burimelne, Picotesmelne, Duae aquae (Two Waters), Follingmilne and Welpesburnemilne. Thus there were two on the upper Gade, Burymill (near the manor house or 'bury') which was in existence until 1962, and Piccotts mill, where there is still a mill building although it is no longer used as such. At the confluence of

Gade and Bulbourne was Two Waters mill, a mill site well into the twentieth century, and a little below the confluence was the fulling mill, possibly on the site of the later Frogmore End mill. Higher up the Bulbourne at Bourne End was Welpesborne mill, also still a mill site, These two rivers were favourable to mill construction because of the irregularities in the slope of their courses. Levelling along their banks has shown that they each have an upper gentle section near their sources followed by a steep irregular section and then by another very gently graded stretch which is broken again just below their confluence. The Gade, for example, has a smooth gradient from Hudnall to Great Gaddesden, falling from 385 feet to 352 feet in two miles. Between 352 feet and 286 feet, about three miles downstream, there is a very irregular section which has marked steps at 344 feet, 321 feet, and 303 feet. The last two breaks are associated with, and may even be partly a consequence of, their use as mill sites, Noakes Mill and Piccotts Mill. This section ends at Burymill with a relatively sharp drop on to the long flat aggraded stretch which extends to Two Waters at 264 feet. Between the mill at this point and Frogmore End mill at 256 feet is another irregular section, the canal having two locks to cross this short stretch. On the Bulbourne, breaks occur at 300 feet (Bourne End mill), 309 feet (Barmill), 329 feet, 341 feet (Berkhamsted mill) and 352 feet, and then there is a straight section up to 373 feet corresponding with that on the upper Gade. Apparently it was not the increased velocity of the river at these 'knick-points', as the breaks of slope are called, which made them suitable for mill sites, but the steeper gradients below a gentle one assisted in the damming back of the river to give a good head of water above the mill dam. In other words, the mill pool was the essential feature. Even where the buildings have disappeared, widenings in the river betray their sites.

The settlements around Grove mill in Watford, Hunton Bridge, Kings Langley, Apsley, Northchurch and Berkhamsted, as well as those in Hemel Hempstead, are all at similar knickpoints on the river.

The presence of so many mills, only one of which was a fulling mill processing wool for local cloth making, gives some idea of the productivity of the surrounding soils and in the Middle Ages they must have provided a valuable source of income to the monastery of Ashridge. By 1650 some of the mills were double ones. The Parliamentary survey, or valuation, that was made at this date gives interesting descriptions of the buildings standing in the meadows at Two Waters, Frogmore and Piccotts End. The two in the main valley were obviously larger than the latter though the valuation was not lower.

'All those Fullinge Mills under one Roofe with a Tenement in the occupacon of William Hitchcocks commonly called Two Water Fullinge Mill scituate and being in the parish of Hempsted on a comon called Two Waters Moore on the west side of ye way leadeinge from Hempstead to

Two Waters, consistinge of a Hall, two Roomes below stayres with three chambers over ye same with a little Barne and a small Gardine .... The fishinge within both pitts and at ye Head of Ye Mill soe farre as the Timber extendeth with all Banks Pooles Lakes Waters Watercourses .....' Value £20.0.0. p.an.

The 'two water corn mills under one roofe' called Covent mills at Frogmore End consisted of a tenement with 'a Hall, a Parlour and two Butteries belowe stayres and two little Chambers above stayres with a Corne chamber at the northe end of the said Mill, a Barne, a Stable and two small Outhouses with a gardine on the west side of the mill bounded with the river northe and the highwaie south ...£30.0.0. p.an.' There were also two sets of grinding millstones at Piccotts End but the buildings were less substantial consisting of two small rooms downstairs and one above with an 'old stable and woodhouse' and a small orchard. However it was valued at £20.0.0. p.an. It is possible that there was some decay in the actual production of the mills at this time, unless there is some other explanation for the fact that the Commissioners making the 1650 survey, note that the annual rents being paid by the current lessees was only £12, 'but they are worth upon improvement as by the particulars before apperenth over and above the said rent p. annum £64'.

The modern paper mills which are described later in this book are thus the descendants of medieval corn and fulling mills, whilst mills such as Piccotts End and Bourne End must have been grinding corn for nine centuries. The latter is the best preserved, its pool and an early wheel being intact, now incorporated in a Motel.

Thus the earliest inhabited site in the large parish lay either side of a road crossing the Gade in front of the mill, at a point where it was crossed by another track coming down the Gade valley. It was a comparatively restricted site, enclosed between meadows and steep chalk slopes, and while settlers continued to colonise the rest of the parish this central vill remained small until it began to expand into a town in the later sixteenth century. Near the mill was the manor house or 'bury', the 'fortification' consisting, as would be expected on this flat valley floor site, of water courses drawn from the nearby Gade. The large stone Norman church immediately to the north of the 'bury' testifies to the comparative prosperity of this corn growing and milling community.

The population recorded in Domesday Book presents something of an anomaly, being so small in relation to the cultivated area, and this is discussed more fully in a later chapter. It is not easy to estimate the population of the village in the Middle Ages. Hemel Hempstead is missing from the poll tax returns of 1377, and in the thirteenth and early fourteenth century subsidy rolls the returns are not made separately but included in the Liberty of Ashridge with Little Gaddesden and other Ashridge manors. The only return which throws any light on the number of households is that made in the tax roll of 1295 when 92 names appear under 'Hemelhamstede' and 74 under 'Bouendon'. The Bovingdon total appears, from the surnames which occur, to contain the Flaunden inhabitants also. This does not give an absolute figure of population as not everyone possessed sufficient land or goods to be taxable, and evasions of payment might exclude others. However, it does seem certain that at least ninety-two families were living in Hemel Hempstead at that time, though not all in the central village, as there were by this time several hamlets. If the Bovingdon figure is included it appears as one of the largest communities in this part of Hertfordshire. The following table will allow comparisons to be drawn:-

Vill	*No. of names*	*Tax Paid* £	*s*	*d*
Hemel Hempstead	92(?) roll damaged	15	14	1½
Bovingdon	74	15	14	1
Berkhamsted	109	13	8	0½
Halymot of Berkhamsted	43	14	6	7½
St. Albans	163	36	7	1
Tring	93	20	7	0
Watford	71	14	12	3
Flamstead	76	20	5	8¼
Abbots Langley	65	11	0	1½
Kings Langley	37	6	10	1¼
Great Gaddesdon	55	9	7	2

This hierarchy in size is little different from that indicated in the Domesday Book and judging from other medieval and Elizabethan Subsidy Rolls, as well as sources for seventeenth century population numbers it remained much the same for the next five hundred years. In fact the order was little different until the rapid economic changes of the early nineteenth century changed the agricultural basis of the original hierarchy.

In 1539 the monastery of Ashridge was dissolved and its lands, including the manor of Hemel Hempstead, were scattered under new ownerships. A new form of over-lordship had to be found for Hemel Hempstead, now held by the crown. It was not thought that the 'urban' functions of the community were sufficiently well developed to warrant a full borough charter with mayor and corporation, though recognition of its more than village size appears in the grant of a market charter with a bailiff to oversee the market courts.

Some indication of the increasing wealth and multiplying functions of the inhabitants is shown in the 1542 Lay Subsidy. Here the distribution of wealth, as indicated by the assessments made on lands and goods, shows a larger number of people that can be classified as belonging to the craftsmen and lower middle class groups than to the labouring population. Nevertheless it appears to be smaller than many other country towns of the same period, with few really wealthy men. There were only six paying £20 or over in 1542, and some of these were farmers in Bovingdon and Flaunden. In 1523 a survey of the manorial rents was taken and some direct indication that the village was expanding by building north of the church can be seen in the two or three references to tenements newly built in Chirchfield. Altogether there were ten tenements in Chirchend, and another cluster in Burymillend - the two 'ends' of the then built up area. The new market led to further building in Chirchend and by the seventeenth century what is now known as the old High Street with its Inns and timbered buildings had come into being as the urban focus. The development of the town from this date is dealt with more fully in the relevant chapters.

The Rural Landscape

From the valley floor with its village, mill hamlets, meadows and marshlands, chalk slopes rose quite steeply towards the flat clay or gravel-covered summits of the plateau. Along the margin between these two rock types where the arable lands or shrubby commons gave way to more closely wooded lands on the heavy or arid soils, was a zone of hamlet and farmstead settlement which can be traced back into thirteenth century documents, the earliest ones still existing. Owing to geological factors there is a variety of soils in this marginal zone, and this, plus the fertility of some of the clays and ease of access up the streamless valleys which cut the edges of the main valleys, seems to have determined their sites. Fig. 1 shows the position of these settlements with the dates of their earliest traceable entry into written records. It is obvious that the large area of woodland which covered the west Chiltern plateau in Domesday times was no longer inhibiting occupation by the mid-thirteenth century, for the position of the farmsteads shows that cultivation extended by then to the outer limits of the vill territories. Many of the farms which were founded at this time have been engulfed by the New Town development but a few remain on the outer edges such as Eastbrookhay, St. Agnels, Woodhall and Boxted. 'Eastbroc' was one of the earliest submanors and lay with its hamlet of tenants on a clay-covered spur between two chalk valleys in the far north-eastern corner of the parish excluded by the present boundary. In 1204 thirty acres of assarted land (land newly cleared from wood) in the 'wood of Eastbroc' was granted to the convent of St. Mary de Prē. Woodhall can be traced back even further. It formed part of a grant to St. Giles Priory in 1198 of woods, lands and pastures, and the rent of three villeins living next to the wood.

The map of settlement in the early middle ages shows that then, as today, habitations were more numerous and closely-packed on the more diversified soils and more broken uplands on either side of the Gade valley than on the Bovingdon-Flaunden side. (Figs. 1 and 2). Over the latter area the heavy clay-with-flints deposits are much more widespread and less cut up by dry-floored valleys. Also the light soils of the Pebble gravels and Reading Beds are not present on this side except across the site of Flaunden These geological factors are reflected in the relatively later clearing of the forest. The thirteenth century documents all point to the wooded nature of the area around Bovingdon. When the manor of Hemel Hempstead was part of the Honour of Berkhamsted a 'Forester of Bovingdon' was one of the manorial officers, and in the Honour Accounts for 1269 and 1272 the following entries were made:-

Fig I. Early medieval settlement in relation to geology.

Fig 2. Early medieval settlement in relation to relief.

1269	(1)	A new rent of 21s. for 42 acres of assart in Bovingdon this year.
	(2)	Entry fine of £33.16.8d. for 10½ acres of assart in Bovingdon rates at ½ a mark an acre. £85.3.10d. for sale of wood from this assart.
1272	(1)	Sale of Herbage in the wood of Bovingdon 11s. 6d.
	(2)	Sale of crop and lop in the wood of Bovingdon £5.2.6d.
	(3)	Wood remaining to be sold in the wood of Bovingdon £26.0.12d.
	(4)	Wages for the Forester of Bovingdon.

Even in Bovingdon there are few extensive woods today and soon after the thirteenth century clearings, woodland seems to have been restricted to small copses to supply timber for fuel, building and fencing, or to those slopes too steep for agriculture. This is also true of the Hemel Hempstead side. Howgrove, for example, is still there, lying on the steep north-facing slope of a narrow valley near Piccotts End, and was part of the ancient manorial demesne. The suffix 'grove' is a very common one and occurs many times in the 1523 survey; they were small pieces of woodland, two or three acres, attached to some of the oldest tenements and often bearing the name of the medieval holder. This is common elsewhere in the Chilterns.

Bovingdon village today is in two units, one group of houses near the church and manor house (now called Bury Farm) at the head of a long chalk valley, and another group around a triangular green or common pasture half a mile to the south in the heart of the former forest. There are timber-framed sixteenth and seventeenth century buildings in this group too but no ancient farm names remain amongst them to enable them to be traced back beyond a date which their architecture suggests, and it is likely that it is later than the first group. Outside these two nuclei are several isolated farms with medieval foundations and these are shown on the settlement map.

Flaunden remains an enigma. Its links with the manor of Hemel Hempstead are discussed in the chapter on the medieval period, but too few records remain to help explain the mystery of its apparent change of site. There is little today to indicate that it may once have stood on the floor of the Chess valley near the thirteenth century church, of which nothing now remains except an overgrown heap of rubble. The removal, if such did take place, to a higher site on a patch of Pebble Gravels on the margin of chalk and clay soils, must have been an early one, certainly before 1523. The fields just to the west of the present site were called 'Flamredyng' or 'Flaundens Clearing' in 1523, which may be significant.

Felden and Boxhamsted seem to have been the only other settlements of hamlet size in medieval times. Felden is still of that stature, but Boxhamsted has shrunk to a single farmhouse - Boxted. Feldende, as it was called in 1200, lies on a typical marginal site on the clays at the head of a dry valley whose course is followed by Featherbed Lane. Thomas, son of Everard Pudifat of Bovingdon granted some small pieces of land there to Missenden Abbey between 1200 and 1229. The name 'Feldende' possibly derives from 'the end of the fields', that is, when the hamlet was established in a forest clearing it lay above the already cultivated chalk slopes along the south side of the Bulbourne valley. Fields End Farm occupies a similar site on the north side of the same valley. Boxhamsted, as has been said, seems once to have been a larger hamlet and was in existence at least by 1250, for it is recorded at this date in the Missenden Cartulary. It lies on light gravelly soils at the heads of three chalk-floored valleys which dissect the uplands of the Gade. In 1310 it received separate mention in a charter to Ashridge granting freedom of warren in Hemel Hempstead and Bovingdon among other places.

The other units of settlement in existence by 1350 are too numerous to receive separate mention, but it will be obvious from the map that the majority of hamlets and farms lying outside the town today represent the clearings made by medieval peasants. It seems likely that by 1350, on the north side of the Gade-Bulbourne valley at least, little of the original woodland remained except on the most intractable clays or the steepest chalk slopes and the district was becoming as important for grain growing as was eastern Hertfordshire. The clay-with-flints soils, after liming with chalk, were ideal for wheat and barley. The chalk digging which took place has left its mark on the present landscape in the form of deeply wooded hollows called 'dells', some of which are very early ones though many more have disappeared. The suffix 'dell' is ubiquitous in sixteenth and seventeenth century field names and scores of them are shown on the earliest Ordnance Survey maps, pitting the chalk valley slopes. A fascinating insight into this practice is given by Peter Kalm, a Swedish naturalist who visited England in 1748 and spent much of his time at Little Gaddesden with his friend, a renowned 'agricultural improver'. He said in his journal, 'chalk is seen in many places between St. Albans and Hempstead, spread out on a field as a manure. The arable pieces were nearly as white as chalk with it, since it was in some places laid on in tolerable abundance. They intended now at the first opportunity to plough it down. The soil on which it was laid was the frequently mentioned coarse reddish-yellow sand mingled with a reddish clay and fragments of flint. Near to Hempstead we saw an entire Hill which consisted only of chalk'.

As London grew in size, its population increasing three-fold between 1534 and 1696, its demand for food sent corn merchants even further into the Home Counties and South Midlands, and the prosperity of Hemel

Hempstead increased. It was in this period that its status improved, its market was founded, and the inventories of farmers' goods show increasing wealth, and there are more and more documentary references to London.

It was in this period of growth that extensive rebuilding of the medieval tenements took place and new farms were added to the earlier network as enclosure of the open fields by agreement proceeded apace (Fig. 3). Until recently many of these farm buildings were still standing, for example, Warners End Farm, and there are still some left outside the built-up area of the New Town. The seventeenth century Court Rolls are full of descriptions of the property of typical yeomen's farms of about 100-150 acres. The following description of Lovetts End is typical of many of them; it contained 'a hall, chamber next to the well house, milk house wheate barne, chicken house, long hogges stye, pease barne, thrashynge place, well kitchen with a place to washe brewe and bake and an orchard called Woodiche garden under the Hall Window'. The fabric of this and other similar buildings owes much to local geology. Timber-frame building is of course typical of south-eastern England as a whole, but in eastern Hertfordshire and Essex the infilling material within the framework is plaster-covered wattle. In the Hemel Hempstead area however, red sandy bricks or 'brick-nogging' is the common infill, producing a distinctive style of local architecture which can be seen at its most characteristic today in the cottages at Water End.

Instead of thatch, small square tiles are usually used for roofing. The abundance of brick, which was normally a very expensive form of building at this early date, is due to the presence of 'brickearths', a fine-grained silty sediment in the local exposures of Reading Beds. (Fig. 1). The scars of the former brickpits and the street names Tilekiln and Brickmakers Lane are all that remain of an important local industry which lasted until the early years of the twentieth century.

The water supply for these outlying farmsteads presented little difficulty. Where the pebble gravels formed the upper layers or where the clay-with-flints is more sandy, shallow wells were the chief source of water, as they were in the town itself. On the heaviest clays, as elsewhere in the Chilterns and drift-covered chalk hills of East Anglia, the farmsteads depended (for both their household and farm stock needs) on ponds dug into and lined with the water-retentive clays and this remained the case until the modern piped supplies. Many of these ponds can still be seen today although since their disuse some have dried out and their former presence is now indicated by an overgrown hollow by the roadside. At Bovingdon and next to Shantocks were much larger ponds for common use. An isolated pond or hollow is always likely to identify the site of a medieval or Tudor farmhouse nearby. This has been found to be the case in North West Essex, and further evidence shows it to be so in the Hemel Hempstead area. For example, it was suspected from the written records that the hamlet of

Fields End was once larger than it was at the beginning of this century. There are several small hollows and a pond in the immediate vicinity, and the Tithe Map of 1843 shows ponds on these sites as well as buildings which have since disappeared. Cox Pond at Highstreet Green has a similar origin in the water supply for a farmhouse which no longer exists.

A further element in the present day rural landscape dates back in some cases to the middle ages and is directly related to the increasing importance of arable agriculture. The lanes in the clay area of the parish are frequently bounded by wide 'greens'. Some of these are today quite obvious as broad grass verges, but others are partially over-grown so that the lane appears to be bounded by copses, and others are disguised between double hedging. They are very obvious of course, at High Street Green, but many minor lanes such as 'Green Lane' behind Leverstock Green also possess them. They once played an important part in the agrarian economy as wayside pastures or patches of green pasture in an area of predominantly arable land, where grazing over the fallows and stubble would need to be supplemented at certain times of the year. That they were already developing and of importance in the fourteenth century is obvious from the recorded dispute in 1380 between the Abbot of St. Albans and the Rector of Ashridge over rights to pasture their animals 'under' the hedges along the Redbourne road which ran along the boundary between their respective territories. It was finally settled that the boundary between the Abbot's manor of Redbourne and the Rector's manor of Hemel Hempstead lay down the middle of the road from 'La Portdelle westwards towards a stone cross in a corner there and thence northwards to Le Chalkdelle and thence to Holtsmere' and that the Abbot and the Rector were to have rights of pasture for themselves and their tenants on their own halves of the roads and paths. These hedge greens are still there.

It is significant also that as the prosperity of the corn market grew in the late sixteenth and early seventeenth centuries, there was an added incentive to enclosure and towards change in the age old field systems. Although there is little remaining in the present landscape, except perhaps the large size of some of the fields, of the field pattern which emerged from the agrarian economy of the middle ages some discussion of them is worthwhile as so little appears to be known about the field systems in the Chilterns. A great many descriptions of field arrangements have been made in the last ten years, adding to and modifying the definitive work of H.L. Gray in the 1930's. It is now fully realised that what was long thought of as a typical medieval system - a nucleated village surrounded by four, three, or two fields in which a single two-crop-and-fallow rotation was practised - is confined to parts of the Midlands and a few other regions. Elsewhere smaller units of cultivation, the furlong for example, are much more common, especially in large parishes which were wooded until at least the twelfth century. This led to a multiplicity of 'field' names and may be one

Fig 3. Additions to the settlement by the mid 17th century

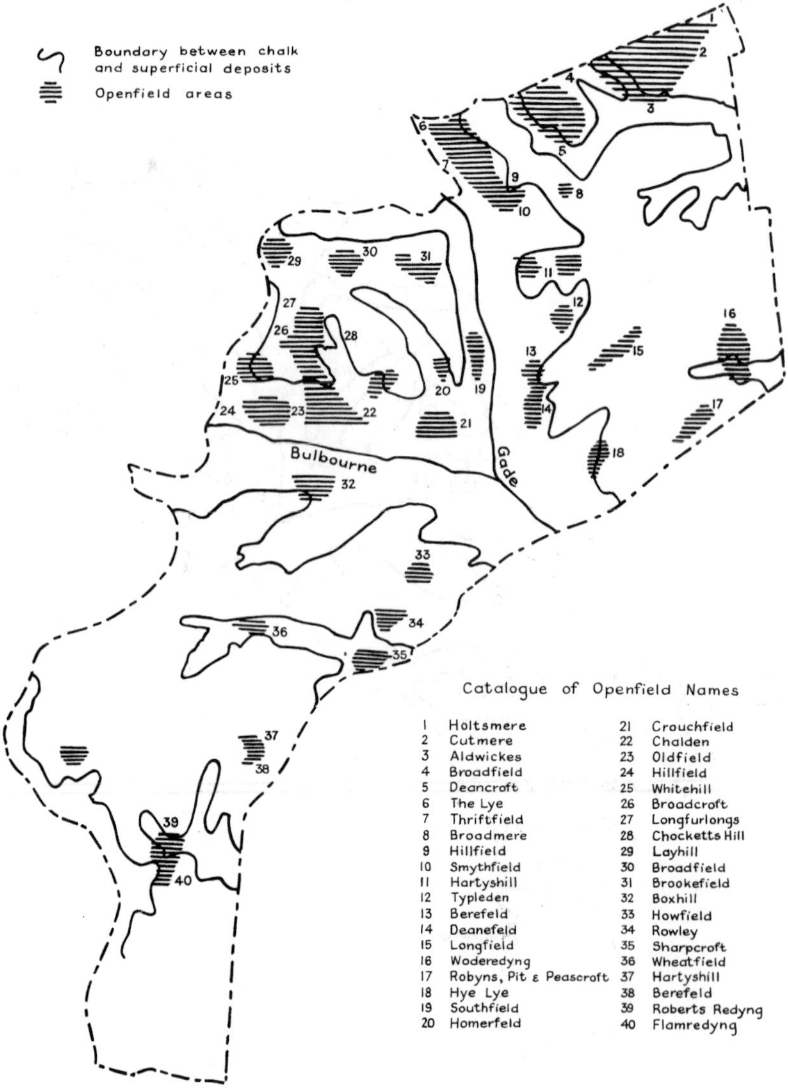

Fig 4. Openfield areas in 1523 in relation to geology.

of the reasons why it has been thought that 'open' or 'common' fields did not exist in some areas. M.S. Beresford's studies of the Glebe Terriers for Buckinghamshire led him to believe that the wooded parishes of the Chilterns probably had no open fields and that the medieval villagers 'were able to maintain themselves by exploiting the resources of a forest economy'. and that later, when clearing took place, it was undertaken more by individuals than communities, and the result was a patchwork of individually owned fields. As far as Hemel Hempstead is concerned this picture needs some modification. Whilst some individual clearing took place, which may be represented by such field names as 'Roberts Redyng' (M.E. ryding = a clearing), community clearing also occurred and resulted in land subdivided into separately owned strips, for instance 'Flamredyng' - Flaunden's (often Flamden in medieval records) clearing. Even Roberts Redyng was subdivided in ownership by 1523. The 1523 survey describes about seven thousand acres of land, of which nearly three thousand appear to be in small unhedged pieces. Many were less than two acres in size and some lay in large unhedged areas of arable land, and others in quite small ones with only three or four other pieces. Some of these subdivided cultivated areas had the suffix 'field' in their names, Deansfield, for example; others 'croft', such as Broadcroft; and many others were without suffixes, such as Le lye or Typleden. Subdivided ownership of the land within these hedged areas appears to have outlasted common rights over them, if they ever existed over all of them, and so, not to confuse further our already complex terminology, one might refer to them as 'open', meaning 'subdivided or land in strips' rather than 'common' fields. The survey itself however uses the words 'in communibus campis' (in the common fields) when referring to small unhedged pieces in contrast to the enclosed or hedged lands. All the terminology associated with an open field system occurs in the medieval charters as well as in the 1523 survey but as the latter is obviously following an earlier survey book (possibly early fourteenth century), it is not clear how much of the earlier terminology was directly taken over by the scribe. More land was enclosed in Hemel Hempstead (nearly 2,000 acres) than in Bovingdon and Flaunden, where it was a little less than a thousand acres. There is not space, unfortunately, to describe in detail the fascinating pattern revealed by the 1523 survey and it must suffice to show the general distribution and a few of the field names on a map. (Fig. 4). It will be seen that there is a fairly close relation between topography and soils and the distribution of open and enclosed lands. The subdivided fields were very largely, but not wholly, along the chalk slopes, the earliest areas of cultivation, and on the least naturally fertile soils in the parish. The field name changed as the slope changed. Other areas lay on the soils derived from the Pebble Gravels, which like the chalk soils would tend to dry out quickly, and which over large parts of the district are uncultivated today (Berkhamsted Common, Ashridge Park). It may well be that in these areas maintenance of common fold rights over the stubble and fallows was almost essential to preserve fertility. Dependence on the manuring by the sheep flocks wandering across the field might at least lower the incentive to enclosure. On the heavier and good corn-growing clays on the uplands, it is possible that in any case common rights would be less firmly fixed, as they, on the whole, represent later intakes from the waste. For the land owners on these higher areas shortage of pasture would in any case not be so acute, as there were the hedge greens and all the incentives would be towards excluding animals from the corn lands. There are many examples of these clay lands, subdivided in the middle ages, being enclosed, or at least remaining in only two or three hands by 1523. By the end of the seventeenth century, when another manorial survey allows a reconstruction of the field pattern to be made, open lands were almost entirely confined to a few chalk slopes. A few of these anomalies persisted into the nineteenth century where they are shown on the 1843 Tithe Map. Two fields subdivided by turf balks, on some of which small hedges grow, can still be seen today - one in Bovingdon and one near Grovehill in Hemel Hempstead.

The nineteenth century Tithe Map, together with those for Bovingdon and Flaunden 1838, because of their scale and completeness give a full picture of the rural landscape at a time of prosperity for Hemel Hempstead. Although, as has been mentioned earlier, industry was developing, the picture is essentially a rural one, a small market town surrounded by acres of rich arable land interrupted only by small settlements clustered around the patches of green common pastures and along broad green ways. The only other grasslands were those of the moors such as Boxmoor, the meadows along Marlowes, the home paddocks of the scattered farmsteads and the parkland of Gadebridge House. At some times of the year other patches of green would indicate the clover and other grasses that provided a rich crop of hay, carried by waggons into London. Almost every farmstead had its orchard, about three acres in size, and amounting to about eighty acres altogether in Bovingdon, where large crops of cherries were also destined for the London market. But elsewhere in the medium to large fields wheat, providing both grain for the corn market and straw for the local plaiting industry, barley for the Hertfordshire maltings and London breweries, and oats, occupied seventy five per cent of the crop acreage. For as Cobbett said in 1822 'the land along here is very fine: a red tenacious flinty loam upon a bed of chalk as a yard or two beneath, which in my opinion, is the very best corn land that we have in England'. This fertility was maintained by chalking, folding by flocks of sheep, and barge-loads of manure brought from London.

There is more grass now, and has been since the general agricultural depression of the late nineteenth century, cattle have replaced sheep as the chief livestock, and barley is more important than wheat, but otherwise

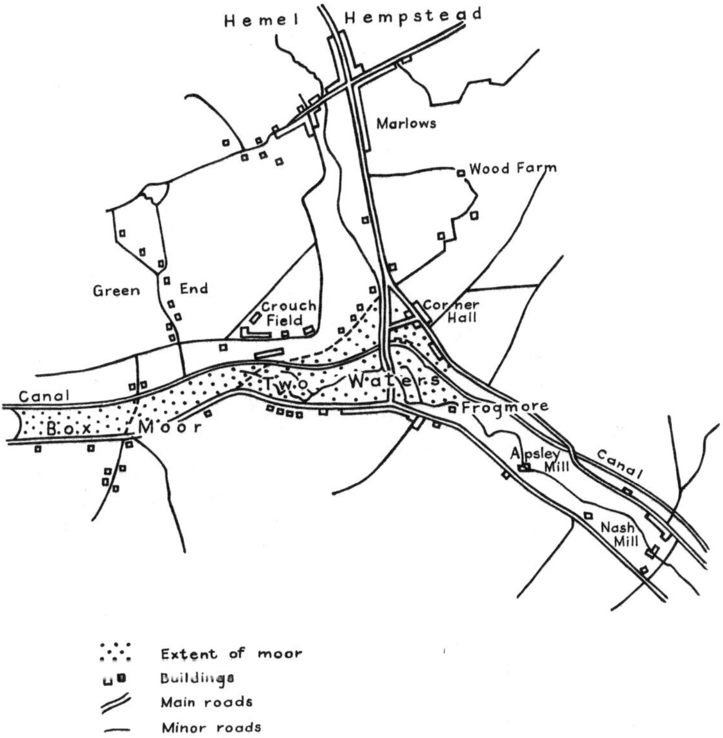
Hemel Hempstead
Marlows
Wood Farm
Green End
Crouch Field
Corner Hall
Two Waters
Canal
Box Moor
Frogmore
Apsley Mill
Canal
Nash Mill
Extent of moor
Buildings
Main roads
Minor roads

Fig 5. 1806-7

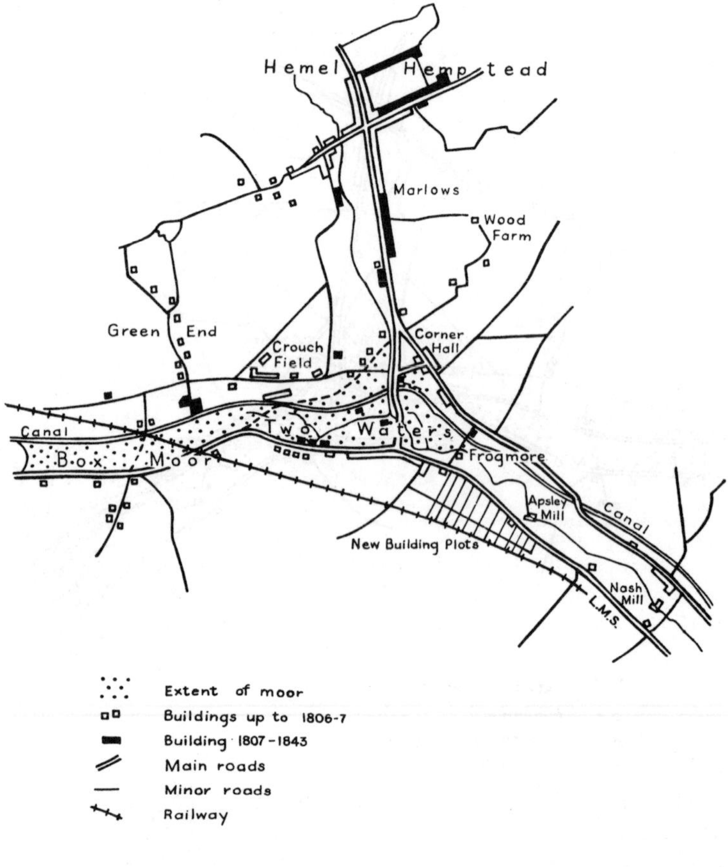

1843 Tithe Map

the aspect of the rural landscape where it has escaped engulfment by the new town estates, as across Bovingdon, is essentially similar to that portrayed above. Some of the medieval farmsteads, Hill Farm for example, were lost during this period of depression, and of course a great many more have disappeared since 1951 but the pattern which developed in the middle ages is still discernible.

Topographically, the eighteenth century appears to have been a period of consolidation rather than expansion. Older timber-framed buildings were refaced or completely replaced by brick structures and one or two new houses were added on the fringes: for example, the beginning of an extension down Marlowes, but in no way was the basic pattern altered. The straw plait industry however was developing rapidly and the phenomenal increase in the population of London in the late eighteenth century with its demands for corn and meat were leading to the industrial and agricultural boom of the early nineteenth century, which together with improvements in communications led to the physical expansion of the old town.

In 1801 there were only eleven parishes in Hertfordshire with over two thousand people. It was still essentially a rural county, until construction of the Grand Union Canal, 1792-1805, the improvement of the Turnpike roads and the early development of railways linking London with the Home Counties, led to the rapid development of the route centres. Along the route of the Grand Junction Canal there was a particularly large increase owing to the developments in the straw plait industry, paper making (Apsley 1804, Nash Mills 1811, Kings Langley 1825), and silk and lace making (Watford and Berkhamsted). In fact by the time of the census of 1841, Hemel Hempstead was even larger than Watford. The topographical expression for this prosperity can be seen in the maps of the period. The earliest to show the extent of building accurately is the initial drawing made in 1801-7 for the Ordnance Survey. As will be seen from the sketch map (Fig. 5) taken from it, this drawing shows the relatively small amount of building in the Boxmoor-Apsley area and the physical separation of the town from Two Waters by the meadows of the Gade valley. The new canal with its wharves is shown, however, and the beginning of the expansion down Marlowes.

By 1841, three years after the London to Birmingham Railway serving Watford, Boxmoor and Tring had come into use, the population of the town had increased from 2,722 in 1801 to almost 6,000, a growth of about 120% compared with the average of 60% for Hertfordshire as a whole. Accessibility had been added to fertile soil and growing local industry, and led to a vigorous expansion, mostly along the line of the main valley in the Boxmoor -Apsley area (Fig. 6). By 1861 another 2,000 had been added to the population and the census report shows that the numbers in the straw plait industry now actually exceeded those in agriculture and the numbers in the paper industry had trebled. A further stimulus to employment was, however the diversification typified by the watercress beds of the Gade valley and the increased acreage of orchards in the Bovingdon-Flaunden area. In the 1871 census a marginal note explicitly states that the increase (by now falling off in rate as a result of the expansion of Watford) had chiefly occurred at Boxmoor and is 'attributed to the proximity of rail and canal'. But by now the straw plait industry was in decline and paper-making was emerging as the main employment outside agriculture. Between 1891 and 1901 the number of employees in this occupation rose by 75%. Meanwhile the completion of the branch railway line to Harpenden in 1877 and the stimulus to the retail trade and minor manufacturing (such as light engineering and brickmaking) caused by increase in population, led to further expansion from the old nucleus of the town, particularly in the Alexandra Road - Marlowes section. Thereafter expansion occurred only on a minor scale until the colossal reorganisation and development following its selection as a New Town.

NOTE ON SOURCES

For evidence on river gradients see an unpublished M.Sc. thesis, University of London, Culling 1953.

For population figures in 1841 see an unpublished Ph.D., University of London, D.J.M. Hoosen 1955.

See also D. Roden, 'Demesne Farming in the Chiltern Hills', Agricultural History Review, Vol 17, part 1, 1969, published since this article was written

CHAPTER 2

Roman Settlements in the Hemel Hempstead Area

The influence of Roman trade and administration was felt strongly by the people of the Gade and Bulbourne valleys, living, as they were, within easy reach of the city of Verulamium and close to Akeman Street which ran through Boxmoor on its way to Corinium (Cirencester). Archaeology in this area has revealed traces of Roman country houses dating from the first to the late fourth century A.D.

These villas were sited in sheltered areas, close to the rivers. The buildings normally faced south to obtain maximum sunlight and were often in naturally beautiful surroundings. Such settlement was made easier as building materials were readily obtainable from the Chiltern Hills, not only timber, which was much used for the earlier houses, but also flint and chalk. Local clay was also available for the manufacture of building and roofing tiles. The first buildings in the Roman style may have been erected by the Belgic farmers of the area who would have been anxious to imitate the living standards of the invaders and who could introduce builders to help in construction, and artisans for interior decoration and the laying of tesselated floors.

Local excavations have shown how building styles developed with the extension of Roman influence and the prosperity of the farms. In the earliest period the buildings were half-timbered and normally comprised a simple range of rooms, perhaps with wing rooms and usually bordered by corridors. Inside and outside the walls were rendered in plaster, the interiors sometimes being decorated with paintings in imitation of marble. A masonry bath house, often with hot, tepid and cold rooms, was sometimes built nearby, its isolation protecting the main house from the risk of fire from the furnaces, and also permitting tenants of the estate to use the baths without entering the villa.

In the second century most timber villas were replaced by houses built of masonry, sometimes retaining the original ground plan. Decorative mosaic floors were sometimes laid in this period and baths were extended to include hot and cold plunges. Now that the main building was of solid construction under-floor heating systems (hypocausts) could be installed so that hot air could circulate below the floors and out through flues set in the walls.

The estates were usually self-supporting farms, often equipped to carry out their own metal-working and other industrial tasks like pottery-making or lime production. They developed to meet changing circumstances and the archaeologist can trace this process in the extensions and changes to the main buildings, the erection of farm outhouses (such as granaries), courtyards and cattle compounds, which took place between the first and fifth centuries as the prosperity and economic circumstances of the occupants altered

Finds at Hemel Hempstead

The first Roman remains discovered in the area in 1837 were two funerary urns from cremation burials, one of which was a globular glass jar. These were found in the churchyard of the small chapel in Box Lane, Boxmoor. With them were grave goods including a terra cotta pot and an iron lampholder.

In 1850 Mr. Byles, who was then the railway clerk at Boxmoor Station, discovered a Roman building and well in his front garden which was situated in the forecourt of the station. His excavation of the well revealed small objects and pottery. In 1851 John Evans, a leading antiquarian, continued the excavation and dug the well to its total depth, finding more pottery, leather fragments including the sole of a sandal, and a coin of the Emperor Nero. Partial excavation of a Roman building was all that was possible, because the structure ran under the exit drive and the railway embankment. Evans' excavation of a building discovered at this time in the grounds of Boxmoor House proved of greater interest. In his report Evans mentions a figurine of Mercury found on the north bank of the River Bulbourne opposite the station, and lists coins found in a field to the north-west of Hemel Hempstead.

No further remains were found until 1962 when, during the construction of the Leighton Buzzard Road, a Roman villa was found in Gadebridge Park, in the same field as the coin hoard mentioned by Evans. This site has now been excavated, as have the remains in the grounds of Boxmoor House (now a school) and the forecourt of the station. More detailed descriptions follow below. In 1966 another Roman building was found at Wood Lane End, Hemel Hempstead, and trial excavations indicate that this may be a mausoleum of second century date with a sunken room.

The Roman Villa at Boxmoor House, Box Lane

When Boxmoor House School was extended in 1966, the opportunity arose to excavate the area once more. The remains proved to be those of a Roman dwelling in which an original timber house had been superseded by a masonry structure in which four periods of rebuilding could be detected.

The timber building comprised a range of five rooms with southern wings at either end and a surrounding corridor. One room had been decorated with wall plaster painted to resemble marble, in this case by the use of mauve paint flecked with white. Other patterning on the walls included red panels bordered with green and white bands which were separated by a band of black colour on which was painted a bird stand.

No articles were found within the remains of the timber villa and thus it

VIEW LOOKING EAST' SHOWING THE PERIOD 5 HYPOCAUST IN ROOM 8.
THE STOKE-HOLE IS IN THE FOREGROUND

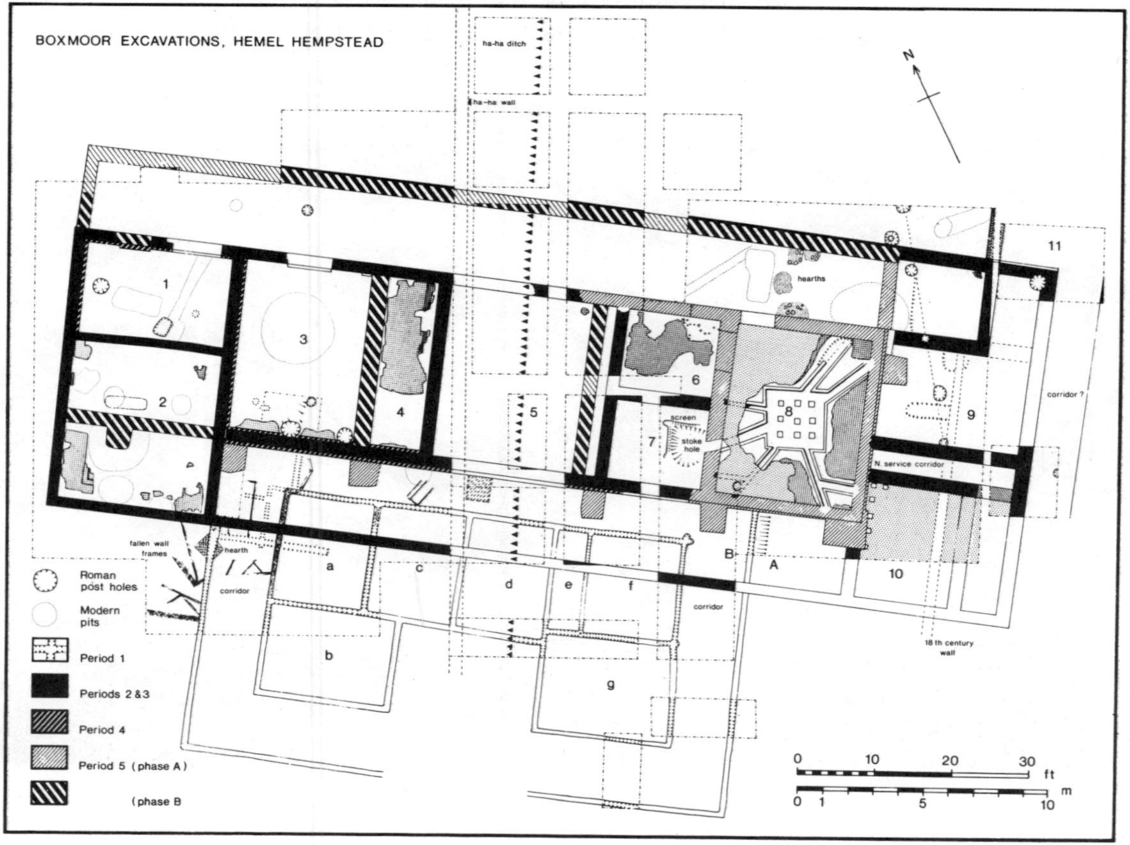

BOXMOOR EXCAVATIONS, HEMEL HEMPSTEAD
N
ha-ha ditch
ha-ha wall
1
2
3
4
5
6
7
8
9
10
11
hearths
screen
stoke hole
C
N. service corridor
corridor ?
B
A
a
b
c
d
e
f
g
corridor
corridor
hearth
fallen wall frames
18 th century wall
Roman post holes
Modern pits
Period 1
Periods 2 & 3
Period 4
Period 5 (phase A)
(phase B
0
10
20
30
ft
m
0
1
5
10

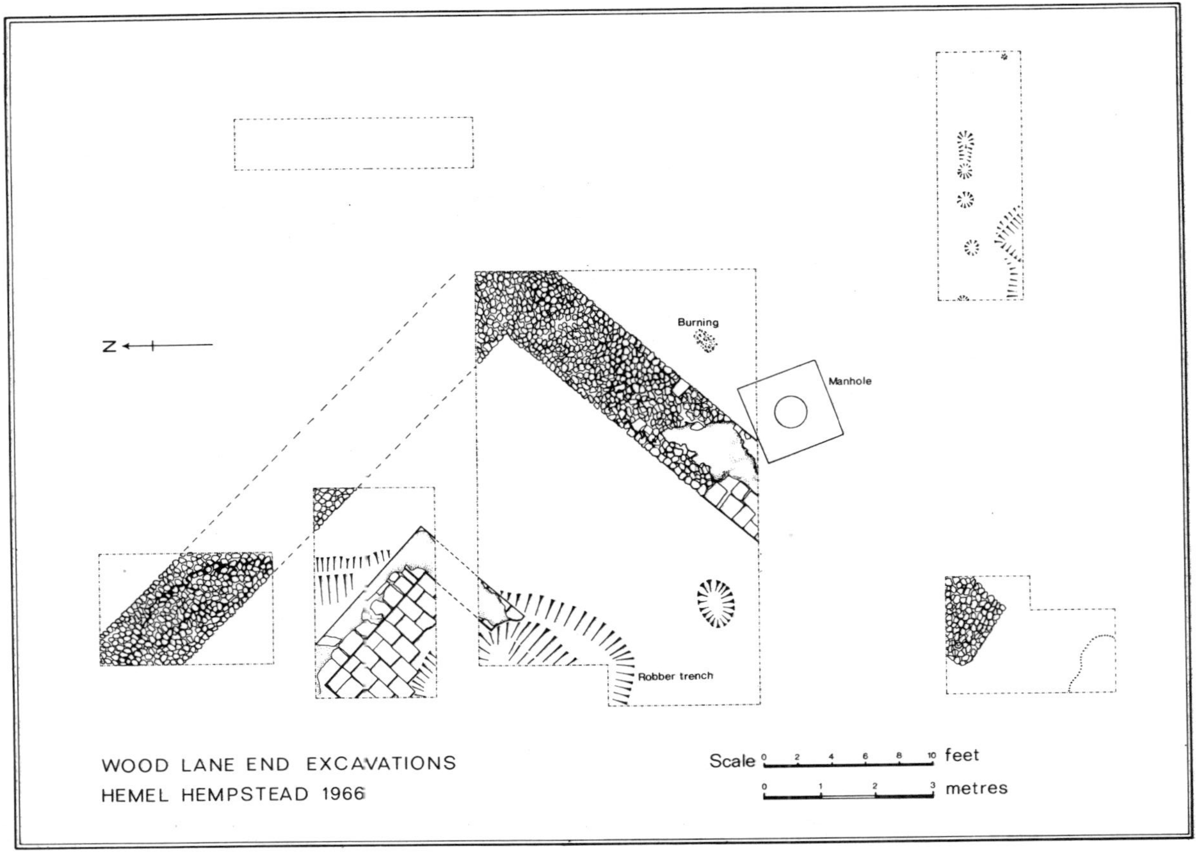

Z
Burning
Manhole
Robber trench
WOOD LANE END EXCAVATIONS
HEMEL HEMPSTEAD 1966
Scale 0 2 4 6 8 10 feet
0 1 2 3 metres

HEMEL HEMPSTEAD STATION 1967

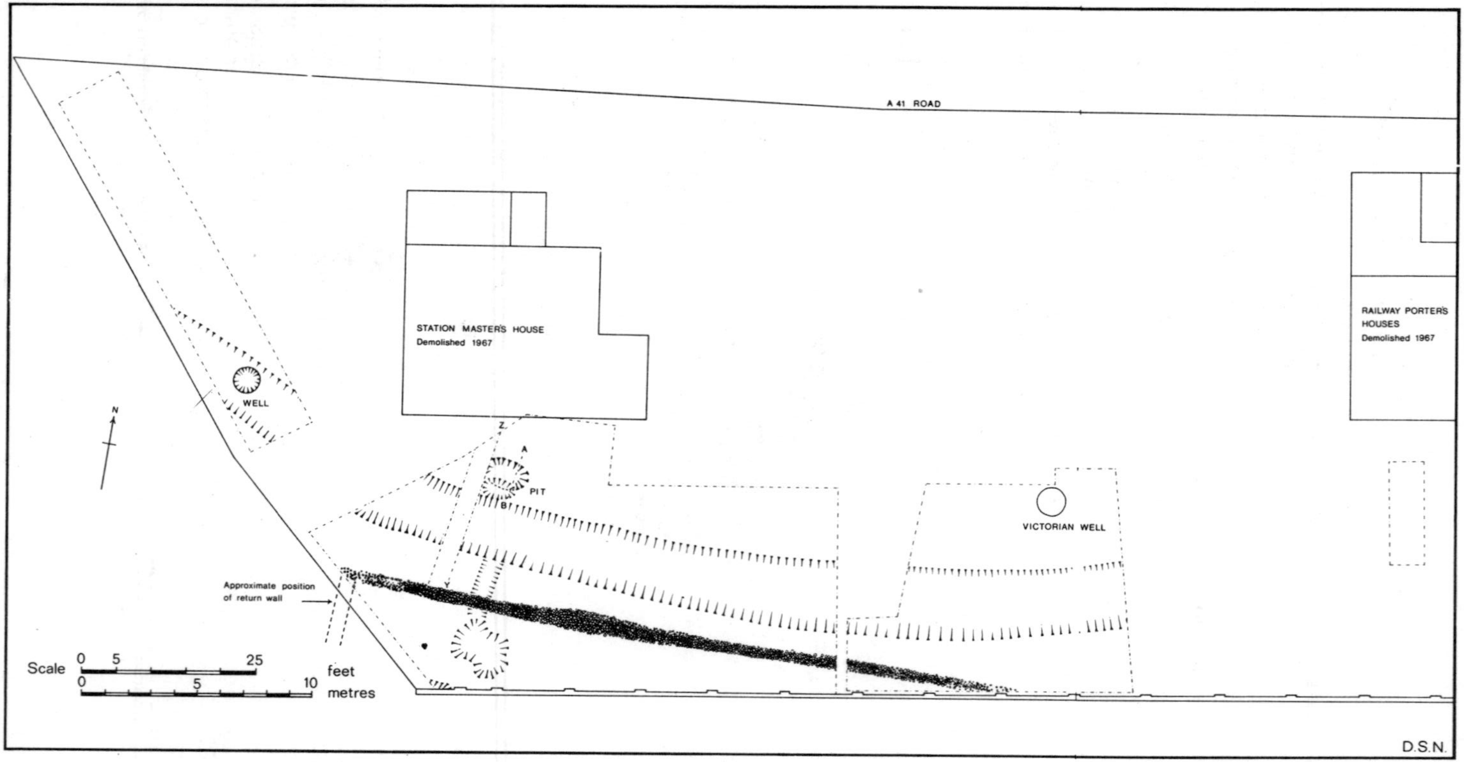

is impossible to date the building exactly. It appears from the collapsed state of the walls and the charring of timber beams that the house may have been emptied and then deliberately destroyed to clear the site. It was replaced by a masonry building with a similar plan and almost the same alignment. In the clay beneath a few second-century potsheds were found.

In the remains of the third house on the same site, probably of mid-second-century date, the room in which Evans had reported the discovery of a mosaic floor was found. The floor must have been lifted at the previous excavation, but the description given in Evans' report survives. The mosaic was nearly 16 feet square made of half-inch tesserae set in reddish cement with a pattern worked in black on white with guilloche patterning in red, black, yellow, white and blue. From this description and the remains of a second mosaic found in another room, the pavements seem to be of mid-second-century date, similar to an example found at Verulamium.

Considerable alterations and reconstructions took place in the third century and later. A hypocaust was put in and coin evidence dates this phase in the early fourth century. It also suggests that the site was inhabited until about 350 A.D.

The Roman Building in the forecourt of the Station

It is possible that this building may have been on the same estate as the Boxmoor House villa and, if so, it was probably associated with the earlier timber building. The 1967 excavation discovered a wall, possibly related to Evans' room, as well as a pit containing an amber glass bowl and quantities of second-century pottery in an adjacent trackway. As no later remains were found it is possible that the site was abandoned.

The Roman Villa in Gadebridge Park

Again a first-century house, probably built of timber and associated with the early simple bath-house nearby, was found to have been replaced by a masonry house a century later when the baths were also remodelled. Flue tiles from the original construction were employed in the drain of the new.

This rebuilt house was made up of a single-storey range of rooms with two southern wings and a surrounding corridor. A basement room also existed as the eastern wing was terraced into the natural slope. This room was variously employed. At one time it was a barn and four large joists were added. These were made from split tree-trunks and appear to have been used to prevent damp from reaching hay or corn stored above, by permitting air to circulate below the floor. Later on attempts were made to overcome the problem of this room becoming flooded by water running down from the courtyard, and a timber drain was laid across the floor. An oven was also installed and the area was divided into the four rooms, the floors of which were scorched by furnaces. Iron slag found there and a tool for cleaning horses' hooves suggest that in the second quarter of the fourth century the area served as a smithy.

The house itself was extended at the end of the second century. New wings were constructed, the south-east range being used as servants' quarters, work rooms and kitchen. The other wing on the south-west was detached from the house and contained a kitchen with three brick ovens, a barn and further servants' accommodation. At one time the barn had an entrance leading to the metalled Roman road which ran outside the villa but this was later closed as the road was subsiding into chalk quarries, and cattle stalls were provided inside the barn, blocking the original entrance. The materials from this wing may have been plundered to help in the fourth-century reconstruction of the main villa.

This later rebuilding seems to be proof of a prosperous period in the estate's history. The wings were extended; the thickness of part of the foundations indicates that the villa may have had upper-storey rooms forming towers at each end, and a gatehouse and porter's lodge gave entry to the inner courtyard of the villa. Hypocausts were installed, the baths were converted and outbuildings erected. In one of the heated rooms the remains of a geometric mosaic decorated with snowflake patterns were found.

In the second quarter of the fourth century the very large bathing pool and massive hypocaust, which are the most remarkable features of this excavation, were built. The hypocaust room, measuring 65 feet by 17 feet needed two stoke-holes to heat it. The bathing pool, 68 feet by 40 feet, only a little smaller than the famous pool at Bath and larger than the public baths at Wroxeter, is bigger than any other pool found on a villa site in Britain. It was fed by water from the River Gade or from a natural spring and a water-lifting device may have been used. In the pool the water was 4 feet 6 inches deep, as was shown by the position of the overflow and by staining on the wall plaster. It was entered by five steps, the lowest of which served as a bench around the interior walls.

Over 160 coins and trinkets, notably rings and coiled bracelets were found in a leat to the north of the pool and it is probable that they were thrown into the water as offerings to a water deity. This bath was far larger than could have been required for the resident family and slaves and it is possible that the estate at this time had become economically dependent on the baths and was not principally a farm. The only comparable baths found are public baths in towns, religious centres or military camps like Caerleon.

It is not known whether the waters in the neighbourhood were regarded as having medicinal properties in Roman times, but they were in the last century as is established by a bill of sale of 1840 which refers to 'Piccotts

VIEW LOOKING WEST OF THE 3rd PERIOD EXTENSIONS TO THE BATH HOUSE

VIEW SOUTH SHOWING MASSIVE PERIOD 6 HYPOCAUST ON WESTERN SIDE OF THE VILLA

end, where there are saline and chalybeate springs, the water of which is said to be similar to that of Cheltenham'.

The prosperity of the villa did not endure, for by about 353 A.D. both baths and villa had been abandoned, only one outbuilding remained in use. The reason for this decline is uncertain but it appears that some farming continued. A cattle compound of timber posts was made at about this time and remained in use until the beginning of the fifth century.

Some other Roman finds have been made in the area, at Moor End Roundabout, Great Gaddesden, Little Gaddesden and King's Langley. Roman tiles can be seen built into the west wall of St. Mary's church. With the growth of Hemel Hempstead other remains may come to light, which will give us a fuller understanding of the pattern of Roman settlement in this area.

NOTE

The full report of the excavations at Gadebridge Park is published under the following heading:-

'Excavations at Gadebridge Park' by David S. Neal,
Society of Antiquaries Research Report No. XXXI.

PERIOD 1 & 2

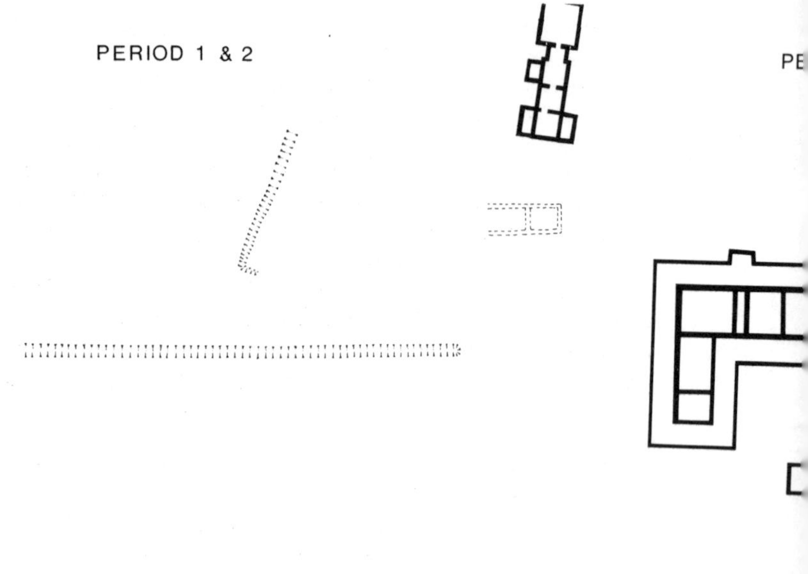

PERIOD 5

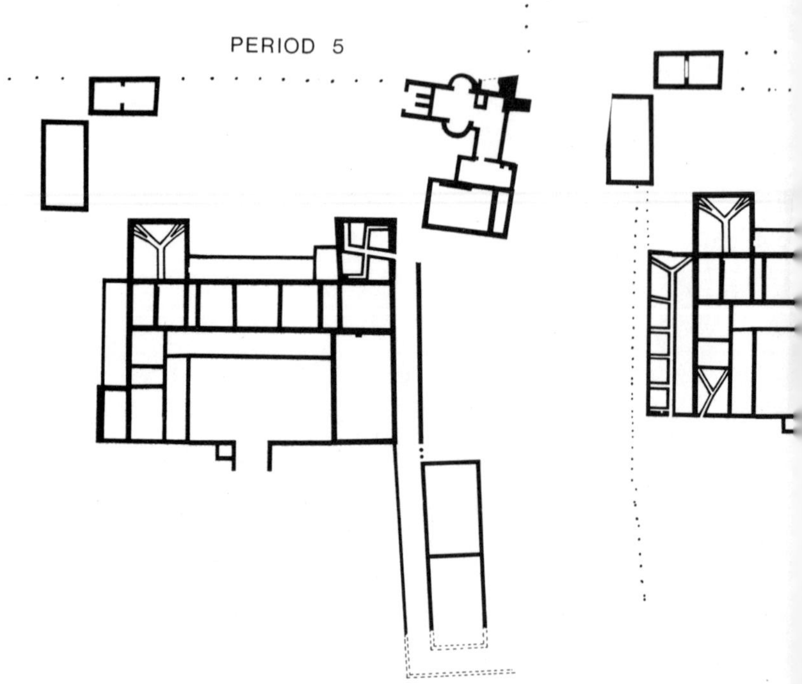

PERIOD 4
6
N
GADEBRIDGE PARK, HEMEL HEMPSTEAD
0 50 100 feet
0 10 20 30 metres

VIEW LOOKING SOUTH WEST SHOWING THE STEPS LEADING INTO THE BATHING POOL.

CHAPTER 3

Medieval Period

From the date at which the villas in the Gade and Bulbourne valleys were deserted, right up to the Norman invasion there is little to indicate the part played by Hemel Hempstead in the story of the Saxon and Danish invasions. There is as yet no evidence of a church earlier than the Norman one and the name of the settlement is perhaps the sole indication of the pre-Norman village. A Saxon charter of around 704-6 A.D. describes the grant of land in the 'regio' called Haemele to Waldar, Bishop of London. The patron making the gift was Offa, King of the East Saxons. This charter refers possibly to Hemel Hempstead, but Edward Miller in his review of the Place-name Society volume for Hertfordshire suggests an Anglian alternative; he prefers a Mercian bishop called Haemele, listed by the annalist Symeon under the year 765 A.D. A personal name seemed more feasible to him than a tribal region. Of course neither of these suggestions may be correct and this remains very much a dark age for Hemel Hempstead. The first glimmer of light comes from the Norman period.

William of Normandy's army, laying waste the countryside as it moved towards London after meeting the Saxon leaders at Berkhamsted, probably penetrated up the Gade valley in search of food and loot and gave the two Saxons who held the village from the Earl Leofwine, Edwin's brother and their men a first taste of the conquest. But it is another twenty years before we hear of Hemel Hempstead's new lord, Robert of Mortain, William's eldest brother. He held it as part of a great lordship in the area and it lay within his Honour of Berkhamsted from which it was his task to police the country round about; at first against local Saxon resistance and then against ambitious barons. At Berkhamsted was the court of the honour, all administration carried out from the castle. The men of Hemel Hempstead probably cursed their new lord and the demands which his military needs made on their husbandry. How well the manor was thriving can in some manner be gathered from the outline account of the place given in Domesday Book:-

'The Earl himself holds Hamelamstede; it answers for 10 hides; there is land for 30 ploughs; three hides are in demesne and there are four ploughs there and two more ploughs could be worked; two Frenchmen with thirteen bordars have twenty ploughs; and four more could be worked; there are eight bondmen; there are four mills worth 37*s.* 4*d.* and two hundred and seventy five eels; there is meadow for four ploughs, pasture for cattle and pannage for 1200 swine. Its value is now £22; when it was taken over it was worth £25 and in the time of King Edward the Confessor it was worth also £25. Two brothers held this manor who were vassals of Earl Lewin (Leofwine).'

This is indeed a very slim account of the manor and there are great interpretative difficulties in rounding it out. On the assumption that the ploughland mentioned represented some 100 to 120 acres, we have a figure of some 3000 to 3600 acres of arable. This however represents the potential whereas the amount actually under the plough in 1086 was only twenty four ploughlands or 2400 to 2880. This probably means that the manor was not being worked as efficiently as it might have been. Compared with its neighbours however Hemel Hempstead possessed a large area of cleared land under the plough. The population figures returned by the commissioners are rather puzzling as the 2 Frenchmen and the 13 bordars (probably cottagers) and their households would have been hard pressed for manpower in working their share of the arable. In neighbouring manors the proportion of men to ploughlands is considerably higher. What seems to be missing is a number of villeins. This is not an isolated example in Hertfordshire and is perhaps due to a scribal error in the compilation of the survey. The eight bondmen have not been included in the above calculation since they were personal slaves of the lord and most likely worked the four demesne ploughs. Two men were needed for ploughing; one led the horse while the other managed the plough. Contrasted with the arable the amount of meadow seems small for the number of plough beasts employed. Hay was probably scarce and the winter diet of the animals was at a later date augmented by oats and mixed corns. The demesne farm had more than sufficient pasture for it is a surplus which is being offered for sale at 2s. The stock of both lord and the tenants also pastured on the wastes and commons in summer and autumn and while it is no longer believed that wholesale slaughter of beasts took place in winter, many animals no doubt suffered this fate and the rest a hungry season. The same woods and scrub which provided food for the cattle also fattened large numbers of swine. The area lying across the Chiltern escarpment was extensively wooded and at Domesday was capable of sustaining big herds. In addition to the 1200 of Hemel Hempstead the nearby villages show similar capacity; Rickmansworth, 1200; Cashio, 1000; Bushey, 1000; Kings Langley, 240; Abbott's Langley, 300; Cheshunt, 1200; Tring, 1000; even the two boroughs of St. Albans and Berkhamsted had 1000 each. Lennard believes that these figures probably represented more than an estimate of the capacity of the woods and were a rough estimate of the swine on the manors.

The four corn mills reflect the productivity of the large area under corn. Apart from Standon which had 5 mills there were only four other manors in the county with an equal number at Domesday.

There is very little to be said about the village in the next two centuries. Only the lovely Norman church gives any idea of the wealth of its lords. The men of Hemel Hempstead lived under the shadow of the castle at Berkhamsted and economically and politically they were affected by its fate. When it was beseiged they suffered; when the lord of the manor mounted his own campaigns they suffered. They were sometimes involved in the fate of kings since the village had many royal lords. Amongst them were Thomas a Becket; Berengaria, Queen of Richard I; Isabella, second wife of King John and his second son Richard, Earl of Cornwall whose son Edmund ended the line of lay tenants and gave part of the village to the church.

Edmund was born at Berkhamsted in 1249 and in 1286 he founded and endowed the monastery or college at Ashridge. Edmund had been in Germany and had brought back with him a holy relic, a golden casket containing some of Christ's blood. Part of it he gave to the monks of Hales Abbey, the rest to his new house of Bonhommes, a minor French order, which had only one other college in England. The date given for the foundation by Dugdale is 1283 and this is also the date of the first charter granting lands and rights to maintain the seven brethren he had installed in the park already existing at Ashridge. His father at his death was said to have held 200 acres of woodland, 3 watermills, 2 fulling mills and rents from his tenants worth £97.3.9½*d.* all in Hemel Hempstead. Edmund's grant probably made this over to the monks together with much other land in neighbouring manors. Edmund's manor did not comprise all the land in the then large parish of Hemel Hempstead, Bovingdon and Flaunden, which was to all intents and purposes co-terminous with the vill. This is clear from the next clause in the charter which granted the homage and services of the holders of three substantial freeholdings given to them by the Earl. His father's mills were then mentioned by name as Picotesmilne, Burimilne, Two Watermilne, Follingmilne and Welpesbournemilne. Next came provision for the shared use of the lord's warren in Hemel Hempstead (which must have been excluded from the grant) giving the monks the right to collect the fines if their tenants are caught by the Earl's bailiffs. Of much greater value to them was the gift of common pasture for all their animals on the Frith or Berkhamsted Common for ever, free of payment. They were also to cut timber from the wood there for their houses and hedges and for the fence around the park at Ashridge.

This was not the end of his generosity towards the newly installed Bonhommes; in 1290 he went to see the King at his royal palace at King's Langley and got from him a licence to grant more extensive lands and rights. These were set down in Edmund's second charter. As well as two burgage tenements in Berkhamsted and a large tract of land in the neighbourhood in Ashridge, he gave all the lands which he held in the vill of Hemel Hempstead. This was probably land withheld in the first grant and now specified as that given him by William Chenduit, William de Bliburgh, John Godsalm and Geoffrey le Somener, together with some lands and tenements which he had wrenched from some freeholders as belonging to his manor. The forest of Bovingdon was now specifically granted to the monks, with the wastes and the assarts which went with it. The advowson of the church which had been purposely excluded from the first charter was now made over to the Rector of the College. Whereas in the first charter common pasture and the right to pasture swine had been reserved to the brethren, it was now extended to all their tenants.

What this meant in terms of the extent, value and position of the lands they owned is impossible to tell. The principal reason for this is that the charter book and central accounts of the Bonhommes are missing, and it is possible to get only intermittent glimpses of the vill and the demesne manor at work in the succeeding years from the few documents which have survived.

Two accounts rendered by the stewards of the Honour of Berkhamsted in 1269 and 1272, together with a description of the Bonhommes' possessions made in 1303 give a rather static view of life in the village and in particular on the demesne farm. A prominent feature of the demesne economy appeared to be the woodland. In 1269 the leasing of assarts, the value of hens and eggs given as rent for the use of the Bovingdon and Eastbrook forests, and wood cut for repairing the Bury mill amounted to about half the value of the total incomings. The return for this particular year, however, appears to have been inflated by the fine for a very large assart of 101½ acres in Bovingdon wood, which shows that the work of forest clearance still continued. However, the woods were considered of sufficient importance to warrant a full-time Forester, whose task it would have been to look after the lord's game, and prevent the theft of the timber and the misuse of pasture. In King John's reign, when it was still a royal manor £7.6.8*d.* was received on the King's account for extra timber sold and there are clear indications that when timber was needed for repairing Berkhamsted castle or the farm buildings within its walls, planks and laths were brought down from Bovingdon.

Despite this apparent stress on the forest, a mixed farming economy prevailed in the village as a whole. The demesne farm still warranted its four full-time ploughmen and there is considerable expenditure on the repair of ploughs, carts, harness and on the shoeing of horses and other plough-beasts. In 1269 the plough-beasts' stable had to be almost completely rebuilt. There was said to be 240 acres of arable on the home farm in 1303 and the grain in the barns was largely wheat or oats. Drage (a mixture of barley and oats) and maslin (a mixture of wheat and rye) were grown to a lesser extent. The oats, the largest crop was used as fodder for the plough-beasts. Some indication of the crops grown by the villeins can be got from the multure claimed by the Lord at his corn mills. This was a certain fraction of the weight of grain or flour ground taken as payment for using the mills. By far the largest proportion was of maslin which was used by the ordinary people in bread-making, followed by almost equal amounts of wheat and malt. Multure in the form of oat flour was also taken. On the home farm some of the grain was kept as seed corn while the rest was used as flour for bread for the reapers at the harvest, and as part of the farm servants' wages, while the malt was made into ale for the harvest time.

The description of the demesne in 1303 lists the services which were due to the lord of the manor in return for land held of him. Although it stated that each of the unfree tenants had to plough 23 acres of demesne land, reap bind and cart 23 acres of oats, thresh 10 quarters of wheat and cart one load of brushwood each year, this probably reflected an earlier period when the work itself was actually performed. By 1303 the full-time servants, a dairy maid, a carter and four ploughmen, helped by an additional ploughman who came for three days when the ploughing burden was at its heaviest got through the major part of the yearly tasks. This use of the 'famuli' was the pattern Levett found on the St. Albans manors combined with the practice of demanding heavy boon-works. These had been performed originally as a favour, but were by this time compulsory and were demanded at the times of the agricultural year when the need for manpower was greatest, i.e., weeding, mowing and harvesting. The lord's reeve could call on 50 men to mow on one day and weed on another. To get in the harvest the lord could command 200 men to attend the Great Boon and 206 to the 'Baggebederep', a reaping boon. Part of the bargain on these occasions, and an indication of their original nature was the provision by the lord of food and drink; the weeders got bread and cheese, while at the harvest feast two sheep were sent from Berkhamsted and ale was provided. As will be seen later most of the villeins had exchanged their labour dues for a money payment and were to a large extent free of servile labour ties. Although the 1303 survey included threshing as a form of work owed to the lord, the earlier accounts show the commoner practice of having it done by wage labour together with the building and thatching of the hayricks outside the lord's great barn. Tasks of a more specialised nature were also done by the wage labour of itinerant craftsmen or local men.

Unfortunately this picture does not disclose anything of the social hierarchy of the village nor anything about the organisation of the farming of the open fields around it. It would be more than a guess to say that the villagers had stock as well as grain. Although the home farm had only 23 pigs in 1269, these would have been only a very small fraction of the number belonging to the rest of the tenants grazing off the acorns and beech mast in the woods. As the lord had his single carthorse and his twelve ploughbeasts so the tenants would possess in aggregate quite large numbers of animals. In addition to the grazing of animals on the wastes there was commoning on the arable in the open fields. In 1286 Ulian Chenduit was declared to have the right to common pasture on his holding of 116 acres in the open fields. The animals fed off the stubble in Hemel Hempstead from November 1st to March 25th after the harvest had been got in. However, Ulian was a freeholder and it is not clear whether all tenants had the same rights. There were still however the common waste pastures. These were named in the late fifteenth century as Castlemead, Bayliemead, Roughdown, Felden Heath, Two Waters Moor and Bovingdon Green. The rights on these pastures were claimed by the Rector as his own in 1499, but the tenants fought him off and some of these areas came later into the hands of the Boxmoor Trust. Although the home farm had no sheep in 1269, almost every villager would have had a few sheep to provide wool for the cloth which was to be made by his wife for their family needs. When the royal collectors of the Ninth on woolfells and lambs came to Hemel Hempstead in 1341, 51 people contributed. The amounts were for the most part small - of the order of two or three pounds (weight), a single fleece. Both the numbers contributing and the amount of wool handed over may not give a fair idea of the pastoral wealth of the village since the villeins complained that there had been an epidemic which had so affected the inhabitants that a thousand acres of arable lay unsown. Undoubtedly this would have affected the attention that they would have been able to give to their animals and losses would have been greater than usual. Although there is no reference to 'murrain' amongst the animals in Hemel Hempstead, both Flamstead and Little Gaddesden claimed that it had struck their flocks and that into the bargain their pastures had been in a poor condition that year. The men of Berkhamsted were in a worse plight, claiming that there were no animals left alive at all. Even discounting the normal reluctance to pay subsidies it is obvious that some calamity had struck both men and beasts. The wool from the local sheep once combed, carded, spun and woven in the cottage had then to be taken as a loose 'web' to the fuller at the mill. In earlier times cloth was fulled, i.e., felted and shrunk to give it greater durability and density, by walking on it in troughs or beating it with clubs, but by the beginning of the thirteenth century the fulling mill was being introduced into England. The lord of the manor probably built the two fulling mills mentioned in 1272 as an investment. The reaction of the villagers was probably similar to that of the men of St. Albans when the Abbot in 1274 forbade them to continue using the older domestic processes and forced them to use his new mill. The Hemel Hempstead fulling mill was situated at Two Waters, a point convenient for all tenants of the parish. There is no trace of profits from the mills in the accounts and this probably means that they were out at lease, a normal practice. The lessees may be represented by Walter Fuller of 1269, Alexander le Foler of 1312 and Ambrose le Fuller of 1314. The fulling mills were still there on a county map in 1676, but a declining cloth industry (as in the Maidstone area) may have resulted in the machinery of the fulling mill being adapted to the manufacture of paper, even earlier than the corn mill mentioned in the chapter on the nineteenth century.

There is no good reason to think that there was any well developed wool trade in Hemel Hempstead; the manufacture of 'coloured clothes' is mentioned at Berkhamsted, but even here there was nothing approaching the scale of trade of the bigger centres. Nevertheless there is a little evidence that there might have been some rivalry between the two places. In 1335. eleven men from Berkhamsted came to the house of John de la March in Bovingdon, smashed up his house, bound him and his mother and took them to Berkhamsted castle where they secretly tortured them to death. On the same day they also went to the house of William Calle in Bovingdon and broke in. Both men were tailors and on each occasion cloth was taken by the assailants. This may be coincidence, but a pointer to some kind of vexed issue in the local cloth trade is the fact that one of the gang was Hugo Stephens le saltere, a cloth worker, a shearman. Perhaps the Bovingdon cloth workers were carrying on their trade outside the guild regulations of Berkhamsted to its disadvantage.

In addition to keeping themselves provided with cloth they could, by keeping a few cattle, maintain themselves in milk, butter and cheese. There is little evidence about the numbers of horses and cattle belonging to the tenants, but it is obvious from the numbers of eggs and hens paid as rent that they needed a fair number, though not all may have possessed as many as Thomas de la Haye of Bovingdon, who lost 13 capons, 20 hens, 2 cocks, 2 ganders and a goose, when thieves broke into his farm. The 'Hens and Eggs' section of the 1269 account reveals the numbers of each paid out as rents:-

> Hens and Eggs. Item, 80 hens as rent and as perquisites of the wood of Bovendon 132 hens; as perquisites of the wood of Est-broc 40 hens; 450 eggs as rent and 200 eggs as the perquisites of the wood of Estbroc.

We can only imagine them as they worked the open fields of the village and carted their produce up and down the sunken lanes in the slopes facing their cottages, but the mills to which they took their grain to be ground loom more substantially. The rule of the manor was that all tenants used the seigneurial mill. The rule was not always observed as 5 men were fined in 1269 for not having their corn ground at the King's mill. The 3 corn mills appear in the minister's accounts, because a certain amount of money was expended each year on repairs to them. The following account was rendered in 1269:-

> Spent in looking after the mills; reckoned for replastering Bury Mill, 15d; for mending the dam at the same mill, 12d; for removing timber and replacing it at the sluice of Pikot Mill, 8d; for repairing the timber at the sluice of Two Waters Mill, 10d; for 'ere' (grease?) bought for Two Waters Mill, 5d, for roofing Two Waters Mill, 10d, for iron for repairing the Bury Mill, 5d,

for sharpening and repairing the picks used in dressing the mill stones, 12d, these with other items make a total of 7s. 10d.

Even when this had been deducted from the value of multure in that year, £6.6.11¼d, a considerable profit was made. When millstones needed to be replaced it entailed considerable outlay: (in 1225, five millstones bought by the Constable of Berkhamsted Castle for the mills of his own vill and that of Hemel Hempstead cost 72s. 6d.). As with the fulling mill it was quite customary for the lord to farm the mill out to someone else; in 1201, a Robert de Wanci was prepared to pay sixty shillings for the farm of one mill in Hemel Hempstead for a quarter part of a year only. A lease of one of the corn mills is recorded in the court rolls for the year 1491. The lessee was to have the mill for 20 years at an annual rent of £4. The terms of the lease stated that the miller was to grind all the Lord's grain free of toll, to be responsible for the repair of the mill dam, to provide at his own expense the cogs, or wooden pegs which fitted in to the driving wheels plus the millstones used in grinding malt. The miller was not even allowed to fish in his own mill dam. In other villages it is common to find the miller in court for either stealing corn or charging excessive toll; the only mention of such an occurrence in the few Hemel Hempstead records is in the court roll for 1491 when two millers were convicted of taking too much in the way of toll. The millers too had their grievances for an ordinance of the court in 1503 forbade the tenants to do their washing on the wooden part of the mill dam, probably because of the damage done by the process. When the College of Ashridge was finally dissolved by Henry VIII the mills were still at farm.

When the Bonhommes took over the demesne farm they probably thought in terms of working the land to provide produce for the consumption of the house and for sale in the local markets of Berkhamsted and St. Albans. Almost immediately they were faced with a problem, which was taxing many other landlords at the same time. The more ambitious men among the villeins were becoming more and more discontented with the system of working for the lord and sought to persuade their masters to allow them to pay in cash for their land instead. The men of Hemel Hempstead seem to have persuaded Richard, Earl of Cornwall to allow them the option of a money payment. This state of affairs caused the Rector to bring Robert de Notteleye before the royal justices in 1286 for refusing to perform his services on the demesne. The Rector claimed that the choice of the mode of payment lay not with the villeins but with the lord. The case was transferred to Westminster where, despite the fact that the outcome is not traceable, the Rector must have won his case, since even after the Peasants' Revolt, during which the local people went to Ashridge to demand a charter, in 1409 justices were sent to enquire into a rumour that the tenants of the house of Ashridge had leagued together to refuse to do their services. In attempting to fight this battle the brothers were swimming against the tide of

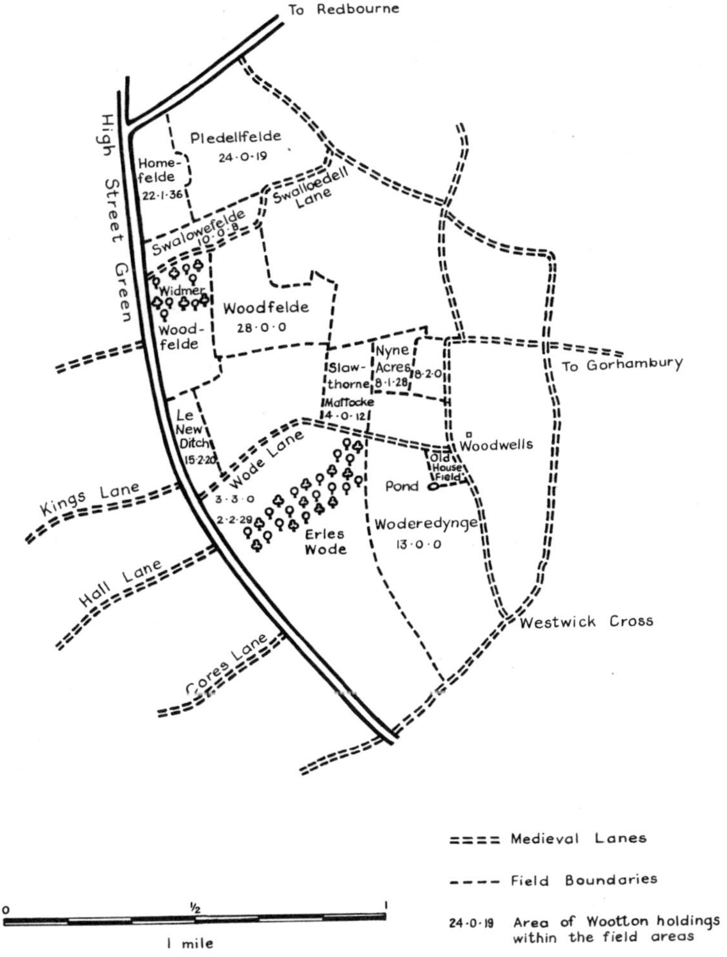

The holdings of Margaret Wootton

BRASS OF ROBERT ALBYN AND HIS WIFE MARGARET, IN ST. MARY'S CHURCH (Photo of an 18th Century engraving)

events, and in common with other religious houses in the early 14th century they were forced to seek permission from the king to lease their demesne because they had not the labour wherewith to work the land. The gains made at the time of the Peasants' Revolt were short-lived, and the shortage of labour produced by the Black Death, so increased the independence of the more substantial villeins that all the lord could do was to fight a rearguard action. The terms of an agreement made in 1418-19 between the lord and his tenants shows the former digging in his heels; if a tenement had a new house built upon it the lord was to have a heriot from the occupiers of both dwellings; no land which owed plough service to the lord was to be divided without first consulting the lord's bailiff; no land was to be granted to a group of men unless the lord had a heriot from them all; no bond land was to be granted to any free man without a licence from the lord and a written statement that the land could never assume free status; no customary land was to change hands outside the three main courts in the year. In each case it seems clear that the tenants were trying to wriggle clear of the restrictions of earlier landholding bonds.

The land market waxed and waned and by 1523 had produced a pattern which it is impossible to account for in detail. It is clear that the older villein holdings of a virgate or a part of a virgate had been for the most part fragmented despite the efforts of the lord to preserve them. However there remain the names of some of the customary holdings, known by the names of their former owners and going back as far at least as the fourteenth century. They are:- Childes, Gouldes, Baldwyns, Poddyfats, Phillips, Lewys, Gawens, Boddes, Whelpleys, Prystes, Springolds, Rantons, Merlers, Netleys, Fordes, Ambroses, Heffes, Bronnes, Catteleys, Newmans, Taylours, Streteleys, Chocketts, Sawceris and Rushemers. Some of these may be as old as the thirteenth century. Although it is in some cases possible to draw up a list of lands formerly held by any one person it is only possible in the case of Margaret Wootton to plot these on a map. This has been done on Fig.11. Added together the lands come to some 150 acres and probably represent the Carucate (theoretically 120 acres) granted to Margaret and her husband Robert Albyn by the Rector in 1335. The lands show an unexpected degree of consolidation, perhaps because they lie in the more recently cleared woodlands where an assart might easily exist as a large undivided close as the one at Bovingdon mentioned in the accounts of 1272. The Albyns were an influential family and Robert was forward in the service of the Crown in the County. There is a brass of both him and his wife in the church of Hemel Hempstead.

The agricultural and social life of the village was complex, comprising an intricate system of strips and furlongs, regulations for pasturing of animals etc. and a complicated tenurial structure. The tenants sought protection both from and against the lord and each other. The lord guarded his seigneurial rights as well as he could in the different manorial courts, which dealt with all kinds of petty offences. More serious offences might be included in the lord's jurisdiction if the king had granted the right to try them; the most common being the right to hold the Assizes of Bread and Ale, which regulated the making and marketing of these staple items of the diet. If the King wished to honour the lord of the manor still further he would grant jurisdiction over crimes normally tried by the royal justices.

Before the manor of Hemel Hempstead passed to the Bonhommes it had belonged to a franchise - an area of special jurisdiction, the Honour of Berkhamsted. What this had meant in practice was that when the royal justices came round the circuit which covered Hertfordshire and Essex, they went first to Hertford where the principal gaol was and then proceeded to the franchises. Berkhamsted was useful to them as an overflow gaol for county offenders from the early thirteenth century onwards. In Berkhamsted they met the Earl of Cornwall's coroner, who declared his lord's right. The king had his own coroner whose job it was to look after the royal judicial interests in the county as a whole, but as a privilege the Earls of Cornwall had been allowed to elect their own. Up at the castle they then tried all cases still remaining within the King's jurisdiction. When Edmund, Earl of Cornwall endowed the Bonhommes he included legal rights enough to create a new franchise, the Liberty of Ashridge. The Rector now elected two of his own coroners and used the royal gaol which was on his own land.

Thus it was that a Hemel Hempstead man might find himself in the local lock-up or the royal gaol depending on the nature of his offence, and although we have not a rich selection of cases before the manorial court, those enrolled in an abstracted form on the two ministers' accounts are fairly representative of the normal business of that institution. Beasts have trespassed into the demesne corn and the woodlands of the lord; in 1269, 26 brewers are fined for offending against the Assize of Ale - this does not mean that there were as many ale-houses, but that at least this many people had a licence to brew, often as a by-trade; a man has encroached on the King's highway; a bond woman pays her merchet for permission to marry; a hedge has been overturned; a local knight has hunted in the King's Warren (Richard was King of Germany); men are not in their tithing groups - units of ten men who were responsible for each other at law; men are fined for non-attendance as suitors at court, a service which went with some tenements. The first mention of this in Hemel Hempstead is of court service attached to a half-virgate of land in Bovingdon around 1200.

As well as service at the manorial court some villagers had to appear at the court of the liberty to present offenders from their vill. Here too they would give their opinion as to the guilt of the accused, but the ultimate responsibility rested with the panel of knights who represented the King. Here cases were more serious; Robert le Archer was convicted of being 'a common associate of thieves and robbers'; Robert Rose had broken into the house of two men; a quarrel in a tavern in the hamlet of Eastbrook had resulted in the death of one of the parties and the flight of the other from the vill without his goods and chattels; there were four murders and the death of one John Nody, drowned in a ditch after falling from his horse. In many of the cases the juries seemed very ready to declare their fellow villagers free of blame and for the most part the justices accepted their findings and sent no-one to the ordeal. One case was however sent to the Hundred court because a point of folk-right had not been observed. By far the most common cases were those concerning freehold land being tried under the older procedures in the earlier Assize Rolls and later under the newer and swifter processes of Edward I. As an example of the kind of case tried; at the same court at which the Rector fought for his right to services from Robert de Notteleye in 1286, John and Agnes Quitseynt claimed that William de Blibery had unlawfully seized Agnes' free tenement in Hemel Hempstead. William did not turn up in court and the jury of local men said that Matilda, Agnes' mother, had given her the land, but that when Agnes and her husband had gone to live in St. Albans they had left the tenement in the custody of the mother. It had been on her death that William had stepped in. Agnes and John were allowed to repossess the property. Many of the cases deal with freehold land in Flaunden and the 1523 Rental reinforces the impression that there was a strong group of freeholders there as does the fact that there is little trace of any copyhold land there in later centuries.

Edward Miller described the estates of the abbey of St. Albans as being outside the orthodox 'Midland' type of manorial structure and saw instead vills with closely dependent hamlets and freemen's holdings inside a none-too-clearly defined manorial structure. Hemel Hempstead accords well with this pattern and had achieved a considerably complex system of manors and freeholdings by about 1300.

Already at the time that the Domesday account was written Hemel Hempstead was divided between two men. What this meant in terms of how the division was made we do not know. Almost equally puzzling is the relationship of the two largest hamlets of Bovingdon and Flaunden to the main centre of settlement. They probably grew up as clearings in the large wooded area lying between the rivers Chess and Bulbourne, but remained in close connection with the main manor; their tenants were still paying suit of court to Hemel Hempstead in 1269. Nevertheless they had their own open fields and they were regulated by the men of the hamlet. Whenever the justices of assize came to Berkhamsted separate jurors came to represent their fellows on trial. Within the vill as a whole we have to imagine an intricate network of feudal tenancies. Any freeholder might be the tenant of several lords; his freeholding might extend outside the vill even. The manor which the monks of St. Albans had at Redbourn had lands in Hemel Hempstead; the Kings Langley manor of Bulystrodes owned land in Bovingdon; Hugo fitz Otto's manor of Latimers stretched across into Flaunden and the manor of Westbrookhay claimed land in Little Gaddesden. When attempting to describe the network of tenancies it is usual to talk of manors and sub-manors to indicate that there were created subordinate but separate holdings usually with a separate court for the tenants. The terms are however used rather slackly and manors are basically collecting points for rent and control of the services due. One manor might well have a full blown organisation with court, reeve and bailiff and its own set of customs, while another might be nothing more than an ad hoc arrangement for working a rather large freeholding with sub-tenants.

TheLittle Benedictine nunnery of St. Giles-in-the-Wood at Flamstead was said to hold 'the manor of Woodhall in Hempsted' when it was dissolved by Henry VIII. The site was somewhere around the present Woodhall Farm and originated in a grant by Agatha, nurse to Eleanor, King John's mother, in 1228. The nuns continued to owe suit to the Rector's court at Hemel Hempstead until the Dissolution.

The site of the present farm of St. Aignels, with the remains of its moat still traceable, probably represents that of the manor of Aignels. The family of this name crop up frequently in the early history of Hemel Hempstead and by 1362 a certain John Aignel is said to have a messuage and garden, 80 acres of arable land in one piece - perhaps an early assart, 52 acres in the open fields and was owed three Autumn boons. Two years later the holding was said to be in 'free socage', a tenure which was not free but had the advantage of money payment in many cases. There is no mention of a manor until 1465. In 1517 it could boast a list of free tenants and copyholders and courts were held in the present farmhouse up to the nineteenth century. Its history is nothing like as clear as that of the manor of the same name in Redbourn.

Another sub-manor which lasted into the nineteenth century with a court and distinct customs was that of Westbrookhay. The de la Hay family is first mentioned as early as 1204, when a William de Haye acted as collector of the King's money in Hemel Hempstead. Robert de Hagh had a hall there in 1238 which was possibly the centre of a manor since the buildings included a chapel. The word manor is first used in connection with the family holdings in 1249-50. It was without doubt situated in Bovingdon and Felden. It is much more difficult to say anything definite about Eastbrookhay on the other side of the parish. In 1442-3 a Richard de la Haye and his wife were granted the manors of Westhay and Estbrokehay. Eastbrook had certainly been a hamlet by the middle of the thirteenth century but there is no trace of a separate manor, and it may be that the sale notice which described the lands put up for sale in the nineteenth century as 'The Reputed manor of Eastbrook' may have been near the truth.

In 1565 the manor of Mareschall in Bovingdon was conveyed to Thomas Penyston and was henceforth known as the manor of Penyston. This same land was described in the 1523 Rental as 'once Bolystrodes and earlier John le Marshall's.' The Marshall family was witnessing charters at the beginning of the thirteenth century in the Bovingdon area. The site of the centre of the holding is perhaps the present farmhouse called Marchants which was called

'Marchaunts alias Marschalls' in a court book of 1676.

Buers or Beavers manor held its last court in 1805 in the half-timbered house known as the Manor Farm which stood at the junction of the London Road and Featherbed Lane, until recently. In 1497 William Bevers died holding a messuage and other demesne lands together with the tenement which had once been Alice Corveyser's. The manor may have been known earlier as Corveyser's since the old name for Featherbed Lane was Corveyser's Lane and the family were holding lands at Two Waters in the late thirteenth century.

In 1523 a large area of land east of Leverstock Green Lane, where the old clay pits and the factories now stand, was called Pleydellfield. Among the lands of the Hospital of St. Mary de Pré in St. Albans, was the 'manor of Playdell in Hemsted.' This nunnery, founded by the Abbot of St. Albans in 1190 was granted 30 acres of assart in Estbroc by King John and 2 acres by Eleanor his mother, and this may have been in Playdellfield. The 'Brothers' of Pré are mentioned in the list of those contributing to the subsidy of 1293 in Hemel Hempstead for this land.

In the 1523 Rental some lands are described as being of the 'Lenvey fee'. They were situated in the main around the church in the older fields and so this fee may have been an early creation. By 1350 a man was claiming that he was bailiff of a manor which belonged to the Lenveyseys in Hemel Hempstead. There is however no further trace of this manor.

Even more ephemeral is the manor of Haybarns or Haybournes which stood somewhere in the Heath Park area. (But see Chapter 10 - 'Boxmoor and its Trust'.)

Apart from this manorial fragmentation there were other considerable freeholders who must have held manors in the vill which have now fallen out of sight. In 1248 Lucas Lovel held a half virgate for the service of a quarter knight's fee. This holding passed to the monks of Ashridge. From the charter of foundation of the monastery this would appear to have been one of the more important grants and his house may have been the present Lockers, since he was referred to as Magister Lucas and in the 16th and 17th century court rolls the name of the house is often spelt 'Lockers' or 'Luckers'. Some men when they wished to endow Ashridge with lands were in a position to make lavish grants: in the fourteenth century one man was party to two such grants involving two messuages, a virgate, 492½ acres of arable, 5 acres of meadow, 10 acres of pasture, 20 acres of wood and rents worth over £1 plus freehold rent of 1 pound of cummin. By means of such grants as these the Rectors of Ashridge gained control of most of the land in the vill. All the land which is recorded in the Rental of 1523 was probably theirs.

The picture of Hemel Hempstead presented by the available sources is one of a village untroubled by national events, but this cannot have been the whole story, for as well as taking part in the peasant rising of 1381, Lollards were to be found at Bovingdon and the frequent sieges laid to nearby Berkhamsted castle must have disturbed the peace of the villagers. The Wars of the Roses were too near at St. Albans to be without effect. Manors, monks and agriculture were not the whole story.

Piccotts End Wall Paintings

In 1953, extensive repairs were undertaken to the cottages in Piccotts End which had housed the original West Hertford Infirmary in 1826 (see p.116). Hidden behind several layers of wall-paper in an upper room the owner, Mr. A.C. Lindley, discovered some late medieval wall paintings of unusual quality. Later investigation revealed that the floor of this upper room was an insertion, and that the wall paintings continued lower down. Two other panels were found in the room below heavily coated with plaster and whitewash.

Structural work on the house showed that the whole row of cottages must once have been one establishment of some importance, a high barnlike structure of wattle and daub on a very heavy oak frame with a steep pitched roof. Inside, the Great Hall was open to the roof, with twin doors at one end, presumably opening into the kitchens, with possibly another hall on the other side of the painted wall. The purpose of the building is not definitely known, but it may well have been a pilgrims' hostel or resting place connected with the College at Ashridge. It stands on an ancient road between Ashridge and St. Albans both of which were centres of pilgrimage.

The paintings consist of five panels in the upper part of the wall and two panels in the lower part. In the centre is Christ in Majesty, blessing with one hand and holding the orb in the other. On the right is the baptism of Christ by St. John, and on the left a pieta, the Virgin holding the dead Christ in front of the cross. In the extreme left-hand panel is St. Peter with the papel tiara, triple cross and keys, and in the extreme right, St. Clement with his symbol of an anchor and the triple cross as Pope. The two lower panels contain figures of St. Catherine with her wheel and sword, and St. Margaret of Antioch emerging from the dragon. (There was a priory of St. Margaret at Ivinghoe.) A curious blank oblong space in the lower wall suggests that there must have been some sort of permanent fitting here, such as an altar.

The costume of the two female saints gives a clue to the date, for they both wear gable head-dresses associated with the early Tudors, and so can be placed in the last quarter of the fifteenth century.

CHAPTER 4

The Sixteenth Century

At the close of the fifteenth century Hemel Hempstead, in the lordship of the Rector of Ashridge, was a large manor supporting an agricultural community whose members held and farmed their land according to recognised rules of long standing, the customs of the manor. These rules, which minutely concerned the day to day running of the estate, were administered by the lord of the manor, through his steward, in the manor courts. The records of these courts, now in the Duchy of Cornwall Office, provide some of the earliest evidence for the history of Hemel Hempstead in the sixteenth century.

The court books and rolls are in fact the records of two separate courts, the court baron and the court leet with view of frankpledge. The court baron was the more frequent of the two. All the customary tenants of Hemel Hempstead owed suit of court 'de tribus in tres', that is the lord could, if he wished, insist on their attendance at the court baron every three weeks. In practice the court was normally held three times a year, once in the week after Michaelmas, once in December or January, and once on the first Tuesday after Trinity Sunday. At these times twelve tenants were sworn in as 'homagers' to act as a jury of presentment, and 'ferrors' or 'affeerers' were appointed to assess the fines. To this court came tenants who wished to make surrenders or exchanges of land and have them witnessed. Those who wished to inherit land came and paid the heriot and the fine for entry and did homage.

Disputes between tenants over boundaries or possession of land were settled there, or if the facts of the case were in doubt a special jury of inquisition was appointed and sworn to discover the truth of the matter before the next court. Sometimes regulations were agreed upon for the use of the common grazing lands. For example in 1531, 'It was ordained by the tenants of the lord by common consent that none of them would put pigs on 'the common mores' unringed from the feast of the Annunciation (March 25th) till the end of St. Michael the Archangel (September 29th) on pain of forfeiting xi*d.* and that none of them would pasture sheep there between those dates on pain of forfeiting the same amount'. Poachers in the waters and warrens of Hemel Hempstead were punished by the court and some cases of encroachment were dealt with, but the most important business of every court baron was the exchange of land.

On the first Tuesday after Trinity the court leet was held before the normal court baron. According to the customs of the manor 'The Lord by his stewards once in the year shall keep his leet with the court baron the Tuesday next after Trinity Sunday, of ould tyme used that season of the year to be kept. To the which leet and court all hedboroughs and other suters shall come and if they make default to be amercied by the same ferors of that same leet and court. And if free suters there come not to the lord's court after they be once amercied then them to be distrained after the course of common law.' In this court twelve capital pledges or heads of tithing, acted as jurors, and all minor offences against the peace of the community were dealt with. Tithings were inspected; breaches of the assizes of bread and ale were punished; those who took excessive profit were fined; those who allowed animals to stray on to the King's Highway were ordered to keep them in check; unscoured ditches had to be cleaned and branches overhanging lanes had to be cut back. Occasionally a case of assault came up, as when 'William Ewer of Felden insulted Henry Howe and drew blood with a stick against the King's peace, xii*d*.' On the whole, however, the offences were minor ones and the powers of the court were not great. The same offenders appeared in court again and again and the only effective punishment was by fines which could be doubled after failure to comply with the orders of the court. Sometimes the career of a persistent troublemaker can be traced through the court records. Nicholas Mason the miller, for example, between 1529 and 1531, was variously fined; for failing to appear in court 2d, for taking unjust toll in his neighbour's flour 20d, for keeping a dog on the King's Highway 12d, for insulting William Paytwin in his own house 8d, for fishing in John Gladman's pond without licence 20d, and for grazing a cow without permission 2d. Finally he was proclaimed a common 'barector (brawler or inciter to lawsuits) et malefactor', fined 12d, and ordered to be of good report in future.

From their absence in the court records, it seems clear that many feudal obligations were obsolete by this date. Although the lord of the manor still had considerable authority as a landlord, he no longer had the control over the private lives of his tenants that some of his predecessors had exercised. Tenants no longer had to pay fines for permission to give their daughters in marriage outside the manor, or to send their sons into the Church. No cases of disputes over labour services occur in the early sixteenth-century court rolls, and all the evidence suggests that by this time all but a very few tenants had managed to substitute money payments for week-work and boon-work. The men of Hemel Hempstead were, in fact, not villeins but free men.

The customs of the manor were not originally written customs and, although both lord and tenants might feel certain that they knew what they were, they did not always remain undisputed. They might be described as 'the immemorial customs of the manor', but they were not, for all that, completely unalterable. Towards the end of the fifteenth century economic changes were experienced which produced landlord-tenant disputes in manors in many parts of the country. Hemel Hempstead was no exception, and the final victory of the tenants in this struggle had far-reaching effects.

In 1499, his last year as Rector of Ashridge, John Witton was at odds with his tenants of Hemel Hempstead. Their grievances found expression in a complaint to the King's Council against the many and great injuries they had sustained at the hands of the Rector to the detriment of the whole lordship. They claimed first that they had rights of pasture in Castelmede (lying next Boxbridge), second that they had free rights of fishing throughout the lordship, and finally that they were entitled to pay a fixed fine for entry into their lands of one third of the annual rent. A committee of the Council, which included Thomas Lovett and Reginald Bray, decided for the tenants on the first two points. They were to have their pasture rights as of old in Castelmede, Bayliemede, Roudowne, Felden heth, and Twowaters More on an annual payment to the Rector of 6*s.* 8*d.* and from the record of the court rolls this payment was regularly made thereafter. They were also to have free rights of fishing without licence from the Rector. But on the third and most important of the points the decision went against the tenants. Fines for entry were not fixed but determinable at the will of the lord.

When this unpopular Rector, John Witton, died he was succeeded by John Berkhamstede, who soon got into trouble with his new tenants for trying to exact £10 from them as a customary gift to the new Rector. When they heard of the proposed tax the inhabitants of Hemel Hempstead 'murmurabant intra se' (grumbled among themselves) and claimed they could not remember ever before having to give a 'recognition' to the new Rector. They appealed to Humfrey Conesby, probably a Justice of the Peace, to arbitrate. He received evidence from the Rector and from a council of ten tenants, but when the tenants saw that their case was not likely to prevail, they made haste to visit the most powerful tenant they could think of, Sir David Phillip, described in the document as 'armiger pro corpore domini regis' (squire of the King's bodyguard). This knight was persuaded by the tenants to come to Ashridge, together with Sir John Verney and Sir Thomas Bryan and a great multitude of tenants, to plead their cause with the Rector. It is not surprising in the circumstances that the Rector immediately agreed to forgive them one half of the money, and then in a further access of goodwill towards David, John and Thomas, forgave them another twenty shillings. One of the most interesting features of this story is that this concession won, it must be suspected, by might rather than right, became thereafter the custom of the manor, and when Thomas Waterhouse, the last Rector of Ashridge, was appointed he received from his tenants not the full £10, but £5.

A third dispute which occurred in 1521 was obviously more serious than either of the others since it resulted in a full record being made of all the customs of the manor. The memorandum concerning this dispute begins as follows: 'Hereafter followeth such orders and directions as were made and awarded by John Broket of Wheathamsted, Esq., in the county of Hertford, John Pure, Thomas Blake, Thomas Stepwith of St. Albans in the county aforesaid gents. arbitrators indifferentlye chosen between John Berkhamstede Rector of the house of Ashridge and the convent of the same place in the same county and their customary tenants of their lordship of Hemel Hempstead in the said county, of and for diverse and manie customs between the said parties late in variance as hereafter it doth appear June 28 12 Henry VIII.' Another version of this award is included in the 1523 Rental and sheds further light on the methods of the arbitrators. They were evidently appointed after a series of hearings 'as well before our sovraigne lord the Kinge his councell as in divers of his courts' had failed to bring about a satisfactory settlement. The four arbitrators therefore decided to 'meete at the courte houlden of the aforesaid maner of Hemelhemsted the Tewsday next after Trynity Sonday in the XII yeere of our said sovraigne lord'. Both parties to the dispute were ordered to meet them there and the final award was made after due consideration of all the 'allegeaunces, titles, answers, replicacions, and rejoynders with such proves as they or any of them could declare or shew either by court copie, customary bookes or other wrytinges or wittnes convenient to be herd'.

A statement of the customs of the manor follows in both versions of the story and contains all the known customs whether they were under dispute or not. First the rules concerning the holding of the manor court are set out. Then a detailed description is given of the rights and duties of copyholders, which incidentally makes it quite clear that all customary tenants came within that category. Surrenders of land had to be made before the correct number of legal witnesses and registered at the next court. A tenant could let his land on a lease of eight or twelve years, and his son could inherit his holding on payment of a relief, a fine and a heriot. This last consisted of the tenant's second best beast or piece of goods, not the best, as was the medieval custom in many manors. Most important of all, the fine levied on all heirs or new entrants to land for taking over an estate was fixed at half the annual quit rent, and was not therefore liable to be increased at the will of the lord. This directly contradicted the award of 1499 and was a most valuable concession to the tenants. It was to ensure in fact that they, rather than the landlord, profited from the steep rise in prices later in the century. It was also of great benefit to the tenants that the arbitrators in this dispute ordered that each tenant should receive a new copy of his tenure. Written title to his land would give the tenant legal protection against an engrossing landlord. The lord was also ordered to make 'a terrier and a Rentall by his counsell on the recognisance of his tenants at this present grant of their copies or at certeyne time after convenyente.' This rental was duly made and what is probably a copy, dating from shortly after 1596, still survives and is a valuable source of information about the organisation of the manor at that time.

The rental is essentially a list of the free and customary tenants of the manor with detailed descriptions of their holdings, giving the approximate acreage of each piece of land and the amount of rent paid for it. The manor is divided into five sub-sections, Estbroke, Boxhamstede, Felden-with-Two Waters, Bovingdon, and Flaunden. In Estbroke there were two free tenants, the heirs of John Spendelowe, who held the sub-manor of Agnells, and the

Prioress of St. Giles, who held the sub-manor of Woodhall. There were no free tenants in Boxhamstede, but in Felden the heirs of Edward de la Hay held the sub-manor of Westbrook Hay and Robert Bevere held the sub-manor of Buers. There were five freeholders in Bovingdon and three in Flaunden. The remaining 134 tenants of the manor were copyholders of varying wealth. The largest single holding was that of Robert Dolt who had 240 acres, but the majority of tenants held considerably less than this.

An analysis of the total holdings in the manor of the tenants of Estbroke and Boxhamstede shows that about 25 per cent. had holdings of ten acres or less, another 25 percent. had between ten and forty acres, about 48 per cent. ranged between forty and a hundred and sixty acres, and only two men had more than a hundred and sixty. Practically all rents were paid in money and not in kind, though a few traditional payments did survive. For example Thomas Munde "for one croft of the fee of Menveys as per containing three acres" paid 1*s.* 3*d.* and one capon, and the total rent of Edward de la Hay amounted to £3.3*s.* 8*d.*, and one pound of cumin. Some tenants paid fixed sums for "works relaxed" or for "one work at the great boon". In Bovingdon there were a few isolated survivals of labour services, that is of people owing in addition to a money rent the work of "one man at the gathering of the harvest". However, there are only two examples of this in the entire survey and it seems probable that commutation of labour services had been generally accepted, and since the demesne was rented out on the same terms as other land it seems likely that for most of the tenants both week-work and boon-work had completely disappeared.

A general picture of the field systems of Hemel Hempstead taken from the evidence of the Rental has already been drawn in the first chapter of this book, and it is a more complex pattern than that presented either by a completely enclosed manor or by an 'open-field' system. On the question of enclosure the evidence of the Rental is not easily interpreted. Many closes are mentioned and some of them are clearly crofts, gardens, and orchards adjoining the tenants' homes. Some, however, are much larger than this, and are frequently subdivided, presumably without fences or hedges, so that, for example, Richard Birchmore could hold 'one acre lying in a close called nine acres'. It would seem therefore that these enclosures were not of the kind normally made by a farmer seeking to consolidate his holding and separate it from the lands of his neighbours. More probably they were survivals from a much earlier period. The acreage which is clearly stated to be enclosed in 1523 is anyway only a small proportion of the total, and there were many tenants of the manor whose lands were 'open' to their neighbours, but this does not necessarily imply an 'open-field' system. There is no evidence that choice of crops or organisation of labour were matters for anyone but the tenants themselves to decide.

The land was good for pasture and for grain crops, but the quality of the land varied from one part of the manor to another. This is reflected in the rents which vary considerably even within one field. The range for arable land was from 2*d.* to 8*d.* an acre. Meadowland was generally more expensive, sometimes costing more than 2*s.* an acre.

From the evidence of contemporary wills wheat emerges as the principal crop, and sheep as the most important livestock. Oats, barley, and pease were also grown and probably rye and vetches which were certainly grown later in the century. Other livestock included small numbers of cows and bullocks, a few horses, and some pigs, goats, poultry, and bees. The people of Hemel Hempstead at this time could therefore, in good years, be almost completely self-supporting. They could provide for their families bread and cheese, butter and eggs, milk and honey, meat and malt, and fresh fruit and vegetables from the orchards and closes near their houses. For surplus produce, before 1539, the nearest market was Berkhamsted, but Hemel Hempstead was soon to become more prosperous than its neighbour.

In 1539 Hemel Hempstead received its charter of incorporation. According to local belief this was granted by Henry VIII out of gratitude to his Auditor, John Waterhouse, who had nobly entertained him at the Banqueting House in Hemel Hempstead. The most important features of the charter were first the right to elect a town bailiff, second the right to hold a fair annually at the feast of Corpus Christi, third the right to hold a weekly market on Thursdays and to enjoy the profits thereof, and finally the right to hold a 'piepowdercourt' to regulate the proceedings of the fair and market and punish offenders against the rules of trade (while the feet of the disputants were still dusty - from the French 'pieds poudrés').

The charter was almost certainly a recognition of the already growing wealth of the town as well as a cause of greater prosperity in the latter part of the century. Before the granting of the charter the nearest markets had been at Berkhamsted and St. Albans, so that it must have been a great convenience to the local population to be able to market their goods in Hemel Hempstead itself. Tolls from stallholders in the market must have proved profitable to the town, and the 'piepowdercourt', an essential adjunct to the market, doubtless brought in a small but steady income in fines, (See Chapter 8).

The right of the inhabitants to choose their own bailiff was certainly valuable, but it is not clear that it was always exercised wisely. The first bailiff was William Stephyns, who appears, from such records as are available to have been influential rather than worthy. He is known to have confessed before the Church Court that he and one William Doughty, servant to Mr Bray, abducted a girl named Cecily and took her to London 'sub spe matrimoni futuri' (upon a promise of marriage.) Furthermore, shortly before his election as bailiff, he and Thomas Halsey were defendants in a Chancery suit. John Wye claimed that one messuage and three acres of land held by his father in fee had never been lawfully given up since there had only been one witness to his surrender of the land, which should therefore be his by inheritance, However, according to his plea before Chancery, William Stephyns and Thomas Halsey 'by the colour of the said unlawful surrender' and 'for their extorts and mighty power have entered into the said premises and keep it from me'. He has, he claims already made one complaint to the court and received from the Chancellor a writ of restoration which was directed to the Sheriff of Hertford, who, 'taking with him divers poor honest men to help him execute the writ", met William Stephyns and Thomas Halsey who "did resiste and would not suffer your suppliant to enjoy his land" and shortly afterwards they did "with force and armye keep the possession of the said house, and they did bette and hurte the wife of youre complainant so that she was in juptie (jeopardy) of her lyffe", and at the last session of inquiry in the said county "they untruly presented and caused me and divers other poor men who came with the Sheriff to be indicted of a riott and trespass, to their utter undoing". In all fairness it must be said that Stephyns and Halsey denied the whole story and said that the land had been copyhold lawfully granted to them by the lord of the manor. The truth of the case is not known nor is the judgment of the Chancellor, but the story does throw some light on the position held by the man who became the first bailiff of Hemel Hempstead.

After the granting of the charter it would be natural to expect that Hemel Hempstead should enjoy a steady growth in prosperity. Yet at no time during the century was Hemel Hempstead inhabited by the great or the wealthy. It is true that John Waterhouse was an Auditor to Henry VIII, but the most distinguished member of the family, his son Edward, did not live in Hemel Hempstead, and after 1540 the Waterhouses seem to have given place to their relations, the Combes. Richard Combe leased the Bury, Burymill, and the Dairy of Hemel Hempstead from the Crown after the Dissolution of Ashridge. He lived in the Bury house and probably rebuilt it. His name heads the subsidy rolls for the town. Nevertheless he was hardly more than a country squire. There is no evidence that he even attained the office of Justice of the Peace.

Later in the century some Hertfordshire towns complained to the Privy Council that wealthy courtiers owned local land, but were only interested in the affairs of court and capital and did all they could to avoid any local responsibilities. This was not the case in Hemel Hempstead. Hence if there was an increase in wealth it was not a case of great fortunes being made or of wealthy people being attracted to a prosperous area, but rather a case of husbandman who prospered so well that their sons called themselves yeomen, and of yeomen whose sons became gentlemen. In fact there is little real evidence for either more or less wealth in Hemel Hempstead during the century. The average value of goods and land left in wills changes little.

Certainly the great majority of people in the parish were below the rank of gentleman and above that of labourer. No more than a handful of men left over £70 in their wills and the great majority left less than £50. The average worth of one styling himself 'yeoman' was just over £53. The great majority of the people were farmers for at least part of their time, and only a very few were entirely occupied in other trades or crafts. Of the eighty-seven surviving wills in which the testator's occupation is mentioned thirty-nine are husbandmen and twenty-six are yeoman; there are five wheelers four carpenters, two tailors, two smiths, two shoemakers, a brewer, a milner, a butcher and a plowright, and finally three labourers, a description that probably implies that they had no land of their own.

Evidence is no more complete for other developments during the century. It is difficult to say, for example, exactly how much enclosure was carried out after 1523. In other parts of Hertfordshire there were riots against enclosure, as at Northaw and Cheshunt in 1547, and at Northaw in 1579; there were none in Hemel Hempstead or at least none of which any record survives. The circumstances in Hemel Hempstead were anyway such as to make enclosure troubles unlikely to be severe. As we have seen, the tenants all had written evidence of their tenancy. There were few wealthy land-owners in the manor, that is men sufficiently powerful to cause suffering to their neighbours. Since, moreover, there was already a good deal of sheep-farming in the manor, Hemel Hempstead was immune to the worst hardships of the time which resulted from simultaneous enclosure and conversion of arable land to sheep-runs. There is no evidence that the corn-market was neglected in favour of wool, and certainly by the middle of the seventeenth century Thomas Fuller was able to describe the market at Hemel Hempstead as "the greatest for wheat in this county". Thus if enclosure did take place during the sixteenth century it seems likely to have been arranged peacefully, by agreement between neighbours, and without causing undue suffering. The only piece of real evidence that enclosure did take place is the fact that when, in 1617, a local jury was instructed to describe the bounds of the manor, they did so almost entirely by reference to hedges and closes belonging to individual farmers.

Enclosure had more advantages for the sheep-farmer than for the arable farmer, and there were certainly large numbers of sheep reared in Hemel Hempstead in the sixteenth century. At least 60 per cent. of the people whose wills have survived had some sheep, and a few owned more than a hundred and fifty. A convenient way of dealing with numerous godchildren was to bequeath "to each of them one ewe lambe", and sheep were often distributed in small numbers to various relations and dependents of the deceased. Sheep were plentiful, relatively cheap, and very profitable, but there is no evidence that wool ever replaced wheat as the main crop. Nevertheless pasture was valuable and evidently in great demand. We have already seen how the tenants were willing to take issue with the Rector of Ashridge over grazing rights.

The commons and pastures then in dispute have an interesting history. From 1499 it was the custom for the tenants to pay to the lord of the manor 6*s*. 8*d.* annually for grazing rights in Castelmede, Bailiemede and Roudowne, and they also had rights in Two Waters Moor and Felden Heath. After 1539 the 6*s.* 8*d.* was paid annually to the Crown, but from the evidence of two indentures written into the back of the surviving copy of the 1523 Rental it appears that some of this pasture land, together with much other property in Hemel Hempstead, was granted by Queen Elizabeth to Robert Dudley, Earl of Leicester on 19th July 1574. The very next day Leicester sold these lands and tenements for an unspecified sum to Francis, Earl of Bedford and Peter Graye of Segenhoe in Ridgmont in Bedfordshire. Seven years later, on 26th May 1581, the same lands were sold by Peter Graye's son Richard for £75 to John Rolfe yeoman, Richard Pope shoemaker, and William Gladman yeoman, all of Hemel Hempstead. The pasture is described in the indentures as "one meadow in Hemelhemsted aforesaid called or knowne by the name of Castle Meade with the appurtenances *alias* Haywards Meade *alias* Bayley Meade *alias* Haybourne". The other lands mentioned are of no special importance.

The next piece of documentary evidence concerning these pasture lands, now known as Boxmoor, is an indenture of enfeoffment dated 26th April 1594 which transfers the lands from John Rolfe (bailiff of the town in that year) and Richard Pope to sixty-seven other inhabitants headed by Francis Combes the younger. This document is quoted in the Act of 1809 governing the Boxmoor Trust, and it is there stated that these commons were "lawfully conveyed and assured to the said John Rolfe, Richard Pope, and one William Gladman, their heirs and assigns for ever, the intent and purpose of which conveyance and assurance so to them made was by a secret trust to them committed to and for the benefit and only use whereby the inhabitants of Hemel Hempstead aforesaid and of Bovingdon their heirs and assigns might and should for ever thereafter have, hold and enjoy the said meadows and all the commodities and profits that might or should arise thereof." It becomes clear as this account proceeds that Pope, Rolfe, and Gladman bought the pasture with money "disbursed and paid at the costs and charges of divers and the most of the inhabitants of Hemel Hempstead and Bovingdon aforesaid". William Gladman died before the other two, and Richard Pope and John Rolfe then legally made the remaining sixty-seven contributors, or their heirs, owners of the land to administer it for the common good. Thereafter any inhabitant might graze an animal on payment of 7*s.* 6*d.* annually, and the profits were to be used for draining and improving the pasture.

All but a few of the inventories for the sixteenth century have been lost, but it is still possible from those that do survive and from the wills to get a vivid picture of the paraphernalia of day-to-day living and to reconstruct in imagination the houses occupied by the Rolfes, Popes, Howes and Fields and their neighbours in Hemel Hempstead, by the Ewars and Lovetts of Flaunden, and the Axtells, Goulds and Shakemaples of Bovingdon. By the beginning of the seventeenth century most people in Hemel Hempstead were living in houses with at least four rooms, generally a hall and a kitchen or buttery on the ground floor and two chambers above. Some had larger houses of six or seven rooms and the vicarage was even larger having eight rooms in all. Over most of England the Tudor century was a great time for rebuilding and for adding new comforts to otherwise humble housing. Hemel Hempstead wills contain several references to "the new parlour" and "the new loft over the kitchen" but it is not easy to tell from these in which part of the century most rebuilding took place.

Dr. Hoskins in 'The Making of the English Landscape' says that "in 1550 most English people were still living in the rather dark squalid and cramped dwellings of their medieval forefathers. These were generally two-roomed houses built of a timber frame with walls of reinforced mud." If this is so Hemel Hempstead was ahead of the times, for many people of quite moderate means were living in three, four and five-roomed houses before that date. Roger Bunne for example in 1543 left to his wife "all my moveables in hall, parlour and chambers".

In 1560 Henry Rose instructed his wife after his death to set up "a barn of iii baies, xii foot a baye and xviii foot wide and ix foot between the joynes and a kechyn at the worke dorė of a baye doble store with a chimney and an oven in it". If a mere barn has a kitchen and a chimney it is hardly likely that houses would be less luxurious. Certainly most people seem to have aspired to the sophistication of having their houses 'chambered over' and some were already in the van of progress having kitchens, chimneys, and glass in their casements.

The outstanding example of rebuilding in Hemel Hempstead in the sixteenth century is the Bury itself. At some time before 1595 Richard Combes pulled down the remains of the old manor house and built himself a new mansion which must have outdone any other in the manor in size and splendour and in the richness of its furnishings. The new house, of which one doorway remains, is partially described in Richard Combes's will. He mentions the hall, the new parlour, his study and eight upper chambers, and though he has no occasion to mention the kitchen or buttery or other domestic offices they doubtless existed. The house probably had at least fourteen rooms in all. The furnishings were splendid. In the "greate chamber" were "a bedstead worth £5 and a mattres or flockbed, a fetherbed, a bolster, two pillows, a paire of blanketts, two pare of sheets 30s. a paire, two pillowberes, a counterpoynte of imagery, a quilt of yellow silke worth £5, three curtaynes of changeable taffata worth £3, two carpetts for windows, two window cushions, one of clothe of silver, the other blue satten embroidered, two chaires, the one fine greene cloth embroidered, the other a close chair of wainskott, a cuppord and a carpett on it, five great chests the one a shippe cheste so called, and the other of red leather bound with iron and three cushions of silke wrought in the lome", Combes also

BURY RUINS, HEMEL HEMPSTEAD

bequeathed to various members of his family two gilt cups, three silver bowls, and sixteen silver spoons, and the remaining rooms were furnished to match the style of the great chamber.

The luxury of the big house may be contrasted to the humbler furnishings of smaller households. In these would be found a homely assortment of simple oak furniture, pewter dishes and brass kettles, fire irons and carpenters tools, tubs and troughs for home brewing, and often timber in the back yard, oak or ash or beech. In the chambers above were large numbers of beds and ample supplies of bedding, indicating that small houses often sheltered large families. All these household articles figure prominently in the wills and, certainly for the poorer folk, more of their wealth was contained in them than in actual money. Possessions were carefully handed on and valued according to the use left in them without apparent regard to current fashions. This applied even to articles of clothing, so that it was not unusual for Agnes Hawkyns in 1537 to leave to her servant Agnes Prat "a velvette kirtell and my best workinday petticoat" or for John Pope in 1558 to give his brother William "my best coat and hat and my buckskyn doublette".

Few people had possessions beyond the necessary equipment for working, cooking, eating and sleeping. Just occasionally in amongst the bolsters and sheets and pewter platters a Bible or some books are mentioned, but they are rare. Ralph Mylwarde in 1569 was the owner of "a bowe and shaftes", but otherwise sporting equipment and weapons are conspicuous by their absence.

It is commonly assumed that for most people life was considerably shorter in those days than it is now, and although many lived long enough to know their grandchildren, there are many indications that people frequently did die quite young. For example it was quite common for a man to die leaving several children under the age of twenty-one. William Golde of Bovingdon in 1568 left to each of his six younger children "xxs., one lamb, one pewter platter, and one sheet" to be paid when they reached the age of twenty-one. Sometimes a man died while his wife was expecting another child and left provision for the "child my wife bears". Further evidence that many died comparatively young is provided by the frequency of reference to remarriage. The man who left money to "my wife's child" and the woman who asked to be buried beside her first husband are obvious examples of people who had remarried. A dying man whose wife was still of marriageable age clearly thought it likely that she would remarry and generally made provision for her only "provided she remayne sole and unmarried". Sometimes it was stated in the will that if the wife should remarry she must take at least some of the younger children with her to her new home.

Generally widows were well provided for, and they were often, as one might expect, the chief beneficiaries of the wills. Where the eldest son received most of his father's wealth and property a clause was normally included in the will granting the widow the use of her own chamber, or sometimes a bay of the house, with the right to come to the fire whenever she wished. The son had to provide meat and drink for her and in some cases, if she did not like what her son provided, she could have money instead. When Robert Pope of Hyllende died in 1544 his wife was probably already an invalid for he left her a room with her son John and "if she call or ask for chykyns, wine or ale, or any spice to comfort her withall I will she shall have her desire whatsoever it be".

When her husband died a wife might expect to receive back the goods she had originally contributed to the setting up of her new home. It was clearly part of the marriage custom of the times that she should make this contribution, generally in linen, brass and pewter rather than in money. It was the poor man's equivalent of a marriage settlement. One husband left to his wife "all that she broughte with her at her wedding daye", another "all she broughte in her bryde carte".

Families were somewhat larger than is common today, so that a man might have to provide for any number of children from one to twelve. The eldest son generally received the largest share of his father's goods, and if he were of age he took his father's place as head of the family and the women folk were expected to accept his authority. William Axtell, who died in 1568, left his daughters in the charge of his son Thomas until they should come of age and said that they were to "obey him and defer to him always duringe the seyd time willinglie, quietlie and gentellye as much as in them lyethe".

If many people died early it would be interesting to know what caused their deaths. Unfortunately it is seldom possible to decide with certainty. Men and women making their wills often describe themselves as "sick in bodye but whole of mind" or even "sick unto death", but it is impossible to diagnose the disease. When a husband and wife, or a father and son, die within a few days of each other some infectious disease is likely to have been the cause, but no further deductions can safely be made. Fifteen wills for 1537 compared with the usual three or four, and sixteen in 1558 suggest minor outbreaks of plague or sweating sickness, but this is mere supposition. However, Hemel Hempstead certainly was visited by plague more than once during the sixteenth century. It was at Bourne End in 1583 when John Cawden, "a laborer of Bourne", hastily made a will leaving all his moveable goods to one Thomas Byggins "for his paynes that he has taken both with me and also with my wife in this time of sicknes of the decease of the pestilence or plauge wherewith it has pleased God to visit us". The will was witnessed by Henry Mayne gent. and William Coop "especially called and desired the daye and yeare above written".

It is not known how many suffered in this outbreak of 1583, but ten years later there was a much more serious epidemic which spread out from London and affected most of Hertfordshire and several other counties. Fairs had to be cancelled at Ware, Uxbridge and Flamstead. The first death in Hemel Hempstead occurred in December 1593 when the parish register records the decease of "Susan daughter of John Dell, carpenter, of the plague". Three more of John Dell's children died in January and February 1594. The plague then departed only to return the following summer. There were twenty-six burials in the August and September of 1594. Eight more people died in the first part of October, and the last of these was Elizabeth wife of Henrie Smith the parish clerk.

At this point the records got out of order. A note in the margin explains that "here som be wanting that dyed in the plague time see the last page", and on the last page:- "Richard the son of Richard Howe was buried the 10th day of October 1594 which was left out of this booke in the extremitie of sickness when the parish clerk was shut up, it being suspected that his wife dyed of the plague a few days before the death of the said Richard Howe as appeareth by this booke. In like manner October 7th Richard the son of Thomas Gladman and Elizabeth the daughter of Thomas Gladman both in one daye." Henrie Smith had in fact been "shutt up" in obedience to orders commonly distributed by the justices in time of plague to prevent the spread of the disease. These were that an infected house would be "shut up and that you appoint a warder at the door to keep them from coming forth and others from coming at them, and that you the churchwardens and overseers of the poor be careful that the parties shut up be sufficiently provided for their present relief and sustentation and further that you cause the said person and his family to keep themselves with their own doors, and that in the meantime he forbear to victuall or let any come into his house till he hath further orders".

The great changes in the religion of the nation during the sixteenth century are but palely reflected in the life of Hemel Hempstead. No riots, burnings or priests-in-hiding are recorded, yet some very significant changes did take place. In the early part of the century St. Mary's clearly had its share of pre-reformation abuses. Masses for the dead must have taken up a good deal of the priest's time since most people left money in their wills to pay the priest to sing "a trygyntall of masses", that is thirty masses for their souls. The church also suffered from the proliferation of altars that became common in England in the fourteenth century. Each altar had a light which had to be kept burning at the expense of the pious or superstitious souls who left their money for the purpose.

In St. Lawrence's Bovingdon there were at least five lights, as is illustrated by the will of Richard Goulde in 1531 who left "my bodye to be buried beside the pychers of St. Christopher, to the roodelighte viii*d.*, to our ladye's lighte viii*d.*, to the lighte of St. Lawrence viii*d.*, to the lighte of St. Nicholas iv*d.*, to the lighte of St. Leonard iv*d.*" In St. Mary's there were at least four principal lights in addition to that of the high altar. There was also the light of St. Uncumber mentioned in the will of Robert Roger in 1537, "I, being warden of St. Uncumber light do owe it xxis." It was believed that wives who prayed to St. Uncumber would be 'uncumbered' of their husbands. The 'brotherhood' is mentioned in several wills and was probably a religous guild formed by some of the wealthier laymen of the parish who employed a priest to sing for their souls and to keep a light burning in the church. This brotherhood survived the dissolution of Ashridge by five years, disappearing only in 1545.

Church ales were commonly held at certain seasons of the year for the purpose of making merry and raising money for the church. Rather lustier ancestors of the vicarage fete, these celebrations consisted chiefly of eating and drinking by friends and neighbours from several miles around. John Eggerton, the priest of St. Mary's in 1527, may have welcomed the addition to church funds but he evidently disapproved of the ales being held in the church itself since they were often accompanied by "brawls, blasphemies quarrels and bad words". Therefore, according to a document copied into the Rental of 1523, he accepted the suggestion of the parishoners and agreed that an old building in the east end of the cemetery should be pulled down and a 'church house' built in its place where it "shall be possible to do their drinking more decently for the benefit of the church". Two wills of 1528 leaving money "to the building of the new church house" show that some at least of the expense was borne by the parishioners.

Up to 1539 the connection between Hemel Hempstead and Ashridge was a close one. The Rector, of course, was the lord of the manor. Pilgrims to Ashridge passed through Hemel Hempstead, possibly resting at Piccott's End on the final stage of their journey. The Waterhouse family, which provided the last Rector of Ashridge, was resident in Hemel Hempstead. This connection with Ashridge did not end with the dissolution of the monasteries. The College of Ashridge came within the terms of the second Act of Dissolution which was passed in 1539 but not actually put into effect until the following year. From the evidence of episcopal visitations early in the century, less prejudiced than the accounts of Cromwell's visitors, the destruction of the College was not wholly undeserved, though its failings resulted rather from slackness and ignorance than from criminality or evil-living. Whatever the justification, the College was dissolved, and the manors belonging to it, Hemel Hempstead among them, became Crown property. The Rector and the brothers were pensioned off.

Two of the brothers found refuge in Hemel Hempstead. Richard Canan and Richard Bedford, still drawing pensions of £5 and £6 respectively, were curates here assisting the vicar John Holland in 1543. Bedford was the last priest of the Brotherhood and Canan later became curate at Bovingdon. Possibly he found the life of a secular priest more congenial, for, according to the visitation records of 1530, he had already proved his unsuitability for the life of the cloister by drinking with other brothers in the dormitory and by habitually slipping off to his home in Dunstable, travelling along the highway without his habit and wearing only doublet and hose. The Rector, Thomas Waterhouse, did not forget Hemel Hempstead, for when he died in 1557, still "a priest of the Catholicke faithe", he asked that his body should be buried in the chancel of St. Mary's "nere to the place where my mother lyeth". He also left to St. Mary's his "stole and fanon sette with pearle".

The accession of Edward VI brought many fervent Protestants into high places, and images and saint-worship, pilgrimages and other popish practices came under official condemnation. In St. Mary's the lights were put out and presumably the subsidiary altars were removed. Official policy was also reflected in the change in the wording of wills. A typical will of the period before 1547 is that of Thomas Felde who died in 1528. It begins, "First I bequeth my soule to almighty God, to our Lady Synt Mary and to all the company of hevyn, and my bodye to be buryede in the parish churchyard. To the high altere in the church xiii*d.*, to the four principal lights in the saide church, to every one of them iv*d.*, to the torches iv*d.*, to the brotherhood there one bushell of wheat that a trygentall be sade in the church". The typical features of this will are the lengthy dedication of the soul including the mention of the "lady Synt Mary", and the elaborate list of pious donations to the church. After 1547 most wills begin much more simply with a dedication of the soul to God (the Blessed Virgin Mary is significantly omitted). The list of religious bequests is also shorter, for the lights, the torches and the brotherhood had disappeared by that date. Donations to the high altar were frequently replaced by gifts to the poor box, and in one will of 1552 money was left not to the altar but to the "table". During Mary's reign the old form of will returned only to disappear again after 1558.

It is difficult to tell what hardships were suffered by the clergy of this period. No record of conflict survives. The resignation of John Holland in 1549 coincided with the imposition of the first Edwardian Prayer Book, but there is nothing to indicate that the two events were connected. Holland's successor, William Wilson, seems almost to have rivalled the Vicar of Bray in digesting the Prayer Book of 1552, the return to Rome under Queen Mary, and the Protestant settlement under Queen Elizabeth.

Although many of the objects of Roman Catholic charity disappeared with the Reformation, people did not abandon the practice of making religious bequests in their wills. Most people chose to leave something to the "poor man's boxe". A man who was himself poor might leave a shilling or half a bushell of wheat. A man of moderate means might will "to be bestowed at my buriall to the poore people in meate and drinke and moneye xx*s.*" A wealthy man might be even more generous and extend his good will to the poor of all the surrounding parishes. Robert Eymes, lord of the manor of Buers and Haybarnes, who died in 1551 left twenty shillings for twenty years to the poor of Hemel Hempstead, twenty shillings to Little Gaddesden, ten shillings to King's Langley and Berkhamsted, and five shillings to Frithsden and Nettleden. Charity sometimes took other forms. Some left money for repairs to the church, others for repairs to the roads leading to the church. It was also an act of charity to prevent a poor man's maintenance being charged to the parish. Thus in 1600 Richard Dolte asked that "John Saunders now in my keeping be maintained so long and so far further as the saide town and parish of Hemel Hempstead may not nor shall not in any wise be charged with his maintenance".

In many parishes a good deal of evidence for church life at this period is provided by the records of the churchwardens, their yearly accounts, their presentations to the church courts, and their returns to the Archdeacon. The churchwardens' tasks were many. They had to see that the fabric and furniture of the church was kept in good repair. They supervised attendance at church, making sure that everyone came to church, that once there the congregation was orderly, and that vituallers and alehouses did not serve anyone during service times. It was also their business to present to the ecclesiastical courts all offenders against the law of the church and the Queen's ecclesiastical injunctions. Unfortunately only a very few fragments of evidence of the work of Hemel Hempstead's churchwardens have survived. From an Episcopal Visitation of 1585 we learn that William Flemes and his wife were excommunicated for not living together. One undated churchwardens' return (probably from about 1595) declares that Bridgett Howe hath made confession of her fault openly before the whole assemblie at morning prayer in the churche of Hemelhemsted the 9th of Julye according as your worshippe appointed her". The rest of her story is unknown.

There is an interesting entry in the Visitation records of 1607. "Robert Besuth and his wife, Francis Morass and his wife, and John Satle [Settle] and his wife have stood excommunicate about half a yeare for not kneeling at communion and still remain obstinate. The forfiture of twelvepence for absence from church hath been demanded of them but not payd they being soe poore as they answer". These three couples were almost certainly puritans and their case illustrates the fact that during the last quarter of the sixteenth century Puritan beliefs had gained many adherents in Hemel Hempstead.

It is possible that the Combes family, who rented the tithes of the rectory, were Puritan in sympathy, but they did not in any case have the advowson, that is the right to appoint the vicar. Since 1544 this had been the right of the Dean and Chapter of St. Paul's. As it happened the Dean of St. Paul's from 1560 to 1602 was Alexander Nowell who had been a Protestant exile in the reign of Mary and was at least a moderate Puritan himself. This helps to account for the fact that three notable Puritans were appointed vicars towards the end of the century though the last two also owed much to the patronage of Lady Bacon of Gorehambury. William Horne (or Herne) became vicar in 1571. He had been a moderator at monthly exercises organised in 1560 by Archdeacon Kemp of St. Albans. Although conservative in conception, these exercises later came under strong

Puritan influence, and were converted into public prophesyings of the type later suppressed by the authorities. In 1574 Horne again acted as moderator in exercises organized by the Bishop of Lincoln. After his resignation of the living of Hemel Hempstead in 1578 he was active amongst a group of enthusiastic Puritan ministers in London who spent much of their time visiting and disputing with Catholic priests in the Tower. Horne was succeeded by John Gibson who was vicar for two years and of whom very little is known.

In 1580 Lady Bacon secured the appointment of Richard Gawton, a well-known Puritan who had been suspended from preaching by the Bishop of Norwich four years earlier because of his objections to certain ceremonies of the church especially the use of the sign of the cross. In 1577 Gawton had added his signature to a letter written by Puritan ministers to the eminent leader Cartwright expressing sympathy with his doctrines.

Gawton's successor was William Dyke, who came to Hemel Hempstead with a considerable record of persecution by the authorities. He was first in trouble in Essex in 1586 when he was suspended from his office at Coggeshall for refusing to wear the surplice and for omitting the sign of the cross and other ceremonies. He removed to Hertfordshire and became vicar of St. Michael's in St. Albans, partly through the influence of Lord Burleigh. Dyke was a convinced Puritan, influential in the movement towards the Presbyterian model of church government. In 1587 he and one Mr. Pigge were appointed to superintend the orders of a national synod which was to be held in Hertfordshire. In 1589 according to Strype "the Bishop stayed him preaching for troubling his auditory with new opinions and notions thwarting the established religion". Thirty-five of his supporters at St. Albans, however, complained to Lord Burleigh, who wrote to the Bishop to ask why Dyke had been prevented from preaching. The Bishop replied that in addition to his schismatic opinions, Dyke was only in deacon's orders and refused to be ordained priest, that he had withstood orders from the Privy Council, that he was guilty of incontinency, and that in any case those who interceded for him were "of the meanest and basest sort". Burleigh, however wrote back completely clearing Dyke of the charge of incontinency and requesting that he might be allowed to preach again although, being only a deacon, he might not administer the sacraments.

It is not clear whether or not Dyke was reinstated as vicar of St. Michael's, but in 1591 he came to Hemel Hempstead as a preacher. He assisted Richard Gawton for three years, then took his place as vicar in 1594. There is amongst the Lambeth MS. a letter dated 22nd January 1596 from the Earl of Essex to the Bishop of Lincoln asking that William Dyke, although still only a deacon, might be allowed to administer the sacraments. This request originated with Lady Bacon who had been largely responsible for securing the appointment of Dyke.

Bovingdon and Flaunden were also involved in the Puritan movement.

Thomas Wilcox, a prominent and active supporter of the classical movement and a prolific author, was appointed curate at Bovingdon by William Horne in about 1573 and remained there until after 1585. Wilcox is held to be joint-author with John Field of the 'Admonition to Parliament' (1571). This was a Puritan plea for a learned minister in every parish, to be chosen by the congregation and not to be ordained by the bishop, and it included demands for the abolition of lay impropriation, kneeling at communion, and lay baptism. Wilcox and Field were committed to Newgate on 7 July 1572 and remained in prison until after October 1573. Wilcox was deprived of his position as minister of God's word in Honey Lane, London, where he had been connected with All Hallows church, and it was probably at this date that he came as curate to Bovingdon, although he was still closely connected with the London Puritans. In 1577 Bishop Aylmer of London recommended that Wilcox and other troublesome Puritans should be removed to Lancashire, Staffordshire, or Shropshire "and such other like barbarous countries" that he might wear out his zeal on the papists. Wilcox still seems to have held a place, possibly unofficial, in London in 1583, but the *Liber Cleri* (Book of the Clergy) of Lincoln Diocese gives his name as curate of Bovingdon in 1584, when he was described as "*Non graduatus nunquam comparavit nec subscripsit*", (a non-graduate who neither appeared nor subscribed to the Prayer Book) and in 1585. He was a friend and counsellor of many influential families, including the Bacons at Gorhambury. A successor of Wilcox at Bovingdon was Nathaniel Walkwood, there in 1597 and 1603, who was suspended in 1605.

In Flaunden, Dyke assisted the Puritan cause by appointing as curate Thomas Scott, who was deprived of his post in the purge of Puritan ministers that followed the failure of the Hampton Court Conference in 1604. Scott was cited with others for "not wearing the surplisse and not conforming themselves to the use of the ceremonies of the churche in the celebracion of divine service and administration of the sacraments accordinge to the booke of common prayer". This may have been the same man who is noted in the *Liber Cleri* of 1607 under Hemel Hempstead: "Mr. Scott their scholemaster teachinge in his owne house sayth that hee hathe a licence but hee is a minister and put to silence and lives as a laye man".

Note on Sources

This chapter draws heavily on three main primary sources:—

Rental of 1523 (a post 1596 copy)P.C.

Will and Inventories, H.R.O., L.R.O. and Somerset House.

Manor Court Rolls and Books, Duchy of Cornwall Office.

But see also:—

J. Strype, 'Annals of the Reformation'.

J. Norden, 'Speculum Britanniae'.

P. Collinson, 'The Puritan Classical Movement in the Reign of Elizabeth I', London Ph.D. thesis, 1957.

Trans. East Herts. Arch. Soc. viii (Act Book of 1590-6).

Hertfordshire Genealogist and Antiquary, i-iii.

'Visitations in the Diocese of Lincoln 1517-1531', Lincoln Record Society, 33, ed. A.H. Thompson.

'Lincoln Episcopal Records 1571-84' ed. C.W. Foster.

'The State of the Church', Lincoln Record Society 23, ed. C.W. Foster.

POSTSCRIPT - CHAPTER 4

The Manor in the following two centuries

Whilst with the passage of time the importance of the manor decreased it continued to play some part in the life of the community, not only in the 17th and 18th centuries but in the 19th and 20th as well; by then it had to all intents and purposes become a recording authority for transactions in copyhold land, until that type of tenure was abolished by the Law of Property Acts of the 1920's.

The Town Council holds seven documents called charters. Only three confer powers on the locality, the remaining four deal with legal proceedings of one kind and another. Two of these four deal with the manor. One, of Elizabeth I and dated 1572, lists the documents by which the various lands of the Manor were given to the monastery at Ashridge by the Earls of Cornwall. The other, of James I and dated 1609-10, records legal proceedings during which the tenants of the manor resisted certain demands made by the Lord of the Manor, the King, or one of his sons.

The royal lord, in order to combat inflation, claimed he was entitled to fix arbitrarily the fines payable by incoming tenants, either on the death of the previous tenant, or when a sale and purchase had been agreed; he also claimed as a heriot the best beast or the best good. The tenants argued that this claim was contrary to the customs of the manor, and pleaded in support the award made by the arbitrators - John Broket of Wheathamsted, John Piers, Thomas Blake and Thomas Stepneth of St. Albans - following the dispute between the Rector of Ashridge, John Barkhamsted, and the customary tenants in 1522 to which reference has already been made (See p. 39) Faced with this decision the King had to give way, and accepted the award and caused it to be enrolled in the Court records. Not only were the Lord's claims rejected but the various customs of the Manor as set out in the 1521 arbitration award were confirmed and recorded, and remained in force so long as the manor continued, and copyhold tenure prevailed.

There was another result, if somewhat indirect. In some other manors it became the practice of the lord, as opportunity offered, to vary the tenure on which his land was held and convert it to leaseholds, either for a fixed term or for a number of lives. When these periods expired the land reverted entirely to the lord, who was able to use it or dispose of it, free of the restrictions which previously existed. However, this did not happen in this manor and copyhold tenure remained until the land was enfranchised by the 1920's legislation.

In these proceedings of 1609-10 the tenants were represented by Robert Shadd (probably Bailiff when the case was heard in the Courts), Thomas Humphrey, William Turner (of Wards End) Francis Howe (of Pix) John Hall (described elsewhere as "Gentleman") and John Gould (of the Streete), all of well known local families and men of substance, (e.g. William Turner who died in 1611 left an estate valued at £280), and all prepared to fight for their rights whenever they were threatened.

The manor probably belonged to James I's elder son Henry, and when he died of typhoid fever in 1612 it was given to his brother, Charles. About 1617 Charles sent a famous surveyor named Norden to make a detailed survey of the manor and its customs and asked a jury consisting of some 29 tenants to answer a set of twenty-four questions. In answer to one question they described in great detail the boundaries of the manor. Answering others they dealt with certain customs, the existence of certain records, the holding of the weekly market and the annual fair and the possession of the market house and churchhouse. It is probable that Norden discovered that certain of the stalls and standings of the market were accommodated on waste of the manor and this led to the negotiation by Dr. Martin and others of the Town Lease dealt with in some detail in Chapter 5. A later Bailiff reimbursed the Doctor for an expense of 6*s.* 8*d.* incurred when Mr. Norden visited Hemel Hempstead.

During the Commonwealth the Government proceeded to sell certain Crown property and ordered a survey to be made of the Manor of Hemel Hempstead with the intention of disposing of it; this was completed in 1650. As a result, part of the manor was sold, and after passing through several hands a moiety of it was acquired by Richard Combes of the Bury *(State Papers Domestic 1655, p.263)*. It was about this time that the Bailiwick acquired the waste of the manor used in connection with the Market as explained in Chapter 8.

At the Restoration the Manor returned to the Crown, and Richard Combes was appointed steward at a fee of £20 a year and the fines of the Court Leet (*State Papers Domestic 1660-61*). Later the Manor formed part of the jointure of Catherine of Braganza when she married Charles II, and in 1676 another survey was made of it which showed there had been considerable changes since earlier surveys were made. From time to time the manor was let to different tenants until it was purchased by the Halsey family in 1815.

Throughout these two centuries the Manor Court continued to carry out its functions. The transactions in copyhold lands were duly approved and recorded by what was known as the Court Baron; and the appropriate fines and fees collected. Every year at the annual meeting of the Court Leet in May or June (this had to be held on the Tuesday next after Trinity Sunday) certain manorial officers were appointed; three men were appointed as constables, one for each of the three divisions of the Towne, High Street side and Boxhamsted side. In addition a varying number of headboroughs were appointed; in 1651, for instance, eight were chosen, one for each sub-district, viz. Towne, Piccotts End, High Street, Corner Hall, Two Waters, Crouchfield and Greenend, Boxted and Bury Mill End. Later the number was reduced to three, and usually the same individuals were elected for a series of years. Besides these, three regular appointments of a fish taster, a searcher and sealer of leather, and an ale taster were made.

Various routine matters were dealt with from time to time. In the 17th century the court was much concerned with the dilapidated condition of the common pound, the pillory and the common cage, and nuisances such as encroachments on highways and common land (e.g. waste), interference with rights of way or of light belonging to the tenants of the manor were investigated and judgment given. Arbitration between tenants was another duty; in 1679 Jonathan Rose asked the court to determine the ownership of an oak tree which grew in his hedge, dividing his land from Joshua Lomase, gentleman. Rose claimed it was "partible", Lomase that it was wholly his, but the court decided after four members of the court had inspected the site, in favour of Rose. Another duty was to see that on the death of a husband in accordance with the customs of the manor a widow had her dower of one-third of the land of her late spouse. This often involved the settlement of trouble between a succeeding son and his mother, although sometimes the widow remarried and her new husband made the claim. In 1691 Mary Thredder claimed from her son John one third part of a messuage and twenty acres of land. Four members of the jury were appointed and reported that to the best of their knowledge they had "set oute the thirds."

But as the years went by these duties fell less frequently on the court, and it became merely a recording agency for sales and inheritance of land. Nevertheless its records are of interest, showing the physical development of the town and certain of the social changes which occurred.

CHAPTER 5

Hemel Hempstead and its People During the 17th and 18th Centuries

Part 1

The granting of the Charter by Henry VIII in 1539 with its market and fair was one of the most important events in the history of Hemel Hempstead; it brought about great changes, especially in the economic sphere. At the same time occurred the dissolution of the monastery at Ashridge which had already begun to dispose of its local property and now suffered the total dispersal of its lands. John Waterhouse, (brother of the last Rector of Ashridge and occupier of the Bury, Hemel Hempstead), and his son-in-law, Richard Combes, acquired a sixty-year lease of the Bury with the land, buildings and stock of the manor, the Bury Mill and fishing rights. This lease was confirmed by the crown in 1540 and in 1557 Richard Combes purchased the property.

The development of the present High Street was set in train by these events. It should be added that about this time there was similar enterprise within the county generally. By this time the effects of the depression caused by the civil wars of the previous century had subsided and, with the growth of the London market, places like Hemel Hempstead, not too far from the capital, were beginning to prosper and develop.

At this time there was no High Street, or Market Street as it was once called, as we know it. This is clear from the evidence given in the case of Oxley v. Partridge (see pp. 182) when in 1677 much useful information about the earlier history of the town was recorded. One important witness was Robert Sawcer (see p. 77), described as a gentleman aged 50 years; he said that he had been told by his father, who had been clerk to the Bailiff and his jury for about 20 years, and by his grandfather "that the ground that is now the market place was in fields that were plowed there and not being above two or three houses ther standing in or near the said place which . . . . were called Churchend, and that when . . . . a market (was) granted . . . . the Market Street was taken out of the fields and built upon."

Another witness, Nicholas Stratford aged 70 years, who had been Bailiff of Hemel Hempstead in 1660, stated that the ground in front of the house of James Rolfe against the Market House was ploughed to the middle of the road and Rolfe claimed it. This house was opposite the Market House, and must have been near the King's Arms as in 1629 the Bailiwick decided that on market days the shoemakers should not stand in front of certain premises including the King's Arms and the premises of Mr. Rolfe. Rolfe, being awkward, was trying, after the street had been made, to exercise some rights which he claimed he had before it existed.

At the hearing of the case in the Court of Exchequer it was stated on behalf of the inhabitants that they hoped to prove that the Market Street was the inheritance of the Earl of Leicester and called Churchfield, and by him or someone interested conveyed to the use of the inhabitants.

The 1523 Rental supports this evidence. In Churchend there were six messuages, (a messuage is the site of dwelling house and its appurtenances), two cottages and one workshop or smithy. Of the six, two have been identified, the Crown Inn and the Cock Inn, both on the east side of what later became the street. The smithy was said to be newly built opposite or near the house of the occupier and next to the cemetery. There were also the vicarage and the Church House. (See Chapter 11 Pt 1.) here was no mention of any street. So we can visualise the scene, a small group of properties near the church and approached by a rough path. There was the smithy and near it the Crown Inn, (the Cock became one later) owned and occupied by William Patewyn, described in his will as a butcher. The Rental also mentions four premises in another field named Churchfield, adjoining Churchend. One was occupied by William Stephyns, the first Bailiff and named as such in the Charter; he had a messuage and 6 acres of land adjoining next to Gydy Lane and he held another 4 acres in the same field. He also held land elsewhere in the parish.

It is probable therefore that the formation of the Market Street and its development arose out of the establishment of the market. It was not long before building took place on the land belonging to the Combes and on the church lands which adjoined. By the beginning of the seventeenth century the records mention the White Hart and a row of dwellings above it on the land in front of the vicarage leading up to the Market House, which by then had been erected on the site of the old Church House. That the White Hart belonged to the Combes is proved by an entry in the Bailiwick records for 1629; the Bailiff wanted to place the smiths during the weekly market against the inn "if Mr. Combes approves". The shambles for the market were in two rows on land which was partly waste of the manor and partly a portion of the churchyard; the back row belonged to the church and the front row to the Bailiwick, but for some period the rents of both rows were collected by the church authorities with the consent of the Bailiff and all the proceeds went to the church.

It may be well to mention here a local legend that at one time the present High Street ran through Gadebridge Park. In a sense this was true inasmuch as before the High Street was made there was "a long alley or walk" mentioned in the Church Terrier of 1625 as belonging to Francis Combes of the Bury.

That the street was formed and followed by building development can be gathered from certain transactions in which property, formerly belonging to the Earl of Leicester, was sold in 1582 to three local men. Seven of the premises mentioned in the deed were in the area of the Market Street and some of them were described as newly built; one was the Cock, occupied by Richard Pope, and another "near unto a lane called Cherry Hill Lane" was probably the Royal Oak. Incidentally, these transactions included land which became part of Boxmoor and this was the origin of the suggestion that this trust be formed to hold lands given by the Earl of Leicester. (See Chapter 10). It may be that the statement made to the Court of Exchequer and referred to above (i.e. that the site of the market and the street had been the gift of the Earl of Leicester) was based on these transactions. That the inhabitants attached considerable importance to the deeds relating to the transactions is evidenced by the fact that they were copied in full into the book containing the 1523 Rental.

Other, if less important results than the development of the Market Street followed the advent of the market. The separation of Hemel Hempstead, Bovingdon and Flaunden, into quite distinct units, already apparent, became more marked. The fact that the benefits of the charter applied only to the inhabitants of "the vill" (i.e. Hemel Hempstead), and were not shared by those of the hamlets, no doubt contributed to this separation.

Within Hemel Hempstead itself were other changes. Hitherto it had been divided into parts, which may well have been the tithings of earlier centuries. The 1523 Rental mentions three districts, Estbrooke, Boxhamsted and Felden-cum-Two Waters. By the seventeenth century there were still three, but they were called the Towne, High Street side (now High Street Green) and Boxted side; the first mentioned was something of an island around the church and the other two seem to have been roughly divided by the river Gade. These divisions were later reduced to two, the Towne area being shared by the other divisions by a line down the middle of the street. The divisions were of some importance and created sectional interests and enthusiasms; separate poor rates were made for each, and parish officers, such as the constables, were also appointed separately for each division.

One further consequence of the rapid development of Hemel Hempstead could have been the division of the Dacorum Hundred into two parts in 1644; the whole parish of Hemel Hempstead with Great Gaddesden and King's Langley was separated from Berkhamsted and its surrounding parishes, and a Chief Constable was appointed for each part. Later when the Poor Law Unions were formed after 1834 these two areas were constituted as separate unions.

Thus by the beginning of the seventeenth century the market had become well established and the Market Street developed. The street itself was narrow, as is proved by frequent references in the Bailiwick records; in places it was only wide enough for the passage of one vehicle at a time, and on either side were some narrow strips of the waste of the manor on which were erected some of the stalls used on market and fair days, and about which there was so much commotion later. The roadway was poorly metalled, if at all, and the users especially the animals, did nothing to improve the insanitary conditions.

Our street was no doubt a picturesque assemblage, having developed in an unplanned manner, a pleasing effect which it has retained to this day. There was no doubt a mixture of old and new in 1600. Some at least of the premises mentioned in the 1523 Rental were still there, and how old they had been then we do not know. There was also the old vicarage which was built of timber with a tiled roof and was soon to be rebuilt. New premises had been erected in the sixty years since the charter, including the market house (See Chapter 8) erected on the site of the church house authorised in 1527. An examination of the backs of some of the existing premises shows the forms of construction in use about 1600 or earlier; there one can still see the half-timbering and the filling, first wattle and daub and later the brick nogging commonly found in Hertfordshire.

A few examples of local inventories will show the type and variety of property in the Market Street in the first part of the seventeenth century, and it must be remembered that as the details were recorded after the death of the occupiers the premises may have been erected very much earlier than the date shown:—

Date	*Name and occupation*	*Total value of goods*	*Accommodation*
1612	Roger Turner Chandler	£39	Hall, kitchen and 2 lofts over. Workhouse & loft over.
1613	George Tompson Joiner	£39	Hall and loft over. Shop in yard, loft over, cellar.
1615	William Smyth Blacksmith		Hall, chamber and new loft over. Blacksmith's shop.
1620	Francis Martin Hatter	£57	Shop, hall, buttery, kitchen chambers over shop, hall and kitchen. Cellar.
1628	Thomas Taylor Clerk in Holy Orders (Vicar)	£145	Hall, parlour, kitchen and 3 chambers above, cellar and outbuildings.
1629	Josias Martin Doctor of Physick	£206	Hall, parlour, study, kitchen and brewhouse, 3 chambers above, 2 attics.
1630	Christopher Besouth Scrivener	£58	Shop with loft over. Hall, kitchen and rooms above. Cellar.

At this time the Market Street had not the continuous line of building it has today; this came later when in-filling took place on the open spaces between the buildings. A number of the properties had substantial gardens which were later built on.

There was apparently no road connection with Marlowes, but probably a footpath, for during the century one authority spent 6d repairing the stile leading to "Marloes". The name must have been that of a local family, probably farmers, to whom frequent references are made in the parish registers about the beginning of the seventeenth century.

Bury Mill End, the district around the Mills, formed part of the Towne area. There was a cluster of dwellings there. The mills were part of the holding leased by Ashridge Monastery to Waterhouse and Combes in 1535. A conveyance of 1678 shows that besides the two water mills there was a flour mill with the following accommodation:

> "On the ground floor the mill house, a hall, two butteries and a brewhouse, on the first floor two chambers, and on the second two garrets."

The Bury has already been described, but mention should be made of the Tithe Barn nearby, with two means of access, one from the courtyard of the house and one over land to the north-east, through what is now Tithebarn Yard, (off the west side of the High Street). There were two barns, the wheat barn and the oats barn. The great tithes, those of corn and hay, originally went to the monastery and were later leased by the crown to the authorities of St. Paul's Cathedral, and then farmed by them to Francis Combe of the Bury. The small tithes, those of lambs, wool, salves, pigs, honey, fruit etc., belonged to the vicar. The great tithes were commuted in 1678 to 2d. per acre for ploughed land and meadows, and the barns, no longer needed, were let. These tithes were valuable, as the Land Tax valuation made in 1691 assessed the vicar for the small tithes at £50, and Combe and another at £245.6.0*d.* for the great tithes.

One or two other features should be mentioned. Beyond the shambles was the cage in which offenders were locked up and which, by the middle of the seventeenth century, had fallen into decay. (See Chapter 9.) Nearby was the pillory which was also neglected; in 1635 the Bailiff spent 6d. on its repair, but in 1651 the Manor Court noted that it was again out of repair and plaintively recorded that "there was never a cuckingstoole".

The pound must have been hereabouts too, although it was later moved to Cherry Bounce. This was also out of repair and in 1651 William Finch, the bailiff of the manor (not to be confused with the Bailiff of the Town), was in trouble for not carrying out certain repairs he had been ordered to do and for which timber valued at £10 had been felled on the Lord's waste; he was threatened with a fine of £5 if he continued to ignore his instruction.

To the east of the street was the Banqueting House, a Tudor building, which still remained in the 1960's. It was reached by a passageway joining the High Street at the Old Plait Market opposite the butchers' stalls. In 1840 or 1850 it was still one house, and the rooms were embellished with carved oak panelling which 30 years later had disappeared. Later it was divided into three cottages. How it got its name and whether it was used for such purposes is not known. According to his will, dated 1734, part of it was then occupied by Francis Moore the elder, a butcher; it had a garden in front which was paled and a great yard before it "extending to the land or passage out of Hemel Hempstead Town" with a stable and hayloft over and a slaughter-house and wellhouse on part of it. What now exists is but part of a much older building or series of buildings.

By the end of the century considerable changes had taken place. Some of the old buildings had been altered or replaced, and new ones had been erected on the vacant plots. More trades were carried on, and to some shopkeepers had come increased prosperity. A number of the newer dwellings were larger; there were more three-storeyed premises and the accommodation was more extensive. A noticeable feature was the increase in licensed premises. A survey of the Manor made in 1676 contains relatively few references to premises in the street, indicating the extent to which so much of the old copyhold land had been converted to freehold.

The eighteenth century saw further development in the town due to increased population and commercial activity. New trades and businesses were attracted and later there was some industrial development. Agriculture also prospered due partly to the expansion of the markets in London. Naturally this expansion was reflected in more and bigger and better houses and shops in Market Street. Existing premises were altered, many of them in the 1720's, for the leaden heads of rain pipes still bear initials and dates. Some reconstruction also followed the great fire in 1749.

New buildings were also erected on such spare frontage land as remained and a continuous building line was established on each side of the street. Cottages were erected and outbuildings converted into cottages in the yards behind the street, creating conditions which developed into slums in the following century. Further building continued up Cherry Bounce and Saffron Lane and also in Bury Mill End, with extensions up Bury Hill and along Bury Road. Towards the end of the century the opening up of Marlowes began with some speculative building to be continued in the next century.

The attempts of the Bailiwick to maintain some measure of control may be seen from odd references in the Bailiwick records. In 1701 the Jury inspected the premises of Walter Oxten and a house newly erected by Zachariah Field, to see if there had been any encroachment on the highway; in 1725 they dealt with another by William Ivory, and in 1753 they agreed that Edward Ivory could erect part of a shed to the blacksmith's shop.

In an area where agriculture was still the principal occupation many lived on or near the farms where they worked, or in small communities not far away. In addition, certain industries like milling, tanning, brickmaking and others had been established and their location was dictated by the requirements of the trade.

Outlying settlements at Boxted, Green End, High Street Green, Felden, Bourne End and Winkwell continued in the seventeenth century to be concerned chiefly with agriculture. In places like Piccotts End, Corner Hall and

Two Waters there was a mixed population of agricultural workers and those employed in trades such as milling and tanning. Piccotts End housed the workers from the farms surrounding the hamlet; Piccotts End Farm, Lovetts End Farm, Wood Farm, and Two Beeches Farm. But other trades developed besides farming and milling; quite early there was a blacksmith and later a wheelwright, and several taverns satisfied local thirst. There were probably two tanneries, one in the hamlet and the other at Waterside near Gadebridge Lane. This tanyard at Waterside was attached either to an old farm house described in 1742 as built with timber, with a brick kitchen or brewhouse adjoining with a room over, or to a brick house newly built there in that year. Neither of these houses has survived.

Another tanyard at Corner Hall was established in the sixteenth century and acquired by the Deacons towards the end of that period. It remained in that family for many generations and was in use until recent years. Waste from this tannery was dumped on Boxmoor affecting both the drainage and the fertility of the ground.

Thomas Deacon acquired property at Corner Hall in 1599. He became affluent and well established there as a tanner and in 1637 he served as Bailiff. His inventory, dated 11th January 1642, indicates his wealth, for it totalled £1,106.15.0*d.* His house consisted of a hall, kitchen and brewhouse, with three chambers above, and a garret above this; he had a tanyard with two sheds which had lofts above. His "butts, hides and skines" were valued at £678 "the Barke beinge allowed." He was also a farmer with crops worth nearly £200, his animals nearly £50 and his farming equipment nearly £20. His house was also well furnished. He left his business to his son, Elisha who was a signatory to the Solemn League and Covenant and may well have been a captain in the Parliamentary Army during the Civil Wars. When he died in 1658, his estate was valued at £635.12.8*d.,* but the house in which he lived was quite different from that of his father. On the ground floor were a long hall and a little hall, with an entry, two kitchens and a buttery; on the first floor were five chambers (one with a little room by it), and there was a garret above; there was also a cellar. The house was much better furnished and in the long hall were some virginals and in the little hall a bandoare, a musical instrument somewhat like a guitar. He had at least two sons and eight daughters. One of the daughters, Sarah, married Daniel Shipton and they lived with her parents. After Sarah's father died they continued to live there and Daniel carried on as a tanner, either on his own account or in some sort of partnership with his brother-in-law. There is ample evidence that the Deacons continued to carry on the business on and off during the eighteenth century. The property remained in use as a tannery throughout the nineteenth century and at the beginning of the twentieth was owned by Henry Balderson.

The leather industry was important locally, as is shown by the appointment of a leather searcher and sealer by the Manor Court: its product served many purposes, not only for footwear but for clothing, for farming purposes such as harness, and in industry for such things as belts, buckets and bellows. It depended mainly on local supplies of hides and needed considerable supplies of water, hence the location of the local works by the River Gade.

Whilst tanning at Corner Hall was an important industry and gave employment to a number of people in the cottages of the hamlet, there were other employment and other properties. According to the 1523 Rental there was an inn there which had then been "newly erected". By the end of the sixteenth century there were at least two farm houses, one occupied by the Besouths, as well as other dwellings. Both farm houses have been demolished although they were there until comparatively recent times. One was called Old Corner Hall and was a substantial dwelling on the west side of the roadway; it adjoined the old tanyard which lay to the south abutting on the one-way street leading to Two Waters Road. The other was on the east side of the Corner Hall street, almost opposite the one-way street and was called Corner Hall. Later, probably in the eighteenth century, another large house was built immediately to the south of the timber yard, first called "The Lawns" and later "Lawn Park"; this too has now gone. There was also a beerhouse called the Horn in the one-way street, and within living memory the trap doors to the cellars were in the highway and were opened periodically when deliveries were made by the brewers. No doubt this and the other tavern (the one which was newly erected in 1523) were well patronised by the papermakers who occupied some of the cottages in the second half of the eighteenth century.

There still remains at least one old building, the Gables, which stands at the corner of Corner Hall road and the one-way street, and was at one time occupied by the Deacon family. Just how it fits into the old pattern is not certain but it remains a good example of seventeenth century Hemel Hempstead.

Nearby was another settlement, Two Waters with its later extensions to Frogmore End to the south-east and along the present London Road in a westerly direction towards Boxmoor. To the south-west lay the small farming community of Felden, or Fields End as it was then called. Two Waters has always been an important settlement. At the junction of the two rivers there was sufficient power to drive two mills, one the old fulling mill, and the other a corn mill; one was at Two Waters itself and the other at Frogmore End. The fulling Mill probably began to function as such in the thirteenth or fourteenth century when similar mills were established all over the country in places where sufficient water power existed. Previously the work had been done by the feet of men treading the cloth in a trough. Now by a simple invention the work of many men was done mechanically with only one individual to supervise the machine. During most if not all of the seventeenth century one or other of these mills was occupied by the Turners.

Other trades also flourished at Two Waters. The usual services were provided by a blacksmith, a wheelwright and a brewer. Another important trade was malting, and papermaking was added towards the end of the eighteenth century. Mention should also be made of the Bell Inn which was there at least from the beginning of the seventeenth century, catering for travellers along the main road. Later, when the road was turnpiked and coaches travelled along it, the Bell was one of the stopping places. There one could change from the London coach to catch one for Leighton Buzzard which enabled travellers to complete their journey to Hemel Hempstead Towne. The main road was a busy one because along it went produce from the local farms to market in London. A directory of the 1790's describes the road as "one of the worst turnpike ways to London". An inventory, made in 1727 of Joseph Weedon, a waggoner of Two Waters, shows that he needed seven horses to service his one waggon.

Away to the north of Two Waters and Apsley was an area stretching from Bennetts End towards Cupid Green, which consisted mainly of agricultural holdings, but scattered here and there were a number of fields from which the clay was excavated and made into bricks or tiles. This kind of work was carried on until the 1930's. One or two places are worthy of note. Tile Kiln Lane is an obvious place and the earliest reference is to Tile Kiln House in the Manor Court Rolls for 1603. This area is still pitted with dells from which the clay has been extracted. Another area is near Swallow Dell Lane and the remains of a tile kiln were found there when the roundabout was constructed a few years ago. Several places along High Street Green have been excavated mainly on land which belonged to the Sanders family who were brickmakers in the eighteenth century.

One brickmaker's inventory survives from the year 1670, that of Thomas Edmonds of Bennetts End who died deep in debt. Nevertheless his inventory shows that he made both bricks and tiles and that his fuel for burning them was wood, not coal.

In this neighbourhood were also lime kilns on land opposite Elephant Farm. (These works were restarted in the 1930's and were operated until the 1939-45 war made it impossible to carry on.) It was said that the chalk found here was of very good quality.

Two other local communities are worthy of mention. The first was in the St. John's Road and Boxmoor area and was called Crouchfield, with extensions on Boxmoor and at Green End. Crouchfield, or Crowchefelde, was the name of a common field which in 1523 had at least 17 tenants with scattered foldings. By 1676, however, part of this field had been built on, accommodating some farm houses and cottages with a tavern or two, a shop and a few craftsmen, including a weaver.

The other area was Bourne End and Winkwell. Here three boundaries met. Winkwell was in the Hemel Hempstead part of the parish, part of Bourne End in the Bovingdon portion and the rest of Bourne End was a detached part of the parish of Northchurch. These parts formed one small community with the mill, farm houses and inns, smithy and cottages. Some of the inn buildings survive to this day.

CHAPTER 5

Hemel Hempstead and its people during the seventeenth and eighteenth centuries

Part 2 The People

Because there were no censuses in the seventeenth and eighteenth centuries we cannot estimate with accuracy what the population was, but certain data still available enable us to make rough calculations of the figures. In 1563 as a result of an enquiry by the Privy Council returns were made in the diocese of Lincoln of the number of families in each parish. In 1603 a return of communicants was made, and another in 1676 gave the number of adults over 16. The figures are:—

	1563 families	*1603 communicants*	*1676 adults over 16*
Hemel Hempstead	144	600	501
Bovingdon	50	no	285
Flaunden	16	separate figures	67
	210	600	853

Using a multiplier of 4½ persons per family, the 144 families of Hemel Hempstead in 1563 give a total population of about 650, with a total of 950 for Hemel Hempstead, Bovingdon and Flaunden. Assuming that about 40% of the total population was below communicable age (15-18 years) the 1603 return would give a total population of 960. Similarly the 1676 return gives us figures of 800 for Hemel Hempstead and 1360 for the three places together. It must be emphasised, however, that these are no more than rough estimates. It is interesting to note that during the hearing of the second Oxley case in 1678 it was stated that about 1620 there were some 500 inhabitants in the Towne; it would be useful to know whether this figure related only to adults (which it probably did) and if it was restricted to those living in "the Towne area". Whatever may have been the actual numbers undoubtedly the population grew steadily throughout the period from the mid sixteenth century to the end of the eighteenth century. At the end of the sixteenth century, and again in the years 1623 and 1624, there were outbreaks of plague, and on each occasion there followed a noticeable drop in the birth rate, to be picked up later. There were movements into and out of the parish, but the net result was a gain, especially after the mid 1600's.

Taking all the known factors into account, rough estimates of the population may be made as follows:

1563	650
1676	800
1790	2400
1801 (census)	2722
1811 (census)	3240

The figure for the 1811 census is given because it is accepted that the 1801 census was inaccurate, the numbers being understated.

The make-up of the population and the different classes to which people belonged are important. That the manor belonged to the monastery until 1539, and thereafter to the Crown meant that the district had no resident 'squire' until the Halseys of Gaddesden acquired the manor in the eighteenth century. Consequently local affairs were generally managed by members of the lesser gentry or others such as yeomen, professional men like doctors and lawyers, and later by the more successful shopkeepers. Some were appointed justices of the peace or to such county posts of importance as High Constable of the Dacorum Hundred. Year by year these and others were elected to be Bailiff, an honour which was usually much appreciated. Naturally the clergy had an influence dependent on the personality of the individual.

During the seventeenth century the most important family were the Combes, yet they never seemed to rise to the status of gentry. At the Restoration Francis Combe was quite content to be appointed by Charles II as Steward of the Manor at £20 a year, no doubt in the hope that he would recover some of the money he had invested in purchasing a part of the manor during the period of the Commonwealth and lost when the property was returned to the Crown on the restoration of the monarchy. Some of the later occupants of the Bury, notably the Gingers who were local attorneys, were also of importance in local affairs.

We cannot deal at length with all the individuals who played an active part in the affairs of the parish during these two centuries, but a careful selection may give us some understanding of the life of the times.

We can start with the Besouths, an old family of which there were several branches. They date back at least to the fifteenth century. John Besouth, aged 42 or more, is mentioned in an Inquisition Post Mortem of 1471-2. By the sixteenth century several branches of the family were established in different parts of Hemel Hempstead.

In 1564 another John Besouth bought the sub-manor of Agnells and was succeeded in 1595 by his son, also named John. The latter took part in local affairs; he served on the Bailiff's jury and most probably had been Bailiff before 1619. He was probably a justice of the peace, and in 1628 was appointed by the county justices to be one of two treasurers for hospitals and maimed soldiers. In addition to farming his considerable estate at St. Agnells he carried on some business in Market Street in a shop he was renting from the Bailiwick when their records started in 1619. He died in

1643, a man of considerable property; apart from his possessions at St. Agnells he had land in the manor of Redbourn and property in Market Street, Hemel Hempstead; his specific bequests in money alone totalled approximately £1,000. One interesting bequest is for £10, to be paid by his executors at the rate of £1 a year for 10 years, to such preachers as his executors might choose, to preach a sermon in each of those years on the anniversary of either the defeat of the Spanish Armada or the discovery of the Gunpowder Plot in 1605. He considered these events to be occasions when this country had been delivered from its enemies by the Almighty, and thus he reflects what must have been the feelings of most men of his time. To the poor of the town he left £5. His widow Amye was probably the last person bearing the name of Besouth to live at St. Agnells; she died in 1647 "being olde and full of dayes."

The Besouths are a good example of how members of important local families frequently intermarried. He had two daughters, Hester and Mary, to each of whom he left a moiety of his manor of St. Agnells and of the residue of his estate. Hester married Josias Martyn, "a doctor of Physick", who took a very active part in the affairs of the town. He was born in 1580, one of the sons of Francis Martyn who "had been a souldier for the towne". Hester was his second wife, whom he married after the death of his first wife, Elizabeth, in 1613. Before his second marriage he lived and practised in Saffron Lane, but afterwards he moved to more substantial premises in the Market Street, a three-storey house, very well furnished. As he was probably the only medical practitioner in the district he had a good practice. and when he died in 1629 he left an estate worth over £200, as well as freehold and other property in Hemel Hempstead and Ivinghoe. His books and the other contents of his study were valued at £50 and his wearing apparel £30. To his son John he left his best sword, his best ring and his best gown, and to another son, Josias, he bequeathed his best cloak, his second best sword and ring, his best Bible and his Book of Martyrs. To the poor of Hemel Hempstead he gave £3. He was one of eleven men who negotiated the lease of the waste of the Manor from the Crown in 1623, against which there was such an outcry in years following. (See Chapter 8).

Hester survived her husband by a matter of 40 years, dying in 1673. They had several children, and one of their sons, Josias, succeeded to his father's practice. In 1683 he successfully petitioned the Government for an M.D. degree, stated that he had been educated at Trinity College, Oxford, and had practised for 20 years. He was not as successful as his father, possibly because of competition from the Smiths who had established a rival practice. When he died in 1672 his mother claimed that all the books and medical sundries were hers as they had belonged to her husband and had only been loaned to her son.

Hester left a substantial estate of her own. To one grandson, Josias, she left £10 to be paid during his apprenticeship and another £200 to be paid to him at the end of it towards setting him up as an apothecary. Josias subsequently practised in Hemel Hempstead for a short time until he died in 1681, described in the parish register as a physician. To another grandson, John, she left £20 towards his present and future maintenance at the University of Cambridge, and £30 towards his degree of Batchelor in Physick, together with "all the books and other goods in the long studdy (except my waters, syrrups and physicall things)".

Her daughter Hester married William Houlker of King's Langley. Through his wife William acquired the moiety of the manor of St. Agnells which had been her mother's; he, together with Francis King, were shown as the owners in the Survey made in 1676.

Before leaving the Martyns mention should be made of other members of the family. Of the other sons of Francis Martyn one, Azariah, was a tailor and another, Francis, was a hatter. The latter's business must have been a precarious one, for of the debts due to him when he died only £3 were said to be good, whilst the bad ones amounted to £43, about which it was recorded "most of the Debtors being dead or worth nothing and other not knowne where they dwelleth." Nothing is known about the rest of Francis's numerous progeny.

John Besouth's other daughter, Mary, married into the King family, and her share of the manor of St. Agnells descended to her son, Francis. He became a man of substance, a Justice of the Peace, Bailiff in 1677, and a trustee for the settlement of the debts of Sir Richard Combe in 1685. He owned and lived in the house called 'the Lockers'.

Among other grandchildren to benefit under John Besouth's will were John and Nicholas King, to each of whom he gave a substantial sum in money and property in Market Street, Hemel Hempstead, including a shop adjoining the Legge, which was next to the Bell. Here Nicholas carried on a business as a draper, and so successful was he that when he died he left well over £3,000, a considerable sum in those days. He had no less than £200 of ready money in his house, and £260 of goods and money in his shop, an interesting comment on the absence of banking facilities at the time. He took part in local politics, was elected Bailiff in 1666, and was one of the defendants in the second Oxley case about the market rights.

Two other members of the Besouth family are worth mentioning. John Besouth was a scrivener and clerk to the Bailiwick in 1619. He died in 1629. Christopher Besouth was also a scrivener, and when he died in 1630 he left books worth £8.9s. and a number of maps. The fact that these individuals carried on the practice of scriveners is interesting. They were in effect attorneys, estate agents and brokers, often arranging loans. Their presence indicates considerable dealings in land, a fact confirmed by other sources.

There were at least two successful farming families of Besouths, one at Corner Hall and another at Heath Farm. The house belonging to the latter farm still stands and is known as Heath Barn. A John Besouth carried out improvements there in the sixteenth century, for in his will of 1586 he refers to the new hall, and mentions "all the wainscotte, seelings and glasse about the house".

Various other members of the family are mentioned in the records from time to time. In 1589 Richard and Robert were concerned in proceedings at Quarter Sessions when one Henry Jones was charged with keeping "a house of play" and the two Besouths were among a number who were engaged in the game. Ephraim Besouth, described as a butcher, was also presented in 1631 charged with poaching in the fisheries belonging to John, Earl of Bridgewater, when it was alleged he had taken and killed eleven trout value 20*s.* and four "pukis" value 6*s.* James Besouth, a carpenter, was Bailiff and churchwarden in 1734.

Other families may be briefly referred to. The Salters were very prominent in the sixteenth and seventeenth centuries. They lived at and owned High Street Farm which in the seventeenth century was at least 260 acres. Hobletts also belonged to them, although the living accommodation there was probably only a cottage then; the so-called Manor House was built later. The Howes were an old family who occupied several substantial farms in the district, notably Gadebridge, Pix and Felden. Several of them were elected as Bailiffs and one was Chief Constable of the Dacorum Hundred in 1647. A Howes family name was Richard, and perhaps the most notable one was he who was Bailiff in 1673 and again in 1689. He took an active part in the fight with Oxley about the market rights and advanced considerable sums to finance the legal costs involved.

Then there was Robert Eymes (or Eames), a yeoman of considerable substance who purchased the sub-manors of Buers and Haybourne during the reign of Elizabeth I, a purchase of which he was obviously proud. In his will he left £20 to the poor of Hemel Hempstead to be paid out at the rate of £1 per annum "in the presence of the overseers or other honest men." He was a sheep-farmer in a big way of business. In the late seventeenth century the manor of Haybourne belonged to Jonathan Pratt; he was a trustee of Boxmoor from 1659, Chief Constable for Dacorum Hundred in 1687 and Bailiff of Hemel Hempstead in 1693. His property included the Black Lyon in Market Street, where he lived and carried on the business of a victualler. He died in 1709.

Two individuals, who may have been Bailiffs before the records started in 1619 and who played an important part in affairs during their lifetime, were Robert Shadd and Francis Mayne. The former led the group of tenants who successfully resisted the efforts of James I in 1609 to increase the rents of his manorial tenants in Hemel Hempstead. Francis Mayne was not so successful when, in 1624, with 26 other inhabitants (including Francis Combe the elder and Thomas Taylor, the vicar) he opposed the Crown's demand that the inhabitants should pay an annual rent for that part of the manorial waste on which the market structures were erected each market day and at each annual fair, a right they had enjoyed without payment for nearly 100 years.

Another family was the Settles. John Settle carried on a business as a barber in Market Street, making a modest living. He and his wife Margaret were respectable and god-fearing folk, but were always in trouble with the authorities; they were dissenters and were frequently presented to Quarter Sessions for not attending divine service. They had a son whom they named Elkanah, who practised as a barber-surgeon in Hemel Hempstead and, for a time, in London. He prospered and acquired considerable property, including Tile Kiln House with some 28 acres of land, the Ship Inn in Market Street and other land at Piccotts End; in 1654 he was elected Bailiff. He took an active part in the fight for the market rights and was a trustee of Boxmoor. In his youth he was not averse to a little sport, and was presented to Quarter Sessions on a charge of poaching. He died intestate about 1683 at the ripe old age of 87.

Nor should we forget the less important and the less successful. When Bailiff Roger Partridge died in 1628, his year as Bailiff was completed by Thomas Lovesay, a shopkeeper in the Market Street. He had married Alice Gardner in 1587 and his first child, a boy, was born in 1588, but lived only a few weeks. Thereafter, over a period of 18 years his wife bore him at least ten children, all girls - 1589 Jane, 1590 Sarah, 1592 Rebecca, 1594 Mary, 1595 Martha, 1598 Elizabeth, 1600 Ann, 1602 Abigail, 1605 Alice and 1607 Phebe. How he must have prayed for a son! Of these ten only two can be traced, Jane who died in 1612 and Sarah who married Henry Long in 1622. We have poor Jane's inventory of her goods when she died which comprised:—

a gowne		18.	0.
3 petticoats	1	0.	0.
3 waistcoates		10.	0.
an hatt		6.	8.
an apron and a pair of bodyes		6.	0.
all her lynnen with some other old apparell	1	2.	0.
money in her purse		1.	2.
	4.	3.	10.

Another case was that of John Wenlock who died in 1622. His inventory showed goods and effects worth £9.17.6*d.*, no money, and debts amounting to £9.16.9*d.* of which £6.15.0*d.* was due to two brewers. He probably carried on a small alehouse. There was much sympathy for his poor widow for on the inventory the Vicar, Rev. Thomas Taylor, wrote the following footnote:

> "I pray you be good to this poore widow sith the case stands so to her as appears by that above written if she be excommunicated at this time she is quite undone."

Excommunication presumably might follow inability to pay the fees of the Probate Court.

The development and changes in the eighteenth century make a selection of outstanding personages more difficult. While agriculture remained the most important industry, the commerce of the Market Street grew. The increase in the value of land and the need for more houses to accommodate the growing population attracted purchasers and speculators some of whom were members of local families.

Thomas Partridge, a member of a family which had lived in the parish for several centuries, became a land-owner of substance and a speculative builder. He was born in 1676 and lived at High Street Green, subsequently moving to Piccotts End where he died in 1753 at the age of 76. In 1741 he paid £10 to the churchwardens and overseers as a fine to secure that he would never be required to fill any public office in the parish. He was already a land-owner of some standing when he inherited more property on the death of his brother Seth, a goldsmith and citizen of London. He was well established socially, for in 1715 Dudley Ryder of Westbrook Hay recorded in his diary that he "went after dinner to Hemstead, we went there to visit Mr. Partridge and his wife, we were treated at his lodgings with tea and fruit and chocolate".

He had one child, a daughter named Elizabeth who married Windmills Crompton, a citizen and haberdasher of London, a man of means, and one of the original trustees of the Sparrow Hearne Turnpike Trust. (See p. 120) The Cromptons inherited the property of Thomas Partridge and added to it. They lived at Piccotts End in the house which was later known as Marchmont House. One of their two daughters married Hugh, the third and last Earl of Marchmont, Elizabeth Crompton died in 1770 and Windmills in 1771, both aged 70. He left a short will leaving all his personal property in trust for his two daughters, having disposed of his real estate during his lifetime. He directed his daughters to "give such part of his wearing apparel as they think proper to my servants in such proportions as they think fit."

When Elizabeth Crompton married the Earl of Marchmont she took with her a good dowry from her grandfather, Thomas Partridge, who had built up a considerable fortune and was no doubt pleased that his grandchild should make such a match. The earl and Elizabeth maintained a large establishment at Marchmont House. The earl sat in the House of Commons for six years and was a keen collector of rare books and manuscripts. In various ways he acquired a large estate, both in England and Scotland, and locally he was buying property almost to the day of his death in 1794 at the age of 86.

The Birches were another local family who improved their circumstances during the eighteenth century. Both John and Thomas Birch were listed in the Land Tax valuation of 1691. Thomas was a successful farmer living at Piccotts End, but occupying land at Felden and at least part of the Bury lands, for his inventory shows his crops stored in the barns there; he was constable for the Towne area in 1699. His inventory of 1714 totalled £616 and among his bequests were £40 to his wife Elizabeth and one dozen napkins, curtains and valances which were of her own spinning and two blankets and "also all the goods which were her own before I marryed her." The rest of his effects he left to his son Thomas, whom he appointed his sole executor.

Thomas carried on a successful business as a draper in premises near the Swan Inn on the east side of the Market Street. He made several additions to the property he inherited from his father. He, rather than his father, was the Justice of the Peace whose name is mentioned in 1700. He died in 1730 and his will showed that he owned the Bell and the Rose and Crown Inns, houses and shops in Market Street, two cottages in Saffron Lane and Barnes Farm in Kings Langley. He was a Baptist and, among several bequests to the movement, he left an annual sum of £3 "to friends for the Minister of the Baptist Meeting new building situate on the Backside of the Rose and Crown to support the interest of the protestant dissenters called Baptists."

His son Richard carried on the business of draper with the same success as his father, and added to the family fortune. Unlike his father he was a member of the established church and was appointed churchwarden in 1735 and 1736. He was made one of the Governors of the Workhouse in 1741 and elected Bailiff in 1745. The Bailiwick was one of his customers and he supplied the Bellman's coat on several occasions.

One man who played a leading part in the life of the town was the Rev. Rowland Johnson M.A., Vicar of Hemel Hempstead 1729-1773, and also a Justice of the Peace. He was a sound old Whig and a stout supporter of the Government, as is evidenced by a letter he wrote to the Lord Lieutenant of the County in 1745 (the year when the Young Pretender sought to recover the throne for the Stuarts). The letter is about a young man, a Scotsman, who was a teacher employed locally in a school for gentlemen's sons. The Vicar enclosed with his letter copies of three affidavits voluntarily sworn before him and Mr. Carpernter of Redbourn (another Justice) in which were set out the efforts of this young man "by soft artifice.... to abate the Fears of the People who look upon the Pretender's son to be a flaming Bigotted Papist by representing him to have been Educated in England and Scotland.... and to withdraw the subject from his natural obedience to King George and to reconcile him to Popery and the Interest of the Pretender by asserting his Right, and by assuring that he personally knew the Pretender and heard him declare that the Liberty of the Subject should be secured to him and his Property as safe as under the present Government." The Rev. Johnson expressed his intention "as a good subject of his Majesty King George in this public time of Danger make known to my Superiors every species of Treason or Disaffection that came within my Cognisance." We do not know who the schoolmaster was or what happened to him, but the letter shows the state of fear and alarm which the Young Pretender created when he attempted his invasion. No wonder that when the result of the battle of Culloden was known the church bells were rung, and the Bailiff paid 10s. to the ringers for their work.

During the eighteenth century buyers of land and other properties were attracted to Hemel Hempstead. One such was Christopher Thomas Tower who came to live at Gadebridge towards the end of the century. In 1774 the house was advertised to let, following the expiration of a previous lease, in the following terms:- "A Genteel House in a pleasant and plentifull country, not half a mile from the church and Market Town of Hemel Hempstead and 29 miles on a Turnpike Road from London to and from which a Stage Coach travels three times a week." There were two parlours, a study, five bed chambers and a store, three garrets, a good laundry and brewhouse, cellars, a brick wine vault, kitchen, pantries "and all other conveniences for a middling family", also stable for six horses and a coachhouse. The grounds consisted of three small gardens planted with good fruit, a wood of about half an acre cut into walks, two closes of pasture beside which was a fine walk of beeches and a meadow in which were two small fish ponds fed by a trout stream.

Gadebridge House, (now demolished) built about the turn of the 17th century, belonged to the Combes. Originally a farmhouse, it was altered and added to from time to time. An early tenant was William Wigg, a physician, who practised here in the early eighteenth century. In the early nineteenth century it was owned and occupied by Sir Astley Paston Cooper, a surgeon on the staff of Guy's Hospital who performed a minor operation on George IV. He founded the Infirmary at Piccotts End in 1826. He and later members of his family made alterations and additions to Gadebridge House and its estate, and when another Sir Astley was the first Mayor of the Borough in 1896, he owned something like a thousand acres in Hemel Hempstead.

It is interesting to note the growth of the legal profession throughout these two centuries. In the early days most legal work was done by scriveners like John and Christopher Besouth. Following the Besouths Henry Sawcer became Clerk to the Bailiwick in 1630 and continued until his death in 1661. He also was a scrivener and signed himself as such when witnessing wills. His son Robert, giving evidence in the Oxley case in 1676, mentioned how he found the first Bailiwick minute book among his father's papers after his death and took care of it afterwards.

The next Clerk was John Allison who was appointed in 1662 and continued until 1678. He was in office when the evidence was taken for the

Oxley case in 1676 and he gave evidence in the course of which he stated that two years earlier he found the book containing the Rental of 1523 amongst the writing of Sir Richard Combe deceased who.... kept most of the writings belonging to the Towne." Now Allison was not a scrivener, but probably an attorney, and his successor, John Crawley, was also an attorney. It appears that the Clerk's work was by this time requiring someone more highly qualified in the law. Crawley's practice was acquired later by William Ginger and Edward Butterfield. The Gingers played an important part in the affairs of the town in the eighteenth century, during which time they acquired the Bury. There is clear evidence that the present solicitor's practice of Lovel Smeathman & Son dates back at least to the time of John Crawley although it has had various names over the years.

The story of the Crawley family is full of interest and extends over a period of more than a hundred years. They came originally from the eastern side of the country, and by the beginning of the seventeenth century we find Abraham Crawley occupying the Kings Arms, Hemel Hempstead. In 1626 he was before Quarter Sessions, charged with permitting his drinking house to be used improperly. He was Constable for the Towne area in 1630. He was succeeded by his son John Crawley I who carried on the alehouse and was also a yeoman farmer on a fair scale. He was one of the subscribers to the fund for the purchase of the manorial waste for use in connection with the market, and was appointed Constable just before his death in 1659.

His son John Crawley II was the eldest of four children and in due course practised as an attorney. He must have been well qualified and astute, and took a large part in local affairs. In 1678 he was appointed Clerk to the Bailiwick, and was probably a Justice of the Peace. During his career he acquired much property. He lived and practiced in a house he owned, which adjoined the Kings Arms. In 1680 he married Elizabeth Salter, but they were unfortunate with their children, none of whom survived them. John died in 1725 leaving most of his property to his wife, but bequeathing to his sister Mary Marlowes House and a cottage adjoining (now known as Old Marlowes).

Crawley's practice as an attorney was taken over by William Ginger and his sons. Later the Gingers sold their share of the practice and it continued to change hands thereafter, but it still remains in existence under the name of Lovel Smeathman and Son although no member of that family is now a partner.

Elizabeth Crawley survived her husband by fourteen years, and was a woman of substantial means. When she died her will named six ladies who were to support her pall and receive a ring worth a guinea and a pair of "shamy gloves". Six men were to carry her to the church and each was to have a pair of black-topped gloves and silk hatband. The Vicar, Rev. Rowland Johnson, was given £2.2.0*d.* instead of his usual fee and she left £50 to be spent on a stone. The will also stipulated that, "to prevent any dispute after my Death touching the Marble Slabs Stone Hearths and Dutch Tiles in the

Chimney, and painted Landskips over the chimney in the House where I live I desire the same may be looked on as standards to the said House and go with the same to my Cousin Sarah Deacon."

With the passing of Elizabeth this branch of the Crawley family died out, but there were other branches of the family which were more fortunate. One of particular interest was established by Thomas, the brother of John Crawley I, (the father of the attorney). Thomas was a yeoman and a maltster, he took part in public affairs and was a church warden and Bailiff in 1691. He was married three times and his third wife, Jane, bore him three sons, Thomas, John and Edmond. The second son, John Crawley III married Elizabeth Deane at Bovingdon in 1699. By foreclosing on a loan made to John Field they obtained possession of a house and 15 acres in Roberts Lane (near Fields End). When Elizabeth died in 1733 she conveyed this property to her son John IV, and it was this John Crawley who fell on hard times.

In 1733 he and his wife, Grace, and their nine children were granted assistance by the Poor Law authorities at the rate of 8*s.* 0*d.* per week and the vestry referred his case to the Justices. Part of the assistance must have been by way of a loan because the Overseers' accounts show a repayment of £2.5.6*d.* In the Freeholders Book for 1736 he is recorded at Fields End and marked "poor", and in 1743 he was before the Court charged with assaulting his wife. By this time things must have become serious and he entered into an unusual transaction; he conveyed his property in Roberts Lane to the Churchwardens and Overseers, provided they maintained his wife and children in the workhouse. Whether this action was due to his poor circumstances, or to the trouble with his wife, is not disclosed. Another factor could have been the house itself; it was a small cottage of but two rooms, and quite inadequate for so large a family.

John Crawley IV and his family were rescued in 1746 by his eldest son, Edmond, when he returned home from the West Indies, whither he had gone as a mariner in the merchant service. Having ascertained his family's circumstances he arranged for his mother and her children to be discharged from the workhouse, repaid the Overseers the costs they had incurred and secured the re-conveyance of the property in Roberts Lane to his father. The latter must have lived in this property throughout these proceedings and continued to do so until he died in 1779 at the age of 78. His wife died in 1778 aged 79. He was survived by four of his children who are described in documents dealing with the disposal of the Roberts Lane property as: Edmond, of St. George's, Hanover Square, London, gentleman; John, of Yarmouth, Nova Scotia, Canada, gentleman; Ann Cooper of Spring Gardens, St. James, Westminster, widow; and Sarah Keep of Tring, widow.

Medical men in the seventeenth and eighteenth centuries were variously described as Physicians, barber-surgeons and apothecaries. The Martins were the first physicians of whom records exist in Hemel Hempstead, and they were closely followed by the Smiths. Arthur Smith must have practised here soon after the first Josias Martin died in 1657, but the Smiths continued to practise well into the eighteenth century. One member of the family became famous in medical circles. He was Hugh Smith, son of another Hugh, who was an eminent surgeon and apothecary in Hemel Hempstead. The son was eldest of 12 children and was born in 1733. He received the rudiments of education from Dr. John Stirling, Vicar of Great Gaddesden, before going on to Edinburgh where he was given his medical training. On qualifying he travelled on the continent where he lectured and gave demonstrations, and was offered a professorship at Leyden in Holland. He refused this and returned to Hemel Hempstead where he assisted his father for two or three years, studying meanwhile, In 1759 he took lodgings in Mincing Lane, and gave lectures and wrote various professional works. In 1763 he was licensed by the College of Physicians and started to practise. The first year his fees were 17 guineas, the second year 175 guineas, the third year 1100 guineas and the fourth 5000 guineas. He continued to prosper, but eventually had to retire, dying at Stratford, Essex, of a slow consumption in 1790.

Other members of the professions were the two Wiggs, father and son, who lived in Gadebridge house in the early eighteenth century; John Hawkins, Charles Cheerington and Elisha Blayney who were all Bailiffs during the second half of the eighteenth century; and Clarke Wilshaw who lived in Marlowes. Elkana Smith has already been mentioned as a barber-surgeon, and another was William Fuller. He came from Watford and established in the Bell, Market Street, where he carried on his profession as a surgeon as well as his business as a publican, brewing his own beer and selling wine and cider. In addition he carried on a business as a grocer and from these varied activities made a good living. The contents of his house, as shown by the inventory made in 1671 just after his death, included;

In ye shopp and sellar under it:

42 spout potts with sirrups, conserves and oyles in them	5.	0.	0.
40 lesser potts with medicine in them	2.	0.	0.
50 glasses with ingredients	3.	0.	0.
Chemical oyle and playstring	2.	0.	0.
Boxes and barrels with ingredients and spices	3.	15.	0.
6 setts of Boxes with ingredients in them	7.	0.	0.
Small gully potts viales, glasses etc.	1.	10.	0.
The Druggs in ye Compter	10.	0.	0.
Sugar with ye Cask	6.	13.	0.
Raisins currans soape salt starch and all other Grossery comodities with boxes, bagges etc.	16.	0.	0.

In ye Sellers the Beere and Cask	13.	6.	8.
Wine and sider with ye cask	10.	0.	0.
His Books in his studdy and other places	6	10.	0.
Cherurgery instruments	4.	0.	0.

The total value of his inventory was £292.

The Bell Inn was let to William Nixon, but William Fuller's daughter removed to the premises of what had been the Leg Inn and there continued some of her father's business as an apothecary and a grocer. She died in 1709.

Hemel Hempstead and its People during the Seventeenth and Eighteenth Centuries

Part 3. The People at Work

Agriculture was both the oldest and the most important occupation of the people at this time and the main body of the evidence concerning the system of farming is to be found in the rentals and surveys which were made from time to time. The Rental of 1523 has already been discussed at some length, (see Chapter 1 and 4). and another was made in 1620, but the details of this have been lost. Another, called a Parliamentary Survey, was made in 1650 when the Commonwealth Government was endeavouring to sell to private individuals what had once been Crown property; this document is still available, but gives little information. A more detailed survey was made in 1676, which shows the considerable changes which had taken place since 1523. With a few exceptions the common fields, with their strips, had disappeared and most of the land was enclosed. Individual holdings had been consolidated into contiguous units and, as a result, the names of the fields had been altered making any comparison with the details in the 1523 Rental impossible. Excluding certain small areas some 68 holdings are listed of widely differing extent:

Under 21 acres	5
21-50 acres	32
51-75 acres	12
76-100 acres	8
101-150 acres	6
151-200 acres	4
Over 200 acres	1

The largest Farm comprised 273 acres and belonged to Richard Salter. It consisted of 197 acres in High Street Green Farm and 76 acres in Hobletts. Each holding, except a few of the smaller ones, had a farmhouse.

The total area of copyhold land was now smaller as some land had been enfranchised and was now freehold. This conversion to freehold tenure had started quite soon after the Manor had been taken over by the Crown; in various wills of the late sixteenth and early seventeenth centuries there is reference to "freehold land". Not all of the land was occupied by the owner; the tenant farmer had appeared, paying rent to his landlord, often someone from London or elsewhere seeking a profitable investment. By the late seventeenth century there were substantial farmers like Michael Mouse and William Nutkine operating on land they rented. By the beginning of the nineteenth century many farms were rented and had assumed the size and form which existed right up to the 1914-18 War.

The re-arrangement of the fields and the enclosing of the land resulted in smaller fields often bounded by hedges. The area remained well-wooded, with trees of value.This is shown by a survey made of St. Agnells sub-manor in 1645, details of which have survived. On fields totalling 149½ acres the timber was valued at £912. The map which accompanies this survey also indicated that there was an area in Piccotts End which was still farmed in strips.

The agricultural implements in use were of a simple kind and showed comparatively little change over the period. The small farmer had few tools, and must have borrowed others if he needed them. The wills and inventories of a few more prosperous yeomen show the kind of implements in use. In 1537 Ralph Hawkyns bequeathed to different persons a dung fork, a mattock, his best shed, a long cart and a dung cart. In 1547 Richard Byrchmore mentions his carts, plows, harrows and harness. In 1623 the inventory of John Howe, a substantial yeoman whose estate was valued at about £400, listed:

Harrows, ploughs, carts and wheels and timber to make and mend carts and ploughs	7.	13.	4.
Axes, bills and other tools		6.	8.

The inventory of William Nutkine the tenant farmer, made in 1677, has more detail:

Two long carts, three dung carts, three pairs of wheels and a water cart	9.	3.	0.
Plows, harrows and plow gears	2.	12.	6.
cart ropes and sacks	1.	10.	4.
saw, hatchet, bills, shovels and two mattocks		9.	0.
Forks, sickles, scythes and peese hooks		14.	0.

During the sixteenth century the beast of burden was most frequently the ox, but it is evident that it was being gradually replaced by the horse during the seventeenth century. John Stone (1623) had horses and harness worth £20. William Nutkine (1677) had six horses worth £30 and harness valued at 30*s.* 4*d.*, whilst Michael Mouse, another renting farmer, had six horses worth £39.10.0*d.* in 1678.

The earlier part of the eighteenth century may well be represented by Joseph Carter, a husbandman, whose equipment is set out in much detail in his inventory of 1718.

4 horses and harness	12.	0.	0.
3 ploughs, 4 harrows 3 carts 3 shares and plough gears and a dungrake	13.	0.	0.
fork shovels and fans		12.	0.
10 rakes, a cutting knife 2 pease hooks and 2 scythes		8.	0.
3 troughs, a wheelbarrow and lumber		5.	0.
3 dozen hurdles		18.	0.
a pitcher, a pillion and cloth and a lanthorn		4.	0.

Unfortunately the practice of preparing these detailed inventories fell into disuse in the eighteenth century and so we have little information about conditions in the later part of the period.

In the seventeenth century, as in the sixteenth, wheat was the main crop and oats, barley and pease were grown to a lesser extent. Sheep were still the most important livestock, with small numbers of cattle, pigs, goats, poultry and bees. With the growing importance of the London market the output of both grain and livestock had considerably increased, and by the beginning of the seventeenth century Hemel Hempstead was already a very important corn market.

That sheep were important too is evidenced by the intention of the Bailiwick to establish a wool market in 1647, but the individual flocks were not generally large. In the seventeenth and eighteenth centuries flocks up to about 120 are shown by the inventories although the usual number was probably nearer 50 or 60 animals (sheep and lambs).

Besides the field crops mentioned above there was other produce which helped to make the farms self-supporting. Inventories frequently refer to equipment needed for cheese-making, home brewing of beer and curing of bacon. Apples and pears were grown in quantities and local names indicate the existence of cherry orchards. In the 1680's sanfoin grasses are first mentioned and in 1720 Zacariah Sanders grew these and had a crop of turnips valued at £12.

(b) **Trades allied to Agriculture**

Blacksmiths were of course indispensable, and this trade was carried on locally by several generations of the Bunn family. In 1621 William Bunn of Piccotts End had

> iron, coals, weights and scales with all the working tools in the shop and a grindstone "as it goeth" worth £22.4.0*d.*

But in 1640 John Bunn had to be content with £11 worth of equipment which consisted of

> iron (unwrought and old) bellows, anvil hammers and other working tools, steel, horseshoes and nails, weights and scales and coals.

The coals mentioned were most likely charcoal.

Another trade was that of the wheelwright. Early inventories show a minimum of equipment and such stocks as spokes, wheels and timber. A much more comprehensive list is contained in the inventory made in 1725 of Thomas Johnson who carried on business in Bury Mill End. In addition to his household effects and agricultural crops and equipment he had

Spokes etc	35.	10.	0.
Elm and ash	7.	10.	0.
Working tools	2.	10.	0.
18 horses	120.	0.	0.
Harness	20.	0.	0.
5 carts	10.	0.	0.
2 waggons	25.	0.	0.
old wagon bodies etc.	3.	0.	0.
Soot sacks	5.	0.	0.

This particular wheelwright seems to have been a carrier as well.

The trade of the maltster only developed to considerable proportions in the seventeenth century. It was usually carried on by substantial farmers of the yeoman class who grew some of the barley they needed and had capital available to buy the rest from other farmers. They supplied mainly the local brewers but in some cases found markets further afield.

The miller followed an ancient and important trade, and we have seen that Hemel Hempstead was well supplied with mills. In the days of the monastery the mills were run by or for the monks, who required their tenants to take their corn to these mills and surrender a portion of their grain as payment for the grinding. Before the dissolution the Bury Mill had been rented to the Waterhouses, who subsequently purchased it and arranged its letting. The other mills remained with the manor and were owned by the Crown. According to his will dated 1583, John Waterhouse of Whitchurche in Buckinghamshire about 1572 took a lease of the two mills at Two Waters and the one at Piccotts End for his life and those of his two sons Henry and Edward. In 1650 the lease was still in force and the corn mill at Two Waters was occupied by John Turner and that at Piccotts End by Thomas Haydon. With the increase in corn-growing the usefulness of these mills had also developed, although much of the grain was sold in London and ground there. Both the Turner and Haydon families contained several generations of millers who profited greatly by their trade. By the middle of the eighteenth century they had been replaced by the Bolton and Tiverton families.

(c) Trade and Commerce

The growth of the market, the increase in the population, and the improvement in the standard of living created better markets for a variety of tradesmen. During the sixteenth century most of the trades mentioned were concerned with agriculture, or with meeting the essential needs of the people. In the seventeenth century the list grew to include tanners, brewers weavers, a mercer, a collarmaker, innkeepers, hatters, bricklayers, barbers, a clothworker, grocer, baker and draper. Some of these trades were late in appearing because previously the work, baking for example, had been done by the housewife in the home.

In the building industry the principal occupation in earlier times was that of carpenter, but in the seventeenth century the bricklayer and the tiler shared in the work and the joiner made his contribution. The bricklayer is first mentioned early in the century, and the name which recurs most frequently right up to the nineteenth century is Chapman. The main family seems to have lived in Saffron Lane (Queensway), but one branch at least lived in Crouchfield. A brickmaking trade grew up in the High Street Green and Tile Kiln Lane areas. The clay there made good hard bricks, forerunners of the multi-coloured Leverstock Reds later made by the Leverstock and Acorn Red Brick Co. The family of Saunders or Sanders made bricks for several generations at High Street Green.

As the century progressed and the standard of housing improved there was more scope for the glazier and plumber, trades usually carried on by the same man. Three such, who flourished in Market Street in the late seventeenth and early eighteenth centuries, were John Duckle (died 1602), Thomas Seare (died 1722), and John Rickson (died 1725), Rickson was also the landlord of the Rose and Crown. Most of his goods related to the inn, but for his plumbing he had 'lead glass and other things'; he also had a horse, bridle and saddle and it is interesting to speculate on a plumber riding a horse to work.

Suppliers of food, provisions and other household goods were well represented. The butchers were early on the scene, some being accommodated in the butchers' shambles which formed part of the market. Bakers came later, and one who lived in the second quarter of the seventeenth century seems to have delivered his bread by pack horse. Grocers, sometimes called chandlers, had arrived by the end of the sixteenth century. They carried on a general trade as is shown by the inventory of Samuel Baker in 1644. He carried on his business on the west side of the Market Street, just to the north of the old Market Square. His stock in trade was so extensive as to make it impossible to list here in full, but it included, besides the usual groceries, Latin grammars and schoolbooks, cloth, tobacco, fish hooks, rat poison and gunpowder. The grocers had considerably increased their numbers by the end of the seventeenth century and most of them were prosperous. William Gladman, who died in 1701, had done moderately well, and his inventory included 15 bushels of salt, pitch and tar, 'Virginnie', earthenware, sugar, plums, spice, hops, soap, allum and brandy, pipes and tobacco, powder and shot, oatmeals, hair cloth, bedcords, small linen and packthread, candle and tallow, and stamp paper valued at £25.

During the seventeenth century the consumption of tobacco increased to such an extent that by 1682 the custom on it brought in the greatest revenue from any such tax. Most of it was sold by grocers, but there were also tradesmen who sold only tobacco. One such was Edmund Sear (died 1689) who had in his backshop one 'Ingen of tobacco with ye press and other necessaries' and in his cellar tobaccos worth £20.

A comparatively large number of tradesmen were engaged in occupations relating to the supply of clothing. There is evidence that many wives and children were employed in carding and spinning raw wool for resale to the clothier. Others were employed in the later processes of cloth-making from weaving to dyeing. Home dressmaking was the rule for many, if not most of the people, but throughout the late sixteenth century there was always more than one person working as a tailor. There were also a number of shoemakers, a glover and a hatter, trades which naturally continued into the next two centuries.

In the early seventeenth century there were tradesmen who worked as weavers. Thomas Bannister had two looms. John Teadure (or Threader) had more than this in larger and more pretentious premises at Crouchfield. About the same time Nehemiah Babbe had two fine looms worth £20 (those of the other weavers were worth only £3 each); he was also a maltster and an alehousekeeper.

We have particulars of two seventeenth century barbers, John Settle (see also p. 74) and Richard Halsey, and in each case the details are very similar. Outside was the sign of their trade, a pole, and inside such equipment as the following:—

> Basins, lavers, chasters and casting bottles
> a headpan and a candlestick
> a box with linnen in it
> chairs, a settle, a bench and a form
> all the pictures and maps
> looking glasses and other glasses, and other
> implements about the trade.

So far we have dealt mainly with the period up to the middle of the 1700's. After then we find many differences. By this time the Market Street had been fully built up, the premises were generally more pretentious and more especially adapted to the particular trade carried on in them. There was greater continuity, the business usually passing from father to son. The trader was more affluent and took a more important part in the life of the community. It was from about the 1740's that the commercial element in the Market Street began almost to monopolise the office of Bailiff. In the middle of the century paper-making was established in the Apsley district and silk-throwing in the Market Street. The latter was introduced by Thomas Hudson, who occupied the premises on the east side of the present High Street in which later Joseph Cranstone started his engineering business.

(d) **Inns, taverns and licensed premises.**

These have played such an important part in the life of the community as to be worthy of special mention. They were not only places of refreshment but premises in which many social and administrative activities took place. Ale was the national beverage for centuries and its brewing was at one time done mainly by women, generally as a home industry. Before the use of hops the product would not keep and so the brew had to be consumed immediately. The housewife gave notice of her brew by exhibiting a piece of brushwood over her doorway. Later the brewing was done by the landlord of the inn, and subsequently the professional brewer arrived. Ale, however produced, had to be approved by a local ale-taster, usually appointed by the lord of the manor who often required the brewing to be done on premises he owned and for which he made a charge. The ale-taster had to see that the Assize of Ale, regulating the strength and price of the beverage, was duly carried out. We find the local manor court annually appointing its own ale-taster right up to the nineteenth century, although in later years his duties were only nominal.

Licensing of premises was brought in by an Act of 1552. (There was an Act in 1495 which enabled the Justices 'to reject and put away common ale-selling' and to take surety of the keepers of ale-houses.) There were three main classes of licensed premises, inns, taverns or wine-shops, and ale-houses, each serving different purposes, but all supplying intoxicating liquors. The Justices of the Peace for the county were the licensing authority, although the Privy Council also made rules concerning ale-houses. Inns which existed before 1552 were exempt from licensing. The Justices' rules required the landlord to provide convenient lodgings, with "good and holsome vitualls fitt to serve all suche as uppon honeste occasions shall repayre unto his house." They define who should use the premises and generally how the house should be conducted; no one should eat or drink there during Divine Service on Sundays or holy days, nor tarry there after 9 p.m. from Easter day to Michaelmas, and 8 p.m. during the winter. The best ale or beer should be sold at not more than 4d. a gallon, with a second quality at 2d. a gallon to be sold off the premises to the neighbours. Games such as carding or dicing were unlawful and so prohibited.

Of the known licensed drinking places in Hemel Hempstead, we shall deal first with those that have not survived, and then with those that are still in use.

The Angel. Situated on the east side of the Market Street, part of the premises is now occupied by a Ladies and Gents Outfitters under the name of Bathe. It was probably in use as an inn in the late sixteenth century and may then have been called the "Tiger" for which Henry Sawcer was licensed in 1617. It was later occupied by Robert Sawcer (Henry's son) who practised as a scrivener and was Clerk to the Bailiwick from about 1629. It ceased to be an inn in the eighteenth century.

The Cock. This was one of the oldest inns in the town and was one of the properties conveyed by the Earl of Leicester to the Earl of Bedford in 1574. It was situated on the lower end of the east side of the Market Street and, although not a large house, was much frequented by the Bailiff and his Jury. In 1632 Richard Turner, then the landlord, was charged at Quarter Sessions with permitting "a certain unlawful game called 'table playinge' to be played in his house.... and that Thomas Bannister...., weaver, was playing the same with him." The house may have been rebuilt during the seventeenth century, for in the early eighteenth century it was of three storeys with a cellar; on the ground floor were the bars, kitchen, brewhouse and other accommodation, on the first floor the quarters of mine host, and on the second floor a number of bedrooms, called respectively the red room, the long room and the gatehouse chamber. The Hearth Tax Return for 1663 shows 8 hearths and the billeting return of 1756 records 4 beds and stabling for 10 horses. Soon after 1851 the house ceased to be used as licensed premises.

The Half Moon. Another seventeenth century house which was frequented by the Bailiff and his Jury and sometimes by members of the Vestry to complete their business and take refreshment. In the 1780's it was owned by Dr. Hugh Smith who left it to his daughter Lydia, and he provided in his will that the then tenant, Richard Sweby, could continue to occupy the premises provided he purchased his beer from Lydia's husband, Mr. Holloway, a brewer who lived and worked at Two Waters.

The Mermaid. (Meremayde). One of the oldest buildings in the present High Street; it was part of No. 75-77, occupied, until recently by, Oliver Gower, ironmonger. In the 1750's it was occupied by Benjamin Puddephat who also occupied the neighbouring premises as a grocer. The Militia Return of 1756 showed accommodation of 6 beds and stabling for 14 horses. There was an extensive yard behind, called the Mermaid Inn Yard, in which were a number of buildings. The inn was empty in 1789, when apparently it ceased to be used as licensed premises.

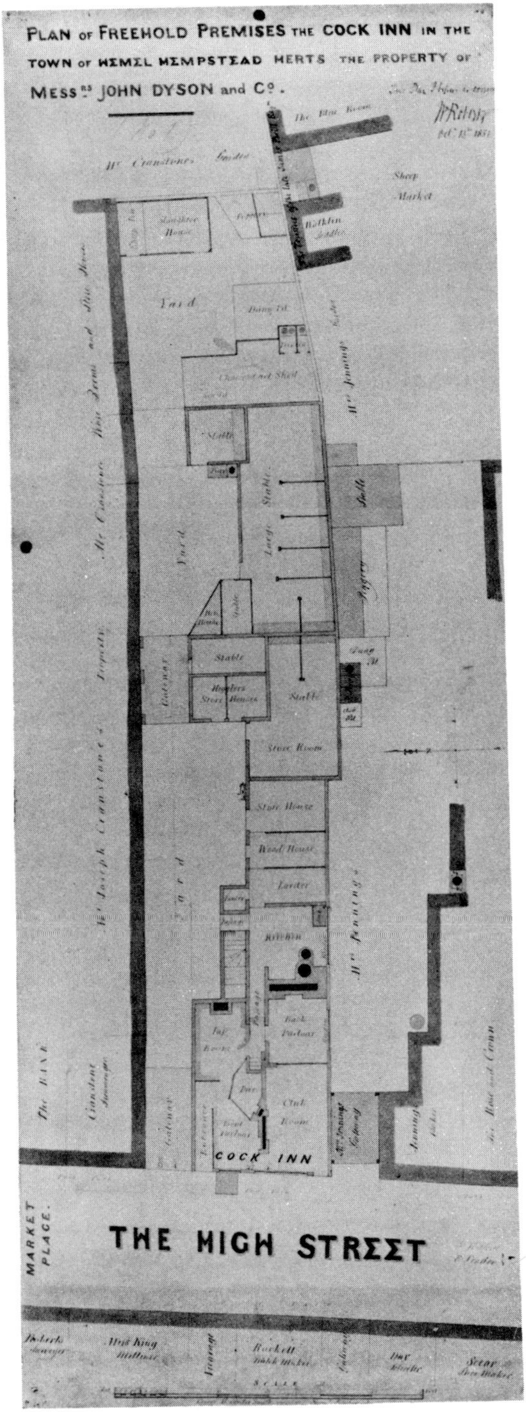

PLAN OF THE PREMISES OF THE COCK INN, 1851

VIEW OF HEMEL HEMPSTEAD FROM THE SOUTH

The Sun. In the seventeenth century this belonged to Francis Oxley (see p.181) who probably acquired it after he returned from service in the King's army during the Civil Wars, and he was succeeded by Henry Fletcher, who also carried on the trade of a clothworker. During the seventeenth and eighteenth centuries it was frequented by the Vestry and the Bailiff and his Jury for refreshment whilst engaged on official business.

The house, which was a fair size in the seventeenth century, was rebuilt in the early eighteenth century. In 1663 it had 6 hearths and in 1756 billeting accommodation was 5 beds and stabling for 30 horses; this accommodation was mainly in premises in the yard behind and was used by the drivers of the waggons on the way to London and on their return. The drivers slept in the room above the stables. The house also possessed 5 acres of adjoining land known, in recent times, as the Sun Meadow.

But perhaps the most interesting feature of this house is that it was the home of an Artisans Benefit Society the rules of which have fortunately been preserved. The Society was apparently formed in 1775 and met every first Monday in the month. There were two feasts each year, in the New Year and in July, and "every member shall come decently apparelled or forfeit the sum of 3d."; they were to pay 2s. each for the feast and a further 2s. to the club, except the lame or the sick. Membership was restricted; no-one over 40 years of age, no tradesman getting more than 10s. a week, and no sick or infirm person could become a member, nor could a landlord, plumber, journeyman, baker, miller or paper-maker. Men who lived wicked or disordered lives were excluded because they were said to be more susceptible to sickness. The membership was limited to 61. The benefits were 10s. a week for 6 months and 6s. a week for a further 6 months in the case of illness; death benefit was £10 in the event of the death of the member and £2 on the death of his wife. In addition, so that the "member may be honoured as well dead as living" all surviving members had to assemble at the Sun, decently apparelled, there to expend 4d. each, and then to attend the burial of the deceased; failure to attend involved a fine of 1s.

There were many other fines, including one of 2d. for each oath uttered profanely, 3d. for being drunk, increased to 1s. for a second offence and on the third occasion exclusion from the Society; if he made dispute concerning the Crowned Head for State Affairs he was fined 6d. Any member who became a bailiff's follower, a soldier or a sailor was immediately expelled, but anyone drawn as a militia-man could continue his membership, and any man who had suffered at the hands of the press-gang could re-join on his return home on paying 1s. into the box.

Whilst we cannot, for want of space, deal with all the inns and taverns to which the inhabitants resorted in those two centuries it may not be amiss to list such as we know were in existence before the eighteenth century.

Location	*Name*	*Earliest reference*
Market Street	Black Lyon	See King's Arms, below
	The Boot	1725 Parish Register
	The Lamb	1709 Bailiwick Records
	The Leg	1637 " "
	Red Lyon	1717 " "
	The Ship, later	
	The Holly Bush	1651 Manor Court Book
	The Swan	1625 Parish Register
	The York	1634 Bailiwick Records
Piccotts End	The Chequers	1714 Parish Register
	The Fox and Duck	1633 Star Chamber Records
	Tom Long the Carrier	1676 Survey of Manor
Apsley,		
Featherbed Lane	The Rose	1714 Parish Register
	The White Lion	1617 House of Lords Mss.
Boxmoor	The Queens Head	1724 Will

We shall now turn to some of the inns which are still in use.

The Bell. (also the Leg) Not the oldest but in its time probably the most important of the hostelries in the old Market Street. According to the Billeting Survey of 1756 it was then the largest house in the town, having accommodation of 9 beds and stabling for 54 horses. It is referred to in the will of John Rolfe of Boxted (1615) and in the Bailiwick Books from 1632, and it appears in the inventory of James Payne (1644) and of William Fuller (1671). From these we learn that it was a house of three storeys with a cellar storing both wine and beer. The house was much used by the Bailiff and Jury and by the Vestry.

Adjoining the Bell to the north was another house called the Leg, at least as old as the Bell and to some extent connected therewith. (See p. 81). It ceased to be an inn after 1671, while the Bell remained in use.

The Bell, Two Waters. This is worthy of mention as one of the oldest licensed houses in the district. It was in use during the sixteenth century and was one of the old coaching inns.

Kings Arms (Black Lyon and Princes Arms). Another old inn dating back to the seventeenth century. Originally it must have been an ale-house, when it was occupied by Abraham Crawley in the early 1600's, but its status improved with the passing years. About 1750 it was called the Princes Arms and the Billeting Return of 1756 mentions accommodation of 7 beds and stabling for 36 horses. During part of the eighteenth century it ceased to be used as an inn and the use and name were transferred to premises just to the south, on the east side of the Market Street, then known as the Black Lyon. Later the King's Arms reverted to an inn and the other premises resumed the name of the Black Lyon. These latter premises were substantial and the 1756 Return records accommodation of 7 beds and stabling for 22 horses.

Rose and Crown. Although the present building is of more recent construction it stands on the site of what was probably the oldest inn in Hemel Hempstead. Certainly an earlier building was there in 1523, occupied by William Patewyn, a butcher. In 1594 Elizabeth Waterhouse of the Crowne was buried, having died of the plague, and in 1599 John Shadde, a substantial yeoman, left to his daughter Ellen a bedstead "standinge in the diamonde chamber at the Crowne in Hempstede." In 1629 the Bailiff directed that on market days the smiths were to stand between the Cock and the Crown. For the whole of the second half of the seventeenth century the landlords were members of the Goodwyn family. In the early eighteenth century mine host was John Rickson, who also carried on the trade of a plumber. When he died in 1725 his widow continued as licensee. It is from Rickson's inventory that we obtain details of the accommodation which may be listed as follows:—

Bedrooms	*Other Rooms*
Red room	Long Room
Lower chamber	Back Parlour
Upper new room	Garret over upper new room
Kitchen Chamber	Little room near street
Blue room	Little room at cellar head
Hall chamber	Brewhouse
Crown chamber	Kitchen
	Wine cellar
	Beer cellar

Outside were a mill house, malting house, glazing shop and other outbuildings.

The inventory of Rickson's successor, John Gray, gives an interesting list of the stock in trade which includes 43 barrels of beer and ale, 8 dozen claret good and damaged, 4 gallons of sack, 8 gallons of rum and brandy and 8 dozen of cider, which together with barrels, jars, bottles etc. were valued at £63.10.0d. The Billeting Return of 1756 shows available accommodation of 4 beds and stabling for 20 horses.

Royal Oak. Situated at the corner of Cherry Bounce and the High Street, it was one of the few premises mentioned in the 1523 Rental which can be identified, although it was not then licensed. It was licensed under the name of the 'Oak' before the end of the sixteenth century. The word 'Royal' was probably added after the Restoration in 1660. It was used as a House of Correction in the eighteenth century, and evidence of this is still to be seen in the cellars. In more recent times it was used as a common lodging house.

White Hart. This is first referred to in a church terrier of 1625 which locates the vicarage "on the north of the signe of the White Hart". In 1655 the landlord, Edward Sage, was licensed by Quarter Sessions to keep a tavern and sell wine, and in 1676 the commissioners used the house to take the depositions in the second Oxley case. The 1756 Return mentions 3 beds and stabling for 10 horses.

Of the six houses dealt with in this group five are in the High Street. There were others scattered around the district, but they were usually small and served only their immediate locality. The following is a list of such of the existing houses outside the High Street as are known to have existed for at least 200 years:

Name and location	*First reference*
Boar's Head, Piccotts End	Manor Court Book 1736
Chequers, Piccotts End	Parish Register 1714
Cupid, Redbourn Road	" " "
Queen's Head, Corner Hall	Billeting Return 1756
Swan, London Road	" " "
Three Blackbirds, St. John's Road	" " "
White Horse, Bourne End	" " "

(e) **Crime**

Almost the only source of information about crime is the Quarter Sessions records and these deal mainly with minor offences, although by modern standards some of the sentences are severe.

In the seventeenth century most of the offences dealt with in Quarter Sessions related to non-attendance at church, irregularities in the conduct of licensed premises, poaching, encroachment on the highway, assault and battery, the sale of unwholesome food and the carrying on of a trade without having served the necessary apprenticeship. Other cases of a more serious nature were dealt with at the Assizes.

An interesting example of poaching is described in detail in a letter dated 1675 addressed to Lord Brackley at Ashridge by someone anxious to secure a conviction against two brothers from Hemel Hempstead named Charles and William Greene. His Lordship was a Justice before whom the defendants would doubtless be brought. The writer expressed his anxiety to preserve the game in these parts for all the gentry in the neighbourhood. The Greenes were described as "mean mecanicks" who spent most of their time, night and day, poaching hares, partridges, pheasants and the like, using dogs for the purpose. The incident which raised the ire of the correspondent was one in which Charles, assisted by his son John, was so impudent as to set a dog on to a pair of partridges near Lord Bridgwater's mansion near Gaddesden. A gamekeeper having observed them, went towards them carrying a gun, but they set about him and took his gun away and kept it for some time thereafter. When called upon to hang the dog involved in the poaching they hanged another dog "in derision". The writer was concerned that their success at poaching might lead the Greenes to further crimes such as stealing horses or breaking in to houses, and concluded "I doubt not of your lordship's justice herein." Whether the culprits received the justice the writer thought they deserved is not recorded.

Another type of offence is illustrated by two cases before Quarter Sessions in 1625 when John Marston, a yeoman, and John Wilkinson, a labourer who was drunk at the time, were charged "for swearing profanely in the name of God."

The information in respect of the eighteenth century is in much more detail and there is a greater variety of cases. The following are a few typical cases:—

Date	*Name*	*Crime*	*Punishment*
1718	Henry Bigg Tailor	Assaulting Nancy Clarke, Spinster	Fined £2.10.0d.
1742	Sarah Ashby	Theft of 1 salt fish and pint of beans, value 10d.	Whipped in House of Correction
1754	John Symonds Cordwainer	Theft of a silver spoon, value 10d.	Whipped on three successive market days and committed to the Bridewell during that time.
1767	George Putman Labourer	Obtaining money by false pretences	Whipped
1768	Elizabeth Griffin	Theft of linen bed sheet, value 2s.	Whipped
1775	John Long Victualler	Assaulting James Chapple	Fined 1s.
1781	John Ellick	Theft of a sack containing a bushel and a peck of wheat, value 4s. 2d.	3 weeks imprisonment and whipped.
1781	Susannah Lee	Obtaining by false pretences 4 yards Irish Linen and other goods	Publicly whipped

1797	James Partridge Butcher	Assaulting Nash, constable, and John Thompson a sheriff's officer, in the execution of their duty.	Four months imprisonment and fined 1s.

Sarah, wife of Samuel Golding, who was charged with stealing some clothes valued 9s., was sent for trial at the Assizes where she could have faced capital punishment. In 1768 William Knight, described as a papermaker, was charged with stealing a pair of worsted stockings, valued at 4s., and was sentenced to be transported for seven years.

A case of some note was that of William Gunston, a labourer. In 1772 he was charged with stealing from Barton Bryers a pair of stays, a black quilted "callamanis" petticoat, some women's stuff shoes and a quantity of linen. The total value of the goods was 33s., a serious offence, but fortunately for him Gunston was found not guilty. In 1777 he was again charged that with James Hoard, another Labourer, he stole 6 hens worth 5s. from Hudson, but again he was found not guilty. However, in 1778 Thomas Trott, victualler, reported that on a Saturday night, between 8 and 9 p.m., he missed from his dwelling house some moneys, especially two silver groats, one silver twopence, one silver penny, one foreign copper coin, one half-crown, two shillings and one farthing, and that William Gunston was in the house at the time and was suspected of stealing the money. Some of the coins were found on Gunston's wife. He was charged and found guilty and sentenced "to work on the Thames" for five years.

The parish registers indicate, as one might expect, a number of violent and accidental deaths. In 1590 John Street, a servant of Francis Combes, was murdered by John Bates, a fellow-servant in the same household. In 1566 Richard Fox from Mr. Slade was killed in a pit and in 1588 Jerome Tuftnell was slain with a horse 'mill' at Mr. Slades. In 1626 two persons were buried who had died of drowning, and in 1628 Margaret, wife of Thomas Rolfe, killed herself. In 1635 George Sawyer hanged himself, and earlier, in 1622, Susan Besouth fell from a cherry tree. In 1727 a child of Woodwards of Two Waters was killed on the road by a waggon and in 1734 a traveller suffered the same fate.

(f) The Working Classes.

Whilst the working classes constituted the majority of the population we know least about them. Having little or no property they left few wills and earned but few mentions in other records. In the parish registers we usually find only their names, although occasionally the entry contains a description such as "poor gardener" or "poor blacksmith" or "poor labourer". From the few inventories available we get a glimpse of the circumstances of some of the better-off workers.

Robert West, 1612, lived in Saffron Lane in a one-roomed house. His furniture was of the simplest, including a table, a form, a few domestic utensils and three bedsteads made with "old boards done together". His tools were worth 1s. 4d. but he had debts amounting to £4.19.0d. due to him. He was probably an artisan.

John Cocke, 1633. His principal goods were 13 hens, a cock and two geese.

Robert Cripps, 1628, farm labourer, unmarried, worked for William Gladman, yeoman of Piccotts End, and lived in. Of a thrifty nature, he had saved £10 which he had lent to Jeromy Rolfe of Nettleden on a bond. He had four sheep which his employer allowed to graze on his land. His only other asset was his working apparel worth 10s.

John Axtell of Two Waters, 1634, described as a labourer, but really a husbandman cultivating a small area of land and hiring himself out as opportunity occurred. He had better and larger accommodation, two rooms on the ground floor with a buttery attached, and the house was better furnished. He farmed a few acres and in June 1634 he had crops of wheat, lent corn, and rye growing in a total of three acres. He had a cow, three sheep and five hens. He and his family used a woollen wheel and a linen wheel for spinning. He had two daughters and five sons, and to each of the latter he left 12d.

Some indication of earnings during the seventeenth century is given in the rates of pay prescribed by the justices in accordance with the law. In 1600 mowers and reapers of corn and grass were to be paid 8d. a day with meat and drink and 1s. without. In 1613 these rates continued, but for the best workers the rate was 10d. with meat and drink. Some agricultural servants were hired by the year and in 1600 were paid as follows:—

	with living	*without living*
Males (of the best sort)	40s.	56s. 4d.
" (of the second sort)	33s. 4d.	40s.
Women	21s.	26s. 8d.

By 1613 these rates had increased to £3 and £3.10.0 for the best sort and towards the end of the century the rates had more than doubled, to £5 for males and £3 for women without living.

For tradesmen such as carpenters there were different rates for summer and winter. In 1613 the summer rate for the best carpenters was 10d. a day with meat and drink and 1s 4d. without, and towards the end of the century the rates were 1s. 6d. and 1s. 10d. The winter rates were 3d. or 4d. a day lower.

By the eighteenth century this practice of the justices prescribing rates of pay had ceased. Towards the end of that period the ordinary work of a farm was carried on chiefly by farm workers who, if married, lived in a cottage belonging to the farm and were paid 6 to 9 guineas a year together with such extras as the farmer provided. The day labourer, working for the same farmer throughout the year, was paid 7s. a week and small beer, except during harvest months when the rate was 9s. It must be remembered that the wife and the children all contributed to family earnings by other employment, often in the home, a particular local source of this kind being straw plaiting.

We do not know what proportion of the total population the working class formed in the seventeenth century, but the proportion had increased during the eighteenth century and in the later half was probably about 70% With most of these the standard of living was low, and there was evidently much poverty, especially among the older people.

How and where these people were housed is a problem which the records do little to solve. Although the population more than doubled during the eighteenth century there is no evidence of any substantial increase in the number of houses. An analysis of the poor rate books from 1758 (the earliest available) to 1801 shows practically no increase in the number of assessments. In the case of the farms many of the workers lived in with the farmer, or in cottages belonging to the farm, and many of the journeymen, tradesmen and assistants, as well as the hostlers and other servants employed in the inns, were similarly accommodated. But many are still not accounted for and these must have lived in houses which they shared with other families, a view confirmed by the entries in the manor court books.

In the nineteenth century the number of poor-rate assessments increased; by 1816 there were over 70% more than in 1758, and by 1832 the increase over 1816 was even greater. The official census data shows a considerable output of new dwellings; in 1821, 846 families occupied 735 houses, and in 1831, 981 families were accommodated in 930 houses. The figures for 1821 disclose a considerable degree of overcrowding, confirming the assumption that the provision of houses for the working classes lagged behind the need.

NOTE ON SOURCES

In addition to the sources in the general list at the beginning of the book the following references are specially relevant to this chapter:—

Calendar of Patent Rolls, Eliz. vol.3, 292. P.R.O.

Conveyance to Sir William Egerton, H.R.O., No. 805 98.

Document in chest of St. Peter's Church Berkhamsted, (evidence of Land Tax valuation of 1691).

Document found in Manor Court Books in the Duchy of Cornwall Offices, London, for the fight over the market rights.

A Survey of the Manor Messuage and Demesne Lands of Agnells H.R.O.

CHAPTER 6

Hemel Hempstead in the Nineteenth Century

The nineteenth century saw the completion of the change from a basically agricultural and market centre to one where industry predominated, above all the paper industry. In the 1801 census the population of the parish – less Bovingdon and Flaunden – was 3,680. By 1851 the comparable figure was 7,948 and 1901, 11,264.

In 1800 the town was practically confined to the old town, with small outposts at Corner Hall, Two Waters, Crouchfield, Leverstock Green and Boxmoor. At the end of the century there were three distinct units, the old town, Boxmoor and Apsley.

The town site was an awkward one for expansion. Squeezed between the river and park of The Bury, the hills, and boggy area of Marlowes, the town was to have difficulty in expanding. When it did grow, it grew in a fashion almost unique, through the inn yards on to the crofts and tofts and meadows behind both sides of the High Street. The influence of this sort of growth is well seen in the narrow strip-like development between St. Mary's Road and Austin's Place.

Transport was in this century a vital factor in the growth of a town. The main coach routes running on the only local turnpike, the Sparrows Herne, from Watford to Aylesbury, passed the town by. In 1799 when the Boxmoor Trustees sold a strip of Boxmoor to the Grand Junction Canal Company, a main line of communication missed the town, as it did again when the London to Birmingham Railway also followed the route of the main road and canal. But this led to the growth of the detached village of Boxmoor, while saving the charm of the High Street and Gadebridge Park. So the north end of the High Street ends where it did two centuries ago, while what was once called the New Town – the area around Alexandra Road – developed after the Midland Station was opened in 1877. Apsley grew with the paper mills, and the industry attracted people into the town.

By 1851 a number of houses had been built at Frogmore End for mill workers. It is interesting to see how many of these were occupied by families who had come into the area. This must have been a substantial factor in population increase in the first part of the century. From three pages in the census figures for Two Waters the men in the family had been born at:- Rickmansworth, Waddesdon, Hatfield, Iver, Isleworth North, Marston, Chelmsford, Bexley, Beirton, Lambeth and Haseley. Some of these newer families in the town had moved around considerably before coming to Apsley. Mr. Pruthero, who was blacksmith, was born in Usk and his children in Bristol and Watford. There are many such examples, especially among those in skilled engineering occupations. In Albion Place, Moses Newton, the iron founder, had living with him a journeyman tailor from Frankfurt-on-Main, Mr. Hooper, a porter at Boxmoor Station, was born in

Launceston, his wife in Edinburgh and their children, then still young, in Carlisle, Middlesex and Boxmoor.

When Cobbett made one of his rural rides in the area in 1822, however, agriculture was still the main occupation. He was very impressed with the quality of the land. Of his journey from Redbourn through Hemel Hempstead to Chesham he writes: "The wheat is good all the way, The barley and oats are good enough until I came to Hemel Hempstead. But the land along here is very fine: a red, tenacious flinty loam upon a bed of chalk at a yard or two beneath, which in my opinion is the very best corn land we have in England. The fields here, like those in the rich parts of Devonshire, will bear perpetual grass... The land is, in short, excellent and it is real corn country. The trees from Redbourne to Hemel Hempstead are very fine, oaks, ashes and beeches. Some of the finest of each sort and the very finest ashes I ever saw in my life."

In the Freeholders List for 1800 there are sixteen farmers and in 1825 there are eighteen. The 1832 register of electors includes fourteen farmers. These are mainly substantial and prosperous men and their numbers remain constant in the first half of the century. Typical of them are Mr. Saunders of Eastbrook Hay who in 1851 farmed 153 acres and employed nine labourers apart from house servants; and Mrs. Mary Varney, a widow, who with her two sons and four daughters had 160 acres at Wood Farm, Piccotts End, and had four labourers and a boy, as well as the Ploughman and horsekeeper who lived in. Arthur Young in his survey of 1804 mentions two of the local farmers as especially enterprising, Mr. John Cotton of Highfield Farm and Mr. Jennens. John Cotton had been a driller for nearly twenty years, using a horse hoe. In 1799 he had six acres of wheat, besides other crops. In 1800 he grew two acres of beans, sixteen of pease, eight of barley, six of oats, all "very straightly and regularly drilled". He estimated his barley at eight quarters an acre. Mr. Jennens was also an ardent driller. Both of them experimented with crop rotation and Young includes their variation on the common Hertfordshire course:- Turnips, barley, clover, wheat, oats.

A great part of the work on farms was done by annual servants who were hired at the fair, held on September 3rd and had no fixed hours of work. In the 1851 returns for the census, Woodhall Farm with its 250 acres had two living-in employees and the Three Cherry Trees with 130 acres had three.

The rates of pay for these annual labourers varied from six to nine guineas a year for a carter or ploughman, and from six to seven guineas for a thresher or tasker. Boys received two to four guineas and maids, who did their share of agricultural work if employed on farms, about five guineas. As well there were the day labourers who worked usually from 6 a.m. to 6 p.m. in summer for eight shillings a week, and 7 a.m. to 5 p.m. in winter for six shillings. If they were taken on for the year, living out, they had seven shillings a week and small beer. It appears that the county average was somewhat higher, ten shillings to twelve shillings. The pay for hay and corn harvest varied considerably with the state of the weather and was paid for by the piece or acreage.

Obviously the lot of the agricultural labourer was not an enviable one, especially in times of depression. In 1851, not a particularly bad year, there were in the Swan and Trout lodging house in Queen Street, twelve Irish labourers, several of them unemployed agricultural workers. The farm labourers lived in the poorer areas of the town. The general picture for the High Street area in the poorer parts, for example Cherry Bounce and the Yards, is of the husband and lodgers working on the land and the wives straw plaiting.

It was in the last quarter of the century that the decline in agriculture became marked. Its extent is revealed in the membership figures of the West Herts Agricultural Society. Its peak membership was in 1874 with 212 members. Five years later this had fallen to 179. Farmer Nash was one of many who became bankrupt and in 1897 the County Court at St. Albans would not discharge him as he had only managed to pay his creditors threepence in the pound. William Field of Revel End went to work as a rough carpenter and managed to be discharged. There was a significant falling off in the Corn and Wool Markets. In 1873 there were 7.000 fleeces, but by 1880 there were under 2,000. Prices fell from 38s. per tod for washed wool in 1877 to 22s. 3d. in 1888 and 19s. in 1898. Only the cattle and sheep market showed stability, Woodman's Christmas Fat Stock Show. started off in 1892 with about £1,000 worth of stock and by 1899 nearly £3,000 was changing hands.

Closely allied to agriculture was the straw plaiting industry. Throughout the century money earned in it must have greatly improved the lot of all the poor sections of the community.

The straw plaiting industry had existed in the south Midlands from the middle of the seventeenth century. In 1860 it was reported that 'as much as £200 had been turned in a market day in straw hats only' in Hemel Hempstead. It was during the period of the Napoleonic Wars, when the industry was protected, that its economic and social significance was most felt. Women could then earn more by plaiting than a man could earn on the land, or than they themselves could earn in service. Arthur Young said that plaiting brought in three or four times as much as spinning. In the early years of the century a good hand could earn 15s. to 18s. a week – the price of thirty yards of the more simple plait and there were women who claimed to earn two guineas a week. The most surprising thing about the industry was the amount that could be earned by children. After six weeks' learning a girl could earn 8s. Children who attended the plait schools could earn 8s. to 14s. after only five weeks.

It was essentially a woman's industry. Men only played a small part in buying the straw and binding it into bundles for the market. Joseph and George Bean who lived at a house at the junction of Winkwell Lane and London Road, Bourne End were two of the local strippers, who stripped and bundled the straw ready for market. The most suitable straws were those which grew long under trees and hedgerows. They had to be hand reaped and kept as long as possible. The dealers purchased the straw at £5 to £10 a ton. When cleaned the straws were bleached in a sulphur box, sorted and bundled. Ann Timms who lived in a cottage in London Road retailed bundles at fourpence each.

The industry was one easily carried out in the home and needed only simple tools. By the early nineteenth century various machines had been invented for splitting the straws, a process previously done by hand. There were two kinds of instruments, a metal hooked stick, and an upright piece of wood on a small stand. Both had little knives for cutting the straws and were known as 'shears'. The split straws were 'splints'.

Before plaiting the straws had to be milled in small wooden mangles, usually screwed to the door post. When flattened the straws were held in the mouth for plaiting. After the plait was made and measured into twenty-yard lengths, it was put through the roller again. Bleaching was done in a box or the bath tub round a tile with some live coals and sulphur on it. Apparently the smell of sulphur was a familiar one in the town and villages around.

Plaiting schools were a marked feature of the industry. Most frequently they were run by women, but some were in the charge of men. There was no qualification for the staff. Elizabeth Watts who had a school in Hemel Hempstead could not read, write, or plait. Her school was probably the one in the old cottage which still stands off the High Street, near the Tithe Barn. Her function was to make the children do their plait. The parents paid a fee ranging from 1½d to 3d a week and they provided the straw. Although the industry was not an unhealthy one, the schools often were. The rooms were crowded and heated by 'dicky-pots' - jars filled with hot charcoal. A good warm room made the straws more pliable. Catarrhal infections and sore mouth were occupational diseases of plaiters and some children had crooked fingers. Children started at the plait schools at the age of four and there were evening schools for adolescents.

The 1867 Factory Acts dealt a death blow to the Plait Schools, but some got away with it by teaching some other subjects. In some cases plaiting had been allowed for some hours in the Parish Schools in an effort to meet the competition of the plait schools. Plaiting was being done in Boxmoor School up to 1878. The closing of the plait schools after the 1870 Education Act was much blamed for the decline in the industry and there were moves to have plaiting taught in board schools as a kindergarten subject.

In fact by the middle of the century, the trade was showing signs of decay. Plaits which sold at 1s. a score in 1838, were selling for only 3d in 1893. Cheap plaits were coming in from Italy and later China and Japan and in 1860 protective duties were repealed.

Since prices were generally higher in the local markets any plaiter who could use them did. The straw plait market was a great feature of Hemel

Hempstead market and regulations were made to deal with sales, especially to prevent forestalling. In 1809 a penalty was imposed for the sale of plait before 7 a.m. between Michaelmas and Lady Day and before 8 a.m. for the rest of the year. In 1813 the market was confined to Collett's Yard and in 1832 to the yard of the King's Arms. Even so the buyers used to meet the plaiters coming to market in Marlowes and Anchor Lane and persuade them to sell their best plait. On market day Marlowes was lined with waggons belonging to the dealers and the public houses were always full.

The plait was sold by the score (twenty yards) and short measure was a constant source of trouble. In an attempt to meet this a Plait Dealers' Association was formed and their inspectors attended all plait markets. These were responsible for many prosecutions, the plait was seized from defaulters and burnt.

Plaiters who did not attend the market, and it meant the loss of a day's work to do so, sold to the local dealers. Often a shopkeeper fulfilled this function and straw plait was exchanged for goods. The late Alderman J. Stone in memoirs tells that his mother (in her girlhood) had to plait a score and sell it before the family could eat.

In the families where women plaited in moderation and the husband continued to work steadily, where plait was held back for higher prices, the general standard of living was raised. There are suggestions however that these were the exceptions. A Factory Inspector's Report for 1869 blamed 'dirty clothes, neglected children, illegitimate births' on the industry. It claimed it made men indifferent to work and that unmarried women could earn enough to bother about nothing but clothes.

In the population returns for 1800, those employed in agriculture are 391, those in trade, industry and handicraft 775. These figures do not point to any one special local industry, employing a number of the population. Until John Dickinson decided to establish his paper mill in Apsley, there was no specialised industrial development. As in all market towns a variety of industries existed to meet local needs, tanneries, breweries, shoe makers, rope works, brick fields and such like.

Already several of the old mills, like others in Hertfordshire, had been converted for paper making. In the eighteenth century Apsley and Nash mills were being used to produce hand made paper.

In 1744 Edward Holmes of Rickmansworth, a paper maker, leased for £100 a year Frogmore Mills with the millhouse, building, watercourse, appurtenances and meadow grounds from Thomas Tower. These had been owned formerly by Ann Puddephat of Hemel Hempstead, spinster. Holmes was allowed to take out the millstones, flour mills, dropping tackle, and sack tackle. It was this lease which passed to the Fourdriniers in 1803, for thirteen years at £130 per annum, from Christopher Tower and Richard Abrook, described as a papermaker. The mills were then called Covent Mills. Henry and Sealy Fourdrinier described as stationers were to take over the millhouse, building, etc. Some interesting items appear in the inventory made when the Fourdriniers gave up the lease at the time of their bankruptcy, such as the elm cistern lined with lead, two double-painted deal half-stuff bins, deal-framed allum cistern lined with lead, three bleach chests lined with York stone, brick salt bin and 2 in. force pump to supply steam boiler. The machine room had a Capital paper machine with a set of three iron drying cylinders and a pair of glazing rolls with gears, wheels etc. on straps.

The first paper-making machine was installed at the end of 1803 at Frogmore Mills, which Messrs. Henry and Sealy Fourdrinier had acquired. The handmakers regarded it as a threat and there were riots. The windows of the mill were boarded and it is claimed that large carboys of vitriol were placed on the roof in case an attack was made on the machine. The idea of machine-made paper was then still very new. In 1805 there were 760 vats in the United Kingdom producing 16,502 tons and only six paper machines producing 527 tons.

The principle of Nicholas Louis Robert's paper machine which had been developed in the Didot paper mills at Essones, a paper-making centre since 1355, was of forming the paper on a woven wire cloth which retained the matted fibres and let the water drain through the meshes. Until this machine was invented the paper had been made by dipping a flat, sieve-like mould into a vat filled with the fibres suspended in water, lifting the sieve and allowing the water to drain from the thin layer of fibres. Henry and Sealy Fourdrinier, with their mechanic Bryan Donkin, built a machine at Frogmore Mill patterned on Robert's. In 1805 Donkin set up a second machine at Two Waters Mill. At first he had two webs of wire one over, one under the paper, changed the next year to the lower web only. The brothers spent about £60,000 on the machine, but as there was a flaw in the patent, they made nothing on the invention and by 1807 machines were being made in England for £715 to £1,040. It was probably 1810 before the machine was working well and by then John Dickinson had patented his cylinder machine. By January 13th 1812 the Donkin machine was working on a sound commercial basis, operated by Marchant Warrell. In his final version the paper pulp was poured on a web of woven wire moving forward with a shaking movement so that the water drained away. The paper was then pressed between rollers and after being separated from the wire was wound on a reel and carried away for drying, this being done by the old method of hanging in the drying loft.

An inventory of August 1837 for Two Waters Mill gives a picture of the machinery and equipment used in paper production then. The rooms in the mill are listed as the machine house, rag house, carpenter's shop, boiler house, glazing room, engine room, water wheel house, steeping room, finishing room, drying loft, bleaching house and yard. The following are a selection of items to be found in some of these rooms.

MACHINE HOUSE	Paper making machine with apparatus complete. 3 Iron drying cylinders. A set of 3 glazing rolls. 2 Expanding riggers. Quantity of old felting cloth round cylinder. A rag basket. A set of cast iron wheels for glazing rolls.
RAG HOUSE	27 deal lattices with wire work for cutting rags. 27 deal rag boxes. Pair of scales with beam and weights.
BOILER HOUSE	10 H.P. steam boiler with brickwork and iron furnace. Force pump. Large iron rag boiler with stages and supports. Iron size boiler with brickwork and supports. Large cistern lined with lead 6ft. long, 10ft. wide and 3ft. 9ins. deep with deal top, sides and support. Double sizing vat lined with lead. Crushing box for resin. 2 lime buckets and 2 lime tubs.
WATER WHEEL HOUSE	20 gallon copper. Copper strainer to the pump. Copper and wood cog wheels, etc.
STEEPING ROOM	3 stout deal steeping chests 12ft. x 4ft. by 3ft. 6ins. Paper lattice.
DRYING LOFT	Stretching bars and rods. 10 deal hanging crosses. Sundry old ropes and hair lines. 3 wood stools on wheels.
BLEACHING HOUSE	Slate tops to bleaching chests, lined with stone and bricks. Lead retort.

John Dickinson was at the beginning of the century in business as a middle man in the paper trade and was working on a machine of his own for paper-making, using the revolving cylinder method. In June 1807 he took out a patent on a machine for cutting and 'placing paper'. This was the first of his many inventions. In January 1809 he patented his machine for paper-making and in May 1809 acquired Apsley Mills. By 1823 there were over sixty men employed at Apsley Mills and a number of women. In 1881 the total number employed at Apsley was 471 of whom 256 were women and girls. The full story of the growth of the mills is told in Joan Evans's book "The Endless Web".

With constant improvements, new processes and new types of production, the mills progressed. In 1825 Apsley and Nash Mills were manufacturing paper under steam power and Batchworth was preparing the half stuff. Then John Dickinson began negotiations with Lord Essex for the purchase of land for a new mill. Home Park was soon completed and work started. Cottages were built and let to the workmen at half-a-crown a week.

In these early days women mostly worked at the unpleasant task of rag sorting. A good worker could sort and cut into three or four inch squares about a hundredweight a day. Hours of work were very long and if production fell both the women and men were liable to be made to work on Sundays. The workers however could be driven too far, as Dickinson found.

The first union in the paper trade, the original Society of Papermakers, was founded in 1800. In 1821 when trade was falling, John Dickinson, in an effort to reduce expenses, lowered the wages of some workers. They had the support of the union and threatened strike action, but Dickinson who would brook no opposition, least of all from his employees, dismissed the leaders and replaced them with men from Abbots Langley. Considerable distress was caused to some families who lived in tied cottages, but Mr. Wright, a machine-man, preferred to go on the Parish with his wife and six children rather than accept the terms offered him. There was a certain amount of sabotage in the mills during the crisis, but gradually the trouble died down and Dickinson personally trained his new men, sometimes staying up all night to supervise them. Not only the men but the new machines gave him trouble. On September 23rd 1823 the big steam engine boiler burst and a new one was found to be faulty, and in 1826 there was considerable trouble with the water wheels and steam engines.

Working conditions in the mills changed slowly through the century, but government legislation led to some improvements, especially in conditions and hours of work for women and girls. The normal working day at Apsley was from 6 a.m. to 5.30 p.m. and these hours could be extended into the night, if there had been machinery breakdowns or there were urgent orders to get out. Half day on Saturday did not come until the 1890's. In 1890 too, the firm gave £100 for the Annual Holiday outing which was then made by wagonettes. In 1894 normal working hours were reduced from sixty to fifty-six and overtime, especially for women and girls, was reduced. The Employers Liability Act of 1898 led to a measure of increased safety. In 1900 employees earning 12s. a week were granted a fortnight's leave a year and those under 8s. a week.

Lads earned 3s. to 4s. a week and would be getting 12s. by the time they were twenty. Machine workers earned 28s. to 30s. a week. Much of the

J. DICKINSON & CO. LTD. WHARF APSLEY MILLS 1901.

W. H. CRANSTONE'S STAND AT TRADE FAIR

work carried small bonuses for extra production and faultless work. Lads producing 20,000 envelopes a day on one machine got a daily wage of seven-pence and one penny per thousand for every extra thousand, or twopence if none were spoiled. Coal came by canal and at Nash Mills had to be wheeled about one hundred feet. The gang of six men who moved the sixty tons was paid about 4s. and six pints of beer a man.

In March 1886 the firm became a limited company and great changes were made. All paper-making was transferred to Croxley and the older mills were turned over to making envelopes and stationery. Considerable alterations and rebuilding took place, a giant envelope machine was purchased and a multicolour printing machine installed. By 1887 three million envelopes were being turned out in a week.

R.H. Ling was appointed manager at Apsley in 1890. The engineering department, of which Leonard Stephenson had been in charge, was transferred from Nash Mills to Apsley, and the former mill concentrated on the production of plate paper. It was there that an experiment was made in 1887 in the 'electric driving' of a machine.

1894 was a bad year in the paper industry, especially, but while many firms had to close down Dickinson's quickly went on to further extensions and improvements. This ability of the paper mills to ride crises throughout the century meant that some of the extreme distress experienced in other towns was less serious here, a fortunate fact in view of the predominance of that one industry.

The foundations were being laid of other industries which have survived into this century. In 1798 Joseph Cranstone came from Horsham to Hemel Hempstead to an ironmongery business in the High Street. The premises were then a house and shop, the front part of which was rebuilt when the Cock Inn was closed. Joseph died in 1811 and his wife and son, George, carried on the business until 1818, when another son, Joseph, took over. In his time the foundry engineering part of the business developed. He built the original gasworks in Bury Road and in September 1867 was advertising that he was ready to execute orders for engines, agricultural equipment and machinery of every description, using his powerful machinery driven by steam. He made the first 'road motor' to travel from Hemel Hempstead to London. It was steam driven and reached London safely, but on the way home ran backwards and was smashed up on Stanmore Hill. However Joseph was unhurt and survived to retire and hand over the business to his son William Henry, who extended the workshops and built a new warehouse in the yard. The Cranstones did not employ a great number of men generally, but in 1897 Cranstone's Foundry took on 120 men to make two-ton bearings for the Admiralty and for a 300 h.p. engine for a Johannesberg gold mine. In this century the business was incorporated and expanded rapidly as the Hemel Hempstead Engineering Company.

Foster's Saw Mill was established early in the century to supply building and fencing timber, general joinery and bent timber for musical instruments. Subsequently the mills were enlarged and modernised, but in recent years, after a disastrous fire, they were closed.

One industry which was important throughout the century but has now completely disappeared was the tannery at Corner Hall. In the Freeholders Book of 1800 Elisha Deacon is described as a tanner and in 1897 Weston's Almanack has an advertisement in which Tom Baldwin, a boot and shoemaker in Cotterells, states that he executes repairs with only the very best leather manufactured locally. By 1832 the copyhold house, tanyard and land at Corner Hall were in the hands of Thomas Elisha Deacon. Waste material from the tannery was thrown on to the moor opposite to it and created some difficulty when the Heath Park recreation ground was laid out in the 1920's and the bandstand erected.

Bricks were made at Cupid Green and Leverstock Green. In the census returns most of the men living in the Tile Kiln area were brick-makers or their labourers. There were lime works on Roughdown Common, drawing their labourers mainly from the Boxmoor area. Iron workers feature in all lists of workers. One iron foundry on the site of the old Apsley Vicarage became a type foundry and is said to be the first place where type was made by machinery.

Maltsters and brewers appear in all lists and registers. They seem to have congregated in the Bury mill area. In 1850 Samual Deacon employed seven men in his brewery there. As vital as the maltsters were the millers. Bury mill was at one stage owned by the Warren family. In 1832 it was assessed for rates with the house and land at over £200 and must have been a considerable property, although it does not seem to have employed more than four or five men.

As well as those working in agriculture and industry, there were throughout the century a number employed in domestic work, not only in the larger houses, inns and farms, but in those of professional men, tradesmen and shopkeepers. From the 1851 census figures we find that Mrs. Grover and her three daughters who lived at The Bury employed five servants:- a parlour maid, cook, dairy maid, servant and groom. At Gadebridge house there were a governess, cook, nurse, lady's maid, needlewoman, housemaid, nursery maid, kitchen maid, two footmen and a coachman. Nearly all the farms had one or more domestic servants. Mr. Merry, the surgeon, had a cook, nurse and groom living in. Quite a number of these, especially in the larger houses, were not from local families. The problem then was to 'place' servants, not to find them. Thus in 1873 the wife of the vicar of Apsley advertised:- "A Clergyman's wife can recommend several girls aged thirteen to sixteen as nursemaids or for other work in quite respectable families. Some are still at school and are good needlewomen."

From freeholders lists and directories it is clear that there were a great number of traders and shopkeepers in the town, as would be expected in a market centre. Pigot's Directory for 1821 includes nine bakers, eleven boot and shoe makers, three blacksmiths, four maltsters, five coal merchants, three ironmongers, one printer, two stationers, one pattern maker, one basket maker, two hairdressers. In the freeholders list of 1825, forty-eight traders are listed. Some of these were very prosperous and their owners lived a very comfortable life compared with that of those in agriculture or industry.

The inventory for Mr. Best's shop in Queen Street which was sold by Mrs. Best to Mr. North, her late husband's journeyman, in April 1844, gives us some idea of the size and contents of these businesses. The rooms listed are the attic, back attic, back chamber, store room, landing, front chamber, best front chamber, dining room, parlour, pantry, wash house, cellar and brew-house. Then there were the plumber's shop and glass room, and the paint and colour shop, as well as the yard, garden and stable. In the best front chamber was the four-poster bedstead of carved mahogany with foot pillars and painted cornice "all tastefully clothed in chintz furniture, lined and fringed throughout with valences." It had a thick new wool mattress and fine goose-feathered bed, with bolster and two pillows in bordered linen ticks. There were a pair of large blankets, one under blanket, a pair of fine linen sheets and a large Marseilles quilt. The bed steps were of mahogany with a "night convenience" and the mahogany easy chair was covered with chintz and had a cushion which covered the convenience. The bidet was also of mahogany and the four chamber chairs painted. The fancy painted wash-hand stand had two drawers and appropriate toilet ware and towel-horse to match. The dressing table was of deal, and the chest of drawers of mahogany. There was a handsome swing glass in a Spanish wood frame, and the fender was of greenwire. The window had painted cornices and holland blinds. The plumber's shop and glass room included such items as:-

2 new glazed hand lights
2 semi-circular fan lights
4 deal painted panelled shutters
1 painter's machine
2 excellent lead figures of Summer and Autumn
Mahogany framed portable water closet
Cast iron melting furnace with grate frame, door and brickwork

Living conditions did not reach this standard for many of the inhabitants. In the middle of the century most of the small cottages, no more than one room downstairs and two up, in Cherry Bounce and Bury Mill End area were overcrowded. One in Cherry Bounce in 1851 had ten, and another family there, husband, wife and a son, shared their home with three lodgers. In one house in Bury Mill End a labourer lived with his seven daughters. Not far away lived an agricultural labourer with his wife, two sons and two daughters, his niece and young baby and a lodger, a widow of 85 on parish relief. Similar conditions were to be found in the cottages around the brick works. In the Inspector of Nuisances reports there is frequent reference to the abatement of overcrowding'. In 1879 it was claimed that the situation was relieved in forty homes.

It is not as easy to obtain information on wages as on prices. The lowest wages mentioned are the 1s. 6d. a day paid by the Overseers of the Poor in 1811. This would, of course be the lowest possible rate paid. But as late as 1889 a sweep was earning 10s. a week and in 1844 a man earning 10s. or 12s. on the roads was summoned for not maintaining his wife, but in the same period the Highway Board said it was paying 3s. 6d. per day to its men and the Burial Board in 1880 employed one man at 20s. a week, presumably a gravedigger. In 1869 the salary of the town's Under-Bailiff (Beadle) was raised from £40 to £45 per annum. In 1875 a pauper girl was being put to service at 1s. 6d. per week, and boy apprentices were getting from 1s. in the first year to 4s. for their last two years, presumably with board.

Those with some skill, though rarely with professional training, earned more. In the eighties a dentist came once or twice a week to a sweet shop to provide teeth at 2s. to 3s. 6d. each. In 1900 a drainage inspector was engaged at £2.10.0d per week. The School Board laid down a scale for teachers in 1893, running from £90 for the Headmaster of Two Waters School to £30 - £40 for ex-pupil teachers and £10 to £20 for pupil teachers per annum. In 1883 a cook was offered £18 per annum and a general servant £7.

What did these wages and salaries buy? We have some evidence from the expenditure of various authorities from the early days of the century and for the second half of the century we have the advertisements of the Hemel Hempstead Gazette and local directories which are a valuable source of information. This paper was founded in 1858, one of the crop of local papers started all over England after the abolition of the newspaper tax in 1855 and it has had a continuous history ever since. Unfortunately no files are available before 1867.

A few of these figures should suffice. In 1838 the Guardians sold 3 pigs for 30s., in 1836 George Rolph was selling Welsh flannel at 1s. a yard and in 1837 worsted hose at 1s. a pair. These would be of the cheapest quality for the workhouse. In 1811 the overseers had paid 2s. 6d. for a leather apron. In 1867 a suit to order cost from 50s., a new piano £28 and the rent of a shop in the High Street was £30, while a sack of flour seized for non-payment of church rates was sold for £2.9.0. E. Rolph, family grocer, was offering good home-cured bacon at 6d. a lb. In 1883 a grocer offered raisins at 4d. a lb., Gilbey's Whiskey at 3s. 6d. a bottle and men's strong boots were 5s. 9d. Rooms were offered furnished from 5s. to £1 (with fire) and kitchen coals were 15s. a ton. In 1887 a detached villa in George Street - perhaps the best residential area - was offered at £25 p.a. and this was about the rate in recently built Alexandra and Midland Roads. Rail fares were not cheap. In 1873 the first class return to Euston was 7s. 6d. while in 1869 a cheap excursion to London cost 2s. 4d. return. The following list of prices from an 1891 Almanac gives an idea of the cost of clothes at the end of the century. The goods were all obtainable from H. S. Fowler, The Cash Clothier in the High Street.

Men's suits from 15s. 11d.
Boy's suits from 1s. 11d.
Men's overcoats from 14s. 11d.
Men's woollen shirts from 3s. 11d.
Men's cotton shirts 11½d.
Men's, Women's, boys', girls' hosiery from 2½d.
Football jerseys 2s. 11d.
Boys' caps 3½d., 6½d., 9½d.

It is clear that the working classes of the area could not be equipped with any reserves to meet the sort of depression which began to hit Hertfordshire in about 1874. The causes need not concern us here, but it was basically an agricultural depression which came at a time when unemployment and sickness insurance did not exist and when poor relief was still a local responsibility.

1873 was not too bad a year. Even in January there were only about twenty-one tramps a week received at the Union Workhouse. But by May 1876 the number was sixty per week and the annual rate was around five thousand. In the nineties the diet was made even more unattractive to discourage vagrants and the work to be done daily was increased from breaking 5cwt of granite to 15 cwt per day. The Christmas Beef Fund distributed beef to 130 necessitous people in 1858, but to 455 in 1878. In that year T. F. Halsey of Gaddesden Place reduced all his rents by one-twelfth. In the 1890's voluntary effort established a soup kitchen selling one pint of hot soup and ½lb. of bread for 1½d. In the 1880's free dinners of this kind were being issued. Hammerfield, which had never been completed and in which about thirty people had had work in a boot factory, was so empty as to be christened "The Deserted Village" in the nineties. By the last years of the century the position was improving slightly. The long delayed sewerage scheme provided work for two hundred men in 1898 and the worst was over.

It had been a difficult time for the poor, though church and other collections and the old-established charities such as Field's and Warren's helped. Benefit Societies also played a part in insuring against destitution and the workhouse. By 1878 there were fourteen lodges of the Independent Order of Oddfellows, one the Royal Philanthropic which met at the Sun Inn increased its membership from 243 in 1867 to 354 in 1881 and in 1882 raised its sick pay to 18s. to £1, which was unusually high. Threepence a week might be a normal subscription.

The churches were active too, in the organising of clothing clubs. There were over sixty members of the Box Lane Sunday School Clothing Club. In 1867 the Hemel Hempstead Dorcas Society was formed to help with cheap clothing. There are many examples of distributions of groceries, tea and coal and of entertainments with meals by individual benefactors and groups. Henry Balderson gave away two hundred tickets for a free hundredweight of coal to celebrate Queen Victoria's Diamond Jubilee.

The late Alderman A. H. Jarman who was a boy in Hemel Hempstead in the eighties and nineties tells in his memoirs of the poverty in the town. His father had earnings of fifteen shillings a week when they lived in a cottage in Plait Market Yard. With seven children to feed, he was too poor to own a clock or watch. A. H. Jarman's first job as a boy at the Posting House (see plate XIV) earned him 4s. for a six-day week, working from 6 a. m. to 8 p.m. His second job at Dickinson's earned him 5s. a week and he worked from 6 a.m. to 5.30 p.m. He and his sisters had to walk to the mills for that early start. Of his education under Mr. S. Seabrook at George Street School, he had a lasting appreciation, especially for the solid grounding given in the scriptures, the boys learning by heart many choice passages from the Psalms, Isaiah, the Gospels and Epistles. He recalled attending the Salvation Army Hall in Albion Hill, where enemies of the Salvation Army gathered outside to deter followers from entering. He recalled too, in the nineties, the Sunday School anniversary services at Boxmoor Baptist church attended by three hundred young people in the galleries, with the body of the church completely filled with adults.

Jarman's eldest brother was one of those who accepted the invitation, frequently given in advertisements of the time, to emigrate to Australia. In 1873 the Hemel Hempstead Gazette carried an offer of free passages to Australia for farm labourers and female servants, while Queensland offered £20 land order warrants to those who paid their passages out.

It was not only in agriculture and industry that hours were long. Clerical workers were not spared. The Post Office was open from 6.45 a.m. to 9 p.m. in 1889 and a further two hours on Sundays. Mr. W. H. Day recalled that when in 1893 aged thirteen, he started work in Lovel Smeathman's (solicitors) office at 2s. 6d. a week, the hours were 8.45 a.m. to 7 p.m. (5 p.m. on Saturdays). As a boy he had been taught to do straw plaiting at the age of four. He also remembered incidentally, collecting quit rents, of as little as a halfpenny from copyhold tenants, and had taken part in beating the bounds of the parish.

Life however was not all hard work. There is plenty of evidence of a variety of social activity among all sections of the population.

National events were always marked. The Bailiwick Record Books for 1832 give an account of a meeting to discuss the celebrations of the Reform Bill. June 15th, the appointed day, was announced by the firing of cannons and bell-ringing. Triumphal arches had been erected and decorated. At 2 p.m. there was a dinner for 1,000 people with roast and boiled beef, bread and vegetables and ale. 1,200 children were given plum cake and ale. There were two bands and sports and the next day the aged and infirm were treated to a liberal allowance of soup and bread. In 1840 for the Queen's wedding a beef and plum pudding dinner was given to 883 children. The Prince of Wales's wedding in 1863 was celebrated with the usual sports, illuminations, dinners and services. The aged poor and children were to be given a dinner, but the committee made it clear that they 'do not undertake to dine the teachers'. On June 20th 1887 all the children marched to the town to take part in the grand procession for the Queen's Jubilee with the usual dinner and sports.

It was customary for masters and traders to give their workpeople carnival suppers. Builder George Attaway decorated his largest workshop in Pope's Lane for his works supper and dance. Henry Balderson gave a supper to all the men engaged in building work in Charles Street in 1881. Shadrach Godwin held his employees' suppers at the Kings Arms.

No doubt the opening of the Town Hall in 1852 gave a stimulus to social activities. The annual November Bailiwick Dinners could now be held there. There are advertisements for concerts there in the sixties. In 1864 a series of philosophical lectures raised £19.1.6d. for the hospital. In 1884, there was a lecture on the Church of England as a national blessing and another on the waste of money through sinecures in the royal household. There were waxworks in the winter of 1884 and comedy, drama and dancing arranged by 'The Winter Social Evening Society'. The parish organist, describing himself as a 'Professor of Music' provided a choral class for 4s. a year. Travelling circuses were also a great attraction. At this period there were also a Natural History Society, a Mutual Improvement Society and some debating as well.

Other jollifications were arranged by such organisations as the West Herts Christian Burial Society, whose second festival in July 1868 provided games in Marlowes Meadows and tea in the Drill Hall. The Society for the Protection of Property held an annual dinner attended by over one hundred members, after which many members sang songs.

There seem to have been activities for the gentry too. At least the Heath Park Hotel advertised itself in 1869 as being "fitted with every appliance for the comfort and convenience of gentlemen and families. It is also within reach of numbers of packs of hounds and being close to Boxmoor Station no difficulty is experienced in procuring ready transit to any part. There is good stabling, etc. attached and plenty of good shooting and fishing in the neighbourhood."

Much of the life of the town undoubtedly centred round its places of worship. Though times were simpler and opportunities for excursions fewer, it is clear from the School Log Books that the children avidly seized the opportunities for amusement offered by such occasions as Sunday School treats, the fairs and even the market, held on Thursdays. The Statute or 'Statty' fair held in September on the Rose and Crown meadow was a great occasion and even at the end of the nineteenth century, it was still customary for hirings of men and girls for the following year to take place there, those wanting to be hired lining up at the top of the High Street.

A good story is told in the West Herts Post of 1888 of a choir outing accompanied by the Vicar, Dr. Robbins, the curate and the organist. A three-horsed van took them all to Windsor where Dr. Robbins decided to take the reins and promptly had an accident. The return home took from 6.40 p.m. to midnight.

In the sixties football was gaining interest outside the public schools. Mr. T. F. Pratt Barlow started a club under Harrow rules which played in a field near Apsley Mills, this club was revived by Mr. Lewis Evans and adopted the association code in 1873. When a County Association was formed in 1886, it included Boxmoor United and Hemel Hempstead. In 1891 the West Herts Association and the West Herts League were formed and the Watford and District Elementary Schools Association in 1899.

On a proposal of Sir Astley Paston Cooper the Rifle Corps was established in 1860. The Drill Hall was used for a number of activities, among them a Gymnastic Club.

Many boys had their first musical training in the Salvation Army band. The Apsley Brass Band was founded in 1894 and in 1898 its members were allowed six half-days leave a year.

When reading accounts of social life in the town, one appreciates the strong local feeling there was behind such activities and the capacity for enjoyment in spite of depressing physical conditions for the majority. Like most towns at this time Hemel Hempstead was lacking an adequate water supply, lighting and sewerage and, although there were frequent outbreaks of fevers, the isolation hospital facilities were totally inadequate.

On March 27th 1835, the Hemel Hempstead Gas, Light and Coke Company was established with works in Bury Road. It was a great event when in September of that same year the first street lamps were supplied. Crowds flocked from all parts to see the sight and later the Bailiff and about forty gentlemen had a Commemoration Dinner cooked by gas. The menu included such items as:-

- a salmon - 16 lbs. boiled
- two large legs of mutton
- a ham - 16 lbs. boiled
- two plum puddings - boiled

Hundreds who were not to share the meal witnessed the cooking by gas.

The works had cost £2,500. There were seven retorts and one gasometer and about two miles of mains had been put down. After four years the

QUEEN VICTORIA'S DIAMOND JUBILEE AT HEMEL HEMPSTEAD, 1897

ARMSTRONG PLACE OFF HIGH STREET.

Company leased the works to Mr. John Cox for twenty-one years at £125 a year. There had been one crisis in the early years when there was a dangerous stoppage and an engineer had to come from Watford. There was no engineer employed by the Company.

The gas supply did not extend as far as Apsley Mills, but in 1851 the firm supplied a private gas works. In 1868 this was extended to Nash Mills. Up to that time the Mills had been lit by hanging oil lamps and candles.

In the middle of the century there was a main sewer in the High Street from houses on one side of the street. It had been laid for £40 out of the Highway Rate. This sewer ran into another one coming down Queen Street and their outfall was into the stream by Bury Mill. The Queen Street section could only take house sewage thrown down gratings in the street. There was another drain in the upper part of the High Street from the Bell Inn to Cherry Bounce, which carried only rain and surface water and flowed into an open ditch. In Chapel Street about forty houses drained into covered cesspools but most of the poorer houses had open pits. Doors and windows in the area had to be kept shut.

Few improvements were made in the next twenty-five years and in 1879 the town was quoted in the General Board of Health Annual Report as having a particularly high death rate from fever. The population of the area covered in that report is 15,493. There were 276 deaths, 60 of those children under one year old. The high death rate and frequent outbreaks of fever were due to insanitary conditions and pollution of streams. Damming back of water by the mills was an added problem. Albion Mill in particular interfered with the drainage of the lower part of the town and there was frequent flooding at Two Waters.

Of the twenty-five samples of water analysed in 1879, five were bad and eight doubtful, but that was claimed to be an improvement. Bovingdon's supply came from one well and rain water. A new well had been sunk at Hemel Hempstead in 1868. It was about 182 feet deep, but the depth of tubing was later found to be inadequate and it was probably not watertight so that there was always the danger of pollution.

A few of the items from an Inspector of Nuisances report in 1879 speak for themselves:-

Privies emptied - 232 (exclusive of 257 earth closets)
Bedding disinfected or destroyed - 13
Houses cleaned or disinfected - 48
Manure heaps removed - 22

But there is a hopeful note in that water was laid on to 26 houses and eight water closets were erected.

As late as 1892 the need for proper drainage and increased accommodation in the isolation hospital was stressed. The resources of the hospital were severely strained in January that year, when there were sixty-two cases of scarlet fever admitted and seventeen cases of enteric fever. There were in fact 162 cases of scarlet fever in the area. The old pest house had been in Pest House Lane, later called Wood Lane End. The isolation hospital at Highfield Lane had replaced it but was still only equipped to deal with one type of fever at a time.

In 1896 the much needed sewerage scheme was in hand. The death rate, in 1899, 19.2/1,000 was still higher than average, but slowly the position improved. There were in that year thirteen dairies and milk shops in the borough and fifteen cowsheds. These were all regularly inspected as were the fourteen slaughter houses and three common lodging houses. Hemel Hempstead was more fortunate than many areas in that it had one of the first cottage hospitals where the sick poor could receive free attention.

At Piccotts End in January 1827 a hospital was opened for the 'gratuitous relief of the necessitous poor'. In its first Annual Report tribute was paid to Sir Astley Paston Cooper for the great part he had played in the venture. During the first seven months 336 out-patients and eleven in-patients were cared for by Mrs. Howarth, the matron, and Mrs. Benwick, Mr. Stell and Mr. Smith were the visiting surgeons.

An annual subscription of £1 or more entitled the subscriber to be a governor and recommend one patient to the out-patients' department. While a subscription of £5 or more gave the right to recommend an in-patient. There were complaints that the right to recommend was abused. Governors were not supposed to send their domestics, only those who were too poor to get any other medical advice.

Soon other inhabitants felt that the poor were receiving treatment that they themselves would benefit from, although there are indications that patients were not always appreciative. Permission was given for others to attend out-patients and contribute to the Charity Box. By 1839 there was a feeling that the contributions had not always been fair and in future the matron gave out 5s., 10s., and £1 for private patients.

The cost of alterations to the cottages, furnishing the hospital and running it for the first year were as follows:-

Repairs and alterations	£178. 10. 10d.
Furniture and fixtures	£149. 1. 8d.
Rents, rates, salaries and wages	£77. 3. 4d.
Medicines and use of surgery	£53. 6. 9d.
Trusses and other instruments	£4. 5. 8d.
House expenses	£49. 13. 8½d.
Printing and sundries	£33. 6. 11d.

By 1879 the expenses had risen to £2,129. 4. 3d.

In the first half of the century a high proportion of the expenses was devoted to the supply of trusses. Probably this is an indication of the heavy manual labour performed by the patients, not only in agriculture, but in the construction of the canal and railway.

Full details of the diets of in-patients are included in the reports. The diet varied little throughout the century and this for 1847 is typical:-

Full Diet 14 oz. of bread, 1 oz. butter, 1½ pints of beer
Breakfast - milk, porridge or gruel.
Dinner - 6 ozs. meat dressed with vegetables every day except Wednesday. On Wednesday broth and boiled rice.
Supper - broth or gruel or 2 oz. cheese.

Low Diet 6 oz. bread, 1 oz. butter, arrowroot, tea and sugar.
Breakfast - milk, porridge or gruel.
Dinner - broth or ½lb. beef for beef tea. Wednesday, boiled rice.
Supper - Gruel or barley water.

Milk Diet 12 oz. bread, 1 oz. butter
Breakfast - milk, porridge.
Dinner - 1 pt. milk.
Supper - gruel or 1 pt. milk.

For all diets there was ale or wine as ordered by the doctor.

The small hospital at Piccotts End was soon outgrown. In 1831 Sir John Sebright was "building a handsome and substantial infirmary in an excellent situation at the entrance to the town". The first stone of the new building was laid by the Countess of Clarendon that May and in 1832 the building, now known as Cheere House, was opened. £13,000 had been spent on the building and equipment. There the work of the hospital went on for forty-five years until increasing population and demand made extensions necessary. Eventually a new building containing fifty beds was erected. This building, now the central part of the present hospital, was opened in 1877 by the Duchess of Teck.

These extracts from the costs of that building are interesting:-

Payment to contractor	£7,600
Levelling and doing grounds	£100
Additional furniture	£150

In 1888 the three old nurses were given a gratuity and dismissed and were replaced by trained 'Nightingale nurses.' It was decided that they should be given a uniform and pointed out that this change would involve at least £60 a year. Two years after the hospital started to train nurses.

The extent of local support for the hospital was most generous. The annual reports had long lists of subscriptions, but even more interesting were the donations and gifts. In 1835 an 'electrical machine' was presented. In 1836 Sir John Sebright paid for a gas light in the porch and gas cooking apparatus in the kitchen. Gifts such as those in this list for 1864 appear every year:-

A number of rabbits
Surgical instruments and crutches
12 dozen Old Rousillon Wine
3 copies of Old England and Her Worthies

In 1878 the list included a text for every bed and one shilling given as a gratuity for picking up two sovereigns!

Bazaars were held frequently. The Countess of Clarendon's Bazaar at Bushey in 1829 raised £647.11.6d. Regular yearly collections were held in the churches and in 1879 they brought in £242.16.6d. Of course at intervals there were difficulties in getting subscriptions in. In 1831 this was put down to the "protracted session of parliament and consequent absence of so many principal families from the neighbourhood."

From 1849 there was a chaplain who had his own comforts fund and subscription list. He was appointed at a salary of £50 and was to hold no other appointment in conjunction with his hospital one. His duties were to hold one full service on Sunday and one other day in the week, "to attend the institution at least three days in the week and whenever called on."

The hospital's work was considerably increased while the London to Birmingham railway was being laid. Between July 1836 and July 1837 there were one hundred in-cases, of these forty-three were from railway accidents, six of which were fatal. The Directors of the railway gave a donation of £21 in the first instance, but as the number of accidents increased they agreed to pay 8s. a week for any employee sent into hospital. Cubitts, the contractors, made the same arrangement. The governors were so impressed by the "numerous and dreadful cases" that they recommended to the employers concerned that a ganger or some intelligent workman be instructed in applying a temporary Tourniquet. Transport of cases to the hospital, especially from the Tring cutting was made along the new line and then by cart and if no first aid had been given the patient often died from loss of blood.

The West Herts Hospital was one of the first to have an X-ray machine. A Rontgen Rays apparatus was purchased in 1899 and was put at the disposal of any medical practitioner in the area.

The hospital provided some care in sickness for the poor citizens of the town, relying on voluntary contributions. In the same way until 1870 the education of their children was dependent on local effort.

Warren's Charity of 1796, which had been given for teaching thirteen poor boys and fifteen poor girls, was granted between 1815 and 1839 to the National School for the boys, and to the School of Industry for the girls. The latter was held in the Bailiwick Court Room in 1813 and the girls were taught what was useful for domestic servants to know.

The National Schools were founded by the National Society to teach children cheaply and in large numbers according to the ideas of the Church of England on the system developed by Dr. Bell. The corresponding schools for nonconformists were the British Schools on Dr. Lancaster's system. Both systems used monitors - children previously instructed by the masters - who taught the others in groups of about ten, while one master supervised possibly several hundred children. A National School was certainly in existence in 1832 and this is doubtless the school, which as two schools, was rebuilt in George Street in 1855.

In 1841 a National School was opened in Boxmoor and in 1847 John Dickinson provided a school at Nash Mills; Apsley National School followed in 1869. All these schools are now county primary schools, except Apsley which was recently demolished and Nash Mills, a church school. In Marlowes, Hemel Hempstead, there was a British School. By a curious chance we know something of this school as at the age of over eighty a man named J. Borwick,, who had been appointed master of the school in 1834 at the age of sixteen, wrote his reminiscences. He was still wearing a short jacket at that time and had recently been head monitor of five hundred pupils at the British School in Borough Road, Islington. He found it quite a task to classify the newcomers, but he selected a few sharp lads to train as monitors after school. Discipline was a problem for he was too small to beat the boys even if he had been allowed to. The committee consisted of Quakers and other nonconformists. An 1820 map shows a school in Bury Road which could possibly have been the boys' school. The girls' British School was in Marlowes and in 1868 when Matthew Arnold inspected it and its 96 pupils, he condemned it.

Sunday Schools had very large enrolments and we hear of one in the Bailiwick Court room as early as 1823. Some idea of numbers can be obtained from the Bailiwick's arrangement for celebrating the Prince of Wales's wedding in 1863, when we gather that the Marlowes Baptist chapel had 370 on roll and the National School, 540. Even Box Lane had 61. To celebrate the passing of the Reform Bill in 1832, 1,200 children had been invited to a meal.

There was no grammar school at Hemel Hempstead, though one private school at Heath Brow called itself by that name at the end of the century. Boys who wanted any advanced education went to Berkhamsted Grammar School, which catered very cheaply for local boys until in 1876 its fees were raised from £3 to £12 and the boarding side was developed in a deliberate attempt to exclude the lower social grades. Some boys went to Watford Grammar School.

It would seem from census returns that most of the poorer children were working at the age of ten in the first half of the century. Only their younger brothers and sisters are described as scholars. On the other hand there was plenty of provision for those who could afford to pay.

Pigot's Directory of 1826/7 records two private academies for gentlemen and one for ladies. By the end of the century there were many such and the advertisements in the Hemel Hempstead Gazette give us some idea of them. In 1867 a Mr Halsey was advertising his Marlowes Academy for Boys. His wife ran a Ladies' School also in Marlowes. At Olive House, George Street, Mr. Payne conducted a boarding and day school for young gentlemen. He was "assisted by a well-qualified resident tutor (Latin and French)". In 1877 George Street boasted Mrs. Keene's "Young Ladies' School for boarders and day scholars." The branches of education proposed to be taught (with the assistance of one or more accomplished governesses and educational masters) were English, including History, Geography, Arithmetic, Reading, Writing and Drawing. Extras were French, Music, elementary Latin, German and Mathematics. In the eighties there was a so-called Hemel Hempstead College for Girls, a school at 37, George Street and another called Arnold Hall in Alma Road.

When the period opens the main link with the world was still the Sparrows Herne Turnpike Trust route through Two Waters. There was a proposal in 1819 to make a new turnpike road from Woburn to Hemel Hempstead through Leighton Buzzard which would link up with this road and afford a new route to London. The first eight miles of the proposed road from Hemel Hempstead to Dagnall were described as good hard road and close to plenty of materials for repairs. The scheme was defeated and at a public dinner in Woburn, over which Lord Charles Russell presided, R. A. Reddall Esq. was thanked for his exertions in getting the bill thrown out. Tolls, of course, had to be paid for the use of the turnpike. There was no toll gate near; to the south one was sited near the park at Watford and to the north there was one near Wigginton. The tolls, until 1823, were - "wheel carriage, chariot, calash, chaise or hearse 3d. (raised to 4½d in 1823), with broad wheels 1½d.

- horse laden 1½d.
- meat cattle 10d. (a score, etc.)"

Pigot's Directory of 1826 mentions coaches leaving the King's Arms at 7 a.m. and 9 a.m. to Snow Hill and London and at 3.30 p.m. to Holborn and 5 p.m. to Gaddesden. There was a carrier to London on Mondays and Thursdays.

Between 1837 and 1859 the tolls had to be halved owing to railway competition and in 1873 the road was de-turnpiked.

The Canal was authorised in 1793 to connect London and the Midlands. In September 1797 a committee was formed to execute the sale of land belonging to Boxmoor Trust to the proprietors of the Grand Junction Canal. The deed is dated 14th September 1799 and the price agreed was £900.3.10d for about 25 acres.

As the canal follows the course of the Bulbourne River not much excavating or banking was necessary except at the locks.

The navvies who constructed the canal lived in encampments, one of which was on Roughdown Common and disturbances among them were frequent. The bridge over the canal near Pix Farm was known locally as Battles Bridge, probably because a fierce argument took place there and a labourer lost his life.

The opening of the Grand Junction Canal in 1804 made more difference than we now realise, as it was used for a wide variety of goods. At the beginning of the century, Arthur Young complained that large quantities of hay and straw went to London in carts from the very banks of the canal and manure was brought back. He advocated the canals should be used more widely and quoted the case of a farmer who brought raw stable dung, night soil and street sweepings in sixty-ton loads by barge and found it very profitable. This practice increased and later in the century there were frequent complaints about the smell from barges tied up for the night. In 1887 the Parochial Committee minutes there is a statement that scarlet fever had broken out near the wharf where manure was unloaded and it was agreed that all manure unloaded should be removed at once and that the wharf should be disinfected and deodorised.

Coal was carried by barge. As much as sixty tons were unloaded at one time at Winkwell for Westbrook Hay. There was said to be much rejoicing by the outdoor staff when it was all carted up to the house and stored for the winter. In 1822 Mrs. J. Dickinson sent to her daughter at boarding school six chickens, some asparagus, 2 dozen cabbages, fruit, jam and a nosegay and all went by boat. Dickinsons relied on the canal, in spite of disputes over the use of the Gade's water, the firm wanting it for water-wheels and the canal company to maintain its water levels.

Another episode from the story of Dickinsons illustrates the difficulty of travel before the railways came. In 1826 John Dickinson left for Edinburgh. He went by road to London where he took a steam packet which was tossed in a storm for 66 hours till it finally put in at Bridlington. John Dickinson then had to catch a coach from York to Edinburgh, which he was visiting because of the important market for his paper represented by its publishing firms. However in 1837 another of his daughters was able to return home from school by the new railway - in a first class open carriage at 20 m.p.h.

There was no station at Apsley till the 1930's and the firm continued to use the canal for much of its traffic. Coal for the mills came from Staffordshire in narrow 30 ton boats, the horses being changed half-way. In the 1880's this only cost 6s. a ton on the boats. Paper went to Paddington by 25 ton boats which left Apsley at 5 p.m. each night, called at the other mills and reached London about 7 a.m.

Directories advertise water conveyance from Boxmoor, Crouchfield, Frogmore and independent wharfs to London, Birmingham, Dudley and to Aylesbury, Coventry, Leicester, Market Harborough, Northampton and

Manchester.

Opposition to the building of the railways was strong, not only from local landowners who petitioned parliament, but from canal owners, the turnpike trusts and highway commissioners. Robert Stephenson's original plan of the line had included a suggestion to take it through Dagnall Gap and Hemel Hempstead. This scheme met with strong opposition from Sir Astley Paston Cooper and the Earl of Brownlow, on whose motion the first bill was rejected in the House of Lords. The ordinary citizens of the town did not support them. In the minutes of the Company there is a letter from Mr. Smith of Hemel Hempstead, dated February 2nd, 1833, saying that nine-tenths of the inhabitants would petition in favour of the railway if the line were carried in the direction first proposed - through Hemel Hempstead and the Dagnall Gap to Leighton Buzzard.

In 1833 the Act for the construction of the London and Birmingham Railway was eventually passed and on July 13th 1837 the Euston to Boxmoor section of the line was opened. Originally the terminus had been planned at Camden Town. Mr. George Buck was the resident engineer for this section and Cubbitts the contractors. The making of the cutting nearly two miles long and the building of the embankment were great feats of engineering. One contemporary writer recommended "all men of science" to visit the bridge over London Road - a wonderful 'oblique arch bridge'. Materials had to be brought by canal and road from far afield. Best Burnt Dorking Cement and Roman Cement, wrought iron from Staffordshire and South Wales, Bramley Stone from Yorkshire. Timber and ballast were locally obtained. The Earl of Essex sold three acres for a ballast pit and in 1846 sleepers were obtained from Mr. Handscombe of Apsley. According to Stephenson's estimates made in 1833, the engines on the line cost £1,000 each, waggons £30 and the coaches £200.

Most of the labourers on the railway were drawn from the local population, although there was some Irish immigrant labour. It was a time of agricultural unemployment and the 18s. to 24s. a week paid to the railway workers helped considerably. Work on the 'horse-runs' with pulleys and barrows was dangerous and as we have seen special arrangements had to be made to treat casualties at the local hospital.

In the first year, excursions were run on the line to Boxmoor Station and a large marquee erected on Roughdown Common where refreshments were provided for sightseers.

The average daily number of passengers in the first month was 1423 and the daily receipts at Boxmoor were £153. Bradshaw's Guide for September 1843 to August 1844 quotes the following fares from Euston to Boxmoor:—

1st class car (6 inside by day)	...	6s. 6d.
2nd class car (closed by night)	...	4s. 6d.

"The 3rd class train takes passengers, private carriages

BOXMOOR EMBANKMENT 11th JUNE, 1837

THE STATION BUS

and horses from London to Birmingham"

Passengers	... ...	14s.
Carriages	... ...	£3
Horse Box	... ...	£4

At that time there were six down and up trains calling at Boxmoor and the time of the journey to Euston varied from 57 mins. to 80 mins. Fast trains to Watford were doing the journey in 1844 in 35 mins. In 1845 third-class fares from Euston were 2s. 1d., first-class 5s. on a 'mixed fast train and, 4s. 6d. on a mixed 'stopping' train.

The story of the Midland railway line to Hemel Hempstead is an interesting one. The idea began as a scheme by Mr. Grover to build a line himself from Boxmoor to Bury Mill End, but Mr. Stallon called the project 'puny' and revealed that there was also a scheme for a line from Boxmoor to Harpenden to join the L.N.W. and Midland Railways. A big meeting in 1862 attended by men from Redbourn favoured the through route, but Messrs. Grover and Barrow continued first with the scheme to join the town to the L.N.W.R. However the latter company, which incidentally owned the horse bus which served Boxmoor Station, did not favour the idea. The line was never joined to the L.N.W.R. for passengers, but was continued from the Midland Station in an easterly direction and after being fourteen years in the building was finally opened not to Harpenden, but to Chiltern Green north of the town, as if it was intended to serve Luton traffic. However, it was hoped at the time that London commuters would come and build homes in Hemel Hempstead. The railway was opened in 1877 by a procession led by the Berkhamsted Rifle Corps Band up a very muddy Alexandra Road. After a trip by the Bailiff and others to Luton and back a champagne luncheon was served in the Town Hall.

The line was at first leased to the Midland Railway and in 1886 absorbed by them. In 1887 the town asked to have the final section of the line diverted to Harpenden to give a better service to London. In 1877 there were four trains a day each way. One left Hemel Hempstead at 7.55 a.m. and arrived at Luton at 8.35 a.m. By changing at Chiltern Green one could be in St. Pancras at 9.49 a.m. In 1884, by contrast, the L.N.W.R. offered ten trains each day to London, the 7.55 a.m. arriving at Euston at 8.42 a.m., but it was necessary to take the horse bus from the Posting House (now Dacorum College). The trip cost 6d. and there were fifteen services a day to Boxmoor. By 1900 the 9 a.m. train from Boxmoor was reaching London at 9.35 a.m., while via Harpenden (30 minutes) the M.R. had seven trains a day giving (with a change) timings such as 7.27 a.m. from Hemel Hempstead, St. Pancras 8.42 a.m.

In 1887 there was a scheme for a steam tramway to connect Chesham, Boxmoor, the Mills, the town and, via Alexandra Road, the M.R. Station. The bill for this scheme actually had a second reading in Parliament. The scheme, with electric trams instead of steam ones, was revived in 1900 but the opposition of the Boxmoor Trustees and of Paston Cooper was decisive. The latter said he never wanted to go to Chesham and did not see why anyone should want to go!

Although Watford had a small motor bus as early as 1898, Hemel Hempstead seems to have waited till 1910 for a motor bus which gave twenty-one services a day to and from Boxmoor Station.

Horse-transport survived longer than one might think. Mr. W. F. Williams of Eastbrook recalls an occasion before the first World War when horses were hastily removed from wedding carriages to be used to pull the fire engine, whose pumps were then steam operated. In 1884 when fire broke out in a barn at Westbrook Hay, the Bailiff rode to Berkhamsted to procure assistance, while a boy was sent to Boxmoor Station to telegraph to Hemel Hempstead for the fire engine. Nash Mill's steam fire engine joined in too, but, not surprisingly, the three brigades were only in time to save the seventh hay rick out of seven.

Most people, except for an occasional excursion by wagonette, used their feet, but for the richer or more enterprising, the Heath Park Hotel and Bell Inn yard offered a light fashionable landau, broughams, with wagonettes and dog carts for hire, and H. Wright of Lower Marlowes offered tricycles, also for hire; while as early as 1869 Cranstone's foundry was offering French velocipedes for sale - "They are worked by the feet placed upon the double cranked axle of the large or front wheel and are guided by the steering handle fixed over this wheel. With a little practice a speed of eight to twelve miles per hour can be easily attained."

The local government of any town in the nineteenth century is complicated and as the century goes on, more and more authorities were created but were often superimposed on existing and more ancient organs of government. The Bailiwick itself is not easy to understand. It owed its origin to the charter of 1539 when a market and fair were granted. The town was not created a corporation, but was given a body corporate, as far as can be seen, to control the market and fair and to administer any income arising therefrom. The body consisted of the bailiff and his jury who also acted as the jury of the Court of Pie Powder (or Dusty Feet) to deal with market offences. Though it continued to meet throughout the nineteenth century it rarely transacted any business, but survived to be one of the last two courts of Pie Powder in England. The jury were the leading citizens, acting as a self-perpetuating corporation, and until there was again a contested election in 1832, no doubt a consequence of the Reform Bill agitation - they selected the Bailiff from among themselves. The Under Bailiff was merely the Beadle, who would accompany the Bailiff on his tour of the market, help with the the inspection of weights and measures and act as the town crier.

From about 1798 the Bailiwick accounts and minute books show a considerable widening of the sphere of activity and interests of the Bailiwick.

Up till then the usual expenditure had been on stalls, the fire engine and the bailiff's and jury's expenses. The income came chiefly from the stall and fair dues. One new self-imposed task was the provision of a town hall. There was already a Jacobean Market Hall and Court House on the present site, mounted on a wooden colonnade. This was repaired in 1825, but in 1851 the Bailiwick started (and completed in 1852) a Town Hall designed by Mr. George Lowe, which is the building to the north of the main Town Hall entrance, but not including the part touching St. Mary's Close. This upstairs hall was throughout the rest of the century used for most of the town's social activities and also occasionally for services, for Sunday Schools, and a School or Industry. The Boxmoor Trust helped to finance the hall, the cost being £1,278. It was originally built over an open colonnade which was filled in in 1857 to make a Corn Exchange. The J.P.s met in the hall for Petty Sessions, until a rival establishment, also paid for by the Boxmoor Trustees, Boxmoor Hall, was opened in 1890.

In 1861 a Reading Room (now a committee Room), and a Vestry Room below it for the Vestry Meetings were constructed to the north of the 1852 building at a further cost of £463, the Vestry Room being let to the parish at £15 p.a., paid out of the parish rates. The Bucks and Oxon Bank (formerly Grovers and now Lloyds) helped to finance the extension by way of a loan. In 1867 part of the old Market House which was used as a corn loft was pulled down and a new corn loft (later the Council Chamber and the robing room, etc.) and a turret for the market bell were built. In 1888 the Lamb Inn, which belonged to the church, and the old insanitary Butchers' Shambles were pulled down and the present St. Mary's Close constructed partly over the churchyard, as a market place, together with another range of Bailiwick buildings beyond it, with shops below. The street was slightly widened. In 1895 there was still a debt of £1,500 owed to the Bank as a result.

The last few years of the Bailiwick saw a decline in its financial fortunes due to the agricultural depression and to the opening of Boxmoor Hall, a rival for lettings, and to a decline in its importance in local government after the institution of a Parish Council in 1894. However, when the Borough Charter was granted in 1898 it was quite natural to combine the office of Bailiff and Mayor, as the leading citizen.

In the early years of the century the vestry functioned as the unpaid general duty organ of local government. It was concerned with the appointing of parish officials - the constables, the churchwardens, the overseers and the parish road surveyor, or stone warden. It also passed these officials' accounts, and authorised church rates. The latter were levied on all and dissenters here, as elsewhere, often refused to pay them. In theory the vestry was a meeting of all the male parishoners in fact it was a much more select body. In 1841 a Highways Board had taken over the duties of the old surveyor and the Poor Law Reform of 1834 had set up Unions of parishes controlled by Guardians to direct the administration of relief and of the Union Workhouse, although at Hemel Hempstead overseers continued to be appointed by the Vestry largely for the purpose of levying the rates. After 1894 the vestry was left almost functionless except for ecclesiastical business.

When the century opened law and order were still dependent on the local unpaid constables. In Hemel Hempstead two men were appointed to carry out the various and trying duties of the constable in addition to their own work. It was an office which all sought to avoid, for until the reform of the Poor Law in 1834 it involved unpleasant duties for the overseers. Although the constables had the support of the J.P.s and the right and duty to present cases at petty sessions and the support of a high constable of the Hundred, the system was quite inadequate to maintain order as the area became more urbanised and distress more general. In an effort to check crime, heavier and heavier penalties were imposed.The late thirties were an especially bad time, for crime and in the County Sessions Book for 1837 we read of George Proctor and John Dennis, both labourers of Hemel Hempstead, sentenced to ten years transportation for stealing 19s. 1d. from the person of James Ringshall. This was probably a second offence, as from other cases it is clear that transportation was not given for first offences. George Higgins of Hemel Hempstead, a labourer, was given one week's hard labour in 1833 for stealing thirty pounds of coal valued 6d from William Cole, grocer, and the same year William Coker got three months' hard labour for being idle and disorderly.

So serious was the menace to property that the well-to-do local inhabitants founded a property protection society which eventually turned into a dining club or little more and survived till recently.

London had acquired the first modern police force by Peel's Metropolitan Police Act of 1829. Hemel Hempstead started its own police under the vestry in 1837 consisting of a superintendent and two privates. The force was established under the Lighting and Watching Act of 1837. The sergeant was paid 30s. a week and the privates 25s. They had to find their own uniforms and were stopped 2s. a week to pay for them. Nine inspectors were chosen by the vestry, three of whom retired annually. In 1839 the chairman of the inspectors reported that the "inhabitants seemed generally satisfied with the efficiency of the force, only one written complaint having been made within the two years against the officers. The number of robberies and depredations in the parish are decreased, many bad characters driven away. Mendicity is much prevented and the agricultural property better protected, there is less fence-breaking and trespassing of stray cattle and most of the farmhouses and land in this extensive parish are visited once in twenty-four hours either day or night."

After the County Police Act of 1839 had been adopted in Hertfordshire, Captain Archibald Robertson was appointed as chief constable in 1841. The new force was to be responsible to the J.P.s and the cost was met by a threepenny rate. By 1843 there was a County force of sixty constables and

HEMEL HEMPSTEAD, HIGH STREET IN 1882

FIRE BRIGADE AT THE BEGINNING OF THIS CENTURY

their officers, who wore blue uniforms with white buttons and embroidery. Strict rules were made and enforced for the new constables. No member was to keep a dog, pig, fowls, or any stock. After patrol they were to stay in their house of lodging where they could easily be found.

Apparently there were heavy arrests in all areas in the first years of the force which called forth the following advice from headquarters:-

> "The constabulary must bear in mind that a heavy calendar or numerous arrests by no means prove the presence of a vigilant police; the absence of the cause of arrests, committals and trials best shows the well working of the force."

In 1859 at the station in Queen Street there were an inspector, Edward Samuel Evans and six men. The status of the area was considerably increased when in 1881, as a result of reorganisation in the County Force, Hemel Hempstead became one of five divisions - D Division with a superintendent in charge. A horse and cart were then provided for the division's use. In 1860 the old quarters in Queen Street had been left for a building in Bury Mill End which had been converted and let to the constabulary at £30 per annum.

Pay increases in 1881 resulted in superintendents getting £120 a year, inspectors £95, sergeants 28s. 0d. a week, and constables 21s. 7d. From the beginning of the force there was a superannuation scheme. Every sergeant and constable had to attend church every Sunday in uniform, but the next year they were granted one day a quarter as a rest day. The life of the constable remained strictly supervised. In 1890, if he contemplated marriage, he had to sign a declaration to say that he was free of all debt and had £20 in cash or furniture to that value. Recruits to the force were mainly from farm labourers, although there were a number of grooms and a few craftsmen among them. (Typical of the career of a constable of the time is that of P.C. 53, Berry Thomas. He was a labourer and joined the force in December 1863 when he was 22. He remained at Hemel Hempstead until 1881, when he moved to Brent Pelham. Two years after he retired with a pension of £35.2.0d. a year.)

The Volunteer Fire Brigade was formed in November 1845 after outbreaks of incendiarism in the area. Two manual engines were available, one supplied by the Phoenix Fire Insurance Company and maintained by Mr. Cranstone and the parish engine in the care of Mr. Hales, who was paid £6 a year. The brigade was made up of twelve gentlemen volunteers and twelve paid men. The volunteers wore brown leather belts and the others webbing belts. After 1884 the paid brigade ceased to function. Funds were raised by social events. In March 1884 the Phoenix Engine was recalled and the parish engine after forty years needed an overhaul. This cost £47.10.0d. The first steam engine was purchased in 1905. One of the last calls on the old manual engine had been to a fire at Gaddesden Place, where there was extensive damage.

Among the extra bodies created to meet the growing demands of local government in the century, the biggest spenders were the Poor Law Guardians who controlled, after 1834, a union of parishes of Hemel Hempstead, King's Langley, Flamstead, Flaunden, Bovingdon and Great Gaddesden. One of their first tasks was to pull down and rebuild the old workhouse in Redbourn Road inherited from the overseers. They had the help of a loan from the Exchequer Bill Loan Commissioners - an early example of this method of financing local government. They also sold off the parish lands for £837.6.8d., lands which the overseers had previously used for settling paupers in Bury Road.

These Guardians met fortnightly and must have given a good deal of time to the work. Nor were they unimportant people; their chairman in 1838 was the Hon. G. D. Ryder of Westbrook Hay. They discussed small details of relief, payments of 6d. per week by a son to help support his father in the workhouse, they asked for tenders for coffins for paupers, arranged for the removal of the insane, instructed and paid Medical Officers at fees from £25 - £75 p.a. and paid a midwife for paupers, a woman who could not, incidentally, sign her name. Some very hard cases came their way, for instance in 1841 they were asked to accept Sophia Barnes of Flamstead and her four illegitimate children. She thought she had married Edward Bishop of Redbourn, but he had a former wife and family and was by 1841 in gaol for leaving them a charge on the parish. They paid a chaplain to the workhouse too. They paid £5 each for three pauper girls of 13 to 15 to be 'apprenticed' to Tring Mill in 1846. In 1845 they appointed one William Hawtree as Schoolmaster and Tailor to the Workhouse at £12 per annum and double rations. By 1848 out relief for two weeks came to £103.15.8d. and Workhouse provisions to £50.17.8d. In the course of time workhouse standards became less strict and in 1883 the Guardians were in trouble with the Local Government Board for over-indulging the paupers in the Workhouse with 38 pts. of wine, 68 pts. of gin, 162 pts. of Brandy, 1167 galls. of malt liquor in six months at a cost of £71.8.0d. It was pointed out in defence that this was not only for the ninety inmates but also for the staff!

Until the establishment of a Parochial committee especially concerned with public health, the Guardians seem to have concerned themselves with such problems as nuisances, etc. Round the middle of the century the total budget for the union was about £2,500 p.a.

Up to the winter of 1853 public lighting was defrayed from market profits at the command of the High Bailiff. Street lamps were lit for eight months of the year from sunset to 2 a.m. with the exception of two nights before and after the full moon. There were thirty-nine of these lamps, fifty to eighty yards apart. The annual charge for each was £2.17.0d.

In 1856 the Street Lighting Act had been adopted. A lighting rate was levied in October 1867 of one penny in the pound on land and three pence on property other than land.

The Boxmoor, Two Waters and Crouchfield, Gas Light and Coke Company was founded in 1868 with a capital of £3,000. It entered into an agreement with the Inspectors of Lighting for the Parish to erect and light thirty public lamps in Boxmoor and Two Waters. In 1878 this company was amalgamated with the Hemel Hempstead Company to form the Hemel Hempstead District Gas Company. Up until 1902 the district accounts and collections were contracted out on commission to Mr. Charles Collett Jones of Marlowes.

Of all the special local government bodies, some of the most interesting were the School Boards. They were set up, one for each parish, under the 1870 Education Act with power to levy rates for aiding or providing elementary schools for children up to the age of twelve. The implementation of the Act changed the picture of elementary education. The existing National Schools were aided and Two Waters British School was taken over, but new schools were needed. George Street Infants were moved to a new school in Queen Street in 1878. In 1877 Bury Mill End School was built to serve a rapidly growing district and Piccotts End School opened.

As in all areas, the schools were overcrowded and amenities few. Salaries were very low and conditions difficult. In 1876 the salary of assistants was raised from £26 to £30 p.a. and all the schools depended partly on pupil teachers.

The log books of the schools show how crowded they were, although on wet days, fair days and market days numbers might shrink to half, or less, even after 1880 when attendance was compulsory. In George Street girls' school with perhaps 70 girls on roll, many were absent on 2nd May 1870 "to go Maying" and on 27th October only one child in the first class was present. In 1889 with 167 on roll only fifty were present one day and several girls were said to be too weak for regular attendance. This was in the days of the agricultural depression and children walked from as far as Cupid Green. The 167 had to be accommodated in two rooms, small weekly fees of a few pence were paid until 1890, the guardians paying the fees of the poorest.

The School Board itself regarded economy for the rate payers as its main duty. Most of the local 'big-wigs' were members, including Lewis Evans, who in his election statement in 1883 declared that Board Schools should teach the Three R's and let the children off school in the busy seasons.

Some information from the log books of local schools will give a vivid idea of conditions between 1860 and 1900.

Boxmoor National School (Girls)

1863 dimensions - school room 45½' x 20' 10", classroom 15' x 9'.

1863 numbers of 119 yet still taught by a mistress and one pupil teacher.

1868 new pupil teacher taken on at 4s. 0d. a week till she passes the examination.

1870 several children away with ringworm.

1889 (N.B. school attendance is now compulsory).
September 6th - 18th children had not yet returned after the holiday and many were away gleaning, but the school attendance officer, here mentioned for the first time, fails to visit any of the children pointed out to him.

Boxmoor Boys C.E. School
1877 6 boys in Standard 1 do not know the alphabet.
1879 Headmaster asks for partitions between the seats of the privy.

George Street Girls' School
1872 Payment by results is worked out thus for a national grant:
38 (average attendance) at 6s. - £11.8.0d; of 22 presented for examination to H.M.I. 22 passed in reading, 20 in writing and 15 in arithmetic - 57 at 4s. 0d. - £11.8.0d. 1 extra at 3s. 0d. Total grant £22.19.0d.
1875 H.M.I. reports an increase of a large number of unruly scholars. The room is too full as the average number is over 100.
1877 H.M.I. reports "a lavatory should be provided during the alterations."

George Street Boys School
1897 H.M.I. says both classrooms 'somewhat overcrowded' as there are about 200 on roll.
1900 H.M.I. reports the illegal employment of many boys some only nine. who are, as a result, late or absent.

Two Waters British Schools (i.e. Nonconformists in control)
1869 1 girl removed through the influence of a clerical manager of a national (i.e. Church of England) school, against the wishes of her mother but she was not in a position to protest.
1870 Work of first class includes English, Saxon and Danish History, Physical Geography, maps of England and Asia, Singing, Weights and Measures, multiplication tables and the Early History of France, read for a composition the next day.
1878 The new school opened.
1895 Mistress of the infants teaches needlework three afternoons from 2 to 4 p.m. in the Senior School and leaves over eighty infants to a pupil teacher and a monitor.
1898 The school's grant was cut because of bad discipline in the lower standards.
1899 Forty were being taught in a room built for twenty-four.

In the last decade before Balfour's Act of 1902 reorganised public education, some steps were taken to improve the educational ladder. In 1893 the County Council offered twenty £10 scholarships, probably for intending teachers and there is mention of continuation schools for the first time, helped out of public funds by the Technical Instruction Committee. Yet in 1894 the Hemel Hempstead School Board is asking the (Government) Education Department to relax the regulations for examination of Pupil Teachers at the end of their engagement. Grants from the national funds depended on satisfactory reports from Inspectors. The whole product of the school rate in the town in 1896 was about £430.

Some of the special bodies, such as the Burial Board, which arranged for the establishment of the cemetery in 1878, and the Lighting Inspectors, need not detain us. The Board of Surveyors is more interesting. Samuel Stallon was chairman in 1870 and was still chairman when its work was merged into that of the Borough's Highway Committee in 1898. The road mending methods were clearly primitive and consisted chiefly of turning cartloads of flints, bought at 2s. to 4s. a load, and sifted sand on to the roads and of watering them to keep the dust down. Scraping the top off was sometimes carried out. The late Alderman J. Stone in his memoirs recalls picking up stones at Leverstock Green at 1s. a cartload.

Even in 1880 the Highway rates totalled only £1,326.3.8d. The men worked from 6 a.m. to 5.30 p.m. with one hour off for dinner. After the borough took over, a correspondent to the Gazette implied that the road mending methods had not changed. He wrote about Boxmoor roads, "stones half the size of bricks and larger are allowed to be thrown on the roads together with a bountiful supply of clay and weeds."

The establishment of the County Councils from 1888 had in some ways eased the road problem, as they took over the main roads from the local Highway Boards and had a county rate to spend. Till 1884 the J.P.s meeting in Quarter Sessions had been able to give some oversight as they had done for centuries, to local government and especially to the maintenance of bridges and law and order.

During the last thirty years of the century as the number of special authorities increased further, there was less chaos than might be expected as the clerk to most of the bodies was usually a local solicitor, Mr. Day or Mr. Grover, or after 1883, Mr. Lovel Smeathman, Grover's successor. In his office much of the work was dealt with over many years by a chief clerk named Stallon (formerly Stallion) who also entrenched himself securely on most of the committees being chairman of several and eventually became one of the borough's first aldermen. His position was an ambiguous one but, in spite of criticism in the local press and by hand bills, apparently almost unassailable. Many local tradesmen served on several of these committees and Stallon had a bloc of supporters among them. The same leading citizens were meeting very frequently in different committees to transact business. Some, such as Stallon himself, were also shareholders or directors of the Waterworks Company formed in 1865, or of the Boxmoor Gas Company which issued shares in 1868. This too, produced an undesirable situation when at the end of the century the costs of these two services were frequently discussed. The new borough in fact bought the waterworks company in 1900 at considerable profit to the original investors.

The story of the granting of a Borough charter to Hemel Hempstead is as follows. The idea was first suggested by Mr. E. Pearman in 1866 and 1876 at the time of the election of Bailiffs, and he raised it again at the Pie Powder Court in 1886 after a Municipal Reform Act had been passed. A Civil Engineer, J. Harris, urged incorporation in 1894, after doing a careful study of the town's charters, but he failed to secure these from the vicar's custody. A much respected headmaster, Henry Dowling, was Bailiff 1895 to 1896 and during this year Harris and the Reverend D. Tatton, Congregational Minister, petitioned the Bailiff to call a meeting to consider incorporation. There was considerable feeling in the town at that time about the control exercised by a small group led by Stallon. Eventually he was the only person on the special committee to oppose the petition for a charter sent to the Privy Council in 1896. In July and October a Court of Enquiry was held. By the end of that year the matter was practically accomplished and Sir Astley Paston Cooper became the first mayor when Hemel Hempstead in 1898 achieved the direct transition from parish to municipal Borough, the only town to do this.

William Randall, who was one of the last Bailiffs and first Mayors of Hemel Hempstead and who gave Randall Park to the town, was its first County Councillor. Until 1939 County Council meetings were held in London because of the difficulties of cross-country travel.

For parliamentry representation Hemel Hempstead voters helped to elect two (later three) members for the County of Hertfordshire. By the Redistribution of Seats Acts 1885 the county was split into four divisions with one Member of Parliament each. The town then found itself in the western or Watford division, while several of the nearby villages were in the Mid-Herts division.

Until the Ballot Act of 1872 voting was not secret and until the Reform Act of 1832 at any rate it was normal to compile a poll book showing how many people were going to vote and sometimes how they did vote.

In the famous election of 1805 there were forty-five men at Hemel Hempstead listed as voting though some of them did not live here but held their 40s. freeholds here. Of the forty-five voters one was a parson (Dr. Bingham of Great Gaddesden), only two were esquires, eleven of whom did not live here) and one, Harry Grover, was described as a gentleman. The rest were not apparently entitled to a description of quality. William Baker Esq., with 1556 votes and the Hon. Thomas Brand with 1072 were elected for the county, and of Hemel Hempstead's forty-five, twelve voted for Brand and the rest for Baker.

In 1833 in the first election after the Reform Bill there were 133 voters on Hemel Hempstead's list. The numbers polling for the county are interesting.

Sir J. S. Sebright received 2154 votes, N. Calvert Esq. 2141, Viscount Grimston (Lord Verulam's heir) 2074 and R. Alston Esq. 2007. The first two were elected.

In 1902 the Western division was still represented by Hemel Hempstead's Lord of the Manor, the Rt. Hon. T. F. Halsey, P.C. of Gaddesden Place. T. F. Halsey was also vice-chairman of the County Council at the time, while Sir John Evans of Nash Mills was Chairman. As William Randall was still a Councillor, the town was well represented on the County Council.

Hemel Hempstead in the nineteenth century was neither an important nor a fashionable centre, but its life was active and particularly for the leading tradesmen, who served on many committees, intrigued and argued, it was no bad place in which to live. For many there was hard work and poverty, but because of the particular nature of the town's industrial growth this was never so grim as in many parts of the country.

NOTE ON SOURCES

In addition to sources in the general list there are many records which exist only for the nineteenth century and later. These are listed here in full:-

Primary Sources

Hemel Hempstead Guardians Reports, H.R.O.

Hertfordshire Roll Books 1805 & 1833, H.R.O.

Surveyors Minutes 1870-83, B.A.

Burial Board Minutes, B.A.

Parochial Committee Minutes, B.A.

Parish Meetings Minutes, 1894-8, B.A.

Parish Council Minutes, 1895-8, B.A.

Gas Inspectors Minutes, 1875-1895, B.A.

Fire Brigade Minutes, B.A.

Public Health Report on Hemel Hempstead, 1854, B.A.

1879 Sanitary Report, B.A.

Overseers Accounts, 1838-58, P.C.

Charity Commissioners Reports.

Pigot's Directory, 1826/7.

Cassey's Directory, 1864.

Kelly's Directory, 1890 & 1902.

First Report of Hemel Hempstead Borough Council Engineer, 1900. H.R.O.

Sparrow's Herne Turnpike Trust Record, H.R.O.

Minutes of London-Birmingham Railway Company, pamphlets, bills, time-tables, etc. at Railway Archives.

Police Records and photographs at Police Headquarters, Hatfield.

West Herts Hospital Minute Books and records kept at the Hospital.

Boxmoor National School Log Book.

Two Waters School Log Book.

George Street Boys' School Log Books.

George Street Girls' School Log Books.

School Board Minutes, 1893.

Congregational Church Minutes from 1874.

Friends' Meeting House Records.

Baptist Church Records

'The Charter of 1898' – special booklet issued to mark Charter Celebration.

Bills belonging to George Rolph Ltd.

Cobbett's 'Rural Rides' vol. i.

Gerish Collection of Newspaper Cuttings, H.R.O.

Memories of Alderman Jarman.

Reminiscences of the late Mr. W. H. Day, the late Mr. J. Stone, Mr. Williams.

'An Octogenarian's Reminiscences', J. Borwick, 1902.

'Old Hemel Hempstead' - W. Winter, Herts Constitutional Magazine, vol. II.

Borough Almanacks for 1897 & 1891.

Parish Assessment Lists, 1804, P.C.

The County Chronicle and Weekly Advertiser, 1816, H.R.O.

Hertfordshire and Hemel Hempstead Gazette, from 1867, in B.M.

Secondary Sources

D. G. Kaye's lecture on 'The Great Depression in Hemel Hempstead).

Smiles, 'Lives of the Engineers - R. & G. Stephenson.'

Smiles, 'History of the Midland Railway'.

Articles in the 'Hertfordshire Countryside'.

Joan Evans, 'The Endless Web'.

J. Cannon, 'The Nicky Line (H.H. to Harpenden Railway),' Baracuda Press.

CHAPTER 7

The Twentieth Century

Part 1 - 1900-1918

The first decade of the twentieth century brought unrest in many industries, activity from the suffragettes and shadows of the coming war, but from the local papers and from memoirs one gets the impression that these took second place to local affairs and the problems facing the new borough.

The Town Council and its health officials were forced to devote much thought to the problems of infectious diseases. At nearly every meeting there were cases of diphtheria, enteric fever, or scarlet fever to report; often all three occurred at once and many of the epidemics were serious. Apsley End was especially liable to outbreaks. In October 1923 there were 11 cases of diphtheria, 3 of scarlet fever, 1 of enteric fever, 2 of erysipelas and 1 of pulmonary tuberculosis. No doubt this and other outbreaks in that area were due to the bad state of the waterways and ditches. Complaints of flooding were frequent and the local council carried on a long argument with the County Council over responsibility for cleaning them. Meanwhile local inhabitants and those who travelled to work at the paper mills had to put up with the bad state of the roads and footpaths. There was still a risk too, of well water becoming polluted from cesspools; an outbreak of typhoid fever at Adeyfield was traced to supplies of milk where the water was infected.

The closing of schools because of epidemics of infectious diseases was still quite a common occurrence. In February 1914 there was a diphtheria outbreak at Apsley non-provided school when 12 cases were reported and the school had to be shut for a time. Again in November there were further cases of diphtheria and 27 cases were taken to the new isolation hospital at Bennetts End. By December the number of cases had risen to 45. In April 1916 there was a serious outbreak among children at the Hemel Hempstead Institution. Bennetts End Hospital could not accommodate them all and the old hospital in Highfield Lane had to be fitted up and nurses engaged to look after them.

To this new hospital in Bennetts End many hours of planning and discussion had been devoted before the foundation stone was laid in August 1914. The choice of site brought local objections. There was a ratepayers meeting at which feelings ran very high and finally a Local Government Board Inquiry was held.

Although diphtheria remained a problem, the new drainage system, connections to which were made in 1900, had certainly helped to solve the old problem of typhoid fever which haunted the town in the nineteenth century. Samuel Rawson, the Sanitary Inspector, was able to report that from 1892 - 1907 there were, on an average, 19 cases a year, but from 1902

- 1912 that figure had dropped to an average of 2.27.

In management of town affairs, whether on the Council, School Board, Boxmoor Trust or Guardians of the Poor, the same people gave faithful service. In fact it was sometimes difficult to find people willing to serve, except on the School Boards where differing religious groups gave strong support to their candidates.

The first election for the Boxmoor Trust for 22 years was held in 1913 but did not arouse great enthusiasm. The same year there were 13 candidates for the election of Guardians of the Poor. Only 693 voters out of a possible 2195 voted for the nine members. The Gazette complained that there was no campaign and the voters appeared apathetic. The Council was often sharply divided between those who wanted to see industrial development in the town and a group strongly opposed to anything that could possibly lead to any rate increase. In 1911 an active Ratepayers Association was formed.

Feelings between the two wards, north and south, often ran high, especially when members were being selected for the various committees. The Coronation celebrations of 1911 were the occasion of one of these rivalries, which was eventually solved by Apsley deciding to hold its celebrations independently.

There was considerable discussion on the need for an extra ward, but after several schemes had been drawn up, the Council in 1913 voted against the formation of a third ward.

Feelings ran higher over parliamentary elections. The West Herts Division then included Watford. Sir T. F. Halsey held the seat for many years for the conservatives. There was much local interest when John Marnham, a prominent local non-conformist contested the seat; he did not get in, but later it was won by another liberal and non-conformist - Nathaniel Micklem. The election campaigns of 1910 were among the livliest and most keenly fought.

The effect of the political crisis over Lloyd George's 1909 Budget was so extensive that there were two General Elections in 1910, one in January and one in December. The issues involved were such that they were the subject of a great deal of controversy and debate, both nationally and on the local level. Colonial Preference, Free Trade, the powers of the House of Lords, British Patriotism against the increasing naval strength of Germany, the extent of taxation on food, Old Age Pensions and Home Rule for Ireland were all put forward for the consideration of the electorate. Hence at both elections it was not surprising that political meetings were usually noisy and even violent.

Hemel Hempstead and the surrounding area was no exception. One meeting at High Wycombe was so violent that the Riot Act was read. There were two candidates for this division of Hertfordshire, both of them barristers; the Liberal incumbent, Mr. Nathaniel Micklem was challenged by the Tory, Mr. Arnold Ward. Both these candidates gathered around them groups of leading local figures to lend support and add a certain lustre to their individual campaigns.

Not unnaturally, Mr. Ward was befriended by the leaders of local industry since the Tory party was the party of Tariff Reform, protection and colonial preference, which would tend to boost the profits of British Industry. Amongst the most prominent of the Tory supporters, then, were Mr. Barton Kent of the brush factory in Apsley, and the directors of Dickinson's Paper Mills. Many of the speeches during the Tory campaign meetings were aimed at informing the public of the benefits which these industries would reap from the 'great Unionist policy of Tariff Reform'. A certain emphasis was laid on the fact that if the Liberals had their way and introduced Free Trade, the Kent Brush Factory would suffer severe set-backs from an influx of imported brushes from Europe at lower prices. Threats of unemployment and reduced wages were used to persuade the working men of Kent's to vote Tory. A similar method could be employed with Dickinson's. The mills, too, or so Mr. Ward and his associates maintained, would suffer if Free Trade allowed an unchecked flow of imported paper at cheap rates without a reciprocal abolition of tariffs on the part of other nations. It would be 'a waste of national wealth and prosperity for us to wait on the supposition that (foreign countries) will ultimately adopt Free Trade principles' said the writer of a letter in the Hemel Hempstead Gazette of 8th January, 1910, criticising Mr. Micklem. Throughout the January and December campaigns, the correspondence in the Gazette included a large number of very heated letters from members of the public and the candidates themselves disputing the various election issues.

This degree of interest and involvement was mirrored in the heckling and excitement of some campaign meetings, and was typical of election campaigns before the 1914-18 war. One can find similar scenes in electioneering during the last few decades of the 19th century.

The Liberal platform at the 1910 elections dealt not only with Free Trade but also with the new proposals for Old Age Pensions, charges by the Tories that the Liberal government had neglected the army and the navy so that Britain was now inferior to Germany in military strength, and of course with 'Peers against the People'. This was the slogan coined by Lloyd George for the constitutional crisis which had forced the 1910 elections, and was concerned with the extent of the House of Lords' powers, particularly in vetoing Bills sent to them from the Commons.

The Liberals under Lloyd George had turned the rejection of the 1909 Budget by the Lords into a grand election issue and Mr. Micklem in Hemel Hempstead made the most of it, laying stress on the idea that the Lords - by implication, the Tory party - were not interested in the welfare of the people. Mr. Micklem produced arguments very similar in sentiment to support the Liberal belief in Free Trade. He spoke of 'taxes on the people's food' because of 'government by the peers' and appealed to local interests by citing the paper making industry. Here, he claimed, the Tories were keeping out foreign paper by duties and by raising prices in Britain. 'Artifically they were going to put more money in the pockets of men making large fortunes..'

The January campaign lasted about three weeks. The issues mentioned but briefly here were tossed back and forth between the candidates, and accusations became increasingly vehement. Mr. Ward said that the Liberals were destroying the Empire, even in the face of Germany's increasing power; but one Liberal supporter described the Tories as a 'War Party' who were trying to drift into war with Germany.

However, the debates had to stop and when polling Day arrived on the 27th January, people were taken to the polls from the factories and each party recruited as many vehicles as possible to bring in their supporters. There was, in fact, a very high turn-out of voters, with an estimated 90% at Hemel Hempstead.

At the previous election of 1906, Mr. Micklem won with a majority of about 1400, but this time, at 'the most momentous election that has ever claimed the attention of the electors' he was defeated by a similar number of votes. Mr. Ward managed a vote of 8,782, whereas Mr. Micklem polled 7,231. In fact, all four electoral divisions of Hertfordshire returned Conservative members. The rejoicing was great. Mr. Ward went on a tour of triumph, making speeches in several of the villages, accompanied by a procession of decorated vehicles. He was preceded into Tring by a brass band playing 'See, the conquering hero comes'.

The December campaign covered most of the same issues with apparently equal controversy and interest. Now, however, there were Tory accusations that the Liberal Party had managed to pass their Budget 'by a series of contemptible bargains', 'by concession and mutual arrangements between Radicals, Socialists and Irish Nationalists'. An advertisement in favour of Mr. Ward announced that every vote given to Mr. Micklem would be a vote 'to destroy the Constitution and break up the British Empire by giving Home Rule to Ireland. Yet he dares to fly the Union Jack, the flag of the United Kingdom'.

Once again, Mr. Ward won, but with a reduced majority of 883. Once again, however, the Liberal party had the majority in Parliament.

To give a few more indications of the way elections were fought and won in the early years of this century, it is possibly worth describing the December homecoming of Mr. Ward. In the words of the Gazette, 'The newly elected member and Miss Ward then entered a carriage decorated with blue flags; ropes were attached and a happy body of young men - and maidens, too - pulled the victor along Marlowes and into the town'. He spoke in Watford, and motored through Kings Langley, arriving in Apsley at 6 p.m. Speeches were made outside Dickinson's and Kent's before Mr. Ward travelled on to Berkhamstead.

Both the campaigns were recounted in great detail in the local newspaper and all the main meetings received full coverage. They were typical campaigns but have the feeling of the end of a particular era when the Liberals were accused of being Socialists and appeals for maintenance of the Empire could still arouse passionate support. But it was only a few years before the Great War and far-reaching changes in political and social life.

The hospital remained a most important institution in the town. From its foundation many charitable efforts were devoted to raising funds for it. The name was changed to hospital from infirmary in 1908. Each year the Friendly Societies held a Hospital Church Parade in aid of the hospital and the Oxford Brotherhood's Parade for it was one of the events of the year. Subscriptions from individuals and groups and gifts in kind were constantly received. Mrs. Drake's Coronation Fund for the hospital raised £1,517.6.8d. In December 1909 there were 39 in-patients. The demands on the Out-Patients Department were high, but were relieved when the National Health Insurance Scheme was introduced. In January 1913 the majority of doctors in Hertfordshire decided to serve on the panel.

Soon after the outbreak of war 20 beds were offered to the British Red Cross Society. The out-patients' waiting room was converted into a ward for the soldiers. It was possible to use this as the number of out-patients had diminished. There were generous gifts to the soldiers, who had much greater freedom than ordinary patients. Private cars were sent to take them out and they were invited to homes for meals. A smoking room and games room were made for them and tickets sent for the grand new Princess Theatre.

The workhouse was another institution to which charitable efforts were devoted. Christmas was always a time for extra gifts to the inmates and for a special party. Dinner at 12.30 usually consisted of roast pork, roast beef, vegetables and plum pudding. Oranges, apples and nuts were distributed as well as tea, sugar and tobacco. One of the guardians carved and local ladies helped to prepare the food. After tea there was an entertainment and a popular event was a gramophone performance given by Mr. F. P. Thurnham.

Mr. Baines, the Master of the Workhouse, gave some interesting figures to a meeting of the guardians in 1912. These covered the years from 1904 and show a steady increase in the number of inmates up to the time of Old Age Pensions in 1909.

Dates	*Inmates*	*Tramps*
1904	4785	1391
1905	5500	1444
1906	5610	1514
1907	5615	1994
1908	5731	1430
1909 (just before Old Age Pensions)	6114	1260
1910	5896	1637
1911	5521	1787
1912	5121	2026

He had some interesting comments to make on this point soon after the scheme came into force, when he reported that of the 5 pensioners who had left in January 1911 only 2 had stayed out. He said that he asked one old man why he had returned and he replied that he had been sleeping with a man who wanted "a four-acre field to himself." He was "glad to get back to Home Sweet Home and when he died he should leave the Old Age Pension to the House of Lords." Tramps were a constant problem especially on a Sunday when some other institutions would not take them and during the war years there was a constant effort to encourage any able-bodied ones to useful work.

Hemel Hempstead was the only borough in the county that decided to exercise its powers as a primary education authority in 1902. There was a keenly-fought election in that year for a seat on the Hertfordshire County Council. Religious instruction in schools was a burning issue and Mitchell-Innes stood as representative of the Anglican Party and Alfred Marnham for the non-conformists. This election aroused great interest and a crowd gathered to hear Mr. Marnham declared elected.

With an increasing population, there arose an urgent need for more school accommodation. Inspectors' Reports which were published in full at the beginning of the century, made frequent reference to lack of space and equipment. School grants from the Board depended on these reports and they contain threats of "a lowered grant if defects are not remedied." After much deliberation it was decided to build a new school at Two Waters to relieve the pressure on all the others. By 1913 this was completed and in use. The total cost for the new school was £3,362.3.0d. £106.1.8d. was spent on equipment and furniture and £186.16.5d. on tar paving. The school provided for 60 children in each classroom, 9 square feet being allowed for each infant and 10 square feet for juniors.

During the war some parts of the schools were used by the military. Attendance was slack. Children were kept away to help on the land and those over 12 who had reached a required standard were allowed to work.

The beginning of the century saw the connection of the much-needed sewerage scheme and an increased use of gas for home and street lighting. The affairs of the Gas Company continued to flourish and it was able to reduce the price and set up a reserve fund of £250. There came rivalry in 1909 with an application from Chesham Electric Lighting Company for a provisional order to supply electricity; this was granted but in fact never exercised. In the same year another bore hole was sanctioned for the water works and the supply had to be further increased when soldiers were camped in Gadebridge.

At the beginning of the century, too, a number of new houses were built, especially at Apsley End where the demand for labour at the mills increased steadily. Weymouth Street, Orchard Street, Henry Street and Durrants Hill were expanding housing areas where villas let at about £25 a year. At the same time new houses were going up in Boxmoor, in Kingsland Road and Horsecroft Road, which benefited from proximity to the station. In 1909 land was sold for the development of the Ellingham Estate.

By 1910 there were about 12,000 inhabitants in the borough. The question of street repairs and paving was one which arose often. Marlowes in 1913 was still not paved in parts; the state of the roads in Apsley was a constant source of concern, especially as motor traffic increased. Kent's was one of the first firms to use motor transport.

The whole situation was made much more urgent after 1914 with so many military vehicles in the area and could only have been slightly mitigated by daily use of the water cart. At the end of 1914 there was a particularly heavy storm when many houses in Apsley were flooded. A barrier had to be built at the Bell to hold back the flood water.

Traffic on the canal reached its peak in 1905, both Dickinsons and Ovaltine using it for coal supplies well into this century. In 1910 there were 21 motor bus services a day running between Hemel Hempstead and Boxmoor Station, the journey to London then took about 38 minutes. To avoid the bus journey people from the town could travel via Harpenden and arrive at St. Pancras taking about 1 hour and 20 minutes. An advertisement of the West Herts Motor and Carriage Manufactory in 1910, "Motor bodies built for any make of chassis" was a pointer to the future.

The Borough Council in 1913 adopted the policy of municipal housing with a plan for houses at Wood Farm. Some members questioned the necessity and pointed out that there was little demand for cottages that had been built at Chipperfield. Although there were labour problems and other delays, in 1915 24 houses were ready and there appeared to be no difficulty in letting them.

Throughout the early years of the century, John Dickinson's continued to expand and the mills employed many people in the area. In 1904 there were 1,283 workpeople and 209 clerical staff at Apsley, by 1911 these numbers had risen to 1,658 and 304. Improvements were made and new buildings added to all the mills. Developments were made which laid the foundations for overseas trade. The use of electrical power and motor transport pointed to the future. A new dock and wharf were built in 1904 and an electric crane purchased. In 1905 Salmon Meadow was bought and a new power house built with three generators. In 1907 Apsley Mills was connected to the new sewer and in 1911 came a link up to the system of the National Telephone Company. In 1906 three new beaters were put into Nash Mills which was concentrating on pulp board manufacture.

There was considerable concern about safety in the mills. A fire main was laid at Apsley in 1901 and five pumps set up. Later a sprinkler system was added. At the same time an underground fire main, which completely enclosed Nash Mills buildings was installed.

There were efforts to improve hours and working conditions. In 1903 a scheme was introduced to avoid Sunday labour. At Nash Mills, the mills were to shut down at 9 p.m. or 10 p.m. on Saturday night and preparations made for Monday morning, thus allowing the men to go home at midnight.

The mills were not free from labour problems and unrest in the pre-war years. In 1911, a year of general unrest, there was trouble in the Envelope and Book Printing Department at Apsley. In 1913 factory hours were changed and rates adjusted so that no-one lost wages. It was during the war years that union activity increased. In April 1915 the National Union of Paper Workers sent their organising secretary down. Many meetings were held and employees signed as members, especially at Nash Mills and Home Park. In 1917 a new system of war bonuses was started and in November two unions in the industry demanded that war bonuses should become part of the standard wage. Union demands did much to even out wages among various types of workers in the industry.

At the outbreak of war, Lewis Evans, then Chairman of the firm, was High Sheriff and had to spend much time on official duties. Men in the mills were encouraged to enlist after consulting their foreman. They were promised that places would be kept open for them and half wages paid to those who were married or had dependants, and quarter wages to unmarried men. On return they were to have a bonus of one month's wages. By 1917, 1,500 men had joined up and 130 had been killed.

Meanwhile the mills had to make greatly increased use of women, even as sales ladies. Especially in the later years of the war there was a great shortage of raw materials. In 1916 wood pulp and paper were severely rationed and in September local trees were used on a large scale. Mobile lumber camps were set up, trees felled and barked by women.

Parts of the mills were used for war work. Trench bombs and small shells were made at Apsley.

At the beginning of the century another industry was moved to Apsley. William Kent had founded a brush making firm in London 1777. The original business was moved from Westminster to Great Marlborough Street by William junior and then in 1901 the factory at Apsley was built by G. B. Kent, with two houses in the grounds and five cottages for employees in Kents Avenue.

Around these two main industries Apsley continued to develop. Several shops were built, as well as the new houses and cottages. There was a strong sense of community which found jubilant expression when Apsley Football Club won the County Cup in 1906.

There was no marked increase in wages generally up to 1914. Most of the advertisements in the local papers were for domestic servants. Cook-generals in a small family were offered about £20 a year, a nursemaid with some experience of children got about £14 and a good general servant about £24. These salaries include free board and lodging. In 1910 an uncertified teacher at George Street School was paid £65 a year and the salaries of supplement tary teachers varied from £25 to £30 a year.

Agricultural wages changed little from those of the previous century, but the decline in the demand for straw plait meant that women no longer contributed as much as previously to the family income.

Rents too remained fairly steady until there was a demand for houses out of London after war broke out. In 1910 a semi-detached villa with seven rooms in Durrants Hill could be rented for 6s. 6d. a week and cottages were available at 2s. 9d. Lodgings with board, could be had for 14s. a week.

Prices of ordinary goods varied little in the early part of the century. The following were obtainable in The Clothing Store in 1912:-

Women's, Girls', Boys' Black Stockings at 1¾d; 2¾d; 3¾d; 6¾d;
Men's Wool and Merino pants and vests: 6¾d; 7¾d; 8¾d; 10¾d;
Boys' Shirts from: 4¾d;
Men's light and dark cord trousers from: 2s. 11¾d;
Boy's suits from: 1s. 3¾d;
Men's tweed suits from: 7s. 11¼d;
Men's and Boys' silk lined caps from: 1¾d;

At Bagnall and Oakley's Winter Sale in 1909 dress lengths, with about 6 yards in each, were reduced from 7s. 10½d. to 4s. 11½d. Frister and Rossman's sewing machines cost £3. 7s. 6d. and could be obtained from H. & A. Flint the Ironmongers. Housewives too must have been tempted to try the 'Daisy' vacuum cleaner, model 2 at 3 guineas, or model 'A' for 6 guineas.

Food prices showed no appreciable rise until the war years. At the beginning of the war maximum retail prices were fixed for three days and these give a fair idea of current prices, such as:-

Granulated sugar	4d. per lb.
Lump sugar	5d. per lb.
Butter	1s. 6d. per lb.
Cheese (colonial)	9d. per lb.
Margarine	10d. per lb.
Lard (American)	8d. per lb.

Howe's special blended Scotch Whiskey was obtainable from The Swan Hotel at 20s. per gallon, or 3s. 6d. per bottle. From Balderson's at Boxmoor Wharf Gin was obtainable at 2s. to 3s. 6d. per bottle.

Hiscock's Gramophones cost 29s. or 5s. deposit and 1s. per week, records were 1s. and 1s. 6d.

For the motoring enthusiast in 1912, an 8 horse power Rover two seater in perfect condition with hood, screen, 4 lamps and tools, cost £120. A 9 h.p. Darracq in good running order with hood was £30, and a 4½ h.p. De-Dion two seater with good tyres was going for £15.

At Joseph Kinnick's shop in the Broadway a single diamond 18 ct. gold ring could be got from 21s. upwards, one with five diamonds (special value) cost 4 guineas. With every ring there was a handsome gift.

During the war years prices rose rapidly and there were serious shortages of food and fuel. Meat was only obtainable at high prices and poorer families had to rely on the soup kitchens; peanut butter had to be used instead of butter and supplemented with dripping from the butchers. Readers of the local paper were given useful hints and recipes. They were told to save coal and burn wood and peat, to keep pigs, poultry and rabbits. Recipes for bread making use of boiled potatoes, barley meal and fine oatmeal appeared regularly.

Amusements and leisure activities of all kinds flourished in the town. The Fire Brigade Fancy Dress Ball was one of the important events and early in the century the Annual Horse Show and Fete in Gadebridge Park drew large crowds. School children looked forward to the 'Statty Fair' especially if going to it included a trip on the Midland line from the Heath Park Station.

For special events such as coronations and Empire Day, celebrations took on a traditional form. For Empire Day 1910, school children marched to the market square, or the Moor, where they saluted the flag and sang the Empire song; refreshments were then given to them at the Corn Exchange or Boxmoor Hall and then they all joined forces on the Moor to receive enamel Empire flags and brooches and compete in sports.

Coronation Day in 1911 started with a peal of bells at 6 a.m. and ended with a torchlight procession and flight of rockets from Roughdown. In between there were a civic service, a dinner for 500 old people in the Drill Hall, a procession tea for schoolchildren, sports, baby shows and games.

Concerts and amateur performances of every kind are reported in the local paper with full details of the artists and programmes. At these Dickinson's Silver band and the Salvation Army Band were frequent performers. One such event was held in the Drill Hall in March 1909 in aid of the genuine unemployed and necessitous poor of the Borough and District. Band of Hope groups and Church Lad Brigades all held their own events at which there seemed no dearth of local amateur talent for solos or monologues, with such intriguing titles as "The Electric Light Scheme", "The Groom's Story", or "Nobody Knows, Nobody Cares".

The programme of local events for 1909 is typical. The Church Missionary Society Meeting was held at Westbrook Hay, the Rose and Sweet Pea Show at the Marlowes, the London City Mission Meeting at Boxmoor House, while in Leverstock Green there was a Garden Fete in aid of the Parish Room Fund. The Hemel Hempstead District National Association Fete was held in Gadebridge Park and Apsley had an Athletic Festival. This was the time of year too for parish picnics and outings and firm outings. Dickinsons excursions were a very popular event. In June 1908 they went to Weston-Super-Mare and several hundreds went on the Boxmoor Excursion to Yarmouth.

The inmates of the Workhouse were not forgotten either and had their

Annual Treat and entertainment. Surplus food from Annual Parish Teas and such events were always carried to the Workhouse.

Randall Park provided extra space for sport and relaxation. Alderman Randall purchased 6½ acres on Beehive Hill in 1909 and he presented this to the town for a public park with a sum of money to lay it out. In 1913 the park was said to be in a deplorable condition and it was a constant problem to keep it tidy in the war years. A Bowling Club formed in May 1913 played there. Local children could use it in place of the streets where already the motor car was becoming a menace. There were cases of speeding, especially in the High Street, and children had been killed on the roads.

The Broadway hall in the Parade, Two Waters, owned by Mr. Weston, with its "halls, pleasure gardens and skating rink" was a popular centre in the 1910's. Skates could be hired for 3d. except on exclusive evenings when they cost 6d.

A great event was the opening of the Princess Theatre in Marlowes in 1913. In 1914 you could see such films as "The Fall of Troy", "In the Coils of the Python", "Victory and Death", "The House of Temperley", "Amid Raging Beasts", or Charlie Chaplin for 3d., 6d. and 1/-, or have one of the boxes for 5/-.

In 1914 the Hemel Hempstead and District Swimming and Life Saving Society held its first of many successful galas and raised over £10 for the Prince of Wales' Relief Fund.

Events such as a flying visit of General Booth in July 1908 when he gave an address to the inmates of the workhouse, or a series of speeches by the Berkhamsted Suffragettes in December 1912, when they spoke from a conveyance in the Market Square under police escort, always brought out the crowds, and gave scope to the local wits. The Gazette reported fully, including comments from the audiences. On the latter occasion one young man walked around the audience ringing a hand-bell all through the speeches.

For those interested in intellectual activities there was the active and popular debating society and the lively meetings of the Oxford Brotherhood The following is a list of societies which were all well supported and flourished over a number of years:-

Plate Glass Society
Tradesmen Protection Society
Building Society
Town Cricket Club
Town Football Club
Hemel Hempstead Institute
Harriers and Athletic Club
Bible Society
Floral and Horticultural Society

Liberal and Radical Society
Womens Liberal Association
Hemel Hempstead Conservative and Unionist Association
Property Protection Association
Debating Society

One gets the impression that for a section of the community these were highlights in a life which was a hard struggle. For working-class mothers with large families living in poor cottages, keeping their children fed and clothed and free from disease was a constant worry.

Advertisements for patent medicines proliferate in the local paper, as in the national press of the time. Often they take the form of personal local stories of cures and appear in the ordinary news columns. In a time of poverty and consequent low health especially among women, Dr. Cassell's tablets, which it was claimed, were good for everything from nervous breakdown to spinal and nerve paralysis, Zam-Buk, for any and every skin complaint, especially ring-worm, very prevalent among children, Eade's Anti-bilious Pills, Eade's Gout and Rheumatism Pill or Harriette Metas Hair Tonic ('grows new hair in 30 days') were held out as panaceas.

People here were more fortunate than many in that treatment was available at the hospital, but even so, hard-earned money must have been spent on useless self-doctoring.

In September 1913 the town was in state of great excitement because of army manoeuvres taking place in the area. There were camps near Randall Park on Mr. Grover's land at Highfield, Gaddesden Place, Boxmoor and Shendish and big siege guns arrived at Midland Station.

The outbreak of war brought the immediate fixing of retail prices for three days, the billeting of soldiers in empty houses, the Town Hall, Boxmoor Hall, the Brotherhood Hall and Corn Exchange. By September over 100 men had been recruited. The Herts territorials were in action in November and lists of casualties lengthened in the local papers.

Early in the war refugees from Belgium appeared and in August 1915 the Relief Committee was formed. Energetic efforts were made to help all relief funds and firms contributed generously to such causes as The Prince of Wales' Relief Fund, and Lord Roberts' Indian Fund.

There was general excitement and often entertainment at recruiting rallies. A party of the Herts Regiment accompanied by its band came to Boxmoor in June 1915, but met with little success as many men had joined the regular recruiters earlier in the year. There was another rally in October, a month before Lord Derby's scheme came into operation.

As the war dragged on, problems at home became more acute. Food was very scarce and there was a problem in distributing what was available in a fair way. Butter cheese, margarine, lard, bacon and especially meat, were in short supply. On January 12th 1918, the local paper reported that the

HARVESTING AT BOXMOOR

PEACE DAY AT HEMEL HEMPSTEAD, 1919

market "gave a better appearance than the previous week, as cattle numbered 5 as against 2 poor specimens and there were 70 to 80 sheep, compared with 40 to 50." All of these were handed over to the local Butchers' Association for distribution, but even so there was not always enough to go round. Communal kitchens were opened. The one in the Corn Exchange set off in February with soup, fish pie and ginger pudding for 6d. The Apsley kitchen never got going successfully and was constantly up for discussion at Council meetings. When rationing was enforced, shortage of supplies still made it difficult to meet needs.

Increasing taxation, higher rail fares, cuts in trains, and the increase in postage rates to 1½d. for a letter, all added to the difficulties of ordinary people who were very war-weary and tired of economy and salvage campaigns and the constant need to 'make-do'; but even so support for the hospital, the Institution and local charities continued in a generous way.

As it became clear that the war was nearing an end, there were signs that the town was looking to the future. Housing and education schemes were discussed. The November meeting of the Guardians considered alternative schemes being discussed nationally, for the care of the poor. In March there was a meeting at Broadway Hall to form The Hemel Hempstead and District Trades and Labour Council and Labour Party which aimed 'to better the conditions of labour educationally, politically and municipally and last but not least the working conditions and wages.' In September the Labour Party decided to fight the forthcoming election locally and adopted Mr. Jesse Hawkes as their candidate. There was considerable union activity at this time among the paper and agriculture workers. The organiser of the National Union of Printing and Paper Workers was active at the mills and wage increases were negotiated.

The Armistice was greeted with spontaneous enthusiasm. At Apsley Mills, and Kents there was no more work that day and people streamed out into the streets while the church bells rang. Dickinson's band marched through Apsley playing patriotic songs and everything, cars, prams, dogs, horses, was decorated with flags and emblems. The paper reported that 'there was no horse play or disgraceful scenes, but a feeling of restrained joy and thankfulness as though the populace had awakened from some dreadful dream.' There was a service of thanksgiving in St. Mary's Church and the Mayor addressed the crowd in the Market Square from the "motor belonging to the fire brigade" and later a huge bonfire was lit.

This restraint carried over to the election. During the campaign, attendance at meetings was not so great as before the war. Although there was some vituperative correspondence in the local paper and strong views expressed in letters from men still at the front, there was not much apparent interest, even from the newly-enfranchised women. The local paper put this down to 'gratitude to Lloyd George' and the conclusion was foregone, victory for the Coalition candidate, Mr. Talbot.

Much more interest and feeling was aroused when Two Waters Mill was destroyed in an explosion. The mill was used at that time for the extraction of fats from wood and in the process carbon bisulphide was used. The mill was destroyed, leaving only the great chimney, 130 feet high. There was no loss of life, but the cottages opposite were wrecked and the road and bridge in a bad state for weeks.

At the end of this eventful year some men were already returning to their homes and plans were afoot for suitable memorials to those who would not return. There were great problems to be faced as the town returned to peacetime conditions, above all much-needed improvements in the living conditions of its working inhabitants and adequate provision for the education of its children.

The Twentieth Century

Part II - The Inter-War Years

As we have seen, the first major political event after the war was the General Election held in November 1918, often called the Khaki Election. In 1912 the County had been divided into four constituencies with Hemel Hempstead in the Watford Division. Now there were five divisions, the fifth being Hemel Hempstead comprising Hemel Hempstead Borough and Rural District, Berkhamsted Urban and Rural Districts, and Harpenden and Tring Urban Districts. The successful candidate, Gustavus A. Talbot of Piccotts End, was a Conservative and Mayor and Bailiff of Hemel Hempstead. He held the seat until he died in 1920, when he was succeeded by John J. C. C. Davidson, who was returned unopposed. Later Mr. Davidson was elevated to the House of Lords, and his wife was elected the member. Except for a short break in 1923 the Davidsons held the seat in the Conservative interest until after the 1939-45 War.

The occasion of the break was the election of 1923 when Mr. Baldwin, the Prime Minister, decided to go to the country to seek support for a system of tariff reform as a remedy for the growing unemployment. Free trade versus tariff reform had raised great political passions before the war and some of these feelings remained. Also there were some signs of a Liberal revival, and the Liberals were staunch free-traders. When the Prime Minister made his decision, the local Liberals, who had no candidate and practically no organisation, decided to contest the local constituency. They produced as a candidate J. Freeman Dunn, a city banker. He brought with him a team of young Liberals, including University undergraduates, and with their help and that of local Liberals built up an organisation, with headquarters in the High Street, he ultimately won the contest, but by a very narrow majority. After recounts the figures were announced as follows:-

J. F. Dunn	8,892
J. C. C. Davidson	8,875
Liberal Majority	17

Mr. Dunn's victory was short-lived, for in less than twelve months another General Election was held and Mr. Davidson was returned in a three-cornered fight with a majority of 4,991.

During this period of election activity, and in the years that followed, the constituency was visited by a number of eminent politicians, including Lloyd-George in the Liberal interest, Stanley Baldwin for the Conservatives and his son Oliver on behalf of the Labour Party. In 1922 Bernard Shaw was a notable visitor, addressing a meeting for the Labour Party.

Like all towns and villages the borough wished to raise a memorial in honour of those who had fallen in the War. There was some argument as to the form this should take and several proposals were made. Eventually it was decided to erect a simple stone cross near the centre of the Borough on part of Boxmoor where the roundabout at the end of Marlowes is at present. But it was not until June 1921 that the memorial was publicly unveiled by Lt. Col. Lovel F. Smeathman, D.S.O., M.C. It bore the names of 420 men and women who had paid the supreme sacrifice. In the meantime Apsley, with its independent spirit, had provided its own memorial in the shape of a memorial hall, a wooden building intended to serve the locality as a place of meeting and a centre of social activities.

An observant visitor to the Borough in 1919 would have noted a number of features. First, that the community consisted of several distinct parts each with its own characteristics and in some ways antagonistic to each other. This no doubt arose out of the manner in which the various districts had developed in the past; Hemel Hempstead, the old town, was dominated by the shop-keeping element, Boxmoor was mainly residential and Apsley industrial. Outlying hamlets like Bourne End and Leverstock Green were again small separate communities extending beyong the Borough Boundaries. Secondly, he would have observed the way in which the borough was almost cut in two by the canal, which left the main railway station, the main London Road and the principal industrial area to the south, approachable only by quite inadequate bridges over the canal. Thirdly, the lack of adequate transport arrangements would be evident, a somewhat unusual road pattern having evolved, with badly-paved and poorly-lit streets; fourthly a lack of amenities and social services Finally he could not fail to observe that the boundaries of the Borough were so drawn as to exclude the main place of employment.

The different divisions of the town had created a demand for a redivision of the wards for municipal election purposes, on the ground that the representation on the Borough Council was disproportionate. This agitation had begun before the War and was renewed when peace returned. The town was divided into two Wards, North and South; the former being the old Hemel Hempstead and the latter Boxmoor and Apsley. Even at the time the Borough was incorporated in 1898 the figures were

North Ward	931
South Ward	1306

and with later development the difference became more marked. Any attempt at revision was stoutly resisted by the North Ward councillors anxious to preserve their vested interests. Eventually however with the defection of one North Ward councillor a redivision scheme was made the subject of an Order in Council in 1924. This act, together with the influence of an increasing population, did much to remove the antagonism between the different parts and the needs of the area were dealt with from a general standpoint.

The Town Council, moving with the spirit of the age and conscious of the needs of the district, undertook a forward programme and carried out many improvements. Early consideration was given to the problem of the bridges over the canal and in due course the three principal ones, Durrants Hill, Two Waters and Fishery Bridges, were all reconstructed and widened to take the increasing volume of traffic. The old bridges had been sufficient to carry the traffic at the time the canal was constructed, but were totally inadequate for twentieth century conditions. Other improvements were made in several roads and defective paths improved and street lighting extended.

One service which attracted much public attention was Education. The Borough was the only area within the County where the district council was responsible for elementary education. The County Council was in charge of what was then called "secondary education", but its efforts were mainly confined to providing some scholarships to Berkhamsted School and Watford Grammar School and a few evening classes. The facilities offered by the Borough Council were far from adequate; they were mainly in old school buildings, with no facilities for teaching domestic science and handicrafts, poor playing accommodation and overcrowded. At an inquiry in 1921 the Headmaster of St. John's School, Boxmoor, gave evidence to the effect that he had not sufficient room in which to seat all the boys in his school, but there were spare places in other schools. Various proposals were made especially in connection with the provision of higher education. Strong representations were made to the County Council but it was not until 1927 that a site was acquired on which to build what is now the Hemel Hempstead Grammar School in 1929-30. In the meantime the Borough Council established a selective Central School of 100 places in Two Waters School.

As to elementary education the major need was a general re-organisation with a break from junior to senior schools at the age of eleven. No existing building was suitable for use as a senior school, but the church authorities which had several church schools in the Borough insisted that one of their buildings should be used as one of the two senior schools. This view was advanced very strongly and delayed the introduction of any scheme of re-organisation. Eventually this objection was overcome and a new school was built at Corner Hall, with separate departments for boys and girls, and opened some time before the war broke out in 1939. Some of the old schools were closed and others were improved.

Housing was another urgent problem. The town had many houses that had outlived their usefulness. Some were very old; others of poor quality built in the early 19th century; some were conversions of old stabling or similar buildings especially those in the yards behind the buildings in the High Street and elsewhere. These were cleared away either by major Clearance Orders dealing with groups of houses, and others by appropriate notice relating to individual houses or small groups of premises. The occupants were rehoused mostly in Council houses.

The bringing of a supply of electricity from Watford to the Borough and part of the surrounding rural area was proceeded with. Originally the district was included in the area of supply of the Chesham Company, but it took no action in the matter. In 1921 the Borough Council started discussions with the Watford authority and eventually the Chesham Order was revoked and the area brought within that of the Watford Undertaking which took immediate steps to bring a supply to the town.

The gas undertaking, owned by the Hemel Hempstead Gas Co. also saw changes. The industry generally was being rationalised and in 1931 the Hemel Hempstead Co. was amalgamated with the Watford and St. Albans Gas Co. It is interesting to recall that the Hemel Hempstead Company was itself an amalgamation of the Hemel Hempstead Gas Light and Coke Company, founded in 1835 and of the Boxmoor, Two Waters and Crouchfield Gas Light and Coke Company, formed in 1868; the marriage took place in 1878. In 1904 the Hunton Bridge and Abbots Langley Gas Co. had also joined the family.

In 1929 Parliament passed the Local Government Act which brought about many changes here as elsewhere. One was the reform of the Poor Law as recommended in the Minority Report of the Royal Commission made in 1909. The local Board of Guardians was abolished and its powers transferred to the County Council. There were Boards of Guardians involved locally, those of Hemel Hempstead and Berkhamsted. In their stead the County

Council appointed one local committee to serve the whole area. It also decided, after detailed study, to close the workhouse at Berkhamsted and concentrate the care and treatment of the inmates at Hemel Hempstead. This caused great concern to the people of Berkhamsted who made vigorous protest to the County Council and elsewhere. But the County Council adhered to its decision and the change was made. The merging of the areas had a certain historical interest; in earlier times the whole area formed the Dacorum Hundred, but in the 17th century it was divided into two - Berkhamsted and Hemel Hempstead - and separate Chief Constables were appointed for each division. When the Guardians were established under the Poor Law Act of 1834 for their respective Unions the two divisions of the Dacorum area were adopted. Now by its action the County Council reversed in some respect those decisions of the past.

The Act also resulted in alterations to the boundaries of many local authorities. The County Council was required to examine the circumstances of the different district councils in the county, and to make proposals for alteration of boundaries and otherwise. These proposals were to the Minister of Health, who ordered a local inquiry and in due course in 1935 made an Order bringing the County Council's proposals, so far as he approved them, into force. Much controversy was caused and strong local feelings were roused. The outcome locally was that the mills at Apsley were brought within the Borough, the different parts of the hamlets of Leverstock Green and Bourne End were united and included in the Borough as was an area of fringe development in the Box Lane area. A large area of purely agricultural land to the north of the Borough was transferred to the Rural District. The Act also made various changes in the financial work of local authorities; these came into force soon after the passing of the Act and were of decided benefit to the inhabitants of Hemel Hempstead.

During this period the health of the population was on the whole good, although from time to time there were outbreaks of infectious diseases such as diphtheria and scarlet fever and the sufferers had to be nursed in the Isolation Hospital at Bennetts End. On odd occasions there were suspected cases of smallpox. But in 1927 a more serious epidemic of para-typhoid struck the district - both Borough and Rural areas - and a large number of cases were diagnosed, eventually totalling between 150 and 200. These were nursed in a number of hospitals here and elsewhere. Fortunately the disease was a mild one and no fatal cases occurred. Various suggestions as to its cause were made, one alleging an infection of some of the milk supply to the area.

Throughout our period the work of the Borough Council continued to grow in volume and importance, and schemes of improvement and development were undertaken. In 1929 it broke fresh ground when it decided to confer the freedom of the Borough on Lovel Smeathman, its first Town Clerk. Mr. Smeathman was greatly admired in the borough and had been a great public servant having filled a number of public offices during his professional career. He had taken an active part in the negotiations with the Government which led to the incorporation of Hemel Hempstead as a borough in 1898. At the ceremony when the freedom was officially conferred the Mayor and Bailiff, Councillor Maurice Alston, spoke feelingly and truthfully of Mr. Smeathman when he quoted some lines from Shakespeare:-

> "Exceeding wise, fair spoken and persuading,
> To those men that sought him sweet as summer"

Later that year Mr. Smeathman presented to the Council the silver mace which now precedes the Mayor on all civic occasions.

Besides the official bodies the town was well served by a number of semi-official organisations. First and foremost, especially in the public's imagination, was the West Herts Hospital, whose origin and development have already been described. A voluntary hospital, it depended on public support and subscriptions, and it needed ever-increasing funds if it was to meet the needs of a growing population and keep pace with the developments in medical science. From a variety of organisations and in different ways the money came, although at times economic difficulties had their deterrent effect. From time to time major schemes with special appeals were launched, e.g. in 1921 a new Nurses Home was opened by Lady Halsey. In 1926 a more ambitious scheme was prepared to mark the centenary of the opening of the hospital in 1827. A sum of £15,000 was sought to construct and equip a new maternity ward, provide proper heating and lighting of the hospital and to carry out a number of urgently needed improvements. Public support was forthcoming and in July H.R.H. Prince Edward, Prince of Wales laid the foundation stone of the new ward. On that occasion the town was in festive mood and the Mayor supported by the members of the Council and other dignitaries and by a large crowd received the Prince on the old Market Square in the High Street and presented an official address of welcome to which the Prince suitably replied. The new maternity ward was named after Miss Markham, a late member of the Committee and a lady who had been a great supporter of the hospital. The ward was formally opened in July 1927 by the Marchioness of Salisbury.

By 1932, the sources of income on which the hospital depended proving insufficient to meet the increasing needs, a contributory scheme was introduced under which by a weekly contribution a subscriber was entitled to treatment in the hospital when it was needed. This produced an increased income and enabled the hospital to carry on until the war and then post-war legislation brought the changes which established the National Health Service.

One other major scheme should be mentioned - the erection of the block which includes the X-ray department and the private wards, an extension of the nurses home to accommodate 36 nurses and the erection of a new children's ward. Originally H.M. Queen Mary had agreed to open these premises but unfortunately was prevented by illness. In her stead she asked H.R.H. Princess Marina, Duchess of Kent to act for her; this she did on 1st October 1938 when she opened the new block, laid the foundation stone for the new children's ward and received purses and other tokens from representatives of the various districts.

Another semi-official organisation of long-standing was the volunteer Fire Brigade, This continued to serve the district with the enthusiasm and spirit which had become its tradition. There was never any lack of volunteers for the Brigade. Earlier in the period the apparatus was housed in the premises adjoining the entrance to Gadebridge Park, but these were so inadequate that the Council acquired a building in Alexandra Road and adapted it to provide a modern station, providing much better accommodation for the equipment together with proper facilities for training and practice.

There were many other organisations seeking to meet the needs of the townspeople. Music always found supporters. In December 1919 the Hemel Hempstead Music Society gave a rendering of Edward German's "Merry England" in the Drill Hall, Bury Road; there were four vocalists from Queen's Hall, London, a chorus of 85 voices and an orchestra with 30 performers. The prices were 3s. 6d., 2s. 4d., and 1s. 3d. respectively and special arrangements were made for heating and lighting the hall. The review in the following week's Gazette was very complimentary. Again, in 1922, the Society rendered Sterndale Bennett's "May Queen" in St. Mary's Hall.

In 1925 the Hemel Hempstead Operatic and Dramatic Society was formed and this developed into the flourishing concern which exists today. Its first major work was "The Pirates of Penzance" which it was originally proposed should be publicly performed in 1926 in the new cinema then in course of erection in Marlowes. However, the building was not completed in time and so use was made of the Guild House at Apsley Mills: this was in May 1926 and the profits went to the West Herts Hospital. In the following January the Society rendered "The Yeomen of the Guard" this time in the new cinema then known as the "Aero". Then followed a regular annual series, including "The Gondoliers", "The Geisha" and other well-known musical plays. Usually three performances were given which were well supported and universally popular. In 1930 a more ambitious programme was adopted when the cinema was engaged for the whole week for performances of "Floradora". From time to time the Society put on dramatic plays such as the three short plays by W. W. Jacobs performed in 1929 at the "Aero" for one night only.

There were other musical societies and groups rendering all sorts of music. In the 1920's there was a Literary Society which met fortnightly in the Town Hall and discussed various topics. From time to time it was addressed by prominent people in the literary world, such as L. J. Hammond and C. H. B. Quennell. The Society lasted for a few years and in 1931 a new one was formed called the Hemel Hempstead Debating and Literary Society. This was well supported for several years, but eventually this too ceased to function.

Entertainment was also afforded by the local cinemas. This was the period in which the silent film was eclipsed by the talkie. There were two cinemas, the Princess Theatre in Marlowes and the Aero Cinema originally in Albion Hill and later in a new building in Marlowes.

The Aero was the more go-ahead of the two. The premises in Albion Hill were small and had previously been used by the local Salvation Army as its headquarters. In 1925 the proprietors of the cinema decided to build a more palatial building in Marlowes in which to provide a variety of entertainment including films and variety turns. It was opened in 1926 and the well-known soprano, Carrie Tubbs, gave a performance at the opening. In 1930 it was renamed the Luxor Theatre, and retained this name until it was demolished when the Development Corporation developed Marlowes as a shopping centre. For a time the proprietors of the Aero used the Apsley Memorial Hall as a cinema.

A society which claimed to be the oldest Association in Hemel Hempstead was the Hemel Hempstead Association for the Protection of Property which was formed in the 1850's for the good old Victorian principle reflected in its name. For its annual subscription the members were supplied with posters offering rewards for information about persons damaging property of members, and the right to attend the annual dinner, usually a very convivial event.

An Arts and Crafts Committee organised exhibitions of local work. These were well supported and helped to foster interest in the arts and crafts. Evidence of considerable local skill and craft was forthcoming on each occasion.

Sport was catered for in a number of ways. Little accommodation was provided by the local authority. In 1919 it had but one small recreation ground, Randall Park, poorly maintained and often misused; the goal posts provided were frequently damaged and had to be replaced and in the end they were removed.

A somewhat more ambitious proposal was adopted soon after the war to provide recreational facilities on part of Boxmoor at Moor End, and a local committee was formed to raise funds and carry out the necessary works. Some levelling was done and a concrete base for a bandstand was laid, but the tennis courts and bowling greens that had been projected were never realised because of lack of funds. Later the land was transferred to the Borough Council which converted it to a garden and pleasure ground.

Boxmoor was the principal playing field for the town. At Heath Park the Hemel Hempstead Cricket Club had its grounds and there, season after season, played that village-green type of cricket which is still so attractive. Many well-known figures in the cricket world have been pleased to show their skill on this pleasant corner of the Moor. Elsewhere were other cricket pitches used by different clubs.

Football too was played on the Moor, but the major club had its site on the Salmon Meadow near Apsley Mills. The Apsley Football Club were members of the Spartan League and in 1932 were promoted to the Premier Division and about this time moved from the Salmon Meadow to its present ground off Crabtree Land.

Other sports were played but mostly in private clubs on private grounds. One such club was the Old House Club which was established in Marlowes as a social and recreational Club. It had previously been an Institute in premises in the High Street and when it moved to its new home its activities were extended to include bowls and tennis in the extensive grounds belonging to the Old House. Later when it sold the frontage land for buildings the tennis courts were lost, but the bowling green was left and still remains.

In the 1930's the Borough Council gave increasing attention to the need for more adequate and properly equipped playing fields and but for the outbreak of war in 1939 would have undertaken a considerable programme. A start was made with an open-air swimming pool. Previously the only facility was a cutting from the canal on Boxmoor. In 1934 the house and grounds of Churchill were purchased for £3,500 and on part was erected a first-class pool. Included in the purchase was a hard tennis court which was made available to the public.

The Council also established a children's playing field on part of Boxmoor at Moor End as a George V Memorial Field.

The people of Hemel Hempstead continued to take an interest in politics apart from the recurrent excitement at election times and were favoured from time to time with visits from political celebrities. In May 1926 Ramsay MacDonald, Leader of the Labour Party cut the first sod on the site in Wood Lane on which the Labour Hall was built, followed in July by Lord Hailsham, Lord Chancellor in the then Conservative Government. In November 1929, A. J. Cook the fiery secretary of the Miners' Union was another visitor.

In 1934 a local branch of the British Union of Fascists was formed and blackshirted members were to be seen in the streets selling their newspapers. They held their first public meeting in the Town Hall, when William Joyce, described as the Director of Propaganda, National Headquarters, London addressed a full house. They continued to be active in the town for some time thereafter, but found little support.

Much earlier, in 1921, there was much support for a local branch of the League of Nations Union and considerable propaganda was carried on the pacific work of that organisation. Here again the town was favoured with visits from persons taking a prominent part in the national work of that Union.

During the whole of this period, but especially in the 1920's, the town continued to expand. Fresh areas of development were opened up and more houses were erected, mostly by private enterprise. The various improvements in the social services helped to make the district attractive. The great dependence of the area on the paper mills was generally recognised and efforts were made to attract other industries, and the first major success was the advent of Messrs. Brocks, firework manufacturers. Other smaller concerns also came. Industrially Hemel Hempstead formed part of a much larger area which extended down the Gade Valley to Watford. In this larger area were developments which afforded employment for some of Hemel Hempstead's population. Others made the daily journey to work in London. One difficulty was transport, especially the location of Boxmoor Station. The opening of a new station at Apsley and the coming of long distance buses to and from London were useful improvements.

But like the rest of the country the district suffered from unemployment, although the volume was much less than in many other parts of the country. In fact, from data supplied by the Ministry of Labour, Hemel Hempstead was at times one of the more fortunate areas in the country. The position fluctuated from time to time and the queues outside the Labour Exchange seemed endless; 1921 was a particularly bad year. The Council did what it could to relieve the situation and the many relief schemes provided work and at the same time brought some permanent improvements. The local poor rate as administered by the Board of Guardians until they were abolished, and then by the County Council, also felt the impact of this lack of employment.

During Christmas 1927 the district experienced one of the worst snowstorms in living memory. All road transport was suspended and the two slow lines on the railway between Bourne End and Northchurch were blocked. One of the biggest drifts was at the lower end of Adeyfield Road - then but a narrow country lane; the drift was about 12 feet high completely blocking the road for 100 yards. Council workmen cut a narrow pathway through this length to enable pedestrians to pass. Attendance at the Magistrates' Court was affected; no one from the rural areas could attend and only two Magistrates could be present, Mr. and Mrs. Mitchell-Innes who lived at Churchill. Later further snow fell, which ultimately turned to rain, bringing serious floods in many parts.

One casualty was the weather vane on St. Mary's Church, and steeplejacks had to be called in to carry out the necessary repairs. The bird on the vane measured 2 feet 1 inch from the top of the beak to its tail and weighed 6¾ lbs. and on it were certain inscriptions:

> One side — 'Thomas Kellam and Thomas Carter Churchwardens repaired in the year of our Lord 1778'
>
> and under this
>
> Robert Gregory and Nicholas Sage Churchwardens ANO DOM 1689 - Daniel Feild facet

On the other side:

In the first year of the reign of King William and Queen Mary

Gregory	Bailiff	1690[a]
Kellam		1776
Carter		1770

The bird was regilded and inscribed:

A. F. Robson Vicar
Lovel Smeathman and James
Steptoe Wardens 1928

Mr. Steptoe cut out his own name himself. Whilst the steeplejacks' ladders were on the spire several brave if somewhat foolhardy young men were tempted to climb to the top of the spire, to the apprehension of many people who watched their escapade.

In January 1930 the area was visited by a great gale, during which widespread damage was done. Between the High Street and Water End 15 trees were blown down and the hospital ambulance was hit and one person killed.

This narrative takes us up to a year or two before the war began in 1939. It is of necessity somewhat sketchy and does not purport to be a full description of all that happened during those twenty years between the wars. In the main it ends about 1935, and while the town continued to develop and expand events were increasingly overshadowed by the threat of war. It was in 1935 that the Government asked local authorities to look into the question of air raid precautions and the County Council decided to appoint a County Air Raid Precautions Officer. At first the threat of another World War was regarded with scepticism as in the early stages the emphasis by the Government was on anti-gas measures. But the reality of the situation gradually became apparent and the experience of Spain during its Civil War diverted attention from gas to the effects of bombs. The planning and the preparation became more urgent and proceeded apace. The Munich crisis in 1938 led to the issue of gas-masks to the public and in the following year came the final calamity. The Borough was ready and on Saturday, 2nd September 1939 received its first contingent of official evacuees from London, followed by its first air raid warning the next day. The story of the town during those war years and its subsequent development as a New Town may well be a task which another may wish to undertake.

(a) Robert Gregory was Bailiff of Hemel Hempstead in 1690/91 and died in 1712. He was described as a yeoman and a draper and carried on business as such. He was a man of substance owning property in Hemel Hempstead and elsewhere and was a supporter of William and Mary. There is evidence of strong local support of those joint sovereigns and the bird on the weather vane may have been erected by public subscription as a mark of protestant feeling. Dutch soldiers were entertained in the town in 1689.

PART 2

CHAPTER 8

The Bailiwick and the Market

Henry VIII by his charter of 29th December 1539 made his vill of Hemelhampsted "a vill incorporate of a bailiff and inhabitants within the vill aforesaid for ever and that the Bailiff and Inhabitants within the same vill shall be and ought to be one body incorporate and one perpetual commonalty in thing and in name and fit and capable in law and shall have perpetual succession and that one person successively of the inhabitants within the vill aforesaid every year shall be elected by those inhabitants as Bailiff of vill aforesaid for the governing of the same vill for one whole year".

The Charter also gave a weekly market, an annual fair, and a court of pie powder (or dusty feet) in connection with them. The Bailiff presided over this court which consisted of a number of inhabitants called the jury. Their duty was to decide disputes arising at the market or the fair and to settle them there and then whilst the dust was still on the feet of the disputants, and to manage the market and the fair. There were no recorded rules governing the constitution of the jury; the numbers varied from time to time, the members were not elected and seemed to have been chosen by the incoming Bailiff at the time of his election, with the advice of his predecessor and such other persons as he cared to consult. It is interesting to note that this court continued in existence until 1898, although shorn of most of its powers, and was the last of such courts to function in this country.

The Bailiff was elected by the inhabitants at a meeting held in the Court Loft of the Market House every year on the morning of the feast of St. Andrew the Apostle (30th November). The Charter contained no directions as to the manner in which the Bailiff should be chosen or elected, and the procedure followed was one built up by custom. Such directions as existed were recorded in the minute books (which start from 1619) and subsequently incorporated in certain official Rules made in 1656 and referred to later. Generally the Bailiff was chosen successively from each of the areas into which the vill (as distinct from the parish)was divided, i.e. the Towne, High Street side and Boxted side. The custom was for the outgoing Bailiff to nominate three candidates, one from each of the three areas, and for the nominee from the area whose turn it was to be elected. But in the eighteenth century, when the management of the town's affairs fell into the hands of a clique, attempts were made to confine the appointment to residents of the Towne area only. The Bailiff having been previously selected was thus formally elected at the meeting of the inhabitants held in accordance with the Charter of Henry VIII. This may have been the origin of the phrase used in the twentieth century to indicate the meeting of the senior members of the Town Council to decide who should be put forward for Mayor for the ensuing year, and called the "To-be" meeting. In the middle of the seventeenth century an item appears in the Bailiff's accounts for refreshments "when I was chosen as Bailiff". At first it was a small sum of two or three shillings, but by 1669 it had grown to £1.6.6d. for "breade and cakes and cheese, wine and beare", and this may have been the beginning of a custom which lasted until the nineteenth century of dispensing mulled port to celebrate the election. It grew into much larger sums in the eighteenth century, at the end of which it was described as a feast. Who attended is not recorded. In the nineteenth and early twentieth centuries the Bailiff's dinner became a very important annual social function in the life of the town; although by this later period the governing body was a municipal corporation and the Mayor presided, it was still called the "Bailiff's dinner". The last one was held in 1924. The 1656 rules required that "everye Bailiffe hereafter shall keepe his feaste within the Towne and not in the parish upon payne of xxd. to the use of the poore".

The election was duly announced to the general public by the ringing of church bells, for which the newly-elected Bailiff paid 5s. or 10s. He had to conform to the Test Act, 1672, by taking the oaths of Supremacy and Allegiance, after having received communion and declared his disbelief in transubstantiation. Certificates to this effect from the minister, the churchwardens and two witnesses had to be produced when the Bailiff went before the Court to take the oaths. This was done at Hertford until towards the end of the eighteenth century, when the Bailiff went to London, probably because by then it was cheaper and quicker as the journey could be made by stage coach. The first Bailiff to take the oath in 1673 was Isaac Field, who charged in his accounts -

Expended at Hertford when I went to the Sessions to take the oath of Supreamacie	10s. 0d.

By 1705 it had increased to £1.9.0d. as follows:

For my Journey to Hertford	10s. 0d.
" three horse hires thither	7s. 6d.
" our Dinners horse meat and other Expenses there	7s. 0d.
Paid to the Clerke of the Peace	2s. 0d.
" Mr. Crawley for a certificate	2s. 6d.

(Mr. Crawley was an attorney at law, who acted as Clerk to the Bailiwick.)

In 1765 it still cost £1.9.6d. to go to Hertford but in 1772 the amount for a London journey was only £1. From time to time the Bailiff gave small sums to the poor when he received Communion.

One important duty of the Bailiff was to submit his accounts for his year of office to the next jury for approval. He was supposed to do so within twenty days of receiving a notice to that effect from his successor, but this rule was not always kept. Efforts were made from time to time to enforce the rule and to tighten up the procedure, and the Bailiff was required to submit his accounts within one month from the date on which his successor was appointed and to hand over any balance in hand. Sometimes, with the consent of the jury, the retiring Bailiff was allowed to retain any balance until it was actually required; this was done when an unusually large sum was required for some particular project, and as there were then no banks it may have been one way of reducing the risk of loss. There is no evidence that any Bailiff failed to hand over his balance when required to do so, although a few did so by instalments. In the eighteenth century the occasion on which the accounts were submitted was one for celebration. In 1720 this cost £1.10.10d, but by 1771 it had increased considerably:

> dinner and liquor when the late Bailiff
> gave up his accounts £4.13.6d.

The Bailiff had many duties other than those mentioned above. According to the 1656 rules he had to hold a meeting of the court of pie powder within one month of his election. He had to set out the standings in the market house on the fair days and he was to

> punish all regrators and forestallers according to the Course of the Common Law and the said Bayliffe to be assisted by the whole bodye in the execution of this order and all other orders here sette downe.

A minute of 1637 stated that he was to -

> look to the Assize of Bread and Ale accordinge to the price of Corne upon payne of iijs iijd for defalt thereof.

There were other directions dealing with the detailed management of the market, or about specific matters which are dealt with later.

On occasion the appointment involved some financial burden on the holder. From time to time the accounts disclosed an adverse balance; sometimes this was made good by a subsequent bailiff, although some years might elapse before this was done. Sometimes there was no reference to any recoupment. Again certain expenses were incurred, e.g. those connected with taking the oath, but not recorded in the accounts. Perhaps the situation might be summed up in the words written in the minute book by Michael Jeale, Bailiff 1746/7, when his accounts were approved on the 25th November 1749.

Gentlemen,

In the Page before is the State of my Account received and disbursed during the exercise of the office of Bailiff. It appears the Expenses have exceeded my Receipts a few Pounds Too trifling a matter for me to mention altho I assure my Brethren that I esteem the honour they did me in electing me to so weighty and important a trust is a full recompense for the Ballance in my favour and further give Leave to acquant them that I shall ever have the Interest of this Corporation at hart according to my capacity and my inclination shall always bee ready to assist them whom I hope have the same Interest at Hart as

Your Humble Sevt
Mich: Jeale

The receipts were £43.8.11d. and the payments £50.1.0¼d., showing a deficit of £6.12.1¼d. Michael Jeale's name is recorded in the Freeholders (or Jurors) Books for 1743 to 1749 showing that he was in possession of an estate worth at least £10 per annum (freehold or copyhold property) or was a long term leaseholder of property worth more than £20 a year. He is described there as a "Brandy-man" and was churchwarden in 1739.

As to the jury, the Charter of 1539 gave no directions as to who should be members of it. The rules of 1656 stated that the Bailiff

> within One month after he is elected ...shall Keep a Court and call a Jury of the Cheife Inhabitants, and shall then together with the sayd Jury consult what shalbe most convenient to be done for the government of the sayd Burrough and Markett and what shalbe then agreed by the Major parte then present the Bailiffe is to observe and keepe as much as in him lyeth.

In the seventeenth century there was no restriction on who should attend. The numbers present varied; for example in the period from 1620 to 1660 the average attendance was 20, the largest number being 37 in 1620 and 1621, and the smallest 14 in 1632. As might be expected some were regular attenders; in the eight years 1630-1637 (inclusive) there were ten possible attendances recorded - although there must have been many more meetings - and out of 35 names 19 attended only once, and but 5 had six or more attendances.

But in the eighteenth century occurred changes which affected both the office of bailiff and the membership of the jury. During the first half of the century the tendency was to restrict the persons forming the jury to a select group and to choose the Bailiff from that group; the individuals concerned seemed to be mostly shopkeepers and others living in the 'towne'. On 14th November 1746 at a meeting held in the Bell Inn it was agreed that no person should be nominated for the office of Bailiff unless he actually resided in the "Town of Hemelhempsted" at the time of his nomination, and no-one was to be nominated or chosen by the Bailiff to be a member of the Jury unless he similarly resided in the town. On 21st June 1749 it was "unanimously agreed that Ephraim L. Love of the Town of Hemelhempsted

....Victualler do succeed Joseph Riddell late of Hemelhempsted Victualler, deceased as a Juryman".

From this and other evidence it is clear that attempts were made to create a close corporation typical of the eighteenth century. It is notable that with two exceptions all the Bailiffs from 1741 to 1755 inclusive came from "the Town", and that during this period several attempts were made to ascertain the legal position and the powers of the Bailiff, and as these enquiries were made by the group in power they were intended to support their authority. In 1741 and again in 1744 it was decided to seek counsel's opinion. In March 1749 it was stated "as by the Attorney-General's Opinion the Bailiff is to be chosen out of the Jury annually", and in the accounts for 1751/2 the following payment is recorded to one Butterfield, a local attorney-at-law who acted as clerk to the Bailiwick:-

> for writing out the copy of the Charter in
> Latin and English and for copying the case
> relating to the Charter and Sir Dudley
> Ryder's opinion thereon 13s. 4d.

Sir Dudley Ryder was Attorney-General from 1737 to 1754, when he became Chief Justice in the King's Bench, and lived at Westbrook Hay on the outskirts of Hemel Hempstead.

By this time too the conditions as to the selection of the jury had changed. In the previous century the number of members varied, but by the mid-eighteenth century it was limited to twelve persons selected by the Bailiff. On the first market day after his election he invited such of the inhabitants as he thought fit to meet him in the Court Room over the Market House and then asked the Clerk to record the names of twelve men; these constituted the jury for his year, but whilst the Bailiff had to take an oath none of the jury was sworn. So close had become the Corporation that in 1755 it was recorded there had been little change in the personnel of the jury for the past ten years. The advantages of this to the persons participating, and the reaction of the inhabitants, were brought out clearly in the events connected with the election of Bailiff in 1755. Fortunately there are available several documents setting out the cases to and the opinions of Counsel whose advice was sought in connection with the affair. These documents not only give the facts in the case, but shed an interesting light on the previous practice followed in electing the Bailiff.

The affair was an effort to maintain the group in power and to manipulate the election of a member of the group as Bailiff in spite of the feelings of the townsfolk generally, who wanted to break the hold which had been established. Feelings had been running high for some years and matters were brought to a head by the actions of the local oligarchy in 1755. Some three years earlier someone had taken the Charter of Henry VIII from the chest in the parish church, where it was usually kept, and stated that "it shall never come into the Church again", presumably so that knowledge of the legal position of the bailiwick was denied to his opponents.

Before the date of the election of the new Bailiff the then Bailiff, William Tompson, landlord of an inn called the Red Lion, declared that the Bailiff could be, and could only be, chosen from the 12 men who constituted his jury. This was thought by most of the townsmen to be "a great Imposition", and so the first of the opinions of Mr. Evans, Counsel, was obtained, and he advised against William Tompson and said in effect that the appointment was an open one to be made by a majority of the inhabitants. Undeterred by this the Bailiff, supported by most of his Jury, called a meeting in the Court Room on St. Andrew's Day. This was a Sunday, and so the meeting was held in the forenoon immediately after Divine Service. One of his jury, not named but described as an apothecary, explained the purpose of the meeting and thereupon the Bailiff nominated three persons. The opposition, which consisted of nearly 100 of the townspeople then nominated three others, and a poll was demanded, but as soon as two persons had voted for Richard Walker, one of the Bailiff's nominees, Tompson delivered the staff of office to him, declared him elected, and then with his jury left the room. The townsfolk remained, however, continued with the poll and elected one John Tuffery, a draper, by a large majority; Tuffery then locked up the Court Room and Market Loft and took possession of the Bailiwick.

So the town was blessed with two Bailiffs each of whom took the Oath of Supremacy required by statute and proceeded to collect the income from the Bailiwick property. Each side threatened the other. Walker, with the twelve he had appointed as his jury "threatened to move the Court of Kings Bench next term for a Quo Warrant against Tuffery or otherwise to punish him" and the Inhabitants threatened "to file a Bill in Chancery against Tompson and his predecessors for an account of the Rents and Profits of the Bailiwick for these ten years past which they thought they had a right to". (As accounts for these years are to be found in the Bailiwick records it would appear that they were not submitted to a public meeting as was the normal practice, but only to a meeting of the 'select jury'). So recourse was made again to Counsel, and two opinions obtained, presumably one by each of the contending parties; there was general agreement that Tuffery was the duly elected Bailiff, and so he took over the duties of the office and served for the year.

One objection by the townspeople to the faction which managed the affairs of the Bailiwick was that the annual income of about £40 was spent on feasting and in other ways solely for the benefit of those responsible, and that the old practice of using the annual surplus towards apprenticing a boy or two every year and in assisting the poor had fallen into disuse; at the end of his year Tuffery had a surplus of £5.11.2¾d of which £5 was "laid out in Flour and given to the poor". No money was spent on feasting except 14s. "upon a meeting to consult who to nominate for Bailiff for the year ensueing". But the old custom returned, if slowly, and in a few years the accounts showed several sums spent each year on the old kinds of entertainment.

Another occurrence which added to the popular indignation was the manner in which the then Bailiff, Silvanus Perrott, and his jury dealt with certain property destroyed by a considerable fire on 2nd January 1749. The event is described in graphic terms in the Bailiwick books as "Threatening and Impending Ruin when from the appearance of the flames the whole Town was in the Utmost Danger". Among the property destroyed was the Women's Market House (sometimes called the Boarded Market House) which had been erected on part of the glebe land of the church at public expense, and for which the Bailiwick paid a small rent to the vicar. The antecedents of this building are described elsewhere. In the terms of the resolution of the jury:-

> In consideration of the Usefulness of (the) place to the persons that come to Markett and for the many Services done to the Parish by the Reverend Mr. Rowland Johnson aforesaid (the vicar) and in the faithfull Execution of his Office as one of his Majesties Justices of the Peace for this County ...and ...as a Gratefull Acknowledgment to Almighty God from so signall ...a Deliverance from ...Impending Ruin ...

it was agreed to rebuild the Market House at the Bailiwick's expense, and the thirteen men present (the Bailiff and twelve jurymen) agreed to advance £2.2.0d. each towards the cost, provided these contributions were repaid to them out of future surplus. They made these contributions and the building was re-erected at a cost of £36.10.4d. Two things annoyed the inhabitants; first that the thirteen men present decided that they would not elect as Bailiff anyone who would not agree to provide at least £10 in his year of office towards the cost of the work; and second that the benefit of the new building, valued at £4 per annum, accrued to the Vicar and in no way to the Bailiwick, The Vicar showed his gratitude by contributing £1.1.0d. towards the acquisition of a new clock which cost £3.3.0d. and which was fixed to the Market House (not the Women's Market House). The main point about the first item was the statement that as the Bailiff could only be elected from the jury they, the jury, could exercise complete control in the affairs of the town and could ignore the wishes of the general body of inhabitants. As we have seen the inhabitants did in fact elect their own nominee.

Tuffery's year was notable for two events of national significance. According to one observer, the summer of 1756 was the wettest in the memory of man. "Great quantities of grain perished by the wind and rains" and these calamities must have visited Hemel Hempstead because 1s. was

> Paid to Wm Dell Junior for watching at the Brook (i.e. Bury Mill End) when the Flood was.

The other event was the outbreak of the Seven Years War when the Bailiff paid 2s. for "Hire of Horses when War was proclaimed."

During the remainder of the eighteenth century the Bailiwick continued to function, but its effective powers were gradually taken from it and transferred to such authorities as the Justices. The way in which this happened can be illustrated by certain events connected with weights and measures.

The Charter of Henry VIII created the Court of Pie Powder to manage the Market, and the Rules of 1656 provided that no bread or butter could be sold in the town if it were not of full-weight. It was assumed that this gave the Bailiff power to inspect all weights and measures throughout the town and certain standard weights were obtained to enable this to be done. For example, in 1771-2 it was found that certain persons were selling beer in short measure and the Bailiff inspected and stamped the measures. In September 1785 the Justices for the Dacorum Hundred meeting at Berkhamsted signed a warrant directing the Constable of Hemel Hempstead and Robert Loader, Constable of St. Peters, Berkhamsted, to regulate the weights and measures in Hemel Hempstead. This they proceeded to do but after they had found that the measures at two public houses were inaccurate and taken them away, the Constable from Berkhamsted (Loader) was forbidden by William Roberts, the Bailiff, to continue, and he departed. The Bailiff, who incidentally was a Blacksmith, then proceeded to carry out his own examination, and this work was continued by his successors. The Justices then demanded 10s. 6d. in respect of Loader's expenses, and stated they intended to enforce payment, an action which the jury agreed to resist at all costs. Recourse was once again made to counsel, but his opinion and the following action are not recorded. But this was not the end of the matter; once again in 1812 it was necessary to seek opinion of counsel and this time the advice was short and to the point. The Bailiff had no power to make bye-laws, the 1656 Rules were now void, and in effect the Bailiff had no powers to deal with such matters as weights and measures. Further, that no rate could be levied for the improvement of the Market House. Nevertheless the Bailiff must have continued to attempt control of weights and measures, as the Town Clerk has in his possession certain standard measures bearing the date 1826.

In any case the Bailiff and his jury continued to legislate for the market. In 1808 they dealt with the sale of straw plait, the making of which was an important local home industry. The records recite that great inconvenience and injury arose owing to the straw plait market starting at a "very early unreasonable hour" and so it was ordered that no sales should be made before 7 a.m. in the period between Lady Day and Michaelmas and before 8 a.m. in the period Michaelmas to Lady Day, the penalty for failing to comply being 40s. The Plait Market was held in Colletts Yard, adjoining the premises then occupied by Thomas Sanders. Some other bye-laws related to short weight in sales of butter, stalls in the Market House, the ringing of the market bell and the sale of unwholesome fish. Others prohibited the placing of a stall or booth in the street without the consent of the Bailiff (penalty 10s.) and the making of wood piles or laying any timber, dung or other articles in the streets or lanes (penalty 20s.).

In July 1814 an attempt was made at the Hertford Assizes to enforce the bye-law dealing with the straying of pigs in the streets, and to recover 3s. 6d. said to be forfeited for an offence by one named Cass. But he, supported by his two sisters, proved that the wrong person had been summoned. They stated that the pig in question had belonged to their mother, and that when she died it had been sold to pay the rent which she owed for her cottage. Consequently, the Bailiff and his jury were non-suited and so lost their case. (This case is recorded in 'The Times' for 28th July, 1814.)

To assist the Bailiff and his jury certain officers were employed. From the beginning of the records in 1619 a clerk was employed to write up the Bailiff's accounts each year, for which he was paid 6s. 8d. rising in subsequent years to 13s. 4d. The first men were generally scriveners, but later on the local attorney was employed; he not only wrote up the accounts, but acted as legal adviser, and it was by him, during the eighteenth century and later on in the nineteenth, that cases were prepared for the various counsel's opinions which were sought on behalf of a somewhat litigious administration.

But perhaps the most important officer was the under-bailiff. He was a jack of all trades, and usually combined this office with that of parish clerk. There is no reference to any remuneration, but he was rewarded by fees; for instance he operated the weighing machine and was duly rewarded for his services. Again in 1638 it was agreed that he should "take of butchers in the street 8d. a piece one quarter towards his attendance to waye their meate and keep the wayghtes and scales together". He was paid 1s. each time he called the jury and was paid sums for specific jobs, e.g. for setting up and taking down the stalls at the fair, and for filling the fire engines.

His duties were many. Besides weighing butter and meat he had to proclaim all orders made by the Court, to ring the market bell, to pound hogs, to record details of sales of cattle in a book kept for that purpose, and also enter therein particulars of strays, to cleanse the market house and street every week, and "weekly to close the market house and not suffer any dung to lye there". If he refused or neglected to carry out the orders, or set up stalls contrary to those orders then he "shalbe putt out and another Chosen". He also had to assist with the fair, to warn members of the jury when a meeting was to be held, and, later, to attend to the fire engine. When an under-bailiff was appointed it was an occasion to take some refreshment, as the following entry for 20th February 1733 shows:-

Spent at Robert Gilberts when Wm Dell was Chosen under-bailiff	10s. 0d.

In the eighteenth century another employee was appointed, called the

Bellman. He was an assistant to the under-bailiff, and when in 1733 the town provided some system of street lighting, he was paid 20s. a year for looking after and lighting the lamps. Both he and the under-bailiff were provided with a coat, and from time to time expenditure on purchasing the cloth and making the coats is recorded. Typical entries are in Tuffery's accounts for 1755-6; he was a draper and supplied the cloth for the two coats for £3.3.3¼d. and Frederick Hillary the Tailor was paid 12s. 0d. for making them.

Another officer who ought to be mentioned is the Clerk of the Markets. He was not an Officer of the Bailiwick but was appointed in every county to oversee all measures relating to the Assize of Bread. A number of entries appear during the seventeenth century showing that the Bailiff suitably entertained him whenever he visited the town.

The Market and the Fair

We have no information about the early history of the market and the fair, but by 1619, the year from which the available records start, they had become well established, and we are able to describe the manner in which they were conducted. Both were held in the street, from Bury Mill to the end of the High Street at Cherry Bounce. The facilities were twofold: (1) the stalls and accommodation in the Market House, and later the Women's Market House and the butchers shambles, and (2) the stalls, pens and standings distributed along the street. The first belonged to the Bailiwick and the rents were credited to it, but the charges for the second were paid to the occupiers of the property in front of which the stalls were erected. The Bailiff and the jury, as a Court of Pie Powder, directed where the stalls should stand and made rules and regulations governing the general running of the market and fair. These rules were probably in force from the beginning of the market, amended as necessary from time to time. Later they found that by the statute 19 Henry VII Chap. 7 they should have made them in due form, and so on 29th May 1656 they submitted them to two of the Justices of Assize at Hertford, by whom they were approved; they governed the market and the fair for some 150 years until by the opinion of Counsel given in 1812 it was found they had lapsed and were not enforceable. Towards the end of the 18th century the Bailiwick took over the letting of stalls and received the rents therefrom.

The market was a general one, in which almost everything usually dealt with in such a market was sold — corn, cattle and other animals and general merchandise. Corn was the principal commodity and Hemel Hempstead became known as one of the principal corn markets in Hertfordshire, if not in the country. The Universal British Directory of the 1790's records that it

> has been reckoned one of the greatest markets for wheat in this county, if not in England, 20,000 *L* a week being often returned in it only for meal. Eleven pairs of mills stand within four miles of the place, which bring a great trade to it; but the road is thereby so continuously torn, that it is one of the worst turnpike ways to London.

An earlier document, a church terrier of 1625, speaks of "Hempstead being a great market towne", and about this time John Norden wrote under the heading of 'Market townes' that "(Hertford)shire is well furnished with market townes, the most of them plentifull of all things necessarie for the peoples reliefe, namelie Hemsted on the Thursday."

Besides growing corn the district produced wool. The fulling mills at Two Waters have already been referred to in previous chapters. The bailiwick records refer to a wool market. The intention to set up such a market was first mooted in 1647 when "it is thought a wooll market to be raised here may be beneficall to the towne and countre". But it was not until 1655 that the proposal was adopted, perhaps because of the disturbances during and following the Civil War. Then a further order was made, and the barley market suggested as the place where the wool was to be sold, and the court loft was the "place appoynted for laying upp of the said wooll bought or not sould". Each year the market was to begin on the Thursday after Midsummer and continue every Thursday until Michaelmas.

Before dealing further with the market it may be well to describe certain buildings and other structures connected with the market, and mostly owned by the Bailiwick. The first is the Market House. This stood on the site now occupied by the old Town Hall, and although its origins are uncertain it was probably built towards the end of the 16th century; it was there in 1619 because in that year certain expenditure was incurred for its maintenance, including 2s. 6d. for glazing the windows in the Court Loft. The documents indicate that it was erected on the site of the churchhouse and the last reference to that building was in 1571; so the Market House was built between that year and 1619. It consisted of a court loft above with a covered area underneath where stalls and standings were arranged. From time to time improvements were made: in 1629 the lower part was paved, in 1633 stairs to the loft above were installed, and in 1643 a chimney was built which, with other work, cost £5.5.0d. The Court Loft was used for meetings of the Bailiff and his jury, the Manor Court, and of the inhabitants generally. Those attending had to sit on benches. In 1756 it was described as a large building with eight cornshops over.

No major work on the building was undertaken during the 18th century, and according to a report made by a Committee on the Repair and Improvement of the Market House in the early years of the 19th century, it had fallen into a rather disreputable condition. The back part abutting on the churchyard was in a ruinous condition and needed to be pulled down and the front was irregular with "hanging projecting eaves", which "brings the Corn Market much too forward in the street and causes much stoppage there on market days to the public annoyance and complaint". Part of the building was so dark that it could not be used properly and consequently

MARKET HOUSE HEMEL HEMPSTEAD

persons bringing corn for sale either pitched it in the forefront, or if this was full, into the street itself, leaving the back part of the building unoccupied. Various improvements were suggested, including an entrance to the Church about the middle of the Market House. The estimated cost of these improvements was approximately £400, and it is interesting to note that it was suggested that £138 could be taken from the rents of Boxmoor wharf and cottages. These proposals were adopted and expenditure was recorded in the accounts for the years 1806/7 and 1807/8. But the whole cost was not met at the time and in 1829 a meeting of the inhabitants of the town unanimously voted £100 from the surplus of Boxmoor Trust to liquidate the debts incurred in respect of the repair of the Market House.

About the time these repairs were carried out a contemporary record describes the building as being "of wood, adjoining the churchyard and it exhibits a curious mode of antique architecture; it appears to be the original building constructed in the reign of Henry VIII". Another writer described it as "constructed of wood, without any ornament". It was built later than the reign of that monarch but it continued in use in its ancient form until it was replaced by the present brick structure in 1851. From this description and the illustration in Plate XIX the building as it was can be appreciated.

On 31st May, 1813, the Bailiff and his jury agreed that the Court Room could be used as a School of Industry when it was not required for public purposes, on the condition that the Bailiff approved the entrance to be used which was not to be through the Corn Lofts. This school carried on in the Court Room for several years. Such a school was designed to cater for the children who did not go to work and so were at a loose end during the week. The instruction was occupational and in no way academic. It was hoped that the school would pay for itself from the proceeds of the sale of the articles made by the children in attendance there. What work was done is not recorded.

The Women's Market House (or Boarded House)

This was the building which was burned down in the fire of 1749. It was erected on part of the glebe land belonging to the church in the year 1634/5 at a cost of £22, out of surpluses on the Bailiwick accounts accumulated over the years from 1623/4. To start with, a rent of 5s. per annum, in the nature of a ground rent, was paid to the Vicar, but by the time of its destruction this had increased to 24s. a year. This increase was agreed to in 1687 when a new lease was entered into. It is sometimes described as the New Market House, to distinguish it from the main and older building, but more interestingly as the Butter Market. Previously the butter women had to stand on "a little slipe of land" near the churchyard. The new building was the place to which the women brought their butter and similar products for sale. At the outset there were four stalls producing 30s. a year. The numbers and the amounts grew to eight stalls and £3.11.9d. rent, although there were fluctuations from time to time. It was described in a church terrier of 1708 as containing three bays standing between the house occupied by William Lea and that of John Clifton, both premises being part of the glebe. William Lea had "a workhouse under the Women's Market House for a Tallow Chandler". The building must have been to the south of the main Market House and separated from it by at least one dwelling house.

The Butchers Shambles

Some of these must have existed from the beginning of the market, and were at the north end of the Market House by the end of the sixteenth century. They were in two groups, the front group belonging to the Bailiwick, and the back one to the church. The church terrier of 1625 mentions all the butchers shambles along the churchyard and one of 1638 refers to

> Twelve shuddes used for stoules for Butchers but whether any of these particulars be Churchyard land or not we doe not knowe.

There are several references to them in the Bailiwick books from 1629 onwards and in 1630 the Bailiff and jury decided that all the rents should be taken by the Churchwardens and used for the maintenance of the church; this arrangement was cancelled in 1642 and the rents were then collected for the Bailiwick. From time to time the number of shambles was increased and a church terrier of 1708 mentions fifteen butchers stalls adjoining the churchyard, these no doubt being those belonging to the church; about the same time the Bailiwick accounts list 20 butchers stalls. Originally they were probably of rather crude construction, easily moved, but later they assumed a more permanent character. Apart from figuring prominently in the Oxley litigation referred to later, there is nothing of note concerning them until a reconstruction scheme was launched in 1798. Then a piece of the glebe land, on which stood a number of what were described as "ruinated shambles", was rented from the Vicar for £3.3.0d. a year and it was proposed to demolish these shambles, and also those in the front belonging to the Bailiwick and out of voluntary subscriptions to erect more commodious structures on the whole site. A special committee of five members was appointed to carry out the scheme. The work was put in hand and the new shambles were described as "neatly built of brick". But the subscriptions were not forthcoming and so the Committee in 1800 had to borrow, on the credit of the Bailiwick fund, £30 from one of its members, Thomas Collett, in order to pay the bill of the contractor, William Harvey. The loan was for four years and this was duly repaid, with interest payments of 30s. for each of the four years. At a later date the stalls were similarly concentrated and taken off the street; this must have been finished by 1817 because in that year appeared a new item -

Weekly rents for stalls	£58.13.4d.

The main duty of the Bailiff and his jury was to regulate the market, and particularly to say where the different traders should stand, and this work was dealt with in some detail in the records. The various entries give a useful indication of the kind of traders who sold in the market. Apart from those who dealt in corn and livestock there were fishers (or fishmongers), passing-men, butchers, bakers, oatmeal men, cheesemen, shoemakers, glovers, smiths, root sellers and "such as sell onions" and the women who sold butter; there was a collarmaker and a chapman, and pedlars had to stand where they could.

As Hemel Hempstead was an important market for corn and other agricultural produce there were regulations concerning their sale. In 1633 it was decreed that "noe man shall pitch any wheat or other corne without the eaves of the markett house". In the next year the sale of corn in any house, yard or other place in the town except in the open market was forbidden, the penalty being 12d. per sack; the market house was to be used solely for the sale of corn and neither wheat nor barley could be sold until the market bell was rung.

Various directions were given about animals, especially pigs. In 1628 it was ordered that on market days no hogs were to be brought into the market house between 7 a.m. and 6 p.m., the penalty being 4d. for each animal, the fine to be given to the poor. In 1633 it was ruled that a boar should not be tied or held in the street, but kept in a pen, and later that no swine be allowed in the street without a keeper, and then only when being driven within the town.

Much time and thought were directed to the location of stalls or of particular trades, and different groups were moved from place to place to secure better use of the available accommodation. For example the shoemakers were one such group, moved in 1629, 1633 and 1634. In 1642 out-of-town shoemakers were to stand in the three new stalls which were erected against the church wall and to pay 3s. 4d. for each stall. In 1655 shoemakers generally were to stand under the penthouses and eaves "of Mr. Arthur Smyth and the widdowe Halsey" but the bailiff was to provide tilt cloth of canvas as necessary which he did at a cost of 8s. 8d. The root sellers, the butchers, the bakers and the oatmeal men were amongst other groups who were moved from time to time, and sometimes these moves were occasioned by special circumstances, as when the new or women's market house was opened in 1635.

Attempts were made from time to time to relieve the congestion arising out of the narrowness of the market street. In 1633 no stalls were to be erected "between the Bell dore down to the Cock dore", and the smiths were moved to the end of the butchers shambles. Next year the same stretch was again dealt with, by prohibiting any stalls on the east side without apprentices. Other causes of congestion dealt with were carts, rubbish heaps and even timber, and instructions were given that timber already in the street should be removed before the following Thursday.

A protective policy was followed. Strangers were put at a disadvantage, the best places in the market were reserved for local tradesmen. The Bailiff was required to punish by fine all regrators and forestallers and Quarter Sessions records contain references to a number of these sharp gentlemen. In 1665 for example, information was laid against one, Edward Wright of Hemelhempsted, husbandman, for forestalling wheat and rye there.

There were other duties and orders incidental to the market. There was supervision of the weights and measures used, and the town had its own standards, which are listed in the inventories of goods belonging to the town, the first made in 1658. The under-bailiff was responsible for seeing that correct measures were given. In 1635 he was instructed to weigh the butter and if he found any light weight he was to seize the goods and they were to be distributed to the poor. Bad meat and fish were seized and burnt; in 1681 6d. was paid for carrying "the casalty meate to be burned" and two-penny-worth of straw was purchased to start the fire.

No corn could be sold before the market bell was rung. This was a common practice in markets, and Shakespeare referred to it in the first part of Henry VI when he tells Joan of Arc and her confederates "Enter, go in; the market bell is rung" - (Act III Scene ii 15-16). The under-bailiff had to ring it each week at 12 noon, except on four days in the middle of winter, when he did so at 11.30 a.m. This bell was a constant source of expenditure, and in 1652 was taken to London and recast at a cost of £3.10.7d.; it is still in existence, and is inscribed "B.E. 1652".

The Fairs

There is some uncertainty as to the history of the fairs. Henry's charter gave an annual fair, held on the Feast of Corpus Christi and this must have been held each year until it was discontinued in the 19th century, but no record of any income from it appears in the accounts until the additional fairs were granted by Cromwell in 1656, although there were a few small items of expenditure shown after 1619. Following a petition to the Committee of Trade and Navigation, signed by 97 persons, an inquiry was held by the sheriff of the county, assisted by a jury of 12 men of Hemelhempsted, to ascertain whether additional fairs in Hemel Hempstead would harm any neighbouring ones. The report was favourable and so Cromwell, by a charter, granted three extra fairs, one in October, one in Lent, and one in Easter week. This application may have been inspired by a draft order made about the same time by the justices in Quarter Sessions; in 1656 this was directed to the High Constables of the Dacorum and Cashio hundred, requiring them to appoint "a statute" for hiring servants and one of the three may have been such a hiring fair. Two years later an attempt to advertise the new fairs was made, and 2s. 0d. was spent on having them proclaimed at several markets.

It is doubtful if all these three Cromwellian fairs were held in the eighteenth century, but it appears that at least two were, but which ones cannot be ascertained. The income fluctuated considerably but this may be no indication of the value of the fair or fairs to the inhabitants. What is certain is that by 1753 there was a statute fair and most likely there was also the charter fair. There are a number of entries in the accounts dealing with the advertisement of the former:

1753/4	
Paid for printing the Statute Putting it in the News and for writing the papers and having it cried at several Places	11s. 4d.
1754/5	
Advertising the Statute	3s. 6d.
Crying the Statute	6d.
1756/7	
Man going to Berkhamsted and sending to Chesham Leighton Watford and St. Albans to give notice of the Statute	2s. 6d.

This advertising did not bring any increase in the income.

The next development is in 1802/3 when the accounts for the first time show separate amounts of income for "the Fair" and "the Statute" respectively and there was a large increase in the receipts. From an average of of £5.19.0d. for the decade 1741-50 the figure had fallen to £4.8.0d. for 1781-90; thereafter it tended to increase somewhat but in 1802-3 it jumped to £15.11.8d. for the two fairs and from time to time reached as much as £20.

The Bailiwick records deal solely with the commercial side of the fairs. In the first half of the seventeenth century the arrangements were simple, but later they became more elaborate and considerable preparation was necessary beforehand. Poles, trestles and other articles were purchased and boards were borrowed from local tradesmen for the stalls or to mark out the road for the different purposes, and when the erections were completed men were employed to watch them through the night, and provided with supper. In addition to the various wares sold from the stalls there was considerable business in horses and cattle, and when the three additional fairs were granted new regulations were made. The horse fair was to be kept in the upper end of the town, that part being more spacious; the sheep were in the lower end and the cows beyond them towards the river and mill at Bury Mill End. By the eighteenth century the Bailiff was accustomed to entertain on the evening before the fair when the stalls were let and on the night of the fair - but this official support for what was an important annual event evidently waned as the century ran its course.

Socially of course the fair or fairs were of considerable importance, and people came from a distance to attend them. In addition to the business of the day there was much jollity and conviviality. To the hiring fairs came those seeking employment; standing dressed in their smocks, carrying the emblems of their trade, they offered themselves to whoever would engage them. No doubt here, as elsewhere, the term for which they were employed was for eleven months and three weeks, so that those who were not normally resident in the parish did not acquire a place of settlement and so became a potential liability on the poor rate. An elderly resident, who passed away not so many years ago, and who in his earlier days offered himself for employment in this way has described the feelings and the humiliation he experienced on those occasions.

Although during the 19th century the rents for these fairs ceased to be recorded in the Bailiwick accounts. the events continued to be held, organised by the showmen who provided the entertainment, or by the auctioneers who sold the cattle. A directory of the 1870's mentions an annual fair for sheep and cattle on Holy Thursday, a pleasure fair on the Thursday after Trinity Sunday (the Henry VIII fair) and a Statute Fair for hiring servants on the third Monday in September. Nowadays the only one is held in September, and it is no longer a hiring fair.

The fight for the market rights

During the seventeenth century the inhabitants on occasion had to fight to retain the rights which Henry VIII gave them in 1539, and the strenuous efforts which they made to keep them show how much they valued them, and what they meant to the town.

It started when James I having had the manor surveyed in 1617 tried to increase the burdens on his manorial tenants who successfully opposed him, as recorded earlier. (see pp 56-7). Having failed, the King endeavoured to secure some recompense, however small, out of the Bailiwick and to understand what happened it is necessary to appreciate how the Market Street was created and how it developed. Following the charter of 1539, in the field called Church End houses and shops were erected, but to no formal plan; before this there may have been a rough track leading to the Church, the Vicarage, and the few houses there. Between the new buildings and the roadway were left strips of the field, which were pieces of the waste of the manor. One strip, two feet wide, ran the whole length of the Market House part of which was built on it. On other pieces of the waste stood the shambles, standings, and sheep pens and stalls. The inhabitants believed that the use of these pieces of land was authorised by the charter of Henry VIII, especially as, at the time it was granted, the land formed part of the Manor and was owned by the King. But James (or rather Charles, because by now the manor belonged to him) thought otherwise and in 1623 he granted a lease of the various pieces of waste on which some of the units of the market stood to a doctor, Josias Martyn and ten others for a period of 35 years, at a rent of £1 per annum. Apparently the negotiations for this lease were conducted in secret, unknown to the inhabitants, and when the fact became known there was a public outcry, and a petition signed by Francis Combe Senior, Thomas Taylor, the Vicar, and 25 others was addressed to the Prince protesting against the proposal that their "ancient right should be granted awaie from them" and claiming that the Prince had been misinformed about the matter. A later document states that the then Bailiff and forty others opposed taking the lease and that of the 500 inhabitants none but the eleven who entered into it consented. There is also the suggestion that the Market Street belonged to the inhabitants having acquired it by deed of gift or purchase from the Earl of Leicester; this would have been about the 1570's. (See p.45).

However, the petition from the inhabitants was referred to two referees, Sir John Luke and Sir Richard Anderson, but they were unable to decide the issue; they described it as "intricat and litagious" and suggested that only a court of law could resolve the question. Whatever further proceedings followed, the lease was entered into, and the rent was paid each year in half-yearly instalments, and each time an extra shilling was paid for "an aquitance". To the lease were attached two conditions which could have been onerous; the inhabitants were to provide almshouses for the poor and build a grammar school, but these requirements were never complied with. There are indications that some provision for the school was attempted and this may have given rise to the legend that Hemel Hempstead once had a grammar school. The lease continued in force until the time of the Commonwealth Government, which, in connection with its policy of disposing of certain Crown properties generally, ordered a Parliamentary Survey to be made of the manor of Hemel Hempstead and this was completed in 1650. It mentions the lease and states that the rent of 20s. per annum is "worth upon improvement over the said rent per annum £17". No doubt with this in mind, knowing that the original lease would soon expire, and appreciating the value of the market to the townspeople, the Bailiff and his jury decided to purchase the waste ground of the manor on which the market and the fair were held for £150. They borrowed the money locally, £54 from the four men who negotiated the purchase, and £36 from 36 others, each of whom subscribed £1. These loans were all repaid out of the annual surpluses on the Bailiwick accounts by 1658.

When Charles II was restored to the throne in 1660 the inhabitants fearing they might have upset the King by buying the waste, and might then lose the market rights they valued so much, decided to give back the waste to the King, together with a gift of £100, and at the same time applied for a renewal of the old lease. They borrowed this money from Henry Clarke of London, and among the entries in the accounts relating to this transaction is the following:-

> Paide to Sir Richard Combe which he paide to
> Mr. Barrington upon exchange for gould being
> the 100 l presented to the Kinge £3.15.0d.

Whilst the inhabitants lost no time in returning the waste to the King they were not so prompt in obtaining the new lease; perhaps they thought it would be granted as a matter of course, but they had not reckoned with one of their number, Francis Oxley. He assumed that the town having given the waste back to the King had surrendered the charter rights as well, and so if he could secure the lease for himself he would become in effect the owner of the rights of the market and the fair. Accordingly in 1661 he petitioned the King to grant him the lease. He is variously described as a baker and a yeoman, and is mentioned several times in Quarter Sessions records, including a charge in 1655 of keeping a common alehouse without a licence. He was the keeper of the Sun Inn in the Market Street, and had served in the King's forces during the Civil War, and was actually serving in the Earl of Oxford's Regiment when he petitioned the King. In his petition he stated he was "nowed ruined in his Estate", and he may have been hard up because in 1659 he raised a mortgage of £160 on the Sun, which he subsequently repaid. His petition was referred to the Surveyor General, who, having conferred with some of the principal inhabitants (some of whom were or had been lessees of the stalls), recommended that the lease be granted to Oxley at the old rent of 20s. a year, provided there were no excessive rents charged for the various lettings. This recommendation was approved, and the lease entered into, to begin in March 1662, but it was confined to the stalls, standings, pens &c., and not in so many words, extended to cover the market rights, a factor of material importance as will appear later.

Whilst the inhabitants generally may have had some inkling of Oxley's petition the granting of the lease to him came as a shock and was roundly condemned. The result was a division of the people of the town into two factions, for and against Oxley; sporadic rioting broke out, and in due time many persons were indicted before Quarter Sessions. As during the recent Civil War the majority of the inhabitants had favoured Parliament, and Oxley himself had served in the Royalist forces, the way in which the inhabitants lined up into two factions was no doubt influenced to some extent at least by the divisions which existed during the Civil War. The Oxley faction was led by Oxley himself, supported by members of his family, and particularly his wife Martha who was something of a virago and quite content to do a bit of scrapping on her own account. She was presented to Quarter Sessions that she "stole a hat value 4s., a mattock value 2s., and a ladder value 1s. from Christopher Mitchell" and that she and Richard Oxley, husbandman, "assaulted the said Christopher who also assaulted the said Martha". The other faction, which might be termed the people's group, was supported by the leading inhabitants, but the more militant operations were directed by one, Christopher Mitchell, a sworn enemy of Francis Oxley.

The fighting usually took place on Thursdays, the day on which the weekly market was held, and the combatants were armed with a variety of weapons - sticks, knives, sickles and various agricultural implements. The rioting started when, having obtained his lease, Oxley attempted to enter into possession of his domain in May 1662. He went to occupy the stalls and shambles belonging to the Bailiwick and to collect the rents for them. One of the tenants was John Field, a butcher, whose rent was 18s. a year; he was a man of some substance, and was elected Bailiff the following November. Oxley, having occupied Field's shambles, was promptly ejected by the latter, and with some force.

Oxley then brought an action for trespass against Field, and claimed damages of £10. This was the first of two law suits which arose out of Oxley's efforts to secure the market, and in this case he really tried to obtain the Charter rights. Field acted on behalf of the inhabitants generally. The hearing dragged on for some years but in 1666, after the Bailiff and the townspeople had petitioned the King "that this vexatious suit may be stopped", it was made clear at the Hertford Assizes that Oxley could not acquire the rights which were vested in the inhabitants, and so suffered himself to be non-suited.

The second law suit - Oxley v. Partridge and 16 others - was tried in the Court of Exchequer and related to Oxley's claim to the rents of the stalls and other lettings in front of the various premises in the market street - these rents had been payable to the different owners or occupiers of the buildings behind the stalls. From the answers given to the questions asked at the interrogations taken at the White Hart, Hemel Hempstead, on 12th October 1677, much useful information can be obtained, not only about the case, but also about the market and the street in which it was held. The result was another defeat for Oxley.

In both cases the arguments put forward, and the evidence given, were very similar. What the inhabitants yielded up to the King was only the waste and not the market rights. Oxley alleged they had given up the lot, and that the lease he was granted entitled him to take possession of the various structures belonging to the Bailiwick and to collect the rents for them - also to receive the rents for the other stalls which were placed in the street in front of the houses and other buildings. He must have been fortified in this view by the condition in his lease that he was not to charge excessive rents. He was granted a lease of the waste land, but he was met by the claim that as the various stalls and so on were not fixed to the ground he could not claim them. Much of the evidence dealt with this point and there was considerable conflict about it. There was in fact some pretty hard swearing. It was suggested that at one time the structures belonging to the Bailiwick had been permanently so fixed, and that when Oxley started his efforts they were raised and put on wheels so that they could be moved. But the principal claim that defeated him was that he could not be given in a lease of land rights which had been granted to the inhabitants generally by royal charter.

Whilst these legal actions were proceeding the petition of the Bailiff and the Inhabitants for a new lease was under consideration, and in 1663 one was granted, for 31 years, "of the waste ground in the common street of the town, where their markets and fairs have long been held. Some persons endeavoured to pervert the same by obtaining a grant of the said ground to their ruin, they have hitherto enjoyed it". Unfortunately, there are no accounts in the Bailiwick books for 1660-1 and 1661-2, so we do not know what happened to the rents due to the Bailiwick during those years. The accounts for the next four years are in summary form only but they do show that the rents, or at least some part of them, were received.

Although the town retained its market and its fair the victory had been a costly one. The records are not sufficiently complete to make possible an accurate estimate of the cost involved, but it was at least £400 and probably very much more. To finance the defence money was raised from several sources; some was borrowed, some advanced by individuals to be repaid later, funds were appropriated and a rate was levied. All these sums (except the appropriation) were repaid out of the annual surpluses on the Bailiwick accounts, and completed by 1689. During those years strict economy seems to have been observed in the management of the Bailiwick affairs, and no doubt they were all concerned in securing the repayment of their money as soon as possible.

The rate mentioned is an interesting one. There was of course no statutory authority for it, but the resolution authorising it was in somewhat peremptory terms and full of threats in the case of non-payment. It was at the rate of 18d. in the £ and was decided on at a meeting of the inhabitants held on 5th January 1677, called to consider ways and means of meeting the expense incurred in "defence of their just right and tytle to the markett house, stalls, shambles &c". The rate so levied was repaid in full, probably the only time this was done either in Hemel Hempstead or elsewhere.

One of the leading townsmen was Richard Salter, and he took an active part in opposing Oxley. He advanced something like £100 out of his own pocket. He also held £30 which was described as "belonging to ye school" and which had been deposited with him at 5% interest per annum, to be repaid to the parish on demand. This amount was appropriated towards the legal costs and Richard Salter was authorised to retain it against the money he had advanced to defend the cases.

Altogether the various events relating to the market, from the time it was decided to acquire the waste, cost a considerable sum of money in the value of the currency of the time; it was at least £650, and probably much more, and a reasonable estimate would approach £1,000. This was a considerable sum and quite a burden for a small market town, but it shows how greatly the people valued their rights, and how vigorously they were prepared to fight for them.

From various records, the Bailiwick Books, Wills and Inventories, we can trace what happened to many of the contestants. Most of the defendants in the two law suits eventually served in the office of Bailiff and those whose wills and inventories survive, died in varying degrees of affluence. Two of the principal actors, and certainly the most active, Christopher Mitchell and Francis Oxley, took part in an interesting epilogue. Mitchell, who became a victualler, had a shop in the Market Street, and other property at Corner Hall, was appointed the first keeper of the House of Correction, which the Magistrates in 1664 ordered to be established. He held the office until he died in 1671, and was succeeded by his enemy, Francis Oxley, who retained the post until 1680.

Perhaps at this juncture further reference might be made to "ye school". There has for many years been a story that the town once possessed a grammar school, the rights and assets of which were improperly appropriated by some ill-disposed individuals to the detriment of the town generally, but there is little evidence to support the story. The lease of 1623 required the town to provide a school, but by the time of the Parliamentary Survey of 1650 it had not been provided. Later records however, do refer to a free school in which the Bailiwick was interested. In 1682 there is the reference to the £30 in the hands of Richard Salter, the interest on which at 5% per annum he had to pay to James Francis, the schoolmaster of the "free school". As Richard Salter was allowed to retain the capital he was no longer required to pay the interest to the schoolmaster. In 1694 there was a meeting of the Vestry which required the then Bailiff, Jonathan Pratt, when delivering up his accounts "to pay to James Francis, Master of the ffree schoole such moneys as shall appear to be in his hands in parte of arrears due to him in respect of the ffree schoole". It is further recorded that Mr. Crawley, the local attorney, had been employed by the parish to obtain a decree in Chancery, "settling the revenue of the ffree schoole". As a result of these proceedings Mr. Richard Salter, who held another £60 belonging to the school, was directed to pay £40 to the attorney on account of his bill of £58.10.7d. and the balance of £20 to Francis. A John Southen held £5 of monies belonging to the school and this he was ordered to pay to Francis. The only other entry is a payment by the next Bailiff, David Shipton, of the balance of the fees due to Crawley the attorney. A document dated 1670 in the possession of the Dean & Chapter of St. Pauls comments on the misfortune of the Church of Hemel Hempstead in that the local schoolmaster had never been to a university. But it goes on to declare that the town was full of "schismaticks" who doubtless were joyful that the area was so ill-served. Therefore there must have been a school of some kind, but what it was and what became of it is not known. If the Vestry books of the time were still available very probably we should know.

Hemel Hempstead has been fortunate in the possession of two revenue-earning undertakings, the Bailiwick and the Boxmoor Trust, both of which over the years have provided amenities which other places of similar size were denied. It was the possession of certain properties so provided which earned the town the unique distinction of being promoted directly from a parish, with a parish council, to a municipal corporation, with a mayor and a borough council, in 1898. The late Mr. Lovel Smeathman, the first Town Clerk, who took a very active part in securing the charter from Queen Victoria, recalled that in view of the property which the community owned, and the manner in which it was being managed, some reform was necessary, and the central authorities were of opinion that the only course to follow was to incorporate the town under the Municipal Corporation Act of 1882. The property concerned included the Town Hall, a Corn Exchange, offices and shops in the High Street and the market rights.

But there were other services and facilities which the Bailiwick had provided, possibly with assistance from the Trust, and some of these should be mentioned. The first accounts of the Bailiwick still available are for the year 1619-20, and include a payment of £3.16.0d. to John Besouth "towards ye preachers diett". In the next year there is another payment to the same individual (who was the Clerk to the Bailiff) for £3.2.6d "in full payment of the preachers diett". A good sermon was a great attraction and was usually given at some length. Subsequently the listeners would make their purchases.

Another service was started in 1659 when a fire engine was purchased from Anthony Greene of the Three Candlesticks, Lothbury, London, for £30; a second one was bought in 1676 for £40.13.6d. In both cases the bulk of the purchase money came from voluntary contributions, but the balance, and the cost of maintaining the equipment, was charged to the Bailiwick accounts. Expenditure was recorded in practically every year's accounts; in 1678 £3.5.0d. was spent on a new "tubb" and in 1705 another one was bought for £5. Frequent payments were made for filling the engine and "for beere when the Engine was played". There were payments for repairs and often for mending or replacing leather buckets; in 1717 4s. was spent on mending some and £2 on buying a dozen, together with 8d. for carriage from London. There are references to payments when attending fires, particularly in 1749, the year of the great fire, when the Women's Market House and other property was destroyed. The payments were:

Beer and other liquors when the fire happened	£1.9.0d.
Paid twenty-three men for watching that night	£1.3.0d.
Beer for the men	5.9d.
Beer when the engine was mended	3.0d.

There must have been other items for repairs following this conflagration, but they cannot be identified. The engines were brought out on all occasions of public celebration, "playing them" was one of the attractions; those who carried out these operations were later suitably rewarded with beer and other refreshments.

In 1780 there was a fire at the White Hart and £1.7.6d. was paid to the soldiers who helped to extinguish it. Whether the engine was damaged or found to be inadequate is not clear, but the jury sent the Bailiff to London to enquire about a new one. None was purchased out of the Bailiwick accounts, but one may have been bought out of voluntary subscriptions, or out of another fund such as that of the Boxmoor Trust.

In the eighteenth century the Bailiwick instituted a system of street lighting. On 2nd November 1733 -

> At a publick meeting of the Bailiff and Jurats ...it is agreed that out of such moneys as ...remain in his [the Bailiff's] hands a sufficient number of lamps shall be bought ...and set up in the said Town in such places as upon Survey shall be judged most comodious.
>
> Further agreed that the Bellman be paid a salary yearly of Twenty shillings for looking after and lighting the said lamps ...

The expenditure incurred in complying with this decision was:-

Purchase of lamps	£6.	7.	10
Paid Bellman helping put lamps up & lighting them till St. Andrews day 1733		7.	0.
Carriage of lamps and oyle from London		7.	6.
Oyle and Cotton	£2	16.	7.
Iron work	£4	1.	1.

Spent on Thos. Glover at the Sun when the engines were played and when Order was made for buying the lamps	£2.	7.	0.
Spent at Mr. Sibleys when the lamps were finished		9.	0.
	£16	16.	0.

At first 12 lamps were purchased, but the number was later increased. They were only used during the winter, being taken down towards the end of March each year, and re-erected before the following winter. From time to time some were broken, some maliciously, as warrants were taken out against people who broke them, and sums were collected voluntarily from others. This system continued into the nineteenth century, the accounts showing expenditure on new lamps, repairs, purchase of oil and labour.

Bailiwick funds were also used to aid the poor, and reference is made elsewhere to the purchase of a house for the parish. (See p.197). But assistance was also given in a more direct fashion. During the later seventeenth and early eighteenth centuries each Bailiff usually gave a sum of £2 to £5 to the poor and often bought flour for distribution to them. There are some interesting entries in this connection for the year 1717, when Mark Brickland, an innkeeper, was Bailiff. First he gave the churchwardens £5.14.9d. for use of the poor. Later he gave another 50s. and spent 55s. 2d. entertaining the jury when it was distributed. However, the most important item under this heading was payments to apprentice the children of the poor. The first recorded item was 30s. in 1648 to apprentice John Combes (or Curtis). There were further odd payments throughout the seventeenth century, but during the first few decades of the eighteenth century surplus moneys were frequently used for this purpose. But the practice ceased when the oligarchy already described came into power. There was one more payment in 1777 when £4.2.6d. was paid for putting out John Bovingdon, "a poor boy". Again, from time to time throughout the eighteenth century small sums were disbursed as relief, buying clothing, paying rent and giving money during illness.

There were other payments which today would be classified as public health expenditure, such as work to the roads, remedying nuisances and clearing the streets.

The Bailiff had to deal with offenders and troublemakers. In 1693 the then Bailiff, Jonathan Pratt, paid 14s. 2d. at John Pryor's when he "had a fight with the parishmen". There was more trouble in 1702 when 3s. 6d. was paid "for beere when we went to remove a Pedlar in the Boarded Market House". But a more serious note was struck in 1739-40 by the following entry:-

Spent and gave the soldiers when a mob was expected	13s. 6d.

The cause of the trouble is not recorded, but in December 1739 the weather was particularly severe throughout the country; it was said that hens and ducks, even the cattle in stalls, died of cold, beer and wine froze in the cellars, and crows and other birds fell to the ground frozen in their flight. The following harvest was very late and the price of wheat nearly doubled. Cold and hunger between them raised the number of burials in London and elsewhere, and in Hemel Hempstead in the years around 1739-40 they increased on average from 62 to 81 per annum. Whatever may have inspired the fear of the mob, and the consequent preparations, there is no doubt that the times generally were hard, and there was trouble in many parts of the country.

The accounts contain many interesting entries relating to national events. During the Civil War money was spent on the purchase of powder, bullets and match, and in 1643 2s. 9d. was paid for "two dynners for the souldiers". The same year a man was hired for 1s. "to read a proclamation from the Lord Generall in several places", and 10s. was paid to Nathaniel Nashe, the constable, "for a payre of sheets and blanketts for the souldiers". But in 1645 the town was so burdened with the cost of accommodating a troop of soldiers commanded by a Captain Coleman, which had remained there for seven weeks, that a deputation was sent to Parliament. On May 21st the Committee of both Kingdoms directed Captain Coleman to join Sir Thomas Fairfax forthwith, and sent to the inhabitants a copy of the order against free quartering "to enable them to refuse free quarters".

When Charles II was restored his proclamation was celebrated with the spending of 5s. 8d. The birth of a son to James II on 10th June 1688 was suitably celebrated as is evidenced by the following entries:-

For beere and wood att the time the prince was borne	£2. 12.10.
Payd for beere and wine on Sunday with the Souldiers concerning the Prince	£3. 17. 8.

The proclamation and coronation of William and Mary in 1689 were dealt with on a more lavish scale and the details of the expenditure are interesting:-

Wine and beere and firewood for a bonfire	£7. 0. 0.
Beere for the souldiers	14. 0.
Gunpowder	13. 8.
Wine and beere for the Dutchmen and our souldiers	4. 0.

And money to buy them powder all night		2. 0.
Ringers and Drummers	£1.	15. 0.
Beere for the Dutchmen and souldiers		7. 0.
For beere and firewood when King and Queene were crowned	£1	19. 0.
Gunpowder att that fire		2. 0.
And to the Dutchmen to buy powder		10. 0.
	£13.	6. 8.

During the celebrations the Bailiff's staff was broken, and repaired at a cost of 6d. and the staff today shows how the repairs were carried out. The fire engine also needed repairs costing £3.10.0d. so the celebrations must have been spirited.

The proclamation of Queen Anne cost £11.1.0d. including "a vesselle of beere in the markett, and beere and tobacco and bread and cheese in the house for the souldiers". George I cost £8.17.0d., George II £7.2.3d., and George III £7.10.2d. with £4.8.0d. spent at his coronation.

The accounts also disclose official celebrations when events of national importance occurred. The first entry was in 1690, on a bonfire "when news came that Lymorick was taken". The declarations of war and the signings of peace were always acknowledged as were some of the important battles. In 1733 the bells were rung and the ringers suitably entertained when the news was received that Walpole had decided not to proceed with his unpopular bill to extend the excise. Earlier, in 1720-21, similar recognition was given when the Duke (presumably of Marlborough) "went through Hempstead".

All the entries relating to these different events are expressed in bald and brief language, but with a little imagination one can realise the sort of celebrations which our eighteenth century ancestors enjoyed.

NOTE ON SOURCES

This chapter relies heavily on the Bailiwick records, but for specific points the following sources should also be quoted:-

Report of the Royal Commission on Market Rights and Tolls, 1891, vol.iii, p. 102.

For the Bailiff's election 1755, see the Smeathman Papers in H.R.O. and Draft of counsel's opinion by F. Halsey, Feb. 20th, 1756, in B.A.

For the case of the stray pig, see 'The Times, July 28th, 1814.

Oxley v. Partridge and others 1677, P.R.O. E 134/29, Chas. II Mich. 20.

For the lease of market waste ground, see C.S.P.D. 1663-4, p. 56.

Kingston, 'Hertfordshire during the Great Civil War'.

For free quartering of troops, see C.S.P.D. 1644-45, p. 509-10.

CHAPTER 9

The Administration of the Elizabethan Poor Law – 1601–1834.

The Elizabethan Poor Law lasted for over 200 years, from 1601 to 1834, and played an important part in the life of the nation generally and of this locality in particular. It was administered by the local Vestry, through the Churchwardens and Overseers of the Poor, under the supervision of the Justices. The Vestry consisted of all the householders who cared to attend the meetings, although comparatively few ever did. Later, following the Acts of 1818 and 1819, the local people exercised an option and appointed a Select Vestry, which consisted of a limited number of members appointed annually by the Vestry; the members were the Vicar or the Curate, the churchwardens and the overseers and some 24 others. The overseers, appointed by the Justices on the nomination of the Vestry, were unpaid and were appointed for a year; they ceased to be responsible for the administration of the Poor Law when the unions were formed under the Poor Law Amendment Act of 1834, but they continued to be responsible for certain valuation work in connection with rates, and for the collection of the Poor Rate. The office was abolished by the Rating and Valuation Act of 1925.

The unit of adminstration under the Elizabethan Law was usually the parish, but where, as in Hemel Hempstead, separate hamlets had established their own identities, these were adopted for Poor Law purposes. Hence Hemel Hempstead, Bovingdon and Flaunden were treated as separate units although at that time they formed one parish. There were however some arguments about the division of the work, and about 1618 the judge at the Hertford Assizes had to settle the appointment of overseers for the three parts, and about the same time the Justices in Quarter Sessions had to deal with the apportionment of the local rates between the areas. The records are not very precise as to the points at issue.

As in other areas the overseers were somewhat reluctant to undertake their work under the Acts, and in 1619 Thomas Gould and Henry Baker, the overseers for the year, were presented at Quarter Sessions for not meeting monthly as they were required to do; they should have done so in the parish church at least once a month on Sunday afternoons after divine service.

The principal Act was passed in 1597, and re-enacted in the famous Poor Relief Act of 1601. This required the overseers with the churchwardens to provide for all the various classes of the destitute, whether able-bodied or impotent, children or aged, lame or blind, or otherwise without means to maintain themselves. There was no specific restriction to those belonging to the parish. There was no longer any reliance on voluntary contributions, but the money needed was to be found by a direct levy, weekly or otherwise, upon every occupier within the parish. The overseers were to provide assistance in money or kind, and for the fit, means to enable them to work.

Before proceeding with the operation of the Poor Law one should mention vagrants, treated as rogues or vagabonds. These had always been dealt with harshly; in the period with which we are concerned, should the parish constables discover such an individual in their district they hauled him (or her) before the local justice, who promptly ordered him to be whipped until his back was bloody and then sent back to his own parish, or the one from which he had come. There is a note in the records of 1682 of one interesting case, that of John Yorke. He was apprehended at Tring, duly whipped and ordered to be returned within two days to Bovingdon whence he had come; before going to Bovingdon he had been a vagabond but had settled down there. He had lived there for nearly a year without giving any trouble, attended church, and paid the rent for his accommodation. He had worked for several substantial men in the hamlet. But the Bovingdon people did not want him back and efforts were made by them to get rid of him, and turn him into a vagabond again. Two inhabitants, William Worster and William Smith, were indicted at Quarter Sessions for contempt of the order made by the Justices that Yorke should remain in Bovingdon. Yorke had some influential support and may have been allowed to stay, but the records are silent on this point.

In a work of this kind we can deal only briefly with a subject so wide as the poor law, but it is well to remember that the way in which the administration was carried out, and the spirit which animated the administrators, varied from time to time, usually reflecting locally the national approach to the problem. Sometimes the treatment was harsh and repressive, sometimes less so, but never generous. The poor were a necessary evil and had to be dealt with as economically as possible.

We can find but little about the work in the 17th century; surviving evidence is mostly to be found in the Quarter Sessions records and those of the Bailiwick. For the greater part of the 18th century and the first three or four decades of the 19th detailed records have survived and we can see clearly the way in which the service was carried out. Broadly the work can be dealt with under the eleven heads which follow.

(a) The Workhouse

We start with this because generally it played an important part in the administration. It was not until 1722 that statutory authority was given to establish these institutions but from a report in a book first published in the 1730's entitled "An Account of the Workhouses in Great Britain in the Year 1732" it is evident that some accommodation in a workhouse was provided by the authorities before the statute was passed. The following is an extract from the third edition, published in 1786:

"Hemel Hempstead. May 24, 1724.

In may 1720, the Parish-Officers here contracted with a Person skilled in setting up Workhouses, to take care of the Poor for 3 Years, at the Charge of the Parish, and to allow him or his Deputy for that Service, the Yearly Sum of 40 (£40) and a coat of 30s. value.

This Care of the Poor has so well succeeded, that whereas upwards of 730*L* (£730) per annum was expended before this Method was taken, the Expenses from *Easter* 1721 to *Easter* 1722, including the Steward's salary, was but 388 *L*. 8s. 8d. (£388. 8s. 8d.) and the Poor well kept cloathed, and maintained, as appears by a Certificate under the Hands of the Parish Officers, who have therefore agreed with the Steward to continue his care for a Year after the Expiration of their Contract with him."

But in 1723 the churchwardens and overseers purchased copyhold property in Saffron Lane (now Queensway) near the present site of the White Lion public house; this property is described in the Manor Court books as a cottage or tenement, with a malthouse, kiln house, strawhouse and a barn with two lean-to's and 3 acres of land. It was probably bought out of a loan of £150 borrowed at 5% interest, and was said to be adequate to accommodate up to 60 inmates. It was managed by a Committee of Governors in accordance with rules approved in 1731 by the Vestry which no doubt prescribed the discipline, the hours of rising and retiring, the work and the meals, the housekeeping, and attendance at prayers and at church. The penalties for disobedience included a period in the stocks, some time in a place of confinement, denial of food, confinement to the house, or such other punishment as might be ordered by a justice. These premises continued to be used as a workhouse, sometimes accommodating more than 60, until they were replaced by a larger building up the same road, built for the Union by the Poor Law Guardians about 1837.

The institution was in the care of a Master (sometimes also called a Governor); he was paid £25 a year, which no doubt also paid for the services of his wife. Goody Neale was also appointed to assist the Master at a salary of £5 a year, payable quarterly. In 1741, following the appointment of a new committee of Governors, one Richard Myles and his wife were appointed at a salary of £10 a year, with an allowance of 30s. "for necessary wearing apparel", and they were "to manage the poor at the directions of the Governors and the officers". This appointment was not satisfactory, and in less then twelve months the Myles were dismissed and it was decided to advertise for a contractor to take over the workhouse and "to contract for maintaining and employing the poor of the parish", and this arrangement duly started in 1742.

During the period 1732–1742 all sorts of people were admitted to the workhouse, some individually, others as members of a family. They took their household goods with them, and were allowed to take them away when they left, or, if they died before leaving the house, the goods were handed over to relatives. The parish paid for horsehire to carry the people and their goods into the house. Whilst in the house thay were expected to work if they were fit enough to do so. They were employed on a number of different tasks; some assisted in the house, and others on such jobs as straw-plait making, making tile-pins, weaving, making sacks, gathering walnuts and leaves, gleaning wheat and stonepicking. In 1735 56,000 walnuts were gathered and sold for 16s. 11d. Some were let out to work for local farmers, and in the early years were hired out for 6d. a day, but in 1740 it was decided that such of the inmates as could be so employed should be sent round the district to be employed by whosoever was willing to take them on at the rate of 8d. a day, at the discretion of the overseers. Boys were set to keeping sheep and one lad earned 11s. Until 1741 the poor were allowed 2d. in the 1s. of monies received for their work, but with a change of policy this allowance was stopped and if anyone refused to work he was "to go without his diet".

This diet was not a generous one as may be gathered from the following "Bill of Affair" issued in 1741:–

	Breakfast	*Dinner*	*Supper*
Sunday	Milk Pottage or some spoon meal	Meat & Plaine pudding	Bread & cheese
Monday	Broth	Thick milk & Bread & cheese	"
Tuesday	Milk Pottage	Rice Milk & Bread & cheese	"
Wednesday	"	Hogsheads, liver & mudgeon or Beefe	"
Thursday	Pease pottage or broth	Hasty pudding	"
Friday	Milk Pottage	Bullocks cheekes	"
Saturday	Broth	Thick milk & bread & cheese	"

Hasty pudding was made from flour stirred in boiling milk or water to the consistency of a thick batter. In the north of England it was made of oatmeal, water and salt, about 13 oz of meal to a quart of water, sufficient for a meal for two labourers, at a cost not exceeding 1d. per meal.

About the same time the Vestry ordered the Overseers to buy for use in the workhouse coarse flour called Rand Dan, unless they were able to buy wheat which, when they had ground it, was cheaper than the coarse flour. It is true that on occasion more appetising foods were purchased, but whether for the sick, the staff, or the fit occupants is not disclosed. In the early years of the workhouse some attempt at costing the maintenance of the poor was made, and the average amount for food and other necessaries worked out at about 1s. 4d. per person per week.

The cost of some of the items of food can be gathered from the accounts as follows:—

Mutton 3d. lb, beef 2d. lb, bullocks cheeks 6d each, sheeps heads 4d each hogs pluck 10d. & oatmeal 1s per half peck.

In 'An Account of the Workhouses in Great Britain in the Year 1732". there appears "A Prayer proper to be used in Workhouses". This was used in many institutions and probably Hemel Hempstead's was one of them.

"O Gracious Lord God, who has opened thy Hand, and satisfied us with Good; who has cloathed the Naked, filled the Hungry, and gathered the Poor, who were scattered and solitary, into one House; affect our Hearts with a deep sense of this thy Goodness towards us; and mercifully grant, that always being excercised in good Works, and not cherishing Sin with the Bread of Idleness, we may use thy Liberality to thy Glory, and walk worthy of so great Benefits, in Sobriety of Life, in Obedience to our Governors, in Brotherly Love one towards another, and a constant Obedience to thy Word.

Pour down thy Blessing on this whole Parish; and grant, we beseech Thee, that as our necessities are daily relieved out of their Abundance, so their Wants may be always supplied out of thy Riches; for Jesus Christ his Sake, our Blessed Lord and Saviour. Amen."

The number of inmates naturally varied from time to time. In the early years there were 38 to 43, but the numbers probably increased in later years when, it must be remembered, the population of the town was increasing.

Some attention was given to the education of the children and Goody Barton was paid 4d. a week to teach them some elements of reading and writing. At Christmas time the inmates were allowed something extra and amounts of about 7s.6d. were specially voted.

In 1741 a spirit of economy and reform was abroad; a new committee was appointed, the credentials of non-parishioners were checked and those without certificates were removed to their place of settlement, and the inmates in the workhouses were reviewed, and some were made to leave. It was decided to discontinue out-relief, except in cases of sickness or emergency, and to require all those seeking assistance to enter the workhouse. Accordingly some 15 persons were required to enter the workhouse and to have no other relief; 9 were widows, 2 were old men, 1 child, 1 single woman, a man and wife.

Lastly steps were taken to employ a contractor to undertake the care and employment of the poor, and the first contractor was John Hunt of Henley-upon-Thames, who had already contracted to look after the poor in that parish. The terms of the contract are not known. This arrangement continued with different contractors until 1796, with a few breaks between the terms of the different contractors. The annual payments varied from £550 to £560, and the arrangements were not always successful. Some contractors apparently did not make the profit they expected and either went bankrupt or were given supplementary payments. The arrangement made was said to be "by the lump" i.e. the contractor agreed to maintain all the poor, both in and out of the workhouse. As the paupers could be maintained more cheaply in the workhouse and usually set to work, the incentive to take them in was very strong. The lot of the paupers committed to their care can be imagined.

In 1796 a somewhat different method was employed. The contractor was Thomas Fellows and he was paid at the rate of 2s.6d. per inmate per week, with an addition of 3d. a day for nursing. During his time the workhouse was often overfull and the inmates numbered up to 74, although the capacity of the house was said to be 60. This overcrowding did not last and after about four months the numbers dropped to around 50, whether because of improved conditions of employment or because of Fellows' treatment is not disclosed. Fellows continued for about a year and then the old system was again adopted and the new contractor was paid at the rate of £720 per annum, but after May 1798 the contract method was finally abandoned and the management of the house was taken over by the Overseers.

Naturally, as the contractors were required to undertake the entire work of looking after those unfortunates who had to seek assistance we can find no details as to how they were cared for. The payments to the contractors represented a very large proportion of the total expenditure – usually two-thirds or more – and little was paid out by way of relief. There were other items of expenditure which will be dealt with in the sections of this chapter which follow.

Any wages earned by the paupers automatically went into the pockets of the contractors. It may be assumed that the inmates were fed and accommodated as cheaply as possible and worked as hard as they were able at whatever work could be found for them. It is interesting to note that during the period for which Fellows was the contractor, the Overseers employed a schoolmaster to teach the children; his salary was 1s.0d. a week, later increased to 1s.3d.
The contractors before Fellows must have given a similar service and the Overseers attended at the workhouse from time to time to hear the children read, and to give money to them by way of reward.

After 1798 the general policy changed, in some measure in response to a change in the national approach to the problem, signified in new legislation. Hitherto the emphasis had been on compelling the poor seeking relief to enter the workhouse, but now the tendency was to grant out-relief in suitable cases. The demand on the accommodation in the workhouse was lessened and this may have been the reason why contractors were no longer employed and the institution was run by direct labour. No doubt the circumstances arising from the war with France had some effect. During the period of the war there was little of special interest in connection with the workhouse. In 1799 30 spinning wheels were purchased and from time to time large quantities of wool and hemp were bought. Quantities of sugar were bought each year for the making of cowslip, currant and other wines. The inmates were still employed also on such tasks as straw-plaiting.

After the war the parish was faced with a serious unemployment problem, and the way in which it was tackled is dealt with later. Meanwhile the workhouse remained in use, managed by a Governor and his wife, until the new and larger workhouse required by the Act of 1834 was provided by the Guardians of the Poor to serve what was called the Union, i.e. a combination of the parishes of Hemel Hempstead, Bovingdon, Flaunden, Great Gaddesden and Kings Langley. But in 1832 the authorities had been in some difficulties. First the condition of the workhouse needed attention, and plans and specifications for repairs and alterations were considered, including new building to increase the accommodation for a total of 100 paupers. Their resources were limited and so they could not undertake too big a scheme; but one was put in hand, details of which are not available, but which cost approximately £200. They paid £20 on account from revenue and borrowed £187. 10s. 0d. with which to pay the balance.

The other difficulty was the question of a Master. They decided to advertise in one daily and two county newspapers for a man and wife to reside in the workhouse, the woman to assist in the management of the house and the man to be Governor, Assistant Overseer, Vestry Clerk and to collect the rates. He was to give security for £500. No satisfactory replies could have been received and so the existing Governor and his wife continued in office, but now he was also to act as Assistant Overseer and collect the rates, for which he was to be paid an additional £10 a year. A separate Vestry Clerk was appointed at £25 a year. Then the old building was sold in 1838 and the proceeds used to repay such loans as were outstanding. The parish authorities asked the lord or the manor, Thomas Halsey, if he would enfranchise the property, so that it would have a freehold title and so fetch more money. He regretted that he could not do so, but this decision was reversed by his successor in 1839. The goods in the old house were duly valued at £171. 15s. 9d. and transferred to the new building.

(b) The Parish Houses.

In addition to the workhouse, the parish owned some cottages in which the authorities housed some of their poor. There was the one purchased by the Vestry in 1675 and another bought by the Bailiwick about 1694; two others were acquired by the parish in the 1730's; three were at Bury Mill End and one at Kemps.

From time to time the Vestry proposed to sell these properties, and also the land belonging to the workhouse, but the only property disposed of was the cottage at Kemps. Full use was made of this accommodation and more than one family was housed in a cottage at the same time; e.g. in 1733 it was decided that James Downer, his wife and family were to live with Thomas Brandby, who occupied one of the cottages at Bury Mill End. There was also some interchange of accommodation, presumably to secure the best use of the property available, as in 1735, when the wife and four children of one Babbons were to be admitted to the workhouse, and John Parker, his wife and all their children were to go into the cottage occupied by the Babbons when they vacated it. Later John Parker went into hospital, accompanied by his wife, and their children were admitted into the workhouse.

The Parish was also interested in six cottages mentioned in the Poor Rate Book of 1832 as being on or near Haybarns. At least three of these belonged to the Boxmoor Trustees, for in 1812 the overseers paid three years' ground rent for them to the Trustees, and these payments were continued thereafter. In the rate book the parish was shown as the owner of all six. In 1831 and 1832 some £50 was spent on repairs of some cottages, but which these were is not indicated. It is to be noted that they had thatched roofs.

In 1838 the cottages at Bury Mill End were sold, but no mention was made of the disposal of the cottages on Boxmoor. They (or at least three of them) may have reverted to the ground landlord, the Boxmoor Trustees, or they may all have been demolished when the squatters' cottages on Boxmoor were demolished in 1837. (see page 218.)

(c) Out Relief

It is clear that throughout the period from 1722 until 1796 or 1798 the policy was to give relief in the workhouse wherever possible. In the years before contractors were employed there were many entries relating to grants of clothing, but whether to inmates in the house or persons outside is not shown. It is significant that most of the individuals concerned were either widows or children, and often the latter were described as living with someone, a person to whom they were most likely apprenticed. Other grants in kind include fuel and food and occasionally rent.

Money payments were comparatively few and almost ceased during the contracted years. The amounts were small, generally running from 1s. 6d. to 3s. 6d. a week. Often the grant was to someone sick, maybe sick unto death, as so often the final entry was in respect of the burial of the grantee. The burial grants follow a regular pattern, 7s. for the coffin, 2s. 10d. for the shroud, 2s. to the parish clerk and a varying amount for bread, cheese and beer. Considerable quantities of beer were consumed on these occasions, anything from 10 to 30 quarts.

The practice of boarding out people was adopted, but discontinued for adults when the contractors were engaged. Usually the persons assisted were accommodated with widows and the payments varied with the size of the family. In the case of children the practice was not wholly discontinued and the rate of payment was 9d. or 1s. per week, with supplementary assistance by way of clothing. It was not a satisfactory way of dealing with the children; they were not cared for and the food they should have had was often eaten by the foster parents.

There were several items of interest. Loans were made occasionally and some were repaid. In 1737 £2. 10s. 0d was paid to take John Moor out of prison, and he was sent a further 10s. 6d to enable him to pay his fees. In 1788 £2. 2s. 0d. was "paid to the Poor People at different Times in the hard weather". In November 1788 there was a great frost which lasted till January. There was some relief of the wandering poor, especially of pregnant women, and it is evident that whenever possible they were persuaded to leave the parish quickly, so that their offspring would not be born in it and so become a charge upon it. In 1810 3s. 6d. was paid for "Daniel Young's clothes as was in Pawn". An unusual allowance in kind was a barrel of good beer, brewed by Mr. Goodwin the brewer, paid for by the parish, and given to Sarah Sage in 1733.

After the change of policy at the end of the 18th century the amount paid out in outdoor relief increased considerably. For the first year or two after 1795 the policy varied, first there was considerable out relief, then a contractor was employed and the payments fell. But from 1800 the payments of out-relief continued each year. The figures show the increased burden which the Napoleonic war and the Speenhamland system of relief laid on the Poor Rate.

It is interesting to note that casual relief was given to papermakers and their families as early as the 1760's and that some of these were immigrants whose place of settlement was in another parish, and to which they were returned. Unfortunately the records give no details.

(d) Care of the Sick

From time to time the parish was visited by epidemics. In the sixteenth and seventeenth centuries there were several outbreaks of plague; there was one in 1594, another more serious in 1625, another in 1637 and, of course, one in 1666. Details of these are mainly gleaned from the parish registers and in 1594 the outbreak was such that the incumbent was not able to record at the time all those who died from the disease. (See page 49.) The visitation in 1625 was part of a wider outbreak which began in London in the previous year.

Another serious disease was smallpox. The Poor Law records reveal what a great scourge it was and there were constant references to it throughout the eighteenth century. Sometimes individual families were mentioned, at other times the incidence was much greater. On occasion the first reference to sickness was in a soldier or a traveller, indicating how the disease may have come to the parish. There were such entries as:—

1739	To the soldier having the smallpox	6. 0.
	Widow Bardy for Lodging the soldier	6. 0.
	Gave to her on the Troopers account	2. 6.
1769	Exs. with James Mansell being illegally Brot. with the smallpox from the Parish of St. Stephens and burying	2. 9. 6¾.
	Exs. with a Travelling woman & child with the smallpox	2. 14. 0.

In 1781 there was a very serious outbreak; it affected so many that the isolation accommodation was full and it was necessary to provide nursing in the home; one overseer paid out money for supporting and nursing 37 people in different parts of the parish and the other paid for about another 20 people. The contractor for the workhouse was paid 3s. for each of 51 people. presumably contacts, for maintaining them during a period of isolation. Several coffins were purchased. In the years 1781 and 1782 the burial rate was unusually high due to this epidemic.

Cases of smallpox were treated in a Pest House, maintained by the Parish and situated in the Wood Land End area. A nurse was employed and paid 2s. 6d. or 3s. a week.

In 1833 the Vestry considered the question of vaccination, and decided as follows:—

(1) General vaccination was not at present required;

(2) The overseers were authorised at their discretion to order the Medical Officer to vaccinate the children in a neighbourhood where smallpox exists, and

(3) Steps to be taken to publish the day on which children may be vaccinated at the Infirmary.

Venereal disease also concerned the authorities. References are made especially during and after the Napoleonic Wars when the disease was spread by soldiers returning from service overseas.

The parish medical service dealt with many other ailments, the following are a few of the entries:—

1724	Drawing Goody Trustram's tooth	6d.
1766	Curing Sara Walker of the Itch	2. 3.
1770	Gave Spufford towards Curing his Eyes	1. 0.
1773	Gave James How to go to the salt waters	1. 11. 8.
1775	Dr. Hawkins for curing Austee's Boy's leg and for a steel machine	6. 16. 6.
1806	Curing Monk's child's head	10. 0.
1809	A Truss for Hall's wife	2. 2. 0.
1811	For the soldier that was Bit by a mad dog	2. 2. 0.

Economy was practised in authorising medical attention: for example in 1734 Dr. Wigg was to give something to Henry Babbon for 3s. and Dr. Smyth was to attend to Michael Cobb's wife "as far as 12s."

Expenses were incurred for cases of mental illness, and the treatment varied. In 1767 two men were each paid 14s. a week for several weeks to look after George Binn who was said to be mad. The total cost was £10. Thomas Borrass, who was said to be "disordered in his senses" only cost 13s. 9d. Other cases were sent to Bedlam (Bethlehem Hospital) and what was involved may be gathered from the following entries in 1769 for Ann Lea –

Expenses before she went	1. 18. 4.
Certificate signing & witness	5. 10.
Horse & cart & attending her to London	1. 2. 8.
Expenses with a horse & man to carry the certificate	5. 6.
Paid for her admission	3. 1. 6.
Later Paid for fetching her out	1. 10. 0.

Payments to the Hospital for maintenance was at the rate of 10s. a week. Patients were also sent to other hospitals at the cost of the parish. Midwifery was another service which involved the parish in expense, and the costs for the different cases varied from a few shillings to several pounds. The basis on which the service was paid was not shown in the records until the 1820's Mrs. Mary Troup was appointed as midwife, to deal with all cases within four miles of the parish church, to be paid 7s. for each case, provided that in cases of difficulty or danger she called in a regular surgeon at her own expense. She was required to provide a Bond of £10 for the proper performance of her duties. Later the fee was increased to 7s. 6d. a case, with a guaranteed income of £7. 10s. 0d for the year.

An earlier midwife was Ann Chance who was employed from 1760. Later she fell on bad times for in 1782 (by which time she was a widow) she was indicted on a charge of stealing from Thomas Trott two pairs of copper scales valued at 3s. With her was charged Richard Davies, a razor grinder, for receiving the articles. Ann was sentenced to be privately whipped and imprisoned for three months, while Davies was publicly whipped twice, and sent to prison for six months. In 1786 the parish spent 6d on spectacles for her. She was buried on 14th August 1790, age 68, a pauper.

Details of the expenses incurred in connection with a difficult case may be quoted. They were incurred in 1726 in respect of Bourne's wife, as under:

Paid Mr. Handley for laying Bourne's wife	3.	3.	0.
Paid John Walker going to St. Albans to fetch the man to Bourne's wife and for a horse to carry him home.		3.	6.
Cinnamon water			4.
Sack (2 lots)		1.	6¾
Mrs. Thomas (midwife)		5.	0.
Paid Thos. Rickson 12 quarts of beer at her lying in		3.	0.
Paid John Harding for Beer when she was in labour		1.	0.
Aniseed water			2.
Sack & beer		1.	0.
Paid Hannah Baile for nursing			6.
Eggs			1.
Relief		11.	0.
Paid Thomas Clark for grave for Bourne's child		1.	0.
	£4.	11.	1¾

So that the poor could have some medical attention when needed, the parish employed such medical practitioners as were available. In the first three quarters of the 18th century the services were paid for as rendered, but from about 1775 a salary was paid. Two surgeons were employed alternately for a period of six months, at a salary of £9 per half year, subsequently increased to £10. Then the arrangement was made an annual one, still employing the doctors alternately, at £20 per annum, later raised to £25. For the last 25 to 30 years of the old Poor Law the work was offered to tender, and usually the lowest tender was accepted. The following were the terms of an agreement with Thomas Eagles Prentice dated 2nd June 1824:—

> (he) agrees to execute the office of parish surgeon apothecary, and man midwife — £60 per annum paid quarterly and truly to attend the poor residing in the parish or not exceeding 10 miles therefrom in all cases, including surgery & midwifery, and to furnish medicines — on the production of an order from the Overseers or from the Chairman of the Select Vestry.

In 1826 the duties were defined in more detail; he was to visit the poor house at least once a week and examine the state of the infirm paupers, and where he had an order to visit a sick pauper who was not in the poor house he could also attend any other member of the same family without a further order.

The tenders were usually about £60 per annum, and when the amounts were the same some preference was shown for one particular doctor. In 1824 Dr. Prentice asked for £60 including "Venerials", and Dr. Cherrington £50 excluding "Venerials", and Dr. Prentice's tender was accepted.

(e) Apprentices

One item of relief was the apprenticing of poor children and this was done either voluntarily or by compulsion. Wherever possible the children were bound to masters in other parishes, so that they could secure a place of settlement there and no longer be a possible charge on this parish. A premium was paid to the master, and the child was usually sent with some new clothing.

An example of compulsory apprenticing was given in 1737 when six children were assigned to several persons, and if any of these persons refused to receive the apprentice the officers were "to proceed as the Law directs". This meant that the defaulter could be fined £10. On each child 40s. was to be spent on clothing although sometimes the money was paid to the master as a premium. During the first 40 years of the 18th Century a premium of 40s. seems to have been a standard amount; for one child a sum of £5 was paid, but towards that this widowed mother contributed £2. 2s. 0d. In the long period during which contractors were employed to manage the poor there were very few entries relating to the apprenticing of the children, implying that whatever was done was arranged by the contractor. The odd cases recorded suggest that the children concerned fell into a special category; the premium was usually £10 and some further expenditure on clothing for the child. The Bailiff helped towards this work by paying out of his annual surplus the expenses of putting one child or more out as apprentice.

(f) Bastardy

One serious problem confronting the Poor Law officers was that of the illegitimate child. One born in a parish acquired a place of settlement there and so could become a charge on the parish. Every effort was made to avoid this liability, either by persuading the putative father to marry the woman, or, in the case of a pregnant woman who was a non-parishioner, by passing her on to the next parish, with such temporary relief as would both encourage her to leave and to sustain her until she was likely to get further assistance. If the father could not or would not marry the woman then he was required to make a suitable contribution to the parish funds. In the

16th and 17th centuries some odd courses were adopted. In the Parish Register the following entry dated 19th December 1573 appears:—

> Daniell the son of Thomas Billingham late of Battersey in Surrey and Marie Patewin of Lambeth, in Surrey . . . did undertake before the congregacion in Hemelhemstead for the bringing up of the child not begotten in matrimonie in the matter and fear of the Lorde, but also at all tymes hereafter to discharge the parishe of it.
>
> Witness hereof
> William Horne Vicar
> Thomas Howe & John Hog Churchwardens
> & also Richard Mason.

One feels that the second part of the undertaking was more important than the first. The Patewins were an old local family. William Patewin is recorded in the 1523 Survey as the occupier of a house and land in Churchend, and other lands elsewhere, totalling some 11½ acres. The house in Churchend was the Crowne, later called the Rose & Crown. On his death about 1545 the family was scattered; his eldest son Richard was a Yeoman in Kent, and his daughter Mary in what was then Surrey.

Quarter Sessions records also contain references to cases from Hemel Hempstead. In 1635 William More was held to be the father of the child of Abigail Goodwyn and ordered to pay to the churchwardens and overseers 2s. per week for the maintenance of the child, whilst the mother was committed to the House of Correction for a year. In 1664 Mary Myles was ordered to deliver her child to Edward Seagrave the reputed father, who had previously been ordered to pay 2s. a week for its maintenance. Now, it was said, he had given sufficient security for indemnifying the parish, and so he was to provide for and maintain the infant by having it in his own care.

Another way in which the parish was idemnified is illustrated by the case of Thomas Kentish, a farmer of High Street Green. In the 1680's he was accused of being the father of the child of Elizabeth Coleman, the daughter of William Coleman, an innholder. He disputed the accusation and the matter went to Quarter Sessions when certain justices were appointed to look into it. He must have been found guilty because, according to the Manor Court books, in 1688 he conveyed to the churchwardens and overseers three closes of 14 acres, abutting on High Street Green, to be held by them until the child was old enough to maintain itself, and so the parish was relieved of any chance that it would become chargeable for the maintenance of the child.

But the more detailed records of the eighteenth and early nineteenth centuries give a clear picture of the practice in dealing with this problem.

Various entries show the payment of relief to women in this condition thus

1761	Expenses sending a woman out of the parish	1. 6.
	Relieved a woman with child and sent her away	4. 6.
1771	Relieved a Travelling woman big with child	10. 6.

An entry showing it was too late to try to send her away –

1773	Paid by the Lying In of a Traveller, nurse and midwife & clothing the child	1. 6. 8.

Where the woman belonged to the parish every effort was made to identify the father and trace his whereabouts. The woman was hauled before a justice and made to swear who was the father and that was all the evidence needed. The temptation to implicate the wrong man must have been great in many instances. Having ascertained who he was, the parish officers tried either to marry the couple or to secure payment from the man. This payment could be either a weekly payment or a lump sum, the latter being preferred. This preference was confirmed by a special committee which reported in 1820, on the grounds that the Parish usually suffers

> "from Sessions Orders, either from the escape of the reputed father, his insolvency, or the expense of compelling him to comply with the terms of the Order".

The lump sums were usually £10 or so, but later they were increased to £25 or £30 in some instances, and as much as £40 in others.

Where marriage was possible, and assistance necessary, the parish paid all expenses, including the purchase of a ring, and sometimes grants were made to the man to encourage him to matrimony. If time permitted, the wedding was celebrated after the publication of the banns, but in urgent cases a special licence was obtained, the fee being paid by the parish.

Often the man concerned did not belong to the parish, or had left it; then the Overseers would try to trace him, travelling often considerable distances by coach or on horseback. Having secured their man, they brought him back and committed him to the House of Correction or Hertford gaol until he gave satisfaction. One example may be quoted. In 1789 the Parish Clerk was sent to Sevenoaks to enquire about George Childs, and his expenses were 10s. 10d. His enquiries must have been successful because the Overseers themselves then went to Sevenoaks, but their expenses were £3. 5s. 10d.; they too were successful and the parish received the sum of £13. 13s. 0d. from a man named Childs in respect of an illegitimate child, charged on the parish.

A few excerpts from the accounts may well illustrate what happened:—

1763	Paid Mr. Noyes (a Justice) for examining and Swearing Elizabeth Stirling and Mary Studman to the fathers of their Barstar children and for two warrants to take up Gates and Davis	8. 6.
1776	Expenses in apprehending Obediah Latchford, examination, Licence and marrying.	4. 12. 4.
	Expenses apprehending John Hall, marrying and swearing him to his parish.	4. 7. 11.

It should be added that when the mother was unable to maintain the child, if it was not left in the workhouse, she was usually allowed 1s. a week for its maintenance by the parish.

(g) Settlement and Removal

Reference has already been made to the principle of settlement. Before 1662 this principle did not operate, except for vagrants, and the charge for relief, of whatever kind, fell on the parish in which the recipient then lived. In 1662 an Act was passed which empowered the Justices, on the complaint of the churchwardens and overseers, to return a person to his place of former residence if in the opinion of the overseers he might at some future date need relief from the parish. This did not apply to anyone occupying premises worth £10 or more by the year. There were special provisions for the issue of certificates to persons temporarily staying in a place to assist in the harvest, and later if a man had a certificate from his own parish to say that it would be responsible for any relief given then he was not liable to be removed. This law was strictly applied and the parish officers went to great lengths to carry it out. The accounts contain many items, both of receipts and of payment in respect of it. Here again a few examples may suffice to show what was done.

In 1691, by order of two justices of the County of Lancaster, Joan Knight, widow, and William Graystock, a boy under the age of seven, were sent from Preston to Hemel Hempstead. Later it was found that the woman's place of settlement was at Two Waters, but in the meantime she had died. The boy had been born in Preston and so never had a settlement here, and as he had become chargeable to the parish, he was sent back to Preston.

In 1738 the sum of £7. 1s. 9d. was spent by the overseers going to Nottingham with the shoemaker who married Butcher's daughter, and £3. 3s. 0d. was paid to Robert Eden "for carrying them away". In 1759 the overseers were busy with several cases; they returned John Harbridge, his wife and child to Glen in Staffordshire, a soldier's child to Bilston in the same county , and Mary Smith to Buckland in Berkshire; the expenses of removal were £11. 3s. 4d. and those of the overseers for horseshire and maintenance were £3.

The case of the White family was more expensive. The family consisted of Edward White, his wife Charlotte and his daughter Isabella. In 1773 they were removed to High Wycombe at a cost of £1. 15s. 6d. High Wycombe appealed to Quarter Sessions, won its appeal and so the Whites were returned to Hemel Hempstead. Undismayed, the overseers, determined to lose the Whites, proceeded further as is shown by the following entries:—

For liquor trying to take White		1.	2.
Taking White and keeping him all night and two			
men and attending to Watford and other expenses	1.	2.	4.
Hemel Hempstead expenses to Watford		5.	6.
For a pair of handcuffs		1.	6.
Mr Nichols for advice		6.	8.
For examination and commitment of Edward White		2.	0.
Expenses at Hertford with Edward White and White			
Horse and cart and expenses with Edward White	3.	10.	0.
to Speenhamland in Berkshire.	7.	14.	6.
	13.	3.	8.

In spite of certain of these items Edward White may well have been a respectable artisan.

Another example shows what travelling was involved in cases of this kind. In 1787 the overseers had to go to Northampton and travelled thus:—

A post chaise to Dunstable		13.	0.
By the coach to Northampton — two places		18.	0.
Gave the coachman		3.	0.
By the Mail Coach three places from			
Northampton to Redbourn	1.	19.	0.
Gave the coachman		3.	0.
	3.	16.	0.
Other expenses	5.	17.	5.
	9.	13.	5.

The journeys took three days and they apparently walked from Redbourn to Hemel Hempstead.

It should be remembered that until 1795 the cost of returning a person to his parish of settlement fell on that parish and not on the one returning him.

(h) Finance

Detailed figures of Poor Law finance are not available before 1758, but there are indications that in the early part of the eighteenth century the authorities were becoming alarmed at the rising costs, and were glad to take advantage of the statute authorising the establishment of a workhouse. It was said that this reduced the expenditure considerably, probably by half, which meant a reduction from about £700–£800 a year to something like £400; certainly in 1724–25 it was about £375. By 1739 it had increased again to nearly £500. Soon after this in 1742 it was decided to contract for the maintenance of the poor, but at that point there is a break in the accounts. and so we cannot ascertain what financial benefit accrued. The accounts available start again in 1758 by which time the expenditure was £748. After that it fell to something like £600 a year. The expenditure remained around this level until 1768; then it reached over £800 and for the next 20 years the average annual expenditure was about £850. From 1788 there was a steady increase; 1788–1797 the average was £960, 1798–1807 £1,580 and 1808–1815 £2,295. There the records end until 1828 when for the next seven years until the new Poor Law Act of 1834 began to operate the average was £2,489. The new system soon brought about a decrease, reducing the annual expenditure to about £1,500.

The method of raising money by rates was simple. The rate was always 1s. in the pound and a new one was authorised by the Select Vestry whenever the overseers reported they were running short of money; consequently several rates were levied in the year, sometimes five or six. Collection was not easy; the amounts unpaid were often 10% or more of the sum collectable, even after excluding any charge on poor persons, or on non-parishioners. The assessments were proposed by the overseers but approved by the Select Vestry. In 1835 some attempt was made to revise the Rate Books and a special committee to undertake the work was suggested; but agreement could not be reached as to its composition. The suggested personnel were four farmers, four tradesmen, the Overseers and the Chairman of the Vestry, with the later addition of one gentleman, but apparently some of the persons suggested were not willing to carry out a task so unpleasant and unpopular. Only parishioners were rated and those who were poor were not charged.

(i) The Years of Crisis

It is unfortunate that the records for the years from 1815 to 1828 are lost because it was during that period that expenditure reached its peak, There was a considerable increase in the population of the town about this time and a change in occupations followed, as is shown by the following particulars extracted from census returns:—

		Families			
	Population	*Chiefly Agriculture*	*Trade Manufacturing etc.*	*Others*	*Total*
1811	3240	303	270	87	660
1821	3962	230	528	88	846
1831	4759	268	323	390	981

To what extent and in what manner these changes affected the expenditure under the Poor Law is not known.

The assistance granted to the poor was of four kinds:—

(a) regular payments each week, termed pensions, paid to the sick, the infirm and the unemployed;

(b) payments supplementing wages where they fell below a certain standard, according to the size of the family;

(c) casual payments, e.g. during a short period of sickness; and

(d) maintenance in the workhouse.

At one time the roundsmen system had operated whereby the unemployed were sent round the parish to be employed more or less casually by farmers and others, who paid the parish for the services rendered and the parish maintained the labourers concerned. After the Napoleonic wars this practice was discontinued, partly because many of the parishioners objected to it, and partly because the justices had ruled against it and had threatened to take some action if it were resumed.

It was estimated that in full employment a labourer's wage would average 10s. a week. This could be supplemented by the family's earnings, especially in straw plaiting, where a wife could earn as much as 2s. 6d. a week, and four children could earn an aggregate of 3s. 9d. These figures were given officially in 1832, and the amounts for earlier times could have been less. In the same return the vicar explained that the Select Vestry had adopted a scale of relief considerably lower than that prescribed by the magistrates. He added that "character is always considered and relief refused to those who have wilfully quitted any employment by which they might have maintained themselves". The inevitable conclusion is that the relief was no more than was necessary to save the recipients from starvation.

Some ideas may be gleaned from some rough notes made in 1819. William Moulder, with 5 children, unwell with a bad leg, was allowed 12s. a week, Sarah Cox, aged 23, described as "very unwell", received 3s. a week and Widow Hall with four children got 5s. 6d. a week. Single men invariably received 2s. a week. Robert Grout, "known to be a man of good character", whose wife was very unwell was granted 3s. 6d.

Special cases were dealt with specially. When Robert Green was unwell his sister applied for relief on his behalf; he was granted 3s. and his sister was told that if the application was repeated he would be expected to repay the money paid to him. When William Fawcett was ill in Wigginton, he was granted 12s. a week, and as his wife had undertaken to find the assistance required, an addition of 3s. was made. On the other hand, "owing to the bad character which Joseph Fensom's family bear and the manner in which they conduct themselves", the allowance of 2s. a week was cancelled as the Vestry was of opinion that their earnings were sufficient without any assistance.

One other note mentions Widow Francis, living in Lumworths Yard (off the High Street) who was ill and for whom Dr. Prentice prescribed "a nourishing and cordial diet".

One of the questions asked of the Vicar in the Return already mentioned was:—

Do labourers in your neighbourhood change their services more frequently than formerly and how do you account for that circumstance? And his somewhat irrelevant reply was —

"Living almost entirely at low public houses they become demoralised, addicted to gaming, drinking and debauchery; brutal in their habits and manners; insolent and unruly".

Something of the same mind must havepersuadedthe Select Vestry, when it met in the Town Hall on Saturday, 11th September 1819, to pass, unanimously the following resolution:—

First. That the Publicans be cautioned against suffering the Labourers to tipple in their Houses, or permitting any of them to remain there after 10 o'clock at night, or draw any beer or liquor after that hour, and particularly that they do not on any account draw Beer or Liquor for any Paupers receiving relief from the Parish, a list of whose names will be sent to them from time to time.

Second. And further that if any breach of the foregoing matters is made known to the Select Vestry, such House or Houses will be reported to the Magistrates.

Third. That it be recommended to the Minister of the Parish that he should require the Publicans to attend for his signature to their Certificates at the Meeting of the Select Vestry immediately preceeding the Licensing day.

The Constables were told of this resolution and asked to enforce it, and to report to the Select Vestry every Wednesday on the success or otherwise of their efforts. On the first Wednesday following they made no report but on the second one they reported that whilst William Dean behaved in a very refractory manner the Public Houses were orderly and closed at the proper hour.

In 1820 a special committee was appointed to examine the cost of relief and to recommend proposals for dealing with the problem. From their report one learns that at the most some 80 families were wholly dependent on the Poor Law as a result of unemployment; this represents something like 10% of the population, and does not include those cases for which casual relief was required. The Committee favoured a return to the Contractor system, but realised that it was not practical at the time. They also rejected the Roundsmen's system quoting the objections already mentioned above. They therefore recommended —

(1) the provision of allotments of 20 poles each for each family to enable it to be more self-supporting;

(2) to provide work for 24 men on the roads, improving Boxmoor and working on land already rented from Boxmoor Trustees;
(3) to employ 12 men by purchasing 12 more flax machines and adding them to the machines already installed in the workhouse;
(4) to dig by the spade land occupied by farmers at a charge per acre equal to the cost of two ploughings. (This suggestion had been adopted elsewhere in the country.)

These recommendations appear to have been adopted in the main and continued for a time. The cultivation of part of Boxmoor was discontinued not later than 1828, when the lease was cancelled with the agreement of the Trustees.

Perhaps before we close this section on the old Elizabethan Poor Law we should note what else the Rev. Jacob H. Brooke Mountain, Vicar of Hemel Hempstead & Justice of the Peace told the Commissioners in the replies he gave in answer to their questionnaire.

He said that generally the farms were small; that very few labourers owned their own cottages the owners were chiefly speculating builders; that the families could subsist on the man's earnings if he took home the whole sum, which he rarely did, and that then their diet might be wheaten bread, potatoes, bacon, salt butter, tea, sugar, and a little beer, but, he added, there could be no saving. The final question asked for information about causes and consequences of Agricultural Riots and Burnings in 1830 and 1831 and his answer was:—

"This neighbourhood afforded fewer opportunities for observation than most others. It is certain that there were agitators and that inflammatory publications were circulated amongst them."

(j) House of Correction

One cannot leave the old Poor Law without reference to the House of Correction. This was the first Institution connected with the Poor Law of which mention is made in the local records. Originally such an establishment was a place to which vagrants, miscreants and other unfortunates (not children or the infirm) could be sent to be usefully employed and perhaps reformed, and so the authorities were required to keep stock of wool, hemp, flax, iron or other material on which the inmates could be set to work. But by the end of the 17th century the House of Correction was hardly distinguishable from an ordinary gaol and the inmates were spoken of as criminals.

By the middle of the 17th century the need for such an institution was felt in the Dacorum Hundred. In 1657 the Justices in Quarter Sessions decided to provide one in Hemel Hempstead and they authorised the local justices to appoint a master. No action was taken and a similar decision was made in 1664, when two of the local justices, Sir Richard Combe and Edmond Smyth, were asked to transfer from St. Albans certain stores which had been acquired for the house at Hemel Hempstead. This later order was complied with, for in 1664 Christopher Mitchell was appointed as Master, and was succeeded in 1671 by Francis Oxley; these were two of the principal contestants in the struggle for the market rights in the early 1660's. In 1664 it was also ordered that a rate to raise £30 be made within the Hundred of Dacorum with which to purchase a stock of materials to be used in the House. This institution may have replaced the old cage situated near the market chambers on the west side of the Market Street, provided by the parish for the incarceration of local malefactors and maintained at some small expense by the bailiwick.

Subsequent masters were appointed as follows:—

Joseph Turney	1677
Thomas Flaxman	1702
William Roberts	1741
Joseph Lumworth	1754

In 1763 it was reported that there was no proper bridewell in the Dacorum Hundred and premises were acquired for the purpose in Berkhamsted.

Apparently the master was expected to find his own accommodation. In return he received a salary and was expected to find the rest of his remuneration from the labour of the individuals committed to his care. The facts are brought out in two petitions presented to Quarter Sessions by Thomas Flaxman in 1718. In the first he asks for an increase in salary owing to the size of the hundred and to the fact that some of his inmates were too ill to earn any money for him by their labour. In the second petition he states that when he was appointed no particular place was assigned for the purpose and so he had to hire a special house for the large number of offenders sent to him. He complained that "some of them have beene soe sturdy and ungovernable as to breake your petitioner's said house and make their escape, notwithstanding his strictest care and uttmost diligence to keep them safe and secure, which hath put him to greate cost charge and trouble in pursueing and taking them, your petitioner seldome faileing therein". He added he had never been paid more than £6 per annum and had to find "locks, keyes, chaines, fetters and instruments for the safe keeping and deteyning the offenders sent to him"; many of them had been so lame or sick as to be incapable of work, and much hemp and other material of value had been spoilt or lost. He estimated his losses to be —

Rent	31. 10. 0.
Repairs to premises	7. 0. 0.
Passing re vagrants	6. 0. 0.
Hemp and material spoilt	4. 0. 0.
Provision and maintenance for those unable to work	5. 0. 0.
	£53. 10. 0.

These petitions were duly considered by the Justices in Quarter Sessions and in 1728 (ten years afterwards) his salary was increased from £20 to £34. 7s. 10d. for one year.

In spite of the difficulties experienced by Mr. Flaxman, when he died his grandson applied for the post and in support of his application states that for many years he had been instructed by his grandfather not only in the business of flax and hemp dresses, a trade he had followed, but also in the management and constant employment of the poor persons committed to the house of correction with proper work and labour. But his application was not successful and William Roberts was appointed. This was not a good appointment as in 1743 he was fined £1 for not attending Quarter Sessions, and in 1754 was dismissed because "he hath quitted Possession of the House of Correction and is run away from his Family and hath thereby neglected the Duty of the said office". He was succeeded by Joseph Lumworth, a victualler who occupied the Royal Oak public house, on the corner of High Street and Cherry Bounce. It was here that his prisoners were kept and the remains of the cells can still be seen in the cellars. The building was still in use as a licensed house in 1970, and until the 1939–45 war was also used as a common lodging house.

Although originally intended as places to which the unemployed could be committed to undertake useful work, Houses of Correction soon became places of punishment or something like a modern remand home to which individuals were sent pending re-examination, or to be sent on to another place. Those dealt with there were offenders charged with minor offences, such as stealing goods of little value, leaving a person chargeable to the parish, or a mother of more than one illegitimate child. Often the imprisonment followed a public whipping, e.g.

> 1754 – John Symons of H.H., cordwainer, was found guilty at Hertford Quarter Sessions of stealing a silver spoon of the value of 10d and was ordered to be whipped at Hempstead on each of three successive market days, in open market, and committed to the bridwell at Hempstead during that time.

Remand cases were, however, much more numerous and the largest number of these were vagrants. Under the law of settlement anyone found wandering, or residing in a parish as a stranger and not having certain means, could be sent back to his place of settlement, usually where he was born, and during the 18th century this movement of people assumed considerable proportions. Hemel Hempstead became a kind of station for vagrants being sent north, especially to Cambridge and they were collected here and then sent on to the next station at Newport Pagnell. These persons usually carried a pass, with directions as to the route they were to follow. The numbers passing through Hemel Hempstead about the middle of the 18th century were 600 to 700 a year. Individuals were sent on horseback, parties by horse and cart. The justices laid down a scale of allowances for this work:—

Lodging or relief for		1 person for 1 night	4d
"	"	man and wife, or 2 men or 2 women	6d
"	"	each child	2d

If they were not lodged for the night but passed on the same day, half charge was allowed. For conveying the vagrants the allowance was 3d per mile for each horse and 6d per mile for each cart, but these could only be used when ordered by the justices. In 1742 John Timbs, a vagabond with a pass, was conveyed by horseback to Newport Pagnell and the Master of the House of Correction was allowed 11s. for the cost of conveyance, together with 1s. 4d. for his keep at the rate of 4d. a day for 4 days. In the same year a party of 45 vagrants, 17 adults and 28 children, were conveyed to the same place in five carts at a cost of £5. 10s. 0d, and the justices asked if a "less number of carts were not sufficient" and pointed out that on another occasion he had conveyed 12 vagrants in one cart. Consequently, instructions were given that the Master was not to pass on the vagrants more frequently than once a week, unless the number waiting reached 8 or there were extraordinary circumstances in which event the authority of the justices was to be obtained.

Sometimes the stay of a vagrant was prolonged as must have been the case in 1728, when Thomas Flaxman, the Master, was allowed an extra sum of £5 for the maintenance of Mary Webb, who had an illegitimate child born there. Sometimes the poor vagrant died in the House and was buried by the Master, such a one was Bartholomew Fowler, who died in 1742, and here is the bill which the County Treasurer repaid to the Master —

To stripping the corpse	1.	0.
" the coffin	7.	0.
" wool to cover the corpse	1.	6.
" four bearers to carry the corpse to the grave	2.	0.
" the Minister, Clerk & Sexton	7.	6.

" keeping the vagrant 2 days	8.
" a nurse to attend him for 2 days	2. 0.
	£1. 1. 8.

Other inmates of the House of Correction included deserters from the forces awaiting return to their units and men accused of being the fathers of illegitimate children who might become chargeable to the parish.

Presumably because Mr. Lumworth's premises at the Royal Oak were his own and could not be used as a House of Correction by his successor in the office of Master, the Justices decided in 1763 to establish a House in Berkhamsted. A building was purchased for £112 and altered at a cost of about £120. It was not a satisfactory building and in 1779 was said to be out of repair. A survey was made and disclosed the following conditions. It was very insecure and the rooms for the men and the women needed air. The men's prison was 16'6"x10'6" and the women's 17'x11', the yard 25'x14'. It was very indifferently watered. There was no employment and no furniture. There was a dungeon, "a most dreadful Hole without air, without any light, 9 steps down and in several places the Brick Bottom has perished and is so damp that a stick may be run down a Foot deep in Damp earth".

The keeper was paid a salary of £20 a year and the prisoners were allowed 1lb of bread a day with water. The average number committed in a year was about 14. It was ordered that no prisoner should in future be imprisoned there.

(k) Miscellaneous

There are many items recorded in the accounts to which reference could be made, a few of which are detailed below:–

Military Service

From time to time men were called to the armed forces, particularly the militia. From 1767 there are frequent payments of relief to the wives of men called up, usually 3s. 6d. a week. Later lump sums are paid to the men themselves: in 1778 the amount was £3. 3s. 0d. each, increased in 1781 to £4. 4s. 0d. During the Napoleonic Wars the payment recurs – first in 1797 at £3. 8s. 0d. per head, then £7. 17s. 6d. in 1803 and £10 in 1808.

In 1796 £88 was paid to the County Treasurer, being the average Bounty and Fines for four volunteers for the Army, and earlier in 1794 £102. 12s. 1d. was expended on "attending the finding of three men and a half to serve in the Navy as by Bill."

Census

The cost locally of taking the census in 1811 was £5. 1s. 3d., and in 1831 £22 was paid "for dinners for 25 persons who took the population May 30th".

The Cage

In 1829 there was some £11 spent on the cage; £2. 18s. 0d. was spent on ironwork, £7. 13s. 0d. on carpenter's work and 2s. on straw. The cage was a kind of cell in which defaulters were temporarily confined, but whether it was attached to the workhouse or erected elsewhere is not known. As early as the 17th century the Bailiwick accounts show money spent on a cage which was then sited in the High Street not far from the old Market Square. It may be that the use of this old institution was discontinued when the House of Correction was established in 1664, and when the latter was transferred to Berkhamsted in 1763, some sort of lock-up was needed, and another 'cage' was provided. In a paper given to the St. Albans Architectural & Archaeological Society in 1928 Mr. John Gladstone records that an octogenarian told him he remembered three wheat-stealers being confined in the cage.

CHAPTER 10

Boxmoor and its Trust

Over many centuries the area of land known as Boxmoor has played an important part in the life of Hemel Hempstead and of its hamlet of Bovingdon. Just when the inhabitants of these places acquired any rights over this land is not known since any early records have been lost, but it was probably in the early days when the manor was developing. The earliest record so far found refers to a dispute in 1499 between the lord of the manor, John Witton then Rector of Ashridge, and the tenants of his manor (see also Chapter 4.); this concerned two matters, one of which was the rights which the tenants claimed in certain commons, particularly Boxmoor. They claimed, amongst other things, that they had rights of pasture in Castlemede (or Boxmoor) as well as free rights of fishing there. On appeal to the Privy Council they secured their old rights of pasture in Castlemede, Baylimede, Rowdowne, Felden Heth and Twowaters More, and the fishing rights in the river running through some of this land. For these advantages they had to pay the Rector 6s. 8d. a year. In effect, these rights may be divided into those in what is now known as Boxmoor and those on Roughdown; we will deal with them separately, and first with those on Boxmoor.

It is well to appreciate why the inhabitants placed such great value on these rights. Meadow-land was an important element in the farming economy of Hemel Hempstead at this time and it was usually in short supply. There were two kinds of pasture, that by the riverside and that on the uplands. The latter was more useful for purposes of hay while the former had considerable grazing value. One difficulty was the keeping of livestock during the winter months owing to the shortage of winter foodstuff. Consequently, it was the practice to slaughter some of the animals at the end of the summer, keeping only such as could be fed until the following spring. Their sustenance was inadequate and they were poor specimens when they were turned out in the spring. Where however there were river meadows the grass probably grew earlier by at least a month, to the great advantage of the stock, which recovered that much earlier. They also permitted the keeping alive of a larger number of animals in autumn. So great was the need for this earlier grazing that in some areas special steps were taken to flood the upland meadows so that an earlier crop became available. Thus the meadow afforded good fodder for the animals grazing on it during the spring and summer months, and the type of subsistence farming carried on by many of the small farmers, added value to the grazing rights on the moor.

It is therefore evident how important Boxmoor was to the people, and how anxious they would be to secure the ownership of the land when the opportunity came, and thus to ensure that they could enjoy their rights without disturbance. This chance came in 1574 when, following the transfer of the manor to the Crown in 1538, Elizabeth 1 granted to Robert, Earl of Leicester, certain lands in Hemel Hempstead which included Boxmoor, and he in turn sold it in the same year to Francis, Earl of Bedford and Peter Graye, Gentleman of Segenhoe, Bedfordshire. Peter Graye's share in the property passed to his son Richard, who in 1577 acquired the Earl of Bedford's share. In 1581 Richard Graye (or Grey) sold a number of properties to three inhabitants of Hemel Hempstead all conveyed in one omnibus deed for a purchase sum of £75, and included in the transaction was the land at Boxmoor. Altogether the transaction comprised, besides Boxmoor, at least nine houses or cottages and more than 25 acres of land in a number of parcels. No doubt the three purchasers were more particularly interested in the property other than Boxmoor since these were personal acquisitions some of which they occupied themselves; John Rolfe, yeoman, probably of Boxted bought a house and land, Richard Pope, described as a shoemaker, but who was also the landlord of the Cocke Inn (which stood on the east side of the High Street) acquired this inn and some land, and William Gladman, yeoman of Piccotts End secured houses and land occupied by himself or members of his family.

Anyway, they acquired Boxmoor as a secret trust for the benefit of the inhabitants of Hemel Hempstead and Bovingdon generally, and the proportion of the purchase price relating to this land was subscribed by the people of the two places. Whether the area bought was the same as that for which the earlier tenants had fought, and were required to pay an annual rent of 6s. 8d. is uncertain. It is described in the deed conveying from Gray to Rolfe, Pope and Gladman as "one meadow called or known by the name of Castlemead with appurtenances, otherwise Haywarde Meade, otherwise Bayley Meade otherwise Haybournes." (Later, in the deed of 1594 two more names were added, viz The Common Mead or the Two Waters Moore). It is known that following the transfer of the manor to the Crown there were many transactions in land in Hemel Hempstead, e.g. in his will of 1551 Robert Eyme (or Eames) left to his wife "the reversion of my house landes and meades called Haybournes with all rents (etc.) as of right belongeth by reason of my purchaise of the manere of Bures." So far as can be ascertained he left no offspring and so the estate had to be dealt with when his wife died, and it could be that part or all of the meadows he mentioned in his will were included in the purchase of Boxmoor. Be that as it may, in 1837 the Trustees purchased Haybarns Meadows, containing nearly 6¾ acres for £550 and added them to the Moor, thus extending the boundary of the property northwards between what is now Cotterells and the river Gade, and clearing away the squatters' cottages which fringed the original northern boundary at this point. It could be that in this manner the Haybourn part of the present moor was acquired in two instalments.

On the question of areas certain facts emerge from the documents that exist. In the schedules to the Act of 1809 the area of pasture is shown as about 178 acres, and this excludes some 35½ acres sold to the canal company and others. In the Parliamentary Survey of the Manor made in 1650 it is stated that there are several commons in the parish belonging to the manor, including Two Waters Moor and Boxmoor 120 acres; it adds that these moors with the fishing were claimed by the inhabitants of Hemel Hempstead and Bovingdon. Could it be that the old tenants paid 6s. 8d. a year for 120 acres belonging to the manor and that the rest was acquired from other owners, e.g. the owner of Haybournes?

It should be added that little is known about the manor of Haybournes (Haybarns or Eymes). The manor house stood immediately behind where the Heath Park Hotel now stands and was still there in 1838 but had been divided into three dwellings and used as cottages. The Heath, now known as Churchill, which was built by one William Howard some time before 1830 is on part of the old Haybarns Estate.

In 1594 two of the original purchasers, Rolfe and Pope — Gladman having died in the meantime — executed a conveyance of the land to some 67 persons (including themselves) confirming the secret trust and requiring those named to hold the land for and on behalf of the people of Hemel Hempstead and Bovingdon generally. At intervals of about fifty years between 1594 and 1809 similar deeds were executed, conveying the land to new trustees thereby ensuring the continuance of the trust. The number of persons named varied on each occasion between sixty and eighty and furnishes a useful summary of the leading inhabitants of the district for the time being. (Details of these agreements and the parties thereto are set out in the preamble to the Act of 1809).

The persons named in the deed of 1594 probably comprised at least one representative from every family of importance. As might be expected the Combe family were represented in this, and also in the subsequent deed of 1659, indicating the active interest they took in the acquisition and retention of this valuable property. Francis Combe, the younger, is the first named in the 1594 conveyance; he was not more than eleven years of age at the time, and was probably made a party as the member of his family with the greatest expectation of life. His grandfather, Richard Combe, was still living but was an old man. This and other facts confirm the family's support — that Francis Combe the elder was one of the attesting witnesses to the conveyance to the three original purchasers; that his eldest son was made a party to the original trust deed; that Sir Richard Combe, the great grandson of the first Richard, and Sir Richard's eldest son were two of the new trustees appointed in 1659.

According to these several deeds the rights in the moor belonged in equal portions to all the inhabitants of Hemel Hempstead and Bovingdon so long as they were resident there, and the general management of the trust was to be in the hands of "Twelve of the best inhabitants of Hemel Hempstead and Bovingdon". There are no directions in the deeds as to how these were appointed until the one of 1787 in which it was declared that this committee should be appointed by a majority of the trustees. The fishing rights which went with the purchase were also of considerable value and others than the tenants of the Manor of Hemel Hempstead may have tried to exercise them. In 1521 there was further argument between the Rector of Ashridge and his tenants which led to arbitration and then it was decided that "no tenant nore Inhabitant within this Lordship shall fish in the Lord's several waters, Hunt, Hawk, nore take beasts nore fowles of Warren within the said Lordship, except they obtain licence of the Lord so to do." In this instance the tenants suffered a rebuff, as no doubt the Rector would want some consideration for his licence. Whether the Crown, when it took over the Manor, and those who subsequently owned the land insisted on this practice of licensing is not known. However by purchasing the land the inhabitants clarified the position, so that when the local manorial jury made its presentment in 1617 it did not include the fishing rights as belonging to the Lord of the Manor. Similar rights in the Gade had also been disposed of to the grantee of the Bury Estate. Berkhamsted also claimed a right inasmuch as it was said the tenants of that manor could fish in any brook, water or river within this (Berkhamsted) manor "from a place called Bulbourne Heads, and see along the river and within the manor unto a place called Kinges Langley Parke pale without the boundes of this manor, but within this Honour." This claim is set out in a survey of the manor of Berkhamsted made by a jury of that manor in 1607, and was an interesting reminder of the ancient position of the Hemel Hempstead Manor as a member of the Honour of Berkhamsted. Whether any attempt was made to exercise this right after the purchase of Boxmoor is not known but right up to the end of the 19th century the Berkhamsted Court Leet continued to present these rights as belonging to the tenants of its manor.

Besides Boxmoor the present Trustees own other commons called (a) Down or Roughdown Common and (b) Shothanger and Dew Green Common, containing about 23 acres and 60 acres respectively. Over these the inhabitants had certain rights which may have been as old as those they had possessed over Boxmoor; but the actual acquisition by the Trustees did not take place until the 19th century. These commons were probably ordinary manorial commons in monastic times, and formed part of the property which fell to the Crown at the Dissolution in 1539. In 1544 Henry VIII granted to the Dean and Chapter of St. Pauls in London the rectory and advowson of the vicarage of St. Mary's Church, as well as certain other properties, including these commons, subject to any rights exercisable by the local inhabitants. That they were then severed from the manor is shown by the verdict of the Manorial Jury in 1617 which was to the effect that whilst "Shutthanger, Rowdowne, Dewgreene and Ffielden Hearthe" are within the manor they are not part of it. Towards the end of the 17th century the tenants of Westbrookhay Manor asserted that the western end of

Shothanger was waste of their manor though there is no independent evidence which supports this.

At the time in the late 18th and early 19th centuries when the public were expressing concern about the condition of Boxmoor there was also interest in the Roughdown and Shothanger Group, and suggestions were made that they should be vested in the same people as was Boxmoor. Among the Boxmoor Trustees' papers (now in the County Record Office) is a draft of a petition to the Dean and Chapter of St. Pauls from "the Vicar, Churchwardens, Overseers and Principal Inhabitants of the Parish of Hemel Hempstead and the Hamlet of Bovingdon." It said that the inhabitants were much bothered with poor labourers for whom no sufficient employment could be procured, and that there was a tract of unenclosed land called Shothanger, Dew Green and Row Down belonging to the Dean and Chapter which had lain waste for many years, used only as a sheep walk or common for certain inhabitants living near. It further stated that in late years there had been many encroachments by "several of the lower order of the people" in digging up flints and chalk, and cutting turf, and that William Fensom and Henry Sibley had lately erected cottages in a chalk dell belonging to the land, of a description to invite burthensome and evil disposed people to settle in the parish to the great nuisance and annoyance of the respectable inhabitants. It also referred to the grant to the Dean and Chapter in 1544 and said that about 10 acres of land was profitable woodland then and long afterwards. It sought to acquire the land so that it would "be a beneficial Resource for the Employment of the unemployed Labourers, who might be usefully set to work upon it to some profitable purpose and at the same time would enable the inhabitants to prevent the introduction of harbours for Rogues and thieves by the erection of cottages in such a bye place."

This document was prepared about 1806 at a time when the parish was much concerned about unemployment and the growing cost of poor relief. The idea of using land belonging to Boxmoor Trustees for the purposes of finding work for the unemployed was subsequently adopted during the period of crisis following the end of the Napoleonic Wars.

The eventual outcome of the suggestion that these commons should belong to the inhabitants was that in 1830 the Dean and Chapter leased them to the Trustees for a period of 21 years at a rental of five shillings a year; the lease was renewed in 1851 and in 1886 the Trustees purchased the land from the Ecclesiastical Commissioners for £100, the land continuing subject to the subsisting common rights.

Reverting to Boxmoor we know little about the proceedings of the Trustees and the management of the Trust for the two centuries between 1594 and the coming of the Grand Junction Canal in the 1790's. That the affairs of the Trust were matters of public concern from time to time may be gathered from occasional references in the records of the Bailiwick and the Vestry.

The following entries appear in the Bailiwick Books:—

1659–60	Paid to Mr. Allison for the writings concerning the Moore	1. 0. 0.
1711–12	Paid Goodman Turner for warning the Trustees of the Moor	1. 0.
1727–28	Paid Mr. Gurney when Trustees met there	7. 6.
1756–7	Paid Mr. Ginger for making the writings of Boxmoore	2. 18. 4.
1758–9	Paid at Thos. Killams when Trustees met	Part of a total
1762–3	Spent when Committee was Chose for Regulating Boxmoor	1. 1. 6.

The payments to Mr. Allison and Mr. Ginger, who were both local attorneys and at the time were clerks to the Bailiwick, were no doubt in respect of the transfer deeds entered into in 1659 and 1757 respectively when the existing trustees transferred the ownership to a new set of trustees, and the payment in 1711 to Goodman Turner could have been for calling a meeting to complete the transfer deed of 1711. The last entry relates to the committee of twelve of the best inhabitants, mentioned in the various deeds, whose appointment was later regulated in the deed of 1787.

The Vestry were concerned with the writings relating to Boxmoor. In 1735 they agreed to Richard Salter collecting these from a Mr. Bambrook at the latter's home in St. Albans and to pay such sum as the latter requires; he paid £1. 11s. 6d. for which he was reimbursed, together with his expenses to St. Albans, i.e. 3s. 6d. Subsequently he (Salter) had to deliver the documents at 8 a.m. on a Monday so they could be put into the "chest over the Vestry Room". In 1776–7 3s. was paid to men going round warning people of a vestry meeting about Boxmoor, and at that meeting a further 18s. was spent, but the purpose was not stated.

During the latter part of the 18th century there was increasing dissatisfaction with the way in which Boxmoor was being treated. In the words of the preamble to the 1809 Act

> various Trespasses and Incroachments have from Time to Time been made . . . by Persons who are not Inhabitants of the Parish or Hamlet, by turning their Cattle thereon at Times and in a manner that cannot easily be prevented, by others taking from it the Soil to the Depth of Several Inches, by others constructing Cottages and Buildings thereon, and by depositing Timber, Ashes, digging Saw Pits, and other (similar) Purposes.

The Trustees had no practical powers of remedy, and the inhabitants felt that some urgent action was needed. Various suggestions were made including one that the land should be built on and so provide additional rate income, a suggestion that has been repeated from time to time since. But the matter was brought to a head by the advent of the Grand Junction Canal.

The valley of the Bulbourne is one of the natural gateways through the Chilterns, and so it was reasonable that the Canal Company should bring their canal through it and so through the Moor. The Company was created by Act of Parliament in 1793 and in due course acquired, in all, 25 acres 1 rood 8 poles of the Moor for the sum of £900. 3s. 10d.; about 11 acres were needed for the canal and towing path, and approximately 14 acres were pieces of land severed from the Moor by the course of the canal. The purchase money was later applied towards the cost of constructing Boxmoor Wharf, on the canal near Corner Hall and Two Waters Road. In this connection it is interesting to record the manner in which the proposal to construct the Canal was received locally.

Its advent was welcomed, but concern was felt at its distance from the town, and this was expressed in a petition prepared by the Bailiff for presentation to the Company, in the following terms:—

> "The Inhabitants of the Town have ever enjoyed the advantages of an established market, well known for its extent and importance; and consequently of a considerable trade uniformly attendant on it. At a meeting of the Inhabitants, . . . it appeared to be their unanimous opinion that their market and trade must (be) greatly diminished by the canal passing in the line now proposed, along Boxmoor, leaving this town at . . . about a mile from it; unless by a collateral cut up to the town, they shall be admitted to a full participation of the benefits of its navigation. They are pursuaded that if the canal be brought nearer to Hemel Hempstead than Boxmoor, the difficulty of conveying goods from there to the town by land carriage will (in its effect upon the market) be felt in no lesser degree than if it were from a much greater distance — more particularly in respect of the corn, which is the staple commodity of this market. For it is believed that the ready communication with other neighbouring towns, which must be afforded by their contiguity to the canal, added to the difficulty of providing land carriage from Boxmoor to the Town of Hemel Hempstead, will operate as an insurmountable impediment to the consigning of corn to this market from all the country bordering on the canal; but that it will be found more convenient by the farmers to convey their corn entirely by water carriage to the next market town, although far more distant from them.
>
> They also submit . . . that by a collateral cut to this town, the waggon bringing corn to the market from the north and north east side of the country may have a ready opportunity of loading back with coal or other goods conveyed hither by the proposed navigation. For these and other reasons the Inhabitants (ask) . . . that a collateral cut from the most

convenient (point) to the town of Hemel Hempstead may be included in the concern; which . . . can be the only means of preserving its . . . market."

This interesting document, which illustrates in a number of ways the running of the corn market in the town, was presented to the Canal Company in 1793. At the same time the Company received similar requests for collateral cuts from St. Albans, Buckingham, Dunstable, Chesham and Newport Pagnell, and expressed the view that they were desirous of extending their scheme so far as it was wise and practicable.

But despite the Bailiff's eloquence the Company were unable to grant his request. Nevertheless, the idea behind the proposal was sound. Transport by water was both more convenient and cheaper than the alternative method, by road. The condition of the highways was bad, and the main turnpike road – the London Road, A.41 – was said to be one of the worst turnpike ways to London, a condition partly due to the heavy corn traffic from Hemel Hempstead, which continually tore up the road. It may well be that the development of a wharf on the canal in the Two Waters Road district by the trustees of the Moor was a direct outcome of the request by the Bailiff to the Canal Company and their rejection of it. Consider its location. It was on a site nearest to the town, and on the best road then available. The Canal Company were legally obliged to construct bridges over the canal to carry existing roads and of a width suitable to deal with the volume of traffic at that time; they built five bridges, viz Durrants Hill (or Albion Hill), Two Waters (or Balderson's), Fishery, Cangles and the swing bridge at Winkwell, and of these the road over the Two Waters Road or Balderson's bridge was the widest, narrow though it was. (The first three were reconstructed by the local authorities in the 1920's. They were all narrow and inadequate and so were widened). It was also very near the turnpike road, but this was an advantage shared by the other bridges.

The wharf was built about the end of the 18th century out of the proceeds of the sale of land as already mentioned, and of the annual revenue from it three quarters was to go towards the improvement of the local workhouse, and the remaining quarter to the relief of the poor in Bovingdon. How the wharf was managed is not reported, but it must have been a profitable venture for some £431 were spent on the workhouse in the years 1800–1803.

Since there was doubt as to the legality of the sale to the Canal Company of a piece of land near the old Mill at Two Waters, as well as uncertainty as to the powers of the then Trustees, it was felt necessary to put the Trust on a more substantial basis by means of a special Act of Parliament, and this was done in 1809. Briefly it provided that

(1) the sales of the land be confirmed;

(2) the trust property be vested in twelve trustees named in the Act, they to be succeeded as need arose by new trustees duly elected by the inhabitants;

(3) the Trustees be given powers to make regulations and orders relating to the Moor, but the Act provided no sanctions or punishments for the non-observance thereof; and

(4) various powers of management were to be vested in the Trustees.

One such power was to regulate or stint the quantity of cattle to be turned on the Moor, and this has been exercised continuously since the Act. This control was carried out by means of pasture tickets. To each house existing in Hemel Hempstead and Bovingdon in 1809 was attached a "share Iron" entitling the occupier to receive a pasture ticket. To enable an animal to depasture on the Moor a number of these tickets were needed viz, one for a goose, two for a hog, three for a donkey, heifer or steer, four for a heifer or steer over one year but under two years, five for an ox, cow, heifer or steer over two years, or a yearling colt, six for a milking cow or cow in calf, or mare or gelding and seven for a mare and foal or mare in foal. Graziers then bought these tickets, at whatever price they could get them, from the householders up to the number they needed for the animals they required to pasture. Since 1809 some of the houses then existing have ceased to be and the shares belonging to them have fallen in to the Trustees and are sold by them if an insufficient number of tickets is forthcoming from the householders. As an example, in 1936 96 animals were put on the Moor by 20 people.

The election of the Trustees takes place very infrequently, and although the most recent one in the 1960's was carried out decorously, earlier ones were more like the hustings of old. The last one of this kind was in 1922. The Ballot Acts do not apply and so the ballot was not secret. In 1922 the interest in the election was very keen and many electors were tempted, if not influenced, by the willingness of certain candidates to offer suitable refreshments in the local taverns. Voting took place in the old Corn Exchange in the High Street and, although there were a large number of licensed premises in that street, every one did record business on that occasion.

Having been appointed, the early Trustees set about the work of managing the Trust in accordance with the powers conferred on them by the Act of Parliament. The principal event with which they had to deal in the first half of the 19th century was the advent of the London and Birmingham Railway. Like the Canal this had eventually to go through the same gap in the Chilterns and to do this the railway had to cross part of the Moor. Unlike the canal the railway was not welcomed and the Trustees were uncompromising in their resistance to the transfer of land, but the Company had compulsory powers and in 1835 about 11 acres was taken from the Moor for £992. The Company also made an offer for the isolated strip of land between the railway and the canal to the west of Cangles Lane, but this the Trustees flatly refused. £550 of this £992 was used to purchase about 6¾ acres in Haybarns Meadow as mentioned above.

Another transaction in land was carried out in 1829 when a small piece of the Moor was sold under the Church Building Acts for £71 as a site for a chapel of ease to Hemel Hempstead now occupied by the parish church of St. John, and the purchase money was used for the redemption of the land tax on the Boxmoor Wharf (in Two Waters Road).

For many of the years after 1809 and up to the 1914–18 War the Trust made a surplus, which was divided between Hemel Hempstead and Bovingdon in the proportions laid down in the Act, and devoted to some worthy public purpose. Mention has already been made of the improvement of the old workhouse; after that funds were voted for the improvement of the old Market House. Public lighting, public clocks, public buildings (like Boxmoor Hall) were all supported or provided out of the annual surplus of the Trust; nor was the church left out. In more recent times the Trust has not been so fortunate and on occasion has had difficulty in paying its way. Boxmoor is nevertheless still a great public asset, a wide open space in the centre of a growing urban community.

From time to time efforts have been made to use the land, or part of it, for building purposes but they have always been defeated. The last attempt was about 1930 when a scheme was proposed to build on some of the land in St. John's Road and at Two Waters. The public response was spontaneous and explosive; there was great public outcry, and the slogan "Hands off the Moor" was chalked, painted or published all over the place. There was a public inquiry at which the opposition to the scheme was expressed, and the Charity Commissioners to whom the scheme had been submitted, decided against it. It is doubtful if another such scheme will ever be put forward, but if it were the "Hands off the Moor" slogans would re-appear, and, one hopes, would be equally successful.

A Nineteenth-Century Highwayman
Robert Snooks

No account of the Boxmoor Trust would be complete without some reference to the highwayman known as *Robert Snooks,* whose grave is marked upon the open Moor by two simple stones placed there by the Trustees in 1904. A mail robbery occurred on the night of the 10th May 1801 in semi-darkness as the postboy, John Stevens, mounted on horseback, was carrying six bags of mail from Tring and divers other places towards London. At a secluded spot, adjacent to the Moor, the highwayman waited, and with force and arms did make an assault putting John Stevens in bodily fear and danger of his life, and there did feloniously steal six leather bags from the person and against the will of the postboy. Snooks rifled the bags of mail extracting Bank of England notes of fifty pounds and ten pounds denomination, together with notes of ten pounds issued by the Aylesbury Bank, all of which items appeared upon the subsequent indictments. The frightened postboy hurried to inform Mr. John Page, Postmaster of Berkhamsted, who was also the Chief Constable for the Hundred of Dacorum, and the registered Innkeeper of The Kings Arms, who raised the alarm with the authorities. Meanwhile the highwayman made good his escape and went into hiding at Southwark, leaving the highway strewn with the ransacked mail-bags at Boxmoor. Reward Bills were soon displayed offering three hundred pounds for his capture. After a period of lying low, he sent a servant girl to purchase a piece of cloth for a coat, and gave her what she understood was a five-pound note. When this note was tendered for payment, suspicions were aroused as the maid had a fifty-pound note. She returned to Snooks for an explanation, but he immediately fled, and made off to Hungerford, his birthplace. For a time he eluded pursuit but was recognised and duly apprehended, being lodged in Newgate prison. Trial by jury took place at the Lent Assize at Hertford on the 8th March 1802 before Mr. Justice Heath. In the calender of prisoners presented by Jacob Bosanquet, High Sheriff of Hertfordshire, the name of Snooks appears first on the list, removed on the 4th March 1802 by Habeas Corpus from Newgate to Hertford Jail, charged upon the oaths of John Stevens and others with feloniously assaulting the said John Stevens on the King's Highway in the County of Hertford, putting him in fear, and feloniously stealing from his person several bags of letters which were sent from the G.P.O. and conveyed by the said John Stevens as the postboy employed from Tring to Hemel Hempstead. Snooks was found guilty and sentence was pronounced "to be executed on Thursday next on some convenient place at or near the spot where he committed the robbery".

From a study of the records two interesting facts emerge. The name of James Snooks, not Robert, appears on the court documents, and further that John Stevens did not suffer any bodily injury but was put in fear and danger of his life. It will be noted that Snooks was sentenced on Monday and hanged on Thursday. Thus the order of the Judge of Assize was carried out.

To come to any conclusion upon the convenient place at or near the spot where the crime was committed would be difficult today, or to mark a particular tree from which Snooks was hanged, since the Moor was open and the stout iron fencing along the Berkhamsted Road to prevent the cattle from straying was not erected until 1863/1865, neither was there any public lighting.

Some account of the final scene is described in the Birmingham Railroad Guide Third Edition 1839 on pp.48–51, and this is summarised as follows:–

Snooks was brought from Hertford Jail for the final act which was supervised by John Page the High Constable. The horse was whipped up, the cart drawn away from beneath the gallows tree and Snooks was left hanging. Under the instructions of John Page the grave was dug, and a truss of straw having been procured, a half of it was thrown into the grave, the corpse placed upon it and the other half thrown over the body and the earth cast upon it without further ceremony.

A relevant entry occurs in the accounts of the Overseers of the Poor for the Parish of Hemel Hempstead:—

"Paid Whitely for attending at Boxmoor with Snooks" 7s. 6d. The assumption is that Whitely was the Parish Constable.

Note on Sources

Much useful information for this chapter has been gathered from an unpublished manuscript in the possession of the Hemel Hempstead Local History and Records Society. This is "Hemel Hempstead — an outline of its story from the earliest times to the year 1839." written by H. E. Ellis in the early part of this century.

The papers of the Boxmoor Trustees are in the H.R.O.

Reference has also been made to:—

Canal Company Records, British Transport Historical Records, General Committee, 17th July 1793.

Evidence given to the Royal Commission on Common Land, 7th March 1957.

CHAPTER 11.

Part 1

The Established Church

The early history of the ecclesiastical parish of Hemel Hempstead is difficult to trace. It was clearly closely bound to the history of the manor, for its boundaries were practically identical. Both manor and parish included the hamlets of Bovingdon and Flaunden, the secular manor being in the Hundred of Dacorum and the ecclesiastical parish in the rural deanery of Berkhamsted in the Archdeaconry of Huntingdon within the diocese of Lincoln.

We do not know whether there was a Saxon church in Hemel Hempstead prior to the building of the fine church of St. Mary's the foundations of which were laid about 1140. The earliest written church records concern the advowson of the parish of St. Mary's. In 1209 King John granted this to his second son, Richard, Earl of Cornwall (d. 1272) and from him it passed to Edmund, Earl of Cornwall born at Berkhamsted Castle in 1249. The first six incumbents whose names we know received their livings from these Earls.

By 1235 chapels-of-ease had been established at Bovingdon and Flaunden, presumably to meet the needs of increasing population in these hamlets, for in that year Robert Grossteste, the reforming Bishop of Lincoln, prevailed upon Richard of Cornwall to accept Bernard de Gravelegh as vicar of St. Mary's, and to appoint two fit chaplains for Bovingdon and Flaunden. The two hamlets were to pay 20s. to the vicar of St. Mary's for the support of their chaplains.

The endowment of the medieval parish church came from the tithes and in the case of St. Mary's these were valuable. Edmund of Cornwall was among many in the twelfth and thirteenth centuries who shared in the revival of monastic life by granting lands and manors to the religious orders. In 1286 he founded the College or Monastery of Ashridge endowing it with various lands including the manor of Hemel Hempstead, and by a second charter of 1290 he granted to the monastery further endowments of land together with the advowson of the church. Thus the Rector and monks of Ashridge became and remained for two hundred and fifty years the masters of the parish of Hemel Hempstead. They drew the profits from the manorial lands as Lords of the Manor and, owning the advowson of the church, they also enjoyed the rectorial tithes. Taken together this gave them considerable power and wealth. Edmund's benefaction was truly a royal and generous one. There was one limitation on their authority – the Bishop of Lincoln compelled them to appoint a vicar and to allot him altar fees for his support. An Act of 1402 stated that the "vicar shall be a secular person (not a member of any religious house) that he shall be a vicar perpetual and not removable at the caprice of the Monastery, that he shall be Canonically Instituted and Inducted and be sufficiently endowed at the discretion of the ordinary for these three purposes – For Divine Service, To inform the people and To keep hospitality".

Thus the tithes were divided between the rector and the vicar. The Great Tithes of corn, grains, hay and wool were retained by the monastery whilst the Lesser Tithes of fruit, herbs, milk and eggs were allocated to the vicar. The collection of tithes in kind was a troublesome business disliked by rector and vicar. Tithes were often farmed out to those willing to undertake the burden of collecting them and later commutation into a money payment was widely adopted. When in 1834 an Act of Parliament commuted all tithes to an annual rent charge varying with the price of corn, the figures for this parish of 12,440 acres were:–

Vicarial or Lesser Tithe			
Hemel Hempstead	501	0.	0.
Bovingdon	190	12.	0.
Flaunden	50	11.	0.
	742	3.	0.

Rectorial or Great Tithe	£	s.	d.
Hemel Hempstead	1,818	15.	9.
Bovingdon	710	0.	0.
Flaunden	160	6.	0.
	2,689	1.	9.

It would be safe to assume that less than a quarter of the sum total went to the priest who actually did the work, the rest going to the sinecure rector.

Besides the tithes, the vicar was provided with a house, and an area of land known as the glebe, which was supposed to be twice that normally allotted to a villein. What the allocation was is not known, but there are references in the Rental of 1523 to lands being "of the fee of the parson" scattered over the various fields. On some of the land adjoining the church after the charter of 1539 a number of shops and houses were built the rents of which belonged to the vicar for the time being. The vicar also received fees and other sums from his parishioners, Easter offerings for example.

What was the church like that Ashridge acquired in 1290? It was already about 150 years old, the foundations having been laid c. 1140 and the church finished some forty years later. It had been dedicated to St. Mary in 1150 when the chancel and tower were completed. The building was of flint

ST. MARY'S CHURCH, HEMEL HEMPSTEAD

ST. MARY'S CHURCH, HEMEL HEMPSTEAD

rubble with some Roman brick and with stone dressings. The opinion of G. H. Cook in his work on 'The Medieval Parish Church' is worth quoting; he says "the most imposing parish churches of the Norman period are those that are cruciform in plan with aisles flanking the nave. This form was by no means common and was confined to the churches of small towns. Of those now remaining Hemel Hempstead, Hertfordshire, begun c. 1140 is one of the best preserved".

The basic structure of the church today is still much as it must have looked when it was completed. Certainly it is a sumptuous church for so small a community, but size and magnificence depended on many factors, the prosperity of the area, the piety of the benefactors and the availability of raw materials. Succeeding generations have added and replaced portions of the fabric as the need arose, giving us the variety of styles and furnishings which St. Mary's enjoys.

The chancel was the earliest part of the church, being separated from the rest of the church by a stone screen. In the twelfth century quadripartite groined vaulting was much preferred, and the chancel here consists of two such vaults with stilted cross-ribs. Although the east window of the chancel was inserted in 1880, there are in the south wall two fourteenth-century windows each of three lights with modern tracery. In the north wall is an original round-headed Norman window, consisting of a single light with chevron mouldings inside and out. On this side of the chancel is a seventeenth-century slab 6 feet long by 2 feet wide inscribed - "Heere lyeth interred the body of Thomas Deacon, the sonne of Thomas Deacon and Martha his wife of CORNER HALL, Batchelor of Artes and Student of Physick, who by his extraordinary spare body in respect of breadth being long sick of a consumption and of his extraordinary height being in proportion to the length of this stone might shew the desire he had to heaven and so departed September 28th A.D.16..".

West of this is a blocked fifteenth-century archway originally leading into the chamber beyond. This chamber has in its east wall a fourteenth-century loop light with original stanchions, and below this is a doorway with a shouldered arch, probably of the same date. It was most likely an outer door, but now gives access to a modern vestry. There was formerly a room above this chamber.

The central tower, supported by four horseshoe arches, is 16 feet square and the west arch is enriched with chevron moulding facing the nave. The fine engineering of the Normans is ably demonstrated by the massive piers of half round responds and the angle shafts with their carved capitals. The second stage of the tower has two plain round-headed windows in each face and the third stage has double round-headed windows with circular lights above them. Near the angles are shallow niches with arched heads. Originally battlemented, the tower is crowned by a magnificent fluted leaden spire probably of the early fourteenth-century; itself 130 feet high, the tower and spire reach almost 200 feet to the gilded weathervane.

Justifiably Chauncey wrote in 1700 that "it is a very fair and tall spire covered with lead, which is a great ornament to the town."

The north transept has a fifteenth-century window of three lights and modern tracery. High up on the eastern wall of this transept is a plain round-headed doorway which opened from the former upper room of the chamber into a loft or gallery. The corbels which carried the floor of this are still to be seen.

The south transept has a fifteenth-century window of two lights with a quatrefoil head. There is a modern three light window in the south wall and the corbels of the old gallery removed in 1879 can still be seen above a sixteenth century doorway with modern external jambs. In the west wall is an original Norman window, the arch enriched with chevron ornamentation. In the south-east corner is a small piscina betraying its use in former times as a chapel. The transept roofs are good examples of fourteenth century work with arched braces and traceried spandrels, restored in 1880.

The nave consists of six bays and shows the Norman workmanship of the later period at its best. There has been a local tradition that the twelve arches signify the twelve apostles. The east and west arches of both arcades have chevron ornamentation. The clerestory has on each side six round-headed windows restored. The second window from the east on the south side is entirely new and replaces a larger window, inserted in the fifteenth-century, of which the head only remains. The clerestory walls were raised about two feet in the fifteenth century and the window thus inserted probably was to afford light to the rood screen and figures, which at one time faced the nave. The roof is also fifteenth-century, plainer than those of the transepts but with traces of the original painting.

In the west wall of the nave is a fine large doorway of the twelfth-century with a richly carved semi-circular arch. The carving of the capitals portrays Adam and Eve wrestling with the serpent and, as a background, there is the Tree of Life. Above it is a fifteenth-century traceried window of three lights.

The north and south aisles, have fifteenth-century windows of two lights with tracery all much restored. In the south wall are the sills of twelfth-century windows, and in the west wall of the south aisle is a large slab, removed from the top of an altar tomb bearing two brass effigies of Robert Albyn and Margaret his wife, which date from c.1360. The inscription is in Norman French: (see plate Va) "Roberd Albyn gist icy et Margrete sa femme aveke lui dieu d'lez alm' eyt mercy. Amen." (Robert Albyn lies here and Margaret his wife with him. May the Lord have mercy on their souls. Amen.) The medieval font (with nineteenth-century additions) stands also in the south aisle, and four shields or coffin plates of lead bearing the armorial arms of the Combe family are fixed to the wall of the same aisle.

The north porch has a fifteenth-century doorway, while that of the south porch is fourteenth-century, this time with mouldings of the same period.

As rector of the church the monastery would be responsible for the upkeep of the chancel; the nave by contrast was in the care of the parishioners. Often monastic rectors were negligent of their obligations. There is some evidence of strained relations between Ashridge and St. Mary's. and the fact that there was no large-scale rebuilding during the Middle Ages would seem to indicate that the relationship was not a vital or productive one. Many religious houses were hard put to it to make ends meet, and as landlords, intent on exacting their full feudal dues, they often spent little on churches that were appropriated merely for their tithe value. Under such circumstances it would have been surprising if there had not been strain between the village and the monks of Ashridge.

Possessing as they did the nave of the church, the parishioners looked on it as a social as well as a religious meeting place. It may have been used as a store house, as a market and as a corn exchange. Meetings to elect wardens or to consider parochial matters and the expenditure of money took place in the nave or porches. Legal documents and agreements relating to church affairs and property were probably drawn up in the upper room north of the chancel, there being no need to build over the porch as in so many churches, Aldbury is a local example.

At the great festivals, church ales, feasts of drinking, merrymaking and dancing, were held within the church, Similarly wakes to commemorate the building of the church and its dedication often ended in drunken riots. The ale was mashed at the parish brewhouse attached to the vicarage in Hemel Hempstead the malt having been acquired by the wardens from the tithes. Needless to say such junketings did not meet with universal approval, particularly in churches with monastic rectors, and thus a church house or hall was often provided. This may well account for a grant of 1527 by John Eggerton, Vicar 1520–28, which mentions that the parishioners will provide the land on which to build a Church House "unless by chance that House be partly within my cemetery there and partly outside the precincts". There has been some controversy as to whether the 'Lamb' public house was the building referred to in this grant, but the weight of evidence makes it seem unlikely. The first reference in any document to the 'Lamb' is in the Bailiwick Accounts for 1700, while as early as 1571 it is noted in the Parish Registers that Robert Dain "from the Church House' was buried in that year. Answers of a Jury of the Manor in 1617 to questions refer to the fact that the Town "holde the Market house and Churchhouse by virtue of ancient Graunts formerly made, Graunted and Confirmed'. Several documents during the seventeenth-century mention claims of the Crown that some part of the waste of the manor in the Market Street was occupied by Bailiwick property. Although Church Terriers in 1638 and 1708 make no mention of this, a significant Terrier of 1625 refers to neither the Churchhouse nor the 'Lamb' but it does note a 'parcell of land upon which stands Hempstead Market house for the most part'. From the position of the building and its shape, and from measurements noted when the old Town Hall replaced the earlier Market House it seems likely that the original Church House was taken over as a Market House sometime towards the end of the sixteenth-century With puritan views affecting attitudes to parish ales and wakes, and with the growth of inns and drinking-houses in the seventeenth to satisfy the thirsts of the town-folk the need for a Church House may well have disappeared. Built as it was, partly on church land and partly on manorial waste its structure and its site, which was a natural trading point, made the Church House an ideal Market House for the town. 'The Lamb' was probably originally one of the shops belonging to the Church which were enumerated in the Church Terriers; these shops were obviously both north and south of the space occupied by the butchers' shambles, and which later became the Market Square (now called St. Mary's Close). The local story that the choice of the name 'the Lamb' refers to the 'Agnus Dei' on the seal of Ashridge is, unfortunately, a myth.

Guilds and fraternities played a large part in the life of the community. Acting as benefit societies and burial clubs, they should not be confused with the trade organisations of merchants and craftsmen, though these often had their religious aspects. The former were usually named after a patron saint and part of their function was to celebrate masses for the souls of dead members and their families. In this they were similar to the chantries and sometimes provided an educational service, for a priest not employed continually would often supplement his income by teaching the rudiments of reading and writing. The small chapel which stood where the Victorian vestries now stand may well have been for a guild or 'brotherhood'; wills of the sixteenth-century contain many bequests to the 'brotherhood priest'. (See Chapter 4.)

The holding of fairs in churchyards on Sundays and Saints days was consistently and unsuccessfully prohibited from the Statute of Winchester, 1285, onwards. Often the clamour from without disturbed worship within and it is not coincidental that the site of Hemel Hempstead's old market was to be found just outside the hallowed ground where such fairs had been prohibited. The churchyard was, however, designated butts for archery, a sport continually enjoined upon Englishmen from the thirteenth to the seventeenth-century. The yew trees often found in the churchyards were to provide the wood for the bows.

The life of the vicar in the Middle Ages was hard, with the Devil on the one hand and the harsh, exacting rectors of Ashridge on the other. He had probably to say "morrow mass" at 4 a.m. or 5 a.m. for travellers and pilgrims on their way to Ashridge or St. Albans Abbey, mattins at 7 a.m., mass at 9 a.m. and evensong as the shadows lengthened. Sermons instructing the people "in the vulgar language on the articles of the creed, the ten commandments, the Evangelical precepts, the seven works of mercy, the

THE LAMB INN, CHURCH PROPERTY

THE MARKET BEFORE ITS REMOVAL TO MARLOWES

seven deadly sins, the seven principal virtues and the seven sacraments" were preached on Sundays and at the great festivals. Special services involving processions marked Palm Sunday and Ash Wednesday, and beating the bounds of the parish during the three Rogation Days before Ascension was a religious and gastronomic endurance test. As late as the mid-eighteenth century when such perambulations were not regularly undertaken, the cost to the parish was considerable:—

		£	s	d.
1771	Paid in going in Procession		14	0.
	Paid for liquor at Flaunden	1	17	6.
	Paid for Veal		8	0.
	Paid for liquor at home		9	0.
	Paid for cheese		16	4.
	Paid for second day in the morning		11	0.
	Paid for Leverstock Green		14	7.
	Paid at Corner Hall		4	5.
	Paid for a Ham		16	0.
	Paid at home for beer		14	0.
	Paid for Dinner		17	0.
	Paid for liquor	1	4	6.
		9	6	4.

The Reformation, of course, brought immediate changes to the living. After the suppression of Ashridge in 1539, the advowson passed to the Dean and Chapter of St. Pauls, London, who appointed the vicar on the nomination of the Bishop of Lincoln. John Holland, vicar from 1534 to 1550, the last appointed by the Rector of Ashridge, and James Wilson, 1550–64, seem to have weathered the oscillations of religious practice and belief during the period. The most unfortunate aspect of the religious changes was the destruction of virtually all the early documents relating to the parish which had been lodged at Ashridge. This too must have been the time when the medieval furnishings of the church were destroyed. What remained at St. Mary's after the storms of the Reformation, was systematically destroyed either by the Puritan fanatics of the next century or by the Victorian "restorers" of the nineteenth.

However, it is from the immediately post-Reformation period that most of the documents extant date, for it was in 1538 that Thomas Cromwell made the keeping of parish registers compulsory. In the early years many registers were on paper — even loose sheets — but in 1597 the incumbent was required each Sunday in the presence of the churchwardens to enter in a parchment volume the name of every person wedded, christened or buried during the preceding week. Entries from the old paper books had to be fairly and legibly copied into the new volume. As the entries for Hemel

Hempstead begin in 1558 for burials and 1566 for baptisms it seems that the first loose sheets were lost.

The number of entries in the Baptismal Register marked "Chrisom", those children who failed to survive that dangerous first month and whose christening robes became their shrouds, seems to twentieth-century observers shockingly high. All families, rich or poor, were equally afflicted. For example the Combes family who lived at the Bury suffered with the rest.

The Plague, too, was almost endemic in the sixteenth and seventeenth-centuries. October 1594 : "Elizabeth, wife of Henrie Smith, clerk, was buried of the Plague"; so harshly had it raged that "here som be wanting that dyed in plague time" and the whole family of John Dell were stricken and died between December 1593 and February 1594. (See p. 49) Again on 23rd August 1625 : "I buried today Edward Barker, Elizabeth his wife and Ellen his daughter were buried on their own backside at Two Waters dying of the Plague in the time of the great contagion at London."

Affidavits attesting to burials of the dead in woollens in accordance with the Act of 1666, passed to benefit the wool industry, are duly noted; "26th August 1777 Samuel, an infant son of Richard and Ann Sweby of The Lamb in the town. Affidavit". The Act remained in force until 1814, but the number of affidavits in later years declined sharply.

Other interesting burial entries include that of "Robert whose name was not known, a journeyman shoemaker", dated 27th January 1617, and that of "John Buckmaster aged about 96 years. Mary Buckmaster his wife aged about 88 years. This ancient couple is reported to have lived in wedlock about 73 years but of this there is no certainty". (1st January 1775). Sometimes a death brought benefit to St. Mary's : "Jonathan Rashleigh of Corner Hall, Esq., gave an addition to the Communion Plate of two large silver flagons and two silver salvers. A.D. 1694".

Thomas Taylor, incumbent from 1605 until his death in 1628 carefully inserted the hour as well as the day of birth when his own children were baptised:

> "1613. March 25th. Timothy the son of Mr. Thomas Taylor, Vicar, born the 25th about eleven of the clock in the night 1613.
> 1615. November 3rd. John son of Mr. Thomas Taylor, Vicar, born October 31st between seven and eight in the evening".

In the Barebones Parliament of 1653 the custody of parish registers was transferred from the Church to the Civil Authority and from 1654 until the 1660 Restoration, the Magistrate, not the minister, had the privilege of conducting marriage after the banns had been published in the market place. Only one such instance is recorded in Hemel Hempstead : "Henry Edwards and Winifred Beedmin both of Ivinghoe in the County of Bucks, publication of their intended marriage was made in the market place at Hemel Hempstead, it being the nearest market town to the place of their dwelling which sayd publication was made on three severall market days (that is to say on the 8th day of April 1654, the 10th and 27th days of the same month) according to the Act of Parliament."

Hertfordshire had always been a place where non-conformity was practised. In the fourteenth-century there was much support for Lollardry in Hemel Hempstead and the countryside around, and this continued in some form after it had been officially suppressed. It was natural that the spread of Puritan ideas should reach Hemel Hempstead during the times of Elizabeth I and grow, particularly during the 1640's and 1650's. These ideas were based on a number of objections to the established practice brought about by the Elizabethan Settlement of 1559. The Puritans felt that the Elizabethan church was too much like the Catholic one; they objected to a set form of worship, they demanded the abolition of such things as the sign of the cross in Baptism, the wearing of the surplice, the custom of bowing at the name of Jesus, and the reading of the Apocrypha in church, and they wanted more and better preaching. The main bulk of the Puritans were content to work quietly to achieve their aims but there were a few ardent and intolerant souls who could brook no delay, and some who found membership of the Church of England difficult to sustain.

Locally, a pronounced strain of Puritanism became evident with the appointment to St. Mary's of William Horne in 1573 and Richard Gawton in 1582, whose work was continued by his curate, William Dyke, who followed in the living in 1594. In these and later times the Puritans found support in the leading families in the district, including the Combes. Reference to the growth of dissent in the sixteenth-century has already been made in Chapter 4 and cases of absence from church are mentioned there. Such absences on Sundays, feasts or Saints Days attracted a fine of twelve pence to go to the relief of the poor, and cases were heard before the Archdeacons' Court held every three weeks at Hitchin.

The first vicar appointed in the seventeenth-century was Thomas Taylor, instituted in 1605, who continued in the living until he died in 1628. During his time a number of events occurred in some of which he was involved, including a complaint against him heard in the Star Chamber in 1621. It was in his reply to that complaint that he stated his object had been to maintain "unyty peace and concord" and that he was disliked because he had tried to make some of his parishioners conform. He was accused of publishing libels about certain of his flock; that certain of them lived adulterous lives whilst others were given to drunkenness. The outcome of the proceedings is not known, but Thomas Taylor continued with the living until he died in 1628. It must be said, however, that the complainants were substantial inhabitants and included John Besouth who among other occupations was clerk to the Bailiwick and Thomas Deacon, a well-to-do tanner of Corner Hall who was elected Bailiff in 1637.

It was during his time that the church fell into some disrepair as is evidenced by the presentment of Robert Coleman for irreverently sitting in the church with his hat on at the Gloria Patri. He alleged that he did so because the rain fell on him as he sat in his seat. He was piously admonished and the Vicar was ordered to have the necessary repairs carried out.

Fortunately we have had preserved the will and the inventory of the goods of Thomas Taylor when he died; the inventory deals solely with personal property, mainly in the vicarage, but also indicates that he owned a house at Great Gaddesden. The general household effects were of no great significance and were such as one would expect, but there are several other items of note, as

A muskett, head piece, sword and dagger and other things belonging to them	1. 0. 0.
Due upon a bond	30. 0. 0.
All the books in this study	22. 8. 0.
Accompted for good debt upon his Easter Books	23. 8. 8.
One nagg	2. 10. 0.

The total of the inventory was £145. 8s. 8d.

The item of his 'Easter Books' is interesting and may indicate a greater popularity among his flock than the Star Chamber proceedings would imply. As to the house in Great Gaddesden, his will explains how he had already made this over to his brother-in-law-Knight and William Halsey, in trust for the education and upbringing of his eight children. The rest of his effects were also left to the same two for the same purpose.

During Thomas Taylor's period there were a number of presentments for failing to attend divine service including:—

1610 John Sheppard and Richard Smith of Bovingdon for not coming to our parish church; Michael Humphrey of Felden for not receiving the Communion and Ralph South for absenting himself from church for three months.

1614 Richard Miles and Frances his wife, Elizabeth the wife of Richard Partridge and Marie her daughter, all of Bovingdon — "Sectaries that come not to church".

1622 The old stagers John Settle and his wife Margaret were consistent in their absence from their parish church and in due course were charged before Quarter Sessions.

Thomas Taylor was succeeded in 1628 by John Taylor, who was no relation. He seemed to have been a follower of Archbishop Laud and one for the strict observance of the sabbath according to the rites of the established church. In this he fell foul of his parishioners who ultimately petitioned Parliament for his removal from the living. He became involved in argument and later litigation with Francis Combes. In 1637 he (Taylor) petitioned that Combes was incorrectly assessed for rates on the impropriate tithe – of which Combes was the farmer – and suggested that an assessment of £250 should be £500. Whether it was this matter or another which became the subject of litigation is by no means clear, but a suit was begun against the Vicar and resulted in the latter being fined £50 and costs to Combes. A second suit involved John Ashton, described as the agent of Francis Combes, in fines of £50 and costs to the Vicar. According to the documents of 1639-40 Ashton was then a prisoner in the Fleet. In 1642 Ashton petitioned the Long Parliament for "relief against several sentences of the Court of High Commission of which he has been fined and imprisoned, at the suit of Mr. Taylor, the Vicar, for playing "Stool Ball" with the curate and others on a holiday."

Whatever the outcome of Ashton's petition Puritanism continued to grow, and in the diocese of Lincoln the Bishop had received a number of complaints that communion tables were being moved from the transept or chancel to the east walls of churches, where the old altar had stood, and there protected by rails according to the Laudian fashion. Thus on the 5th of October 1640 a witness stated "I did hear Edmund Ayles say that he was the the Captain of those unruly soldiers that did pull down the rails in our church or chancel, and that those were the last of seventeen that he had pulled down and broken with his own hand. Likewise he said he was one of the two committed by Thomas Conesby, Esq., into prison at Hemsted but he was brought out of prison by the soldiers by force and if at any time he were in distress he could have five hundred to relieve him. I said unto him: 'Suppose you were dismissed from His Majesty's service?' He answered: 'That they would follow their work however and that there should not stand one rail within ten miles of Hemsted' – Jno. Briggs."

Attempts by John Taylor to prevent the spread of such doctrines merely incurred further wrath, and there were clashes between vicar and parishioners over the interpretation of Francis Combe's will of 1641 whereby he charged his estate called Hemsted Bury with the payment of 20 marks a year for ever for a learned and godly man to preach a Thursday lecture. Taylor maintained that he should be the Thursday lecturer, but the parishioners petitioned the House of Commons "that Mr. Phillip Goodwin may be appointed Lecturer to preach on Sunday afternoon and Thursday morning, market day, without hindrance from the Vicar John Taylor."

Puritanism in the town could not stomach Taylor's views and as a result he was turned out of the living. Further petitioning led to the appointment to the living, by both Houses of Parliament, of Rev. George Kendall. Kendall, however, proved to be an Anabaptist who refused to baptise infants and claimed that the Church of England was no Church, and 1643 found him consigned to Newgate prison. On April 8th 1644 it was "ordered that Mr. Kendall now a prisoner in Newgate shall be released of his imprisonment, giving sufficient security in a bond of £500 not to publish any of his opinions either in the prison or elsewhere, contrary to the doctrines of the Church of England."

On the 7th of May 1644 Parliament again considered a petition from the inhabitants of Hemel Hempstead: "Pray that Mr. James Asheton may be appointed their pastor and that power may be given to him to recover all arrears of dues payable since the ejection of the last minister". Mr. Ashton lasted only until 1646 for then it was ordered that the living should stand sequestered unto the use of John Warren," a godly orthodox divine", a man highly esteemed during his ministry until his death in 1657.

In June 1656 John Warren petitioned the Lord Protector Cromwell in the following terms "The parish is large and the market of great public resort. I have a family of ten, have preached nine years, and undergone great hardship rather than remove on the death of the registered incumbent, I have lately paid £40 first fruits, tenths, etc. There are £47 augmentable profits paid in yearly by Richard Combe and one and a half years ago I petitioned the Trustees for Ministers for an Augmentation, but after I spent much time and money they postponed the case and said they must have your special order. This I beg the rather because a Parsonage of £160 a year has lately fallen to the Trustees in the next Parish". The petitioner was successful and an augmentation of £35 per annum was granted.

It is not clear exactly what happened to Matthew Carr,(appointed vicar in 1657 by Cromwell) at the Restoration of Charles II in 1660. At all events in 1661 the Rev. George Screven was at the vicarage and noted in the register "I have not copied out any christenings of the year 1660 which was before my time because I am informed many were set down which were never baptised". Certainly non-conformity was still rife: "27th December 1661, John Wood buryed his wife without Christian buriall". Screven presented before the Archdeacon's Court twenty or more persons for not coming to church, as well as the two church wardens John Curl and James Dagnell for neglect of their duties. Non-payment of tithes by non-conformists, especially Quakers, was a constant bone of contention: "24th October 1673 – Thomas Robins, a husbandman of Hemel Hempstead, was committed to Hertford gaol for a claim of eight shillings tithes at the suit of Joel Jones". (Joel Jones was vicar 1670–1687 and Thomas Robins was a Quaker.)

A demonstration that the church was still a ladder of preferment open to the humblest was the career of Nicholas Strafford, born in 1633, son of a shoemaker in Hemel Hempstead. Christmas day 1682 found him preaching on the Atonement before Charles II at Whitehall and the sermon was afterwards published by special command of the King. "The Lay-Christian's Obligation to read the Scriptures", written in 1687, marked him out as a High Church Tory. In spite of this he was created Bishop of Chester on 15th

September 1689. Strafford's voting in the House of Lords was not sufficiently latitudinarian or frequent to secure further advancement, so he remained Bishop of Chester until his death in 1707.

On Sunday 14th April 1700 he preached at St. Mary's a sermon which was subsequently published and dedicated: "To my Beloved Friends the Inhabitants of the Town and Parish of Hempstead. It was not my intention that this sermon should be made more public than it was by preaching, but at the earnest request of some of you, backed with such reasons as I could not easily withstand, I was prevailed with to send it to the Press. Though I cannot but have a more than ordinary respect for the Town in which I drew my first breath, and for those persons more especially in it, with whom in my early age I frequently conversed, yet should I deny you any assistance by which you might be better enabled to repel and overcome those temptations of the world, you might justly conclude I had but little regard to the salvation of your souls. I therefore recommend this short discourse . . ."

From the documents we can describe two vicarages of Hemel Hempstead. The first was one described in a Church Terrier of 1625 as "consisting of three bayes built of timber and covered with tile, all chambered over and boarded and the whole building disposed into eight rooms, viz., the hall, the parlour the kitchen and a groundseller under, and foure chambers above", with sundry outbuilding, a garden and an orchard. The inventory of Thomas Taylor's goods, dated 1628, and already referred to above, agrees with this description, except that it mentions only three chambers above; one could have been either dilapidated or unused.

This building was probably in poor condition — like the church itself — and was probably erected much earlier. However, the new vicar soon had it replaced by a new building (the second vicarage) described in a terrier of 1638 as containing a hall, kitchen, two lodging chambers and two garrets over, with sundry outbuildings, a garden and an orchard. It also had a parlour on the ground floor, probably omitted in error from the reference in the terrier. This is confirmed in another terrier of 1708 at the time when Cornelius Price was the vicar; this terrier deals with the church and the glebe land in much more detail. The vicarage was built with timber and bricks, and covered with tiles, the parlour had a boarded floor and the hall had a brick one, There was a considerable number of outbuildings, and the orchard, garden, courtyard and back yard contained in all one acre and were fenced with pales.

The 1708 terrier throws an interesting light on the fees the vicar might expect:

"As for the surplice fees what they have been of old we cannot learn, but when Mr. Price became Vicar (1705) Marriage Fees either with or without Licence were five shillings, burial one shilling in the churchyard and two shillings in the Church or Chancel or any part of them and double for all strangers and sixpence for Churching. And as concerning Mortuaries the churchwardens and parishioners do say that no Mortuaries are due or payable within the said parish, but the present Vicar do believe the same to be due and payable according to the statue. Twelve pence for publishing Banns of Marriage."

By the end of the seventeenth-century the interior of St. Mary's can be seen in the earliest surviving prints — horse-box pews, a three-decker pulpit and a choir screen. The organ was placed in a gallery over the west door spanning the nave.

About 1706 a quarrel which had long been simmering between the Chapelries of Bovingdon and Flaunden and the mother church at St. Mary's came to a head and began a movement towards separation, which finally took place in 1833.

As far as the Mother Church was concerned Bovingdon and Flaunden had one parsonage and one vicar — at St. Mary's — and they had to make an annual payment of 20s. besides their tithes. Further, they held that Bovingdon had yearly to repair part of the fence of the mother churchyard and provide a bell rope for one of the bells. Since an agreement made on St. Mary Magdalene's Day 1428, they ought to pay a third-part of the costs in repairing the fabric of St. Mary's. It was strongly maintained that the chapelries were part of the Manor of Hemel Hempstead and were not parishes in their own right for they had never paid separate first fruits or tenths to the King nor procurations, nor synodalls to the Bishop.

Against this Bovingdon and Flaunden argued that the changes wrought by King Henry VIII in fact constituted three separate cures and the vicar had no power over their curates. True it was that they yearly and constantly paid 34s. to the overseers of the Poor of Hemel Hempstead, duly contributed to the repairs of the churchyard fence and provided the rope for the middle bell, but they paid 20s. yearly to the vicar in lieu of first fruits, tenths, procurations, synodalls and all other dues including tithes. Had they not all the essentials of parishes? — Churches where they could christen, marry, administer the sacraments and bury; churchwardens, overseers to care for their own poor, their own rates, in all things separate and distinct from the Church of Hemel Hempstead.

The main contention of the outlying chapels, namely, that they were separate parishes was invalid; but they were correct in saying that they might be used for marriage, administration of the sacraments and burials. When these rights were conferred is not known except in the case of burials in Flaunden which were allowed by Papal Bull in 1478 on the grounds that it was more than five miles from the mother church.

It is curious how long the trifling contribution for a bell rope continued to be enforced. The Churchwardens' accounts for 1741/1742 show that new bell ropes were put to the Hemel Hempstead bells and there was "received of

Bovingdon Parish for last year's bell rope 4s.6d.", and again "spent when the new bell ropes were put on 15s. "

Certainly the chapelries had much of which to complain. Writing of Flaunden, Nathaniel Salmon records in 1728 "This church is hard for a stranger to find and the Curate for want of endowment cannot find the way thither more than one Sunday in a month and that in an afternoon".

"A party of ladies and gentlemen who were visiting in the neighbourhood walked down to old Flaunden Church. 'How very interesting' remarked one of the party, 'I should so like to attend service here.' 'Well, tomorrow is the regular day' replied the woman who was showing them over the church, 'but I do hope and trust it will rain, and then the parson won't come, for I've got one of my best hens sitting on thirteen eggs in the pulpit and she won't come off till Tuesday".

As far as Bovingdon was concerned: "On the appointed fourth Sunday if the weather were fine, a man was stationed on the top of the Tower of Bovingdon Church whence he commanded a view of the road leading from Hemel Hempstead. If he saw the parson or his curate approaching, he would descend and ring the bell to summon the parishioners to Church.

"If it rained or snowed, it was quite unnecessary to place a man on the look-out. It sometimes happened that for three consecutive months there was no divine service held either at Flaunden or Bovingdon. A Labourer, not fifty years old, told me that he had often known a corpse, when become too offensive to keep longer in the house, to remain three, four or five days in the Church before a clergyman from the mother church could be procured to perform the burial service."

Such casual treatment of the chapels indicated the usual attitude of the Established Church throughout most of the eighteenth-century. Certainly there is a self-satisfied complacency about the churchwardens' accounts for the period 1735—1777. (This is the only account book to survive.)

St. Mary's seems to have been a closed vestry, for the same names appear over and over again, some spanning a period of thirty years; Kellam, Perry, Puddephatt, Johnson, Warren. A large proportion of the expenses of the churchwardens was accounted for in attending the Bishop's visitations at Welwyn three or four times a year (the standard expenses were 12s. per visitation) and treating themselves royally on beating the bounds, as we have already seen. Likewise the Great Tithe Banquet seems to have been very largely a self-indulgent affair:

1773	Mr. Perry and the overseers going around the Parish for two days to take an account of the Great Tythe Dinner	.... 6s. 0d.

Paid for liquor in going round the parish for the Great Tythe:

	The first day	5s.	0d.
	Second day for Dinner	6s.	0d.
	And liquor	7s.	4d.
May 8th Dinner for 10		15s.	0d.
	Wine	10s.	0d.
	Punch	7s.	0d.
	Beer	3s.	6d.
	Horse Hire	3s.	0d.
	Ringers	10s.	0d.

On this occasion the Bishop was visiting the parish.

In 1733 a new book of accounts was started and the retiring wardens took an inventory of "Church goods delivered . . . to Thomas Howlett and William Axtel, Churchwardens for the year 1733":

Two surplices
One silver cup and cover
Two silver flagons and two silver salvers the gifts of John Rashleigh, Esq.
One silver spoon
One Holland Table Cloth
Two Diaper Napkins marks with H.H. 1669
One Great Bible
A Brass Pully
6 Keys to the Poor Box and Chest
4 Boxes to gather Collections
Bishop Jewell's Works against Harding
Erasmus — his Paraphrase of the New Testament
The Book of Martyrs
A Cushion and Cloth for the Pulpit
A Carpet to the Communion Table all purple broadcloth
Four Books of Common Prayer of the largest volume
A box on the Stone
A Leadon Standish
A Book of Homilies
An Hood for the Minister
Two Brass Sconces for the Pulpit
The Table of Marriages
Directions for gathering Briefs upon frames.
A Box for the Communion Plate
A Branch the gift of John Crawley, Gent.
A Book to enter Crissins.
(Brass Sconce: hanging or projecting candlestick.
Standish: case for pen and ink.
Branch: chandelier).

Many of the payments made by the churchwardens are dull and routine — the sort of payments always necessary to keep the fabric in decent repair.

May 3rd 1739: Pd. Robert Bigg and William Dell for several days' work in cleaning the church spouts and working in the churchyard . . . 18s. 6d.

During an epidemic expenditure of another kind was involved:

November 1741 :	Paid carrying Eames family to the Post House	1s. 6d.
	Paid carrying Widow Coker to the Post House	1s. 6d.

and regularly a number of these entries:

June 1744/5: Going round the parish several times putting out poor children . . . 3s. 6d.

betrays the practice of clearing the workhouse of pauper children and apprenticing them to masters in the town.

Even the great global struggle against France in the eighteenth-century impinged on the quiet tenor of rural life:

1743	Paid by Mrs. Samuel Hills	
	Paid Mary Hill for Ringing after the B. of Dettingon	10s. 0d.
	Paid the ringers on the King's return	10s. 0d.

Hemel Hempstead celebrated the safe return of George II from what proved to be the last occasion on which a king of England led his troops on the battlefield in person. The heartfelt thanks of the town was shown when in:

1746	Paid Mary Hill for the Ringers on the occasion of the Duke's gaining the victory over the rebels	10s. 0d.

William, Duke of Cumberland's victory over Bonnie Prince Charlie was a profound relief to an anxious nation.

The year of victories in the Seven Year's War, the annus mirabillis of 1759, led to a good deal of expenditure on bellringing:

1759	Paid for Ringing on occasion of Prince Ferdinand of Brunswick gaining a complete victory over the French	15s. 0d.
August 10.	Paid for the Ringing for the taking of Quebec . . .	10s. 0d.

November 19. Paid for Ringing on the Day of Thanksgiving	. . .		15s. 0d.
December 2nd. Paid for Ringing on Admiral Hawkes taking of the French fleet (Quiberon Bay)	. . .		10s. 0d.

The first new king for thirty-five years led to right royal celebrations:

1760	Paid proclaiming the King George III	£5.	8s.	7d.
	To Punch on the King's Coronation	£1.	5s.	0d.
	Beer at the same time		9s.	6d.

The Bailiwick supplemented these expenditures as is shown by their accounts.

On the flyleaves at the end of the Register for Baptisms and Burials 1764–1797 the Rev. Dr. Bingham wrote an account of the preparations made to withstand the threatened invasion of Napoleon: "At a meeting of the inhabitants of Hemel Hempstead convened by the Rev. Dr. Bingham (notice of which had been given in the church the preceding Sunday) on Friday the 5th day of August 1803 at the Town Hall for the purpose of considering of the best method of serving Our King and Country at this important crisis . . .". There followed at length a detailed account of the formation of the Loyal Hemel Hempstead Volunteers and of the Dedication of their Colours in St. Mary's on Sunday the 4th December 1803, together with a precis of Dr. Bingham's sermon and special prayers for this occasion.

Another flyleaf note was made on June 9th 1827 : "A dreadful fire broke out in the middle of the night and raged till morning – two homes destroyed others injured – much property stolen or spoilt".

The eighteenth-century also saw the parish well endowed by munificent benefactors. Thomas Warren, for instance, "by his will dated November 2 1796 gave £1,200 stock 3% Consolidated Bank Annuities in trust to apply the Dividends thereof as follows: £7. 10s. 0d. part thereof to be distributed equally to and between 50 poor widows . . . the residue to be applied in the establishment of two free schools . . . for the education of poor children whose parents are of the Protestant religion . . . Equal pay did not exist as the Master of the Boy's School was to have an annual stipend of £15. 12s. 0d, while the Mistress of the Girls' School was to have only £12. 5s. 0d. This echoed an earlier bequest from Francis Combe for "10 pounds a year for ever for maintaining a Free School for Teaching the poor of this Parish to read, write and cost accounts".

Changes in the Church fabric and furnishings took place too: "Peter de Lamotte, Esq., ciel'd the north and south isles in the body of the Church A.D. 1726." "Bulstrode Peachey, Knight, Esq., Impropriator of the Great Tithe of this Parish gave £20 towards erecting the altar piece, 1730".

Also in the eighteenth-century it was decided to add to the five bells of the sixteenth-century to make the present peal of eight bells: Treble and 2nd, both by Lester and Pack; 3rd by Chandler 1688; 4th by Robert Oldfield 1633:, 5th by John Dyer 1590; 6th by Robert Hot 1604; 7th by Robert Oldfield 1617; and Tenor by Lester and Pack 1717. The Chime barrel was installed in 1761 by J. Eayre of St. Neots and the church clock was a gift from Lord Marchmont in 1784. Many of these changes seem to have been part of extensive alterations and renovations undertaken around 1759, but the faculties are missing and information is therefore scant. The lead of the spire was "repaired by H. Pedley, Plumber 1800" according to an inscription on a portion of lead blown down in a gale in 1938.

An entry from the Vestry Order Book dated 7th June 1819 may record the change from the old box pews. The committee reported that "between the years 1800 and 1810 there was an increase of 400 in the population of this parish. There can be no difficulty in accounting for the numerous applications which have lately been made for pews. About 200 additional sittings will be gained by the plan they intend to propose. They hope that no member of the Church of England in this parish will in future absent himself from Divine Worship because he cannot be accommodated with a convenient seat".

Another extensive restoration was undertaken in 1846 but again evidence is lacking. By this time St. Mary's was beginning to assume the character it now possesses both inside and out,the fields to the south being a fortunate legacy from the reactionary Astley Paston Cooper, Lord of the Manor until 1841. In September and October 1860 it was agreed that the organ and the western gallery be removed and "that the organ be placed in the chamber on the north side of the chancel end of the church". By 1862 a new organ had been installed (itself replaced by the present one in 1910, when it was built into the north transept). In 1879 the vestry again resolved that "it is desirable to remove the pulpit and to place it either in the south-east or north-east corner of the nave . . . To remove the galleries in the north and south transepts". At the same time the chancel was restored with a new roof above the Norman stone vaulting. New gas lamps, a brass eagle lectern (presented by the Misses Hamilton of Marlowes), a reredos from Oberammergau and east window both in memory of the Dowager Lady Cooper, and a jewelled silver gilt chalice and patens (presented by Miss Grover) completed the changes. In 1885 the nave roof was restored and three years later a new west window to commemorate Victoria's Jubilee, and the renewal of the thirteenth-century colouring of the roof and walls of the chancel was completed, (given by the Misses Hamilton and Miss Godwin of Grove Hill). The final changes came in 1897 when the new vestries were built and the choir reseated (the Misses Varney joining previous benefactors) and a little later the painting of the Annunciation placed at the crossing in memory of the Misses Hamilton.

It remains to quote from certain official documents. The Royal Commission on Ecclesiastical Revenues, 1835, states that the gross income of the incumbent was £785, and this related to the whole parish for which there were two curates. The glebe house was said not to be fit for residence. The 1851 Census gives the income in more detail:

	£
Tithe	500
Glebe	100
Fees	25
Easter Offering	5
Rent of churchyard	5
	635

The outgoings then were £190.

The revival of religious faith in the nineteenth century ran concurrently with the expansion of population and this inevitably necessitated new chapels-of-ease to serve a prosperous and expanding area. Eventually new ecclesiastical parishes were carved out of what had been St. Mary's benefice. After the separation of Bovingdon and Flaunden, Boxmoor was created a parish in 1844 and the original chapel of 1829 was replaced by the present Victorian Gothic church of St. John the Evangelist in April 1874. Within the parish of Boxmoor is the church of St. Francis Hammerfield, dedicated in 1914 after religious meetings had been held since 1908 at 7, Glenview Gardens.

Holy Trinity, Leverstock Green, was built in 1849 and became an ecclesiastical parish in 1850. At Apsley, the Church of St. Mary was erected in 1871 and in May 1873 was created a parish from parts of the parishes of Hemel Hempstead, Abbots Langley and Kings Langley. The church was erected largely through the generosity of Charles Longman and his fellow directors of John Dickinson and Company.

St. Paul's, Hemel Hempstead, was first a chapel-of-ease to St. Mary's in 1869 and became a separate parish in 1878, though the two parishes were reunited in 1960. All Saints, Piccotts End, a chapel-of-ease, was consecrated in 1907.

So St. Mary's stands even now at the centre of the spiritual life of Hemel Hempstead as it has stood for over eight hundred years. Perhaps it is no longer the centre of bitter religious controversy, noisy parish pump politics, riotous ales and wakes. Nonetheless the stones still echo to the sounds of long ago and it remains for the spiritual comfort of our souls — the very same purpose that moved the Normans to apply the adze and saw and mortar to the stone than newly-quarried, to build their church in the manor and vill of Hamelamstede.

Note on Sources

In addition to works listed in the general sources, reference has been made to:—

4 Henry IV Cap. 12. 1402
Commons Journals ii. 608, and
House of Lords Calendar 1642 (for the petition against John Taylor).
Lambeth MSS. Augmentation 997 Mar. 11, 1656/7
(for John Warren's petition).
The description of Flaunden and Bovingdon churches in the eighteenth-century are quoted in Cussans, 'History of Hertfordshire'

CHAPTER 11

Part 2

The Rise of Dissent and the Development of Nonconformist Congregations in Hemel Hempstead.

During the reign of Elizabeth I most of the Puritans were content to work quietly for the overthrow of the Establishment and to work to that end within the established church. But there were others, more impatient, who sought to satisfy their religious feelings elsewhere than within the Church of England. This independence of thought arose partly from private reading of the Bible, a practice which developed in the time of the early Stuarts, and which led to private interpretations of the Holy Word. Hence, the desire for independence of worship resulted in the creation of a variety of sects, which became the foundation of nonconformity. During the Commonwealth and Protectorate the number of these independent sects increased, but the main groups were the Presbyterians, the Congregationalists or Independents, the Baptists and the Quakers.

Locally the Baptists seemed to find their main support within the Church of England. As shown in the earlier part of this chapter there was a succession of ministers who favoured the Baptist principles. It was doubtless because of the restrictive legislation passed soon after the Restoration of the Monarchy in 1660 that small groups began privately to meet to worship as they wanted to. One such group is mentioned in the records for 1662.

In September of that year there were presented to Quarter Sessions John Brandley shoemaker; James Robson tanner; Thomas Meare shoemaker; Thomas Halsey, alias Chambers, and John Wood collarmakers; and James Field and Nicholas Clover Husbandmen; all of Hemel Hempstead, and charged that they "unlawfully assembled under colour of exercising acts of religious worship other than those of the established Church of England, and buried the body of John Brandley in an orchard." In October 1662 Brandley, Robson, Meare, Halsey, Wood and Field, together with Samuel and Nathaniel Southing (probably Southen or Southern) were similarly presented for refusing to attend Divine Service. The outcome of these proceedings is not recorded on the calendar of the Sessions Books. But they do disclose that when two years later, one of them, James Field, was again before the same Court he refused to plead, and was fined £10 and committed to gaol until he paid the fine.

In his parish register the Vicar, George Screven, a conformist, recorded the burial as being by "a company of Quakers and Annabaptists." In doing so he probably did not know to which particular sect these people belonged, but used a term then commonly employed to describe non-conformists generally. It might be well to ascertain what we can about the individuals concerned in these proceedings.

The deceased, John Brandley was Bailiff of Hemel Hempstead in 1651–2; he carried on his business in the Towne area. His son (who was charged) continued with the business; he was appointed Constable for the Towne area in 1651 and again in 1659; according to the Hearth Tax Return for 1663 he occupied a house with two hearths. James Robson was appointed Constable for the High Street side also in 1651, and occupied a much larger house, which had six hearths; he owned land in Corner hall, where he lived, and he may well have been interested in the tannery there which belonged to the Deacons. He was obviously a man of some substance. Thomas Meare was probably a craftsman and little is known about him; he was assessed in the rate levied for the Oxley cases at the moderate sum of 5s. 0d. Thomas Halsey had a cottage with courtyard and orchard in High Street Green; it had two hearths. Later he may well have been the landlord of the Ship (later called the Holly Bush) on the east side of the Market Street. John Wood, who was appointed Headborough for Crouchfield and Greenend in 1651 was probably a craftsman. Nothing is known of James Field and Nicholas Clover.

Of the two Southings (most certainly Southern or Southen) it can be said they were members of a well-known and well-to-do local family. Both were yeomen, farming on a good scale, Samuel at Warners End and Nathaniel at Boxsend. The former, who was Bailiff of Hemel Hempstead in 1656–7, had a house with four hearths and Nathaniel one with five.

It is clear that the individuals involved in these affairs represented a cross section of the community and may have been a representative few out of a larger number who shared their religious beliefs. They may have been a selected few who were chosen to be charged. It is equally certain that among the adherents to this sect were men of substance. It is noticeable that several of them held an official position of one kind or another during the 1650's, a period in which the Puritans were generally in authority locally. Whether the persons charged were Baptists or Quakers is uncertain but the evidence points to them being Baptists.

In the next year there were more so listed. These people were undoubtedly the early nucleus in Hemel Hempstead of a non-conformist congregation. To start with they met in private houses or other small buildings to avoid action by the authorities, but later, with the relief afforded by the Toleration Act 1689, they began to assemble more openly in buildings provided for public worship. They must also have enjoyed the support of some of the principal families in the district which would dissuade the authorities from taking action against the dissenters. When these separate buildings for divine worship were first erected, and to what denomination they belonged, is not known, but certainly one of the first was Box Lane Chapel.

Just as Lady Bacon of Gorhambury and the Combes of Hemel Hempstead had earlier helped on the Puritan cause, so now the well-to-do owners of

Westbrook Hay, first the Maynes up to 1642 and then the Lomaxes probably encouraged Puritanism in the Bovingdon area, where the curates (under St. Mary's, Hemel Hempstead) were also of the Puritan persuasion, for outlying daughter parishes were often neglected by the Church of England. The well known Puritan Minister, Dr. Edward Staunton, formerly of St. Albans whence he was ejected with other such ministers after the Restoration) retired to Bovingdon. He preached locally, including Hemel Hempstead, and died in Bovingdon where he was buried in 1671.

The Westbrook Hay area was then a good place for a Dissenting Chapel and Urwick states that there was a meeting place in Box Lane "half a century before the Act of Toleration" of 1689. The present chapel is inscribed "Rebuilt 1690". The Chapel is certainly older than its Trust Deed of 1697, which speaks of the building "as lately erected". Remote sites like this, well away from towns and prying eyes, and if possible under the protection of a local squire, were essential during the difficult years for non-conformists, especially 1662–1689, when their conventicles were illegal and their ministers harassed and not allowed within five miles of their former parishes. Box Lane was reputed to be a bridle path, but it may well have been "the highway which leads to Wycombe" mentioned in the 1523 Survey. Be that as it may the locality was sufficiently remote, and the means of escape – a hatch or doorway at the back of the pulpit – such as to give the worshippers a sense of some security when taking part in Divine Worship of a kind not approved by the State.

When the building which was replaced in 1690 was first erected, and what was its construction, is not known. The chapel authorities, in a brochure published to mark the 350th anniversary, claim that the Rev. Thomas Wilcocks was the founder and possibly the first Pastor; he was an eminent Puritan, who suffered imprisonment and other indignities for his beliefs; he frequently preached at Bovingdon, probably under the protection of the Maynes. He died in 1608. The presentment in 1614 of the Miles and Partridge families as "sectaries that come not to church" bears out the existence of an early Puritan congregation in Bovingdon (See p.238.) The next pastor we know of was Thomas Whitehead who held the office when the Trust Deed was executed in 1679. He was succeeded by Joshua Bayes in 1706, who had been educated at the famous Dissenting Academy at Attercliffe near Sheffield, and was a fellow student there of one of the Lomaxes. By 1715, under its then minister, George Boyde, the chapel had a congregation of 300, an extraordinary number for such a remote chapel. (But see below).

The meeting had usually been Independent or Congregationalist, and the latter sect had been in charge of it for some years. There appears to be some doubt as to whether it was originally Congregationalist or Presbyterian. But in 1706 it was described as being Presbyterian. In the official census of church attendances taken in 1851 the chapel is shown as Independent and as founded in 1714; the accommodation was free, and sixty people attended the morning service and 300 in the afternoon.

This census was taken officially in 1851, the only one of its kind. It sought to ascertain among other things, the origin of the building as a place of worship, the amount of accommodation available, and the attendances at Divine Worship, either on a specified date or by average.

The Quakers had probably been meeting at the Cross Lane Meeting House, Wood Lane End, near to the way to Redbourne (on the site now marked as Meeting House Field) from 1652, and certainly from 1667. In 1684 Thomas Richards of St. Albans wrote to John Chauney, Clerk of the Peace, "my business falls out so that I can not possibly wait on you on Monday, so much desire your pardon for my non-attendance. There is a Quakers' Meeting constantly held every Sunday at Wood End, Hemel Hempstead Parish. Mr. Marston, one of the High Constables of Dacorum Hundred, lives hard by and I don't hear tell ever disturbed them. I thought fit to acquaint you with it that you may admonish Marston." Worship continued there until the beginning of the eighteenth century and then the building remained unused. There was a burial ground attached to the Meeting House and among the thirty-three burials recorded as taking place there were those of James and Elizabeth Stirredge who came to live here in 1688, and found Hemel Hempstead a haven of peace after their imprisonment for their faith in Somerset. Elizabeth found some fame in Quaker circles by the posthumous publication in editions of 1711, 1746, 1772 and 1795 of her "Strength in Weakness Manifest in Life" showing her pious care of her children. She died in 1706, aged 72 years. One local Quaker was James Haydon, a miller of Piccotts End, who died in 1729 and is described in the parish register as having been a Quaker for many years.

With the coming of toleration, and less need for secrecy in meeting, it was decided to move to a more central position, and in 1718 a small plot of land belonging to the Bell Inn, High Street, was bought for £26. 11s. 0d. and on it a new meeting house was erected at a cost of £315. 8s. 1½d. This was restored in 1808 and much improved around 1860. There is much interest in the early records of this meeting house, notably the story of the Quaker schoolmaster, John Owen. He came in 1704 as the result of a proposal, at the Watford monthly meeting, to set up a school in or near Hemel Hempstead for the education of Friends' children. He was to teach "all the learning he is capable of teaching at £30 per annum, (except Merchants' Accounts). He can teach in the Meeting House." He became joint clerk of the monthly meeting in 1706 and was a leading contributor to the new Meeting House. In 1720 he was indicted before the Justices at Hertford for keeping a private school for boys without a licence from the Archbishop, Bishop or spiritual guardian. He was found 'not guilty'. No doubt he was technically guilty, but the Act was being less and less observed. One of Owen's pupils was Thomas Birch (1705–1766) F.R.S., F.S.A., Secretary to the Royal Society 1752–65. He acted at one time as usher to Owen. There are many records, up to modern times in the parish, of Quakers refusing to pay tithe or church rates, and this resulted in the distraint of their goods. An example is shown from Owen's own story –

> 1720 Taken from John Owen by Joseph Carpenter, Warden (i.e. churchwarden) and Ralph Squire, Constable, by warrants – 1 Kettle, 1 Pottage Pot, 1 Chocolate Pot, valued in all at 20 shillings for six shillings demanded for his church rate so called.

This distress was presumably levied at his house at Waterside, Piccotts End.

From 1690 these early Quakers seem to have provided help for their aged members, and, on one occasion at least, paid for half a year's rent of 15s. and fuel for a member. In 1711 they bought a dozen books "against profane swearing." They also showed their high moral principles in 1706 when one Nathaniel Narb, who was not a member but only an attender, was reported to the Friends as having defrauded the Government over the Excise upon malt. Friends were to visit him or "draw up such a paper as may help to clear the truth and let the world know that the man was not in unity with us – we greatly condemn the action." In 1713 Edmond Neale of Redbourn was in trouble with the members for having redeemed his tithe charge and so weakened the Friends' testimony. He must have listened, for in 1715 his wheat was requisitioned for tithe. The meeting closed in 1905, but was re-opened in 1948; there was a burial there as late as 1931.

The Quakers were a small community but their influence was often much greater than their numbers. From time to time the Freeholders Book refers to men as "Quakers". Men of propriety they may have been, but often also men of property. We can mention but a few. First the family of Squires. There is a reference in 1747 to Thomas Squires of Piccotts End, and in 1768 to another Thomas Squires, schoolmaster of the Towne or High Street. Whether these were the same or father and son is not clear, but one or the other or both were owners of property and lenders of money on mortgage. A mortgage on a farm of 60 acres called New House, situated above Piccotts End and near Two Beeches was foreclosed, and a malt house and other property in Piccotts End was acquired. The Dearmers were another eighteenth century family of note.

A nineteenth century family were the Cranstones a number of whom lie in the burial ground of the Meeting House in Bell Yard. They came here in 1798 when Joseph Cranstone senior acquired property in the High Street. He was succeeded by his son, Joseph, who took over in 1818. The father married Maria Lefevre of Staines whose grandfather or great grandfather was one of the French Huguenots who found shelter in this country from the bitter persecutions which followed the Revocation of the Edict of Nantes.

Joseph the younger developed the business, especially the foundry and engineering side, later the Hemel Hempstead Engineering Co. Ltd; he built and owned the original gasworks in Bury Road, was the originator of the Volunteer Fire Brigade, is said to have made the first road motor (steam driven) to go from Hemel Hempstead to London, and died in 1878 at the ripe old age of 85. He was one of the Trustees of Boxmoor and for many years their Chairman; for many years also he was a member of the Board of Guardians and was elected Bailiff for 1839–40; He was succeeded in business by his son, William Henry Cranstone, who also filled the office of Bailiff in 1871–2; he died in 1913 at the age of 72, and was buried in the Friends Burial Ground. His uncle, James Pollard, was another member of the Society. He was a partner in the local bank with H. Grover, the title of the firm being Grover & Pollard. He may earlier have been a draper.

The 1851 Census shows there was seating for 170 in the Meeting House, 140 on the floor and 30 in the gallery. The attendance was 23 in the morning and eleven in the afternoon.

It has already been made clear that at an early date the Baptists were a strong group in Hemel Hempstead. George Kendall, the minister appointed by Parliament in 1642, was committed to Newgate the following year because "he hath been a chief promoter of all the distractions there, he refuseth to baptise any infants, he hath openly maintained the Church of England to be no church" and because the people of the parish were "much possessed with Anabaptism and Antinomianism and other sects." After the Act of Uniformity of 1662 the Baptists had to meet separately and quietly to avoid trouble with the authorities, and this they no doubt did in private houses and other buildings. One such group may have included the party which buried John Brandley in an orchard to which reference has already been made. Another organised group dates from 1679 when some Baptists from the parish of Kinsworth, near St. Albans, moved into Hemel Hempstead with the Rev. Samuel Ewer as their first minister. This group probably met in a house in Wood Lane End, again away from the main centre of the town, which was occupied by the Rev. S. Ewer until he died in 1708; the premises were certified for such use in 1712 when they were still occupied by his widow Sarah.

Other houses were similarly certified in the early years of the eighteenth century and a prominent name among the witnesses is that of John Costard whose house called Waterside House (in Piccotts End) was one to be certified. He has already been mentioned above in connection with his business as a tanner.

The need for a permanent place of worship led to the erection of a chapel on a site which now forms part of the ground on which "Old Marlowes House" stands, but the date of this is uncertain. Later, in 1731 this meeting was moved to a new Baptist Chapel erected in the Rose and Crown Yard, High Street, with a burial ground attached – probably the walled one we can still find there (1960). From there in 1861 they moved to their new large building in Marlowes, a move made necessary by increased membership and the dilapidated state of the old building.

The 1851 Census mentions a Baptist Meeting House at Water End which was erected before 1800. It was described as a cottage fitted up for preaching where persons constantly reside. Services had been held there some 16 or 20 years before 1851 (and probably much earlier); it had free accommodation for 90 persons and this was said to be the size of the congregation at the evening service.

Several of the eighteenth century Baptist ministers supported themselves by teaching, beginning with Dr. Philip James in 1718, who combined preaching, teaching and some practice of medicine.

Baptists can be divided into two groups – General and Strict Baptists. The Marlowes community was and is general Baptist but a little group of Strict Baptists have continued to worship in Salem Chapel, Featherbed Lane since they were established in 1818. The Baptist Church in London Road, usually known as Duckhall Chapel (the local name for the area in which it is situated) was started by a group of Strict Baptists, but came, without dissension, to be of the General persuasion in 1891. The chapel was erected on the present site with a burial ground attached in 1825, and rebuilt in 1864.

The Ordnance maps show that towards the end of the nineteenth century there was a Particular Baptists Chapel in Astley Road, seating some 250. This could have been the iron building which once served the Congregationalists.

The Baptists also had a small burial ground in Bury Road which had at one time been an orchard. It was probably purchased in the early eighteenth century and was shown in the Manor Court books as belonging to "protestant Dissenters called Particular Baptists". From time to time the formal ownership was transferred to different trustees. The deeds are now held by the General Baptists.

A small chapel, an offshoot of the Marlowes congregation was opened in Leverstock Green in 1841.

The strength of the Baptist community in the mid-nineteenth century can be gathered from the following statistics ascertained by the 1851 Census.

Accommodation			*Attendances*				
			Morning		*Afternoon*		*Evening*
Sittings	*Additional Space*		*General*	*Sunday School*	*General*	*Sunday School*	*General*
2493		Whole parish	1110		774		1119
		Individual places in Hemel Hempstead –					
680	–	Rose & Crown Yard	351	200	–	200	487
90	–	Water End	–	–	–	–	90
340	50	Boxmoor	150	150	–	–	300
140	30	Salem	65	–	72	–	–
162	40	Leverstock Green			No figures		

It is not certain what were the beginnings of the Congregationalists in Hemel Hempstead proper. There was a meeting of Independents mentioned in 1690, which may have been the group certified as a meeting of Presbyterians by Joshua Bayes in 1702, for in many parts of England the Presbyterians later called themselves Independent Congregationalists. Some survived long enough to fall under the spell of Wesley and become Methodists. The local Congregationalists eventually settled in the small chapel in Chapel Street – now a low whitewashed cottage, but marked by some burials around it. This was opened in 1836 by the Rev. H. Price, who served as pastor till his death in 1863. He and his wife are in fact buried by the old chapel. This building – still called Independent – was restored in 1867 but soon proved too small. If this was the case, it is not borne out by the figures in the 1851 Census. This shows 110 free places and 130 others, and the attendances were

	Morning	*Evening*
General	90	100
Sunday scholars	90	20
	180	120

In 1879 a site was bought in New Road, (now Alexandra Road), which was being developed on land which the Paston Coopers had sold for the 'New Town' as this area was called. An iron chapel was supplied for this site by Mr. Cranstone of the High Street Foundry, and it was opened in 1880. The present church, replacing the iron one, was built in 1890 under the energetic ministry of the Rev. Dan Tatton – later a moving spirit in the steps to get the town incorporated as a borough and one of the party to receive the charter. The old iron building was sold and served another meeting in Astley Road, and finally came to rest in Bury Road where it was ultimately demolished.

Whilst there is no evidence that John Wesley made any substantial impact locally it is clear that Methodism grew here much earlier than the second half of the nineteenth century, as was once supposed. The 1851 Census mentions a Wesleyan Chapel opened in 1839 with 100 free seats, 170 others and free space or standing room for 100. The attendances based on an average over twelve months were

	Morning	*Afternoon*	*Evening*
General	40	150	150
Sunday scholars	50	50	–
	90	200	150

An official rate notice for 1868 shows that it was published on the doors of the following:—

Wesleyan Chapel, Queen Street
Primitive Methodist Chapel, Albion Terrace
Wesleyan Chapel, Frogmore End
Chapel at Crouchfield

Unfortunately no earlier similar notices have been found. These dates imply that there were earlier buildings in Queen Street and Crouchfield than was once imagined. The Chapel in Albion Terrace had seats for 120. Later it was used by the Salvation Army, then converted to a cinema, and finally became a printing works. The building in Crouchfield belonged to the Primitive Methodists and owed its origins to the evangelism of some St. Albans Methodists who walked over to Boxmoor to sow the seed there.

In 1890 the building in Queen Street was sold for £200 and the larger chapel built in Marlowes. On 20th March 1890 the Rev. C. H. Kelly, President of the Wesleyan Conference, preached in the Queen Street Chapel to an overflowing congregation, and £2,240 was raised for the new building which was opened on 11th November 1890.

In 1867 a new Wesleyan Chapel was built at Frogmore End, Apsley, on the site of the old chapel mentioned above.

It is of interest to recall the early days when the narrow sectarian attitude of the Victorians gave rise to some conflict, and Thomas Collins of Hemel Hempstead, a worthy Wesleyan Minister, wrote a small tract of twenty-four pages, entitled "A Letter to the Curate of Hemel Hempstead, Herts" and sold by John Mason, 66 Paternoster Row, London in 1852, price twopence. The reply to this was a tract issued by a Curate of St. Mary's Parish Church — "A Country Curate's Protest against interference of a Wesleyan Preacher in his Parish."

An interesting aspect of nineteenth century dissent is illustrated by the movement away from the Church of England which led to the foundation of the Reformed Episcopal Church of England congregation here, who built their church, Christ Church, in what was then Lower Cross Road, now Christchurch Road, in 1883.

The Oxford Movement, with its stress on ritual, and the Cambridge-based Ecclesiological Society with its advocacy of re-furnishing churches and of removing the eighteenth century box pews, making everyone face the altar, had little effect in Hemel Hempstead in the earlier days, although the box pews, gallery and three-decker pulpit had been removed by 1860, and the opening of St. Paul's chapel-of-ease (opposite St. Paul's Hospital), now demolished, in 1869 had made the necessary room. However, by the 1870's these movements were having an effect on St. Mary's.

In 1869 we get some sign of this when a letter in the Gazette complained of the curate reading facing east. In 1873 there were letters on the possibility of the Disestablishment of the Church of England. (The Irish Church had just been disestablished). A few years later there were letters protesting against ritualism. The writer appeared in July 1877 to be George Rolph, the High Street Draper, who complained that holy communion was no longer held in the evening, that the new vicar was preaching in a surplice (the last four had done so in a black gown) and that the vicar faced to the east.

The situation which led up to the holding of these services is not entirely clear, but there was a suggestion of ritualism in the parish church and some discord arose. The increasing suspicion about these practices led to the breakaway in October 1878 of some parishioners who were eventually to form Christ Church. Services were held in the Town Hall, and on 11th May, 1879 there was a visit from Bishop Gregg, Primate of the English Reformed Episcopal Church, who preached two sermons in the Town Hall. A temporary church was opened on the 28th November 1879 and a permanent building was dedicated on 20th May 1883. In the meantime in 1879, the Rev. George John Lacell was appointed to be the Minister.

The land on which the church was erected was purchased by George Rolph in 1879, and had previously formed part of the meadow belonging to the old workhouse. Rolph was a leading spirit in the establishment of this church: he gave the money with which to build a rectory or parsonage house on land adjoining the church in 1885, and in his will bequeathed a perpetual endowment of the church.

This was not an area where Roman Catholics were numerous and seventeenth century returns of recusants — those who would not attend church — do not mention them. It was difficult for Roman Catholics to flourish in any area of England where there was not a powerful family to protect them, and in this area the powerful families tended to be strictly Protestant. It was not until 1898 that a Roman Catholic Church was opened in Boxmoor, although Mass had been said occasionally between 1893 and 1898, first in a cottage in St. John's Road, and later within the Presbytery.

For some years in the mid-nineteenth century there was a Mormon church (the Church of the Latter Day Saints) in premises in Redbourn Road, behind the Beehive Public House. It was part of a larger movement in Flamstead. According to the 1851 Census it was established in Hemel Hempstead in 1850 and is one of the places of worship on which the rate notice was published in 1868. The seats were all free and the attendances were 25 in the afternoon and 50 in the evening. The Pastor in charge was a man named Sells, who could have been Charles Sells who probably owned the beerhouse and cottages nearby. Alternatively it could have been a son named William. It is understood that eventually the pastor emigrated to Utah in the United States. At Flamstead the accommodation (180 seats) and the attendances were larger, and there the Presiding Elder was John Burgess who exercised some authority in Hemel Hempstead.

Soon after it was founded by William Booth the Salvation Army came to Hemel Hempstead. In 1883 it occupied what was known as the "Old Glory Shop" in Albion Hill; this building had previously served as a Primitive Methodist Chapel. The Army remained there until 1908, when it moved into a larger and more convenient Citadel on the west side of Marlowes, the foundation stone of which was laid on 17th October, 1906. Despite some early opposition (see chapter 6 p. 112) the Army seems to have been well received locally, and, with increasing membership, extended its scope and activities. In accordance with its usual practice it held its services not only in the Citadel but also in the streets and public places; one such was the old Market Square in the High Street. In these services it was helped by its band, which on occasion was glad to assist in various public functions and events. It is now housed at the corner of the Market.

Some of the various nonconformist sects which have existed in Hemel Hempstead have been mentioned above, but there were others about which no detailed information is available. The Presbyterians were in some strength here, but do not appear to have erected a specially designed place of worship. They appear to have been connected in some way with Box Lane Chapel, but in addition they caused to be certified several private houses in which groups of worshippers could assemble, particularly in the early eighteenth century. From time to time other small groups appeared, and often functioned in small halls in different parts of the town. Some of these groups were essentially local, whilst others belonged to a more widely supported sect. For example, there was a Gospel Hall in Marlowes, on the east side just north of the junction with Hillfield Road; there is no information as to its origin, but it was no doubt built about the mid-nineteenth century. It remained in use until it was demolished some time in the 1940's.

In spite of its various sects and diverse practices it must be remembered that Nonconformity generally was extremely vigorous in nineteenth century Hemel Hempstead and, as so often elsewhere, was strong among the traders. Rivalry with the church was strong and this comes out clearly in the log books of the British (Nonconformist) and National (Church) Schools, which are referred to elsewhere. A sore point with the Nonconformists was when their pupils took off to go to a Church Sunday School treat! Another problem arose if the Bailiff was nonconformist and was expected to attend church.

The Sunday Schools must have played an important part in the life of the town. For many children before the 1870 Education Act and the compulsory attendance which followed in 1880, it was the only schooling they had. No doubt many learned to read there with the Bible as their reading primer. In 1884 the Baptists had 350 scholars and also supported a Ragged School and branch chapel at Leverstock Green. Further examples can be found in the chapter on the nineteenth century.

All in all, the history of Hemel Hempstead gives vivid illustrations of the development of nonconformity, which was plainly more vigorous here than in many places.

Note on Sources

The most important sources for this chapter are:—

Urwick — 'Nonconformity in Hertfordshire' and

The records of individual chapels and churches.

CHAPTER 12

Postscript – The Coming of the New Town.

1. The War years

Hemel Hempstead shared in the effects on the whole country of the war against Germany which began on 3rd September 1939. Men were called to the colours: everyone had to black out their dwellings and the lights of their cars; the air raid precaution volunteers went on duty; and children and expectant mothers, evacuated from London, arrived in the town. The first major task was to find billets for the evacuees, who in the main were received by the townsfolk without resentment. In a few weeks, all the evacuated school children were receiving full-time education in various buildings from the teachers who had accompanied them from London. The larger part of the Great Ormond Street Hospital was evacuated to the buildings in Redbourn Road (now known as St. Paul's Hospital but originally the old poor law workhouse). In addition to those who had been evacuated to the town under official arrangements, people and small businesses moved from the London area to the town; and soon most of the empty houses, shops and offices were occupied. Before the end of 1939, national registration of the population with the issue of identity cards was completed, and food rationing began, followed by petrol rationing.

The 'phoney war' which lasted until May 1940 gave an opportunity for the town to complete the organisation of the mainly voluntary war-time services. The local people responded well to the call to give valuable service voluntarily – in air raid precautions, the auxiliary police, the auxiliary fire service and, last but by no means last, the women's voluntary service. To those were added the Local Defence Volunteers (later the Home Guard) in response to the government's call after the evacuation from Dunkirk. But many mothers and children who had been evacuated to the town during the war's first days returned to London.

When, in the summer of 1940, after the fall of France, the Germans began their bombing attacks on Great Britain, Hemel Hempstead did not escape the bombs but the town was fortunate not to suffer seriously. The casualties were few and the damage was slight, but the town had to deal with refugees from the bombing attacks on London; 10,000 came to Hemel Hempstead in three weeks in September. Rest centres were opened and the various services co-operated fully in receiving them, finding them billets and looking after them. Full-time education was provided for the children. It was during this time that the village of Hempstead on Long Island, New York, U.S.A., presented to the Mayor and Bailiff of the town, a mobile canteen which was in frequent use during the rest of the war. It was last used to provide refreshments for the railwaymen and volunteers working at the site of the terrible train crash at Bourne End in 1945. This gift began a close association between the two towns which continues, with individuals from one town visiting the other as opportunity occurs.

The fall of Singapore in February 1941 brought sadness to many homes in Hemel Hempstead as the Beds. and Herts. Regiment were among those who surrendered to the Japanese.

In 1942 the 8th United States Army Air Force with their flying fortresses took over the newly-constructed airfield at Bovingdon. The American airmen soon made themselves at home and many lasting friendships were made. Many soldiers from various nations came and went from the neighbourhood; and each left their own impression on the people of the town.

In December 1943, the Middlesex Regiment arrived in Hemel Hempstead direct from the battlefields of Sicily after having fought in the 8th Army through the North African desert. They had been sent back to this country in preparation for the invasion of Europe in 1944. On arrival the Mayor and Bailiff entertained them to a tea in the Guildhouse at Apsley which John Dickinson & Co. Ltd. willingly placed at his disposal for the purpose. The officer commanding the regiment (who is at the time this is written – 1971 – Vice-Chairman of the Hertfordshire County Council) in thanking the Mayor and Bailiff for his hospitality commented that it was the first time for months they had been together under one roof. The regiment remained in billets in the town for two or three months before moving away for more intensive training.

The enemy flying-bomb attack on the south of England, following the allied landings in Normandy on 10th June 1944, led to another flood of refugees from London to Hemel Hempstead – rest centres were again opened and the events of 1940 were repeated, although on a smaller scale. In May 1945, the war against Germany came to an end. The town was ablaze with light as black-out curtains and shutters were taken down; many people danced in Lawn Lane until the early hours of the morning and a great bonfire was lit on Roughdown Common. Soon afterwards, the A.R.P. Controller made the following report to the Borough Council:–

"1. With the end of the war in Europe the Council will wish to have this report from me on the extent of enemy action in the Borough.

2. *Number of Warnings* – the number of Air Raid warnings in the Borough was 828, the first being sounded on the 3rd September 1939, and the last on the 29th March, 1945.

3. *Number of Bombs* – in all 90 high explosive bombs (of which 9 were unexploded), 4 oil bombs, 1 flying bomb and about 350 incendiary bombs dropped in the Borough. In the Belswains Lane incident on the 10th May 1941, 3 high explosive bombs dropped a few feet outside the boundary. Of the 9 unexploded bombs the Bomb Disposal Squad exploded 7 in situ and removed the remaining.

The first incident occurred at the Manor Estate on the 19th August 1940, and the last on the 3rd July 1944, when a flying bomb fell at Tower Farm, Felden. One high explosive bomb fell in the Grand Union Canal near Fishery Bridge and that section of the canal had to be emptied to ensure that the bomb had exploded.

4. *Casualties* – in spite of the number of bombs, only one person was killed, 1 seriously injured and 15 slightly injured in the Borough. In the Belswains Lane incident, however, 8 persons (including two wardens on duty) were killed and 14 persons were injured.

5. *Damage* – 4 houses were completely destroyed and 161 damaged. The Corporation's property escaped lightly as only Piccotts End School, the Elephant Farm Cottage and the Felden Water Tower were damaged.

6. *Rest Centre Service* – from the 9th September 1940 to the 19th May 1941, and from the 20th June 1944 to the 14th August 1944, the Rest Centre Service was in operation to care for refugees from the attacks on London.

7. *Emergency Feeding Service* – the Corporation had ready an Emergency Feeding Service sufficient to feed thousands of people, but the only occasion on which it operated in emergency was after the Belswains Lane incident in May 1941."

The war against Japan ended in August 1945 and was celebrated by street tea-parties for the children. The surviving prisoners of the Japanese returned and were reunited with their families. In general, however, it is fair to say that, thankful though everybody was, the event was not greeted with quite the same enthusiasm as V.E. day.

As was to be expected, the basic pattern of town and church administration did not change during the war. However, many societies and clubs withered away or suspended activities as their members entered war service elsewhere. But war savings groups and Dig for Victory parties, in addition to the wartime volunteer services listed before, became strong. Some small cultural and lecture groups and associations with international aims, also developed, (largely initiated by the newcomers to the town). At the end of the war most of these languished and died and some of the pre-war societies revived.

One administrative reform, brought about by the energy of the then Mayor & Bailiff, the late Alderman Henry Fletcher, was the merging in 1939 of various small charities (those bequeathed by Jane Godwin, Benjamin Collett, Thomas Warren, William Norris, Mary Ann Evans and Henry Richard Woodman; and Field's Charity) into the United Charities.

As no general election was held during the war Lady Davidson remained the Member of Parliament for the Hemel Hempstead Constituency.

The early days of the war brought an unexpected blessing. A lorry demolished the old memorial fountain in the middle of the junction of the

High Street and Marlowes outside the old Post House (now the junction of Marlowes and Queensway). For some time it had been an obstruction to traffic but nobody wanted to be the first to suggest out loud that it be removed. It was not replaced.

In spite of the sombre times, life in Hemel Hempstead was not unrelieved drudgery. The events of the summer of 1940 – Dunkirk, the fall of France and the enemy attacks on this country – produced a unity of purpose and a quite illogical exhilaration of the spirit. The influx of people from London and from other parts of the world enriched and enlarged the culture and the quality of life of the town, and this did much to offset the dreariness, sadness and boredom except perhaps for those who lost fathers, husbands, sons or dear friends in the fighting or in the air raids. The country as a whole was of course profoundly affected by the war and suffered unalterable changes. This was particularly true of Hemel Hempstead, not so much in its physical characteristics (unlike many cities and towns) as in its people and their general outlook.

2. After the war

The changes in Hemel Hempstead caused by the war were destined to be eclipsed by the changes which occurred in the early years of peace. During the latter years of the war the local government and central authorities had given thought to what would be the problems of post-war reconstruction. Locally the prime needs were housing and an enlarged and improved water supply. Nationally one of the many problems was the reduction of congestion in the major cities, particularly London, by dispersal of some of the population, by re-habilitation of what before the war had been called the depressed areas, but which had been renamed development areas, and consequently by a rational re-location of industry.

Locally, a completely new water-supply scheme, which had received parliamentary approval in 1939, was re-examined and brought up to date. This involved a new main pumping station at Piccotts End to replace the one established in Marlowes by the former Hemel Hempstead Water and Laundry Co. in the latter half of the 19th century, with new reservoirs and mains. Housing sites were acquired at Belswains Farm, Anchor Lane and Redbourn Road. As a matter of urgency 50 temporary houses were built in Crabtree Lane. Although this meant the encroachment of bricks and mortar on previously open land, the urgency of the need for houses secured full local support for these projects.

The consequences to Hemel Hempstead of the solution found by the central government for this problem of the congestion in London did not find such ready acceptance. In the Greater London Plan prepared by Professor Abercrombie published in December 1944, it was proposed that several satellite towns should be built around London to which industries and people from London should move. One of the sites selected for these satellite towns was called Redbourn, but its centre was halfway between Redbourn and Hemel Hempstead and about one-third of the site was in the Borough. Professor Abercrombie stated that Hemel Hempstead, by reason of its steep hills and valleys, was unsuitable for a satellite town. The Government on the 19th October 1945 appointed a New Towns Committee under the chairmanship of the late Lord Reith of B.B.C. fame. In a remarkably short time this Committee produced a report in three instalments, the last being published in July 1946. Soon after that, the Minister of Town and Country Planning, Mr. Lewis Silkin (later Lord Silkin) announced that he had selected Hemel Hempstead to be a new town to which would be applied the provisions of the New Towns Bill then going through Parliament. In the summer of 1946 he published his proposals for the area of the new town to house 40,000 people, with factories and commercial premises, in addition to the 22,000 already living there. This led to widespread protests in Hemel Hempstead. On 19th November 1946 Mr. Silkin attended a packed and stormy meeting in the Apsley Guildhouse to explain his proposals. The Borough Council possess a transcript of the proceedings at this meeting which makes interesting reading. On the 2nd, 3rd and 5th December 1946 a public inquiry into the proposal was held at which barristers, solicitors and ordinary folk, including the farmers, expressed their objections. In the event the Minister made an order on the 4th February 1947 designating 5,910 acres (mostly in the Borough) as the site of a New Town, but his way was not yet clear because three local residents led by Henry Fletcher of Southridge, who had been Mayor and Bailiff at the outbreak of the recent war, challenged the order on the ground that the Minister had initiated the proceedings for it before the New Towns Act 1946 had become law. It was not until 30th July 1947 that the challenge failed when the High Court gave judgement in favour of the Minister.

In the meantime the Minister had appointed an advisory committee for the proposed new town under the chairmanship of the late Lord Reith. This advisory committee then became the board of the Development Corporation which was formally constituted on the 7th March 1947 to undertake the task of constituting the new town. Lord Reith resigned on 8th November 1950 and Mr. Henry Wells (later Sir Henry Wells) was appointed to succeed him. The board began its investigation and started preparing a master plan for the town which was published in 1949. It was the subject of a public enquiry on the 15th to the 22nd November 1949, at which many criticisms of the plan were heard. A highlight of this enquiry was the appearance as an objector of Nathaniel Micklem, K.C., Mr. Micklem who lived at Northridge, was nearly 100 years old and had been a Q.C. in Queen Victoria's reign. He had also been a member of the committee established in 1896 which secured the incorporation of the municipal borough in 1898 to succeed the old bailiwick. In spite of his age, he put his objections clearly and with force and fervour. A year later the Minister proposed substantial modifications of the plan which were made the subject of public debate. Eventually, a modified plan was approved in 1951. The general pattern of the master plan was that the residential areas should be developed as neighbourhoods, each with its own shopping centre; that a new town centre should be built; and that areas should be set aside for industry and commerce. It did not cover the whole of the Borough; Felden, Bourne End, Piccotts End and Dickinson's factory in Apsley were excluded. It is interesting to note that at the time Dickinson's were the only large employers of labour in the town and still – in 1971 – are one of the biggest. This plan formed the basis of the development until about 1960 when the master plan was replaced by a revised master plan (about which the public were also consulted) which had been made necessary by the realisation that the incoming population (mostly in the younger age ranges) was producing a natural increase which would take the population of the town to 80,000. With the dissolution of the Development Corporation on 31st March 1962 and their replacement by the Commission for the New Towns, the revised master plan was replaced by the town map produced by the Hertfordshire County Council, which contained much the same provisions, although it differed in some details.

The Development Corporation did not await the approval of their master plan before starting development. With the approval of the Minister, they made a start on the Adeyfield Neighbourhood and the industrial area along what is now Maylands Avenue. In addition to providing the roads and buildings for these developments, they had also to prepare plans for and undertake the comprehensive main drainage of the whole of the new development and arrange for the other services, water, gas, electricity, telephone, and public transport, to be available when required. The first house was completed in 1950, when the Mayor and Bailiff, with representatives of the development corporation, greeted the new tenant and his family on arrival and handed him the key of his new house. It would be wearisome to trace in detail the development of every part of the new areas throughout the succeeding years. It will suffice to select some of the events of general interest.

The selection of Marlowes as the town centre was opposed by the Borough Council and the traders at a public inquiry on 29th November 1949 on the ground that it ought to be an extension of the existing town shopping centre in the High Street, otherwise the prosperity of the High Street would languish; but the Development Corporation's proposal was confirmed. When in 1954 the first shops in the new and widened Marlowes opened and the old market moved from St. Mary's Close in the High Street to its new and larger site in Marlowes opposite Hillfield Road, the forebodings about the prosperity of the High Street proved to be justified. Much and continuing effort has since been devoted to restoring the High Street, in particular by the Civic Trust scheme in 1968, but more needs to be done. To some extent, the situation has been eased by the location of the new civic centre between the new shopping centre and the High Street. These comments do not necessarily imply that the original decision was wrong. The growth of traffic might have made a town centre straddling Queensway unsuitable. Complaints have been heard from some quarters that traffic along Marlowes is too heavy. It is interesting that it has recently been revealed that the Development Corporation originally proposed to the Ministry of Town and Country Planning that the Marlowes town centre should be planned as a pedestrian precinct but the Ministry discouraged this proposal. Whether or not the town centre is in the right place or form, it is thriving, and provides a wide range of choice for the shopper and serves a much wider area than Hemel Hempstead. The completion of the Marks & Spencer's store in 1973 has added to the towns attractions. One prominent feature with which nobody quarrels is the water gardens incorporating the River Gade bordering the west of the town centre. Another interesting feature is the use of names in the town centre commemorating men notable in the town's history — King Harry Street, (after the King who granted the town its first charter of incorporation) Combe Street (after Sir Richard Combe first occupant of the Bury) and Stephyns Chambers (after William Stephyns who took office as the first Bailiff on 29th December 1539).

The industrial estate in the north-eastern part of the town has attracted many prosperous firms, some of national and even international repute. There is a continuing pressure to expand.

The residential neighbourhoods were built according to plan — Adeyfield, Bennetts End, Chaulden, Warners End, Gadebridge, Highfield (part by the Development Corporation and part by the Borough Council), Leverstock Green and, finally, Grovehill. In recent years numerous private estates of varying sizes have also been built. For the future, with the move of Brocks Fireworks away from the town, a new estate (of at least 1,000 houses) in the extreme north-east of the town, is expected.

In the later years office building began. Notable are the Transport Ministry building off Marlowes, the McAlpine building in St. Albans Road later extended to form a bridge across Marlowes with a fourteen-storey block on the west making a gateway to the town centre, Lord Alexander House in Waterhouse Street and the nineteen-storey block housing Kodak's United Kingdom head office. The siting of the Kodak building gave rise to considerable controversy.

In 1959 the London-Birmingham Motorway — M.1. — was opened. It passes close to Hemel Hempstead to which it is linked by a new road, Breakspear Way, which was named after the only English Pope, Nicholas Breakspear of Abbots Langley. As part of the development a series of main traffic routes was constructed in the town, including the Leighton Buzzard Road from Moor End to beyond Potten End as a by-pass to the town centre. While this is being written, acute controversy is raging in the town about a proposal by the government to construct, as a bypass to the London Road, a motorway from Hunton Bridge to Tring. Particular concern has been aroused because this road will cross Roughdown Common and the part of the Moor where the body of highwayman Snooks lies.

Because of economic pressures and lack of foresight on the part of the government, the provision of amenities in the town lagged behind the other development. Efforts in the last decade to catch up have by no means fulfilled all the requirements. The two cinemas — the Luxor and the Princess — which served the original town were closed and demolished to make way for town centre development, but the foundation stone of a new cinema was laid in 1959 by Miss Lauren Bacall, a noted film star; and the cinema was opened on the 29th August 1960 by two other film stars, Miss Virginia Maskell and Mr. Leslie Phillips. The Borough Council opened the Pavilion in 1966 for general entertainment and have started to construct a large covered swimming pool at Churchill next to the pre-war open-air swimming pool. At a later stage a sports hall is to be linked with this. Permanent Community Centres have been provided in Adeyfield, Bennetts End, Chaulden, Warners End and Highfield; and a temporary centre (used jointly with the churches) at Grovehill. Plans are afoot for one at Leverstock Green; and later, a permanent one for Grovehill is planned. Sports fields have been provided. When the Elephant Farm Sewage Works were abandoned, that area was selected as the principal sports ground with provision for a running track and stadium. Football pitches have been laid out and the first stage of a large pavilion has been built but the stadium is still awaited. Gadebridge Park was bought by the Council in 1952 from the Paston-Cooper estate and has been enlarged since. The Bury Garden, off Gadebridge Park, was acquired and is well maintained to provide a quiet and beautiful place for rest and contemplation. A large acreage of land belonging to the Commission for the New Towns and zoned as open space in the town map was bought by the Borough Council in 1971 to ensure its preservation as such. A lot of it will probably be kept in its natural state, although some of it, particularly Northridge Park (the grounds and site of Northridge which was demolished after the death of Nathaniel Micklem who had once again become a Q.C. at the accession of Queen Elizabeth II) will be maintained to a high standard.

In 1962 the government decided that the development of the new town as originally proposed had been substantially completed and on 31st March 1962 the Development Corporation was dissolved and its assets and liabilities were transferred to the Commission for the New Towns. The Commission had been established by virtue of the New Towns Act 1959 to take over and manage the property of Development Corporations as the new towns became substantially complete. In 1962 the Commission took over from the Development Corporation at Crawley and Hemel Hempstead to which in 1966 Hatfield and Welwyn Garden City were added. The Commission continued with the development programmes of the corporations they replaced. The Development Corporations had a special position in relation to town and country planning and could buy land compulsorily. The Commission does not have these powers; its position in law is much the same as any large private property-owning company. The Development Corporation had been a self-contained unit within the town itself. The Commission's offices are in London with local offices in each of the towns, each with its own manager and a local committee to look after the Commission's housing activities.

How did this physical development affect the life of the people? A lot of people had to leave their land and homes; and the compensation paid could not in many cases make up for the heartache of those displaced. Farmers in particular came off badly. A sad case was the demolition of Bridge Street, all the residents had to move, many in the evening of their lives, people who had lived there, in some cases, 50 years or more. Although they were re-housed, as were all whose homes were taken, they felt as strangers in their new homes. Happier was the lot of the dwellers in the old cottages nestling under the railway bridge at the south end of Marlowes. They were little better than slums, and when they had to be cleared to enable the road to be widened, the occupiers were not loath to move to other better houses.

What of the life of the people, particularly the newcomers? The resentment felt by many of the 'old towners' towards the new town project did not in most cases extend to the people who came newly to live in Hemel Hempstead; and on the whole they soon came to be part of the town. The new residents had their own problems arising from the incomplete roads etc. The pattern in each new neighbourhood repeated itself. People moved in as the houses were completed. It was still some time before the roads, the footpaths, the street lighting and the landscaping were finished. This led to the formation of active tenants' associations concerned to secure the early completion of these basic facilities and, later, to press for shops, playing fields and a community centre. During this process, the protest associations were transformed, with encouragement from the Development Corporation, into neighbourhood councils and neighbourhood associations which continue on a permanent basis, although, with the achievement of their original aims, their outlook and objectives have changed. An extensive variety of societies and clubs grew up, catering for a wide range of interests. Some were associated with older institutions in the town but most were new. At the start of the development, the Rotary Club sponsored the formation of the Council of Social Service which in its early days played its part in encouraging the establishment of a community life in the neighbourhoods and continues to search for new needs. Under their aegis the Old People's Welfare Council was set up and a Citizens Advice Bureau. The Old People's Welfare Council particularly provided a service which had been lacking. They instituted, with the help of the Women's Royal Voluntary Service, a meals-on-wheels scheme to provide the house-bound aged with hot mid-day meals on several days a week. They persuaded the Borough Council to build an Old People's Day Centre on the site of the Half Moon Yard cottages off the High Street. This centre was completed in

1971 and has proved to be most popular. An old people's harvest tea is arranged and throughout the year visits are paid to the aged and help given where required.

At one time there was a fear that concentration on a pattern of neighbourhoods might make more difficult the achievement of a sense in the new comers that they were part of the town as a whole. But the growth of the town centre and the civic centre had allayed this fear, without detracting from the keen sense of neighbourhood loyalty which exists. An account of the development of the community life and its expression in the growth of Societies can be found in "A New Town Comes of Age" – a report commissioned by the Borough Council, the County Council and the Commission for the New Towns and published in July 1970.

What else has happened in the 25 years since the end of the war? The, 1940's saw changes in the administrative pattern. The West Herts Hospital, which had started as a cottage hospital at Piccotts End 100 years before, was taken over in 1948 as part of the new national health service; and the dedicated men and women who had given so much voluntary service to managing and improving the hospital found their occupation gone, although many of them continued to serve in another capacity on the West Herts Group Hospital Management Committee or on the house committees of the local hospitals. For what it was worth, Hemel Hempstead had two hospitals after 1948, for the buildings at St. Paul's which had over the years been the workhouse, the poor law institution and the public assistance institution then became part of the national health service as St. Paul's Hospital. Although at that time it was a separate hospital with its own house committee and matron, it later became integrated with the West Herts Hospital for Management purposes. With the growth of the population of the town and other areas served by the hospital it was long recognised that it would become inadequate. An area to the east of the present West Herts Hospital is reserved for the building of a completely new hospital, for which plans are being prepared by the North-West Metropolitan Regional Hospital Board. In the meantime, improvements have been made to the existing hospitals, including a large, new out-patients and ward block at the West Herts Hospital which was opened by the Queen Mother in 1959.

The Hemel Hempstead Volunteer Fire Brigade, which had been one of the oldest in the country and for whom the Borough Council had built a new fire station in Alexandra Road just before the war, had been absorbed during the war by the national fire service. After the war, the national fire service was disbanded and responsibility for the fire service was given to the Hertfordshire County Council to whom the fire station was transferred. Modern conditions required a full-time paid service with a much reduced volunteer component. In 1969 the County Council opened a new and larger fire station in Queensway; and in 1971 the Borough Council bought back for £10,500 the old fire station for conversion to use for sports and games.

The first non-commercial building in the new town centre was the new Salvation Army Citadel at one corner of the new market square. This was built to replace the small, decrepit building in Marlowes and has enabled the Army to expand considerably the splendid service they give to those who fall on hard times or are afflicted in any way.

The new civic centre at the north end of Marlowes grew over the years. First came the divisional police station, then the new public library, followed by the College of Further Education. In 1966 the new town hall, the pavilion and the health centre were opened. The centre was completed by the opening of the new courts in 1968.

The Hertfordshire County Council as education authority has risen to the demands of the new town by building 43 new schools of all types and a College of Further Education. The teachers and staff of these establishments have contributed much to the enrichment of the life of the town.

The private schools in the town continued, although with changes. Lockers Park preparatory school remains; Gadebridge preparatory school moved from Gadebridge to Westbrook Hay in 1963, when the Commission for the New Towns moved their offices from there to the newly built office block at Swan Court in Waterhouse Street overlooking the water gardens. The old house at Gadebridge (the former home for many years of the Aston-Cooper family) was then demolished. St. Nicholas School for Girls amalgamated with Abbot's Hill School and its site was developed as a private residential estate.

The old railway between Boxmoor and Harpenden was closed to passengers on 16th June 1947 and to goods traffic on 1st July 1963 but the line to Heath Park had been disused for some years before that. The line was acquired partly by the Development Corporation and partly by the Borough Council. A large crowd gathered at midnight on 6th July 1960 to see the demolition of the high railway bridges over Marlowes. The embankments across the Moor were removed and the soil was used to fill the cutting between Wood Lane and Midland Road.

The 1914–18 War Memorial in Heath Park opposite the old Plough public house had to be moved when the Plough roundabout was constructed. It was re-erected on an even pleasanter site at the junction of Station Road and St. John's Road and the names of those who fell in the 1939-45 war were added.

In 1958, town-wide events (including a Mayor's ball at Apsley Guildhouse) were organised to celebrate the 60th Anniversary of the Municipal Charter. Among the events was a festival of the arts which proved to be so popular that it was repeated in 1960 and 1961. By then it had become so established that, at a town's meeting, the Hemel Hempstead Arts Trust was established which, with financial support from the public authorities, has since gone from strength to strength. Apart from an annual festival in the Autumn, the Trust has organised international weeks in the Spring. So far the art of Hungary, France, the Soviet Union, Italy, India, Mexico and Czechoslovakia has been featured.

The discovery of Roman tiles during the construction of the Leighton Buzzard Road through Gadebridge Park led to the formation of an Excavations Society which, with financial support from the Ministry of Public Building and Works, the Borough Council and various learned societies, has sponsored excavations in various parts of the town. The most important was in Gadebridge Park where the remnants of a unique Roman bathing pool and large residential buildings were unearthed during excavations lasting several years. (See Chapter 2). A full report on these discoveries is to be published soon.

The Churches have not been inactive in this period. In 1960 the parishes were reorganised when St. Mary's parish was enlarged to include St. Paul's parish and parts of the parishes of Boxmoor and Leverstock Green. New Anglican Churches were built in Adeyfield, Bennetts End and Warners End; a new Roman Catholic Church was erected in St. Albans Road; Non-Conformist Churches were established in Adeyfield, Bennetts End, Chaulden and Gadebridge. In 1948 St. Mary's eight bells were removed from the belfry, and sent away to be repaired. They were later re-installed in the belfry. A picture showing the bells, (five of them dating respectively from 1400, 1604, 1688, 1758 and 1767) is displayed in the committee corridor in the new town hall. The spirit of ecumenicalism is strong in the town and all the churches co-operate in many fields. Even closer association can be foreseen if talks which are under way for the joint use of buildings by the various denominations reach a successful conclusion. In 1959 the church-wardens of St. Mary's required the Borough Council to take over the maintenance of the churchyard which had been closed for burials in 1879 by Order in Council. The churchyard was in an unkempt state. A faculty was obtained from the Bishop of St. Albans for the removal of the stones and memorials on the graves and for the reservation of a small part of the churchyard as a garden of rest where the ashes of those who had been cremated could be interred, an agreement was made under the Open Spaces Act 1906 for the preservation of the land as an open space and the Council converted the overgrown churchyard into the green garden which today links the High Street with Gadebridge Park. In 1961 the churchyard at St. John's, Boxmoor (which had also been closed in 1879) was treated similarly.

As the new town grew, it became apparent that the Council's burial ground in Heath Lane would soon be full. The Council had already acquired, by the start of the war, land to the north, partly for an extension of this burial ground and partly for allotments. During the war this additional land was used for the burial of German prisoners of war who had died in captivity and for one British soldier. Even this extension, however, was too small, so in 1955 the Council bought 30 acres at Woodwells Farm, just outside the eastern boundary of the Borough, and laid out 2½ acres of it as a new burial ground. The bodies of the Germans were removed from Heath Lane and re-interred in the German war cemetery at Cannock Chase; the British soldier was buried in the old burial ground. It is doubtful whether the whole of the new 30 acres bought by the Council will ever be needed for burials because since the war cremation has increased considerably rising from 13% of total deaths in 1949 to 53% in 1969. In 1953 the Council joined with thirteen other local authorities in the area to establish a crematorium at Garston which was completed in 1959.

The Boxmoor Trustees have continued strong in their principles throughout the years. Suggestions made from time to time that the Trustees have no place in modern times and that their lands should be transferred to the Corporation with greater resources to manage them, arouse heated feelings and are rejected continually. They have not entirely escaped the effects of the post-war development. Pieces of the Moor have been taken for developments and for road-widening, and the proceeds of these have added to the Trustees' capital. Several elections of new trustees have been held among the householders of the town, and the new trustees are no whit less determined to protect the Moor than were their predecessors. The efforts of the government (which began during the war) to eradicate bovine tuberculosis led to the gradual establishment of tuberculosis-free herds but, to be attested, these had to be fenced off from non-attested cattle. This led to a considerable diminution in the use of the Moor for grazing cattle which was not completely compensated for by its increased use for grazing horses. Of late years, with the success of the government's efforts and the removal of the farming restrictions, cows are again grazing on the Moor. In 1971, 91 beasts were allowed to graze there.

The Territorial Army, who contributed so much in the war were provided with a new headquarters at Handpost Farm at the bottom of Adeyfield Road. It was opened on 17th July 1955 by Anthony Head M.P. the Secretary of State for War, who arrived in the town by helicopter.

The winter of 1947 was hard. The ground was frozen solid from Christmas to March. Fuel ran short and much hardship was experienced. When the thaw came, houses in low lying streets like Mill Street and White Lion Street in Apsley were flooded.

In 1965 the main railway was electrified, entailing the raising of all the bridges over the line. Hemel Hempstead Station was rebuilt to deal with the faster and much more frequent service to Euston.

During the years since the war, the town was honoured by several visits from members of the Royal Family. The death of King George VI on 6th February 1952 was the cause of widespread mourning. The Magistrates Court, when the news was brought, adjourned; and a Borough Council meeting to be held that day was cancelled. The new Queen Elizabeth II, visited the Borough on 20th July 1952 when she laid the foundation stone of St. Barnabas Church at Adeyfield, and afterwards toured Adeyfield and the development at Bennetts End which had just begun. Later, she attended a service at St. Albans Abbey.

On 14th July 1959 the Queen Mother opened the new outpatients block at the West Herts Hospital and then visited homes in Chaulden and Warners End. Princess Margaret opened the new church at Highfield on 6th April 1961. The Duke of Edinburgh came to the Apsley Grammar School (now Longdean Upper School) and the Corner Hall Secondary Modern Schools on 30th October 1959, to see entries for his Awards Scheme. Lord Mountbatten of Burma opened the Mountbatten School on 24th November 1970.

An historic occasion was the distribution by the Queen, of Maundy Money in St. Albans Abbey on 18th April 1957, the first time this ceremony had occurred anywhere other than at Westminster. The Mayor and Bailiff who attended the ceremony received a set of the maundy coins.

The formal connection of the Borough with the Davidson family ended in 1959 when Lady Davidson decided not to stand for re-election to Parliament. In her place, Lt. Col. James Allason, O.B.E., was elected and he has held his seat at all subsequent elections until 1974. Lord Davidson died on December 11th 1970, and his memorial service in Westminster Abbey was attended by the Mayor and Bailiff and the Mayoress with the Town Clerk and his wife.

Sir Alec Douglas Home, the Prime Minister, came to Hemel Hempstead to speak at a general election in 1964. The conservative party lost the election. Mr. Harold Wilson, too, spoke in the town at the 1970 election and the Labour party lost the election. One wonders whether future prime ministers will risk election speeches in the borough. Mr. Edward Heath (who became Prime Minister in 1970) visited the town on 17th November 1967 when he was leader of the opposition and was received by the Mayor and Bailiff in his parlour. Apart from election times, many politicians of both parties have visited the town either to open some important building or to inspect progress or to discuss some particular problem involving a government department.

Soon after the war, the local elections both for the borough council and the county council came to be fought on political grounds. While the county council has remained consistently conservative, the borough council became controlled by Labour in 1956. Labour remained in power until 1969 when the Conservatives obtained a majority. In 1971 the two parties had equal strength – 18 members each. The Council at the start of this period had 24 members – 6 councillors for each of the Apsley, Boxmoor and Hemel Hempstead wards with 6 aldermen. In 1965, after a public inquiry, the Home Secretary made a scheme to take account of the growth in the size of the town providing for 9 wards with 3 members each and 9 aldermen – a total of 36.

What of the future? The answer is scarcely one for a history. But the problems and opportunities which have faced Hemel Hempstead since the war, which have been unparalleled in its long history, are not finished, and controversial issues will continue to arise. In 1974 local government will be re-organised, involving the dissolution of the borough, the revocation of its charters of incorporation and the inclusion of the town in a larger district yet to be defined. The national health service will also be reorganised then. A new hospital will be built, the recent re-organisation of the education of our children will develop and, in the religious field, the widening outlook of the churches and the closer co-operation, and perhaps one day the integration, of the denominations may be foreseen. The town is prosperous. Will its size be kept down to the planned total population of 80,000 or must it grow substantially beyond that? Will the motorway bypass of the London Road be built and, if so, what will its long-term effect be? Will there be a heliport at Leverstock Green? Will Luton Airport expand and, if it does, will all the efforts of so many to make Hemel Hempstead such a pleasant town to live and work in be spoilt by intolerable noise? What progress will be made with filling the gaps in the provision of amenities to enable the young, the middle-aged and the old to enjoy a full and rich life? Perhaps a supplementary chapter to this history will be written in 25 years time to supply the answers to some of these questions.

APPENDIX I

CORPORATION OF HEMEL HEMPSTEAD

Mayor and Bailiff

1939/41	Henry Fletcher
1941/45	Horace Dive
1945/9	Alfred L. Selden
1949/50	P. J. White
1951/52	Herbert Christopher
1953	W. G. S. Crook
1954	Arthur W. Mayo
1955	W. G. S. Crook
1956/57	Gilbert D. Hitchcock
1958	Wyndham Thomas
1959	James F. Reynolds
1960	Gwendolen D. Marshall
1961	Olive Taylor
1962	James Anthony Graham
1963	Frank George Edwards
1964	Robert Leonard Clark
1965	Alastair C. Melhuish
1966	Bertram T. Barrett
1967	Frederick R. Mullin
1968	Maud A. Hannam-Clark
1969	John J. Doyle
1970	William M. Isbister
1971	Peter G. Wood

Town Clerk

1939 –	C. W. G. T. Kirk

HEMEL HEMPSTEAD DEVELOPMENT CORPORATION

Chairmen

1947-50	Lord Reith of Stonehaven
1950-62	Henry W. Wells

General Managers

1947-56	W. O. Hart
1956-62	Brigadier G. B. S. Hindley

COMMISSION FOR THE NEW TOWNS

Chairman of the Hemel Hempstead Local Committee

1962-64	Sir Henry Wells
1964-68	Wyndham Thomas
1968-78	Gilbert D. Hitchcock

Managers of Hemel Hempstead Local Office

1962	Brigadier G. B. S. Hindley
1962-69	A. W. Thomas
1969-78	Brigadier J. R. Blomfield

APPENDIX II

GROWTH OF HEMEL HEMPSTEAD

1947 – 1971

Population		
1947		21,000
1971		69,371
New Dwellings		
Development Corporation and Commission	12,126	
Council	2,744	
Others	2,731	17,601
New Factories		
Number		70
Number of Employees		13,600
Size		3,727,254 sq.ft.
New Offices		
Number		51
Number of employees		3,500
Size		606,936 sq.ft.
New Shops		
Number		304
Size		513,487 sq.ft.

APPENDIX III

Meaning and derivation of some local place-names

Abbreviations:–

E.P.N.S. . . . . English Place-Name Society
I.P.M. . . . . Inquisition Post Mortem
ME. . . . . Middle English
Min. Acc. . . . . Ministers' Accounts
Miss. Cart. . . . . Missenden Cartulary
OE. . . . . Old English
P.R.O. . . . . Public Record Office
V.C.H. . . . . Victoria County History

1. **Hemel Hempstead**
   'homestead in Hæmel'. The district name, Hæmel, probably means 'broken country'. See end note on p. 284.
2. **Bovingdon**
   Bovendon 1200, Ancient Deeds (P.R.O.), Bovyndon 1200, Miss. Cart. E.P.N.S. suggests 'above the down' (OE bufan dune) or 'Bofa's down' (OE personal name Bofa).
3. **Flaunden**
   Flawendene 13c, Ancient Deeds (P.R.O.), Flawndene 1200, Miss. Cart., possibly 'Flaha's valley', OE pers. name Flaha, OE denu, 'valley'.
4. **Adeyfield**
   Possibly Ladyfield, a field-name on the site of Adeyfield, 1523 Rental Adeyfield 1615 Court Roll.
5. **Apsley**
   'prati de Apsele' – Apsley meadow, 1269 Min. Acc.
   'aespe OE – 'aspen tree.'   leah OE – 'a clearing'.
6. **Bennett's End**
   'district, quarter, or part of parish occupied by Bennett'. The term 'End' in Herts, Essex, and Middlesex names usually means 'district' and it does not necessarily signify 'land near a boundary'. Personal name, Robert Beneyt, 1269 Min. Acc.
7. **Bourne End**
   'district near spring or stream'
   le Bournend, 1357 Rental, OE burna, OE ende.
8. **Boxden**
   'box-tree valley'
   Boxdena, 1200 Miss. Cart. OE box, OE denu.
   Box trees were evidently abundant here, cf following names.

9. **Boxmoor**
'marshy wasteland by box trees'
Boxmoor Common, 1615 Court Roll. OE box, OE mor.

10. **Boxsted**
'box-tree homestead'
Boxhamstede, 1230 Pipe Roll, 1309 Charter Roll (P.R.O.)
Boxted, 1599 Subsidy Roll.OE box, OE hamstede.

11. **Bulstrode**
'bull marsh'
Bulestrode, 13c Ancient Deeds (P.R.O.). OE bula, OE strod.

12. **Buncefield**
Personal name, Peter Bunne, 1269 Min. Acc.

13. **Burymill End**
'district by manorial mill'
Burimelne, 1286 Ashridge Charter, Burmilne, c1290 Dugdale
Burry Millend, 1623 Land Revenue Misc. Books (P.R.O.)
OE burh, 'manor, manor house', OE myln, OE ende.

14. **Chaulden**
'chalk valley'
Chalkden, 1523 Rental. OE calc, OE denu.

15. **Cornerhall**
Cornerhall, 1523 Rental

16. **Cotterells**
Personal name, William Cotel, 1269 Min. Acc.
Part of Cotel's tenement was in this vicinity.

17. **Crouchfield**
'field by a wayside cross'
Crowchfeld, 1487 Court Roll. Robert de Cruce, 1314 Lay Subsidy, probably lived here. ME crouche, OE feld.

18. **Eastbrook Hay**
'enclosure east of the brook'
Estebroc, 1199 Cartae Antiquae. OE east, OE broc, OE(ge) hæg

19. **Felden**
'valley with cultivated land'
Felden, 1588 Halsey Deeds, Felddane, 1667 ib.
OE feld, OE denu.

20. **Fields End**
'district or corner containing cultivated land'
Feldende,1200 Miss. Cart. Early forms for 19 and 20 are difficult to keep apart. E.P.N.S. volume is here followed.

21. **Frogmore End**
'district by frog-marsh'
Froggemore, 1357 Rental, Frogmore Ende, 1650 Parl. Survey
OE frogga, OE mor.

22. **Gadebridge**

Gatebryge, 1491 Court Roll.

23. **Grovehill**

'hill by a wood or copse'
William de la Grave probably lived here; he is mentioned 1269 Min. Acc. OE græfe, OE hyll.

24. **Hammerfield**

Holmerfield, 1523 Rental, Homerfield, 1599 Court Roll, Hammerfield, 1681 Court Roll
hol. OE – 'a hollow', mere OE – 'a pond' or gemaere – 'a boundary'.

25. **Highstreet Green**

Highstreet, 1499 Court Roll.
straet OE – 'Roman or paved road'.

26. **Holtsmere End**

Holtesmer, Gesta Abb. 1380.
holt OE – 'a wood', gemaere – 'a boundary'.

27. **Howegrove**

'copse on a hill spur'
Hograva, 1272 Min. Acc. OE hoh, græfe.

28. **Leverstock Green**

Uncertain. Leveleystocke grene, 1551 Sidney Sussex College Documents, is earliest form given by E.P.N.S.

29. **Lockers**

Possibly from Magister Lucas, an important landholder in the 13th century, 1269 Min. Acc.
Lockyers 1491 Court Roll, Lookers 17th century Court Rolls.

30. **Lovetts End**

Personal name John Lovet 1367 I.P.M.

31. **Moor End**

Le More 1523 Rental Moor end, 1633 Court Roll.
the end or edge of Boxmoor.

32. **Nash Mills**

'mills at the ash tree'
Initial N is remnant of ME atten, 'at the', used in such names; it also gives rise to Noake, 'at the oak tree', elsewhere.
Asshemulle, c1300 St Albans Cartulary, Naysshmylle, 1437 Court Roll. OE æsc, OE myln.

33. **Piccott's End**

Personal name, Peter Picot, Pipe Roll 1204.

34. **Pouchen End**

Personal name, Pulchin, Lay Subsidy 1295.

35. **Roughdown**

'rough hill'

Rowdown, 1497 Court Roll. OE ruh, OE dun.

36. **St. Agnells**

From family name Aignell, confused at some period with St. Agnes. William Aignell is mentioned c1200, Miss Cart.

37. **Shantocks**

Probably a personal name. Court Roll 1594.

38. **Sheethanger**

Shotehanger, 1544 Patent Roll.

sceat OE – 'corner or projecting piece of land',

hangra OE – 'wood on s steep slope'.

39. **Two Waters**

'two rivers', meeting-place of rivers Gade and Bulbourne.

Tuewatirmelne, 1290 Dugdale. OE twegen, wæter.

40. **Venushill**

Veners hill 1523 Rental.

Personal name Alex le Venue 1269 Min. Acc.

41. **Warners End**

'district occupied by Warner family'

John Warner, 1609 Court Roll.

42. **Water End**

Court Roll, 1502.

43. **Westbrookhay**

'enclosure west of the brook'

Le Hay End, 1346 Assize Roll, West Hay, 1443 Close Roll, Westbrookhay, 1541 V.C.H. OE west , OE broc, OE (ge) hæg.

44. **Woodhall**

Wudehall, 1198 Cat. St. Giles.

wudu OE – 'a wood', hall OE – 'hall, large house'.

END NOTE

Hemel Hempstead. The first element is *Hæmele,* the name of the district in which the settlement occurred. First mentioned in the 8th century, this name probably means 'broken' (OE *hamol, hamel*). OE *hāmstede,* 'homestead, site of a dwelling' accounts for the second part of the name. The combined form *Hamelamestede* is used in the Domesday Book, and variants, e.g., Hamelhamsted, Hamelhampsted, and Hamelhamstud are found in the following centuries. A shorter form, Hemlamsted, occurs in 1339, further abbreviated to Hempsted by the sixteenth century. In recent times, *Hemel* has been replaced, though the second part has remained Hempstead and has not been restored to its Hampstead form.

INDEX

PREFACE TO THE HISTORY OF HEMEL HEMPSTEAD

This History of Hemel Hempstead owes its origin to the enthusiasm and interest of the first officers of the Hemel Hempstead Local History Society Mr. W. G. S. Crook, Honorary Freeman of the Borough and now President of the Society, and Mr. A. L. Wood, Secretary until shortly before his death in 1971 and formerly Borough Treasurer. The Society owes them both a deep debt of gratitude.

Mr. Wood had written a considerable section of the book himself and was just turning to the editing of it when he died, so it fell to Mrs. S. Yaxley to try to impose some common pattern on our diverse contributions. A work of this kind must inevitably reflect the different methods and approaches of the contributors, so editing is no easy task, but Mrs. Yaxley has tackled it in a very scholarly way and the Society thanks her most warmly. I am grateful, too, that no fewer than four former colleagues at Apsley Grammar School (now Longdean School, Hemel Hempstead) have contributed chapters.

This work could never have seen completion without the active encouragement of successive Mayors and Councils and especially of The Town Clerk, Mr. C. W. G. T. Kirk.

The Society could never have embarked on its publication without the generous guarantees given by the Borough Council and the Commission for the New Towns, whose help and support we most gratefully acknowledge.

Much more could have been written and more was, in fact, written, but the manuscript had to be abbreviated for publication. However it is our hope that this book is full enough and scholarly enough to stimulate the interests and to satisfy the curiosity of generations of Hemel Hempstedians in the history of their Town. May it lead them on to the fuller satisfaction that the study of the history of one's neighbourhood can provide, while those who have not time and inclination for further study, may see in the history of this one place a reflection of much of the history of England writ small.

Hemel Hempstead 1972.

V. J. Wrigley
Chairman, Hemel Hempstead
Local History Society

FOREWORD -

The need for a history of Hemel Hempstead was urged on the Society from a number of quarters, especially owing to the development of the Borough as a New Town under the New Towns Act. The newcomers whom the development had brought were interested in the town in which they had come to live, and the 'natives' (if that word may be used without giving offence) were anxious that the story and traditions of the neighbourhood should not be forgotten. The Society was pleased to embark on the venture and approached both the Borough Council and the Development Corporation for their views, and if these were favourable, for support. Both bodies were in favour and their support, financial and otherwise, was generous.

A team of contributors was formed and work started. Over the years changes took place in the personnel: some for various reasons were unable to carry on, and others having either left the district or suffered from illness were unable to complete their respective tasks, although their work was so far completed as to make the efforts of those who took over very much easier. In view of these and certain other factors it is understandable that the work took much longer than was originally expected. One of these factors was the amount of material found, in a variety of places.

In the beginning it was assumed that the work of the contributors could be so integrated as to form a continuous whole, but experience proved this to be impossible. Accordingly, and on the advice of authorities it was decided to leave the essays as written by the individual authors; this may have resulted in some overlapping and repetition on the one hand, and omission on the other. It is hoped that this will not adversely affect the interest and pleasure of the reader.

The narrative ends with the outbreak of war in 1939. The memory of those war years is still vivid with many, and the relative intimacy of local history could revive feelings which are best left to rest. The coming of the New Town brought drastic changes and the development involved is not yet complete. It was thought therefore that the history of the years after 1939 should form the subject of a separate and later study. However, we have included as a postscript a chapter on the coming of the New Town; this is by Mr. Kirk who is the Town Clerk and was intimately involved in the proceedings connected with the advent of the expansion of the town. So far as possible no reference has been made to living persons.

Spelling is always a problem, especially where there is such a variety as, for instance, in the name of the town. Except when actually quoting from documents modern spelling has been used. The area around St. Mary's Church has always been called 'the Town' both colloquially and in Legal and other documents; here the spelling 'Towne' has been used up to the eighteenth century.

To some there could be confusion about the High Street. Today this is the name of the old market street which forms the centre of the old shopping area around the church. In earlier days this was 'the Towne' and later the market street. The name 'High Street' was then applied to the old Roman road, coming from St. Albans, through Leverstock Green, to its junction with Redbourne Road. This was once the main entrance to the district but is so no longer and is now known as High Street Green.

One would like to acknowledge the help and assistance which have been given by organisations and individuals but they have been so numerous that it is a practical impossibility to list them all. All concerned are conscious of how much this help has contributed to the production of this work and would like their thanks to be extended to all who have been so helpful. Reference must however be made to the Borough Council and the Development Corporation (now the Commission for the New Towns) without whose support and financial aid this work could not have been carried out. The gratitude of all concerned is sincerely extended to the members and officers of those bodies.

Nor should be forgotten the inspiration and encouragement of the Chairman of the Society, Mr. W. G. S. Crook, as well as his many practical contributions to the various sections. To him is due great credit for his work in connection with local history in Hemel Hempstead, not only as Chairman but as author of so many articles which have aroused generally a keen interest in the town's story.

1971 A. L. Wood

CONTRIBUTORS

Brian Anthony Chaplin, M.A. (Cantab)

Dorothy Cromarty, M.A. (London).

Robert Cromarty, B.A. (Oxon.)

William George Seymor Crook, J.P. Mayor and Bailiff of Hemel Hempstead 1953 and 1955, Freeman of the Borough.

Charles William G. T. Kirk, O.B.E., Ll.B. (London), D.P.A. Solicitor, Town Clerk of Hemel Hempstead 1939 -

David S. Neal

Mary Gwennah Robinson, B.A. (London).

Arthur Leslie Wood, F.I.M.G.A., A.S.A.A. (Hons.), Diplomas in General and Local History, London University.

Valentine James Wrigley, M.A. (Oxon.)

Susan Yaxley, B.A. (London).

CONTENTS

LIST OF ILLUSTRATIONS

LIST OF MAPS AND PLANS

Figs. 1, 2, 3, 4, 5, 6, & 11 were redrawn by Mrs. D.A. Brown.

GENERAL LIST OF SOURCES

Abbreviations:– B.A. .... Borough Archives
P.C. .... Parish Chest
P.R.O. .... Public Record Office
H.R.O .... Hertfordshire County Record Office
L.R.O. .... Lincolnshire County Record Office
B.M. .... British Museum

Charter of 31 Henry VIII, B.A.
Inspeximus Charter of Charles II, B.A.
Bailiwick Minute Books & Accounts, B.A.
Parish Registers, P.C.
Church Terriers, P.C.
Churchwardens Accounts, P.C.
Vestry Order Books, P.C.
Poor Law Accounts, P.C.
Rental of 1523, (a post-1596 copy), P.C.
Early Proceedings of Chancery, P.R.O.
Proceedings in the Court of Requests, P.R.O.
Records of the Court of Exchequer, P.R.O.
Lay Subsidy Rolls, P.R.O.
Hearth Tax Returns, P.R.O.
Census Returns, P.R.O.
Halsey Papers, H.R.O.
Wills & Inventories, H.R.O , L.R.O. & Somerset House.
Quarter Sessions Records, H.R.O.
Smeathman Papers, H.R.O.
Agricultural Returns, Board of Trade, H.R.O.
Visitation Papers, L.R.O.
Hertfordshire and Hemel Hempstead Gazette, B.M.
Manor Court Rolls and Books, Duchy of Cornwall Office, London.
Acts of the Privy Council, P.R.O.
Calendar of State Papers Domestic.
Calendar of Patent Rolls.
Boxmoor Trust Records, H.R.O.

Secondary Sources

Victoria County History of Hertfordshire.
J. E. Cussans, 'History of Hertfordshire'.
Clutterbuck, 'History of Hertfordshire'.
Sir Henry Chauncy, 'Historical Antiquities of Hertfordshire'.
H. J. Todd, 'History of Ashridge'.
W. Urwick, 'Nonconformity in Hertfordshire'

ACKNOWLEDGEMENTS OF ILLUSTRATIONS

PLATE I	CHURCH COMMISSIONERS
PLATE II	DEPARTMENT OF THE ENVIRONMENT.
PLATE III	DEPARTMENT OF THE ENVIRONMENT.
PLATE IV	DEPARTMENT OF THE ENVIRONMENT.
PLATE V	DEPARTMENT OF THE ENVIRONMENT.
PLATE VI	DEPARTMENT OF THE ENVIRONMENT.
PLATE VII	LOCAL HISTORY & RECORDS SOCIETY
PLATE VIII	BOROUGH OF HEMEL HEMPSTEAD.
PLATE IX	JOHN DICKINSON & CO. LTD.
PLATE X	HEMEL HEMPSTEAD GAZETTE.
PLATE XI	BOROUGH OF HEMEL HEMPSTEAD.
PLATE XII	LOCAL HISTORY & RECORD SOCIETY.
PLATE XIII	BRITISH RAILWAYS BOARD.
PLATE XIV	HEMEL HEMPSTEAD GAZETTE.
PLATE XV	BOROUGH OF HEMEL HEMPSTEAD.
PLATE XVII	LOCAL HISTORY & RECORDS SOCIETY.
PLATE XVIII	LOCAL HISTORY & RECORDS SOCIETY.
PLATE XX	LOCAL HISTORY & RECORDS SOCIETY.
PLATE XXI	LOCAL HISTORY & RECORDS SOCIETY.
PLATE XXII	LOCAL HISTORY & RECORDS SOCIETY.
PLATE XXIII	LOCAL HISTORY & RECORDS SOCIETY.

PART 1

CHAPTER 1 - Topography & Settlement
Synopsis

A. THE VILLAGE OF HEMEL HEMPSTEAD

1. Major physical features and early habitation
2. Site of the Saxon village.
3. The valley flow - meadows.
4. " " " - mills.
5. Population in the Middle Ages.
6. Expansion.

B. THE RURAL LANDSCAPE

1. Early hamlet settlement.
2. Woods.
3. Site of Bovingdon.
4. " " Flaunden.
5. " " Felden & Boxhamstead.
6. Dells in relation to geology.
7. Agricultural Development.
8. Local Architecture & Geology.
9. Ponds & water supply & geology.
10. 'Greens' on the uplands.
11. Field patterns.
12. Agriculture in the 18th Century.
13. Expansion in the 19th Century.

At first glance there appears to be little left of the past in the rapidly changing brick-covered acres which make up contemporary Hemel Hempstead, but beyond the built-up area there remains a countryside which goes back to the Middle Ages. By-passed by the canal and main railway, the town escaped the nineteenth century's urban and industrial revolution which engulfed Watford and other better-placed Hertfordshire towns. Outside those areas of the parish which have been radically transformed since 1950, is a pattern of farms, fields and lanes, that had quietly evolved from the patchwork of commons, woods, wastes and open arable which are revealed in the earliest manorial documents. In the centuries from 1300 to 1800 change came very slowly; and the interlocking, irregularly-shaped fields and copses, the widely scattered farms and hamlets shown on the Tithe Map of 1843 had only gradually emerged.

The aim of this chapter will be to trace the origin of the major elements in the present landscape insofar as they have been influenced by the physical features of the area over which the parishes of Hemel Hempstead Bovingdon and Flaunden extend, and to show how the modern cultural pattern, which makes this area both distinctive and yet part of a greater Chiltern region, emerged from the changing relationship between man and the land. In other words, to portray Hemel Hempstead as a place, a particular pattern of buildings, roads, lanes, woods and fields, whilst succeeding chapters describe its inhabitants and its economy.

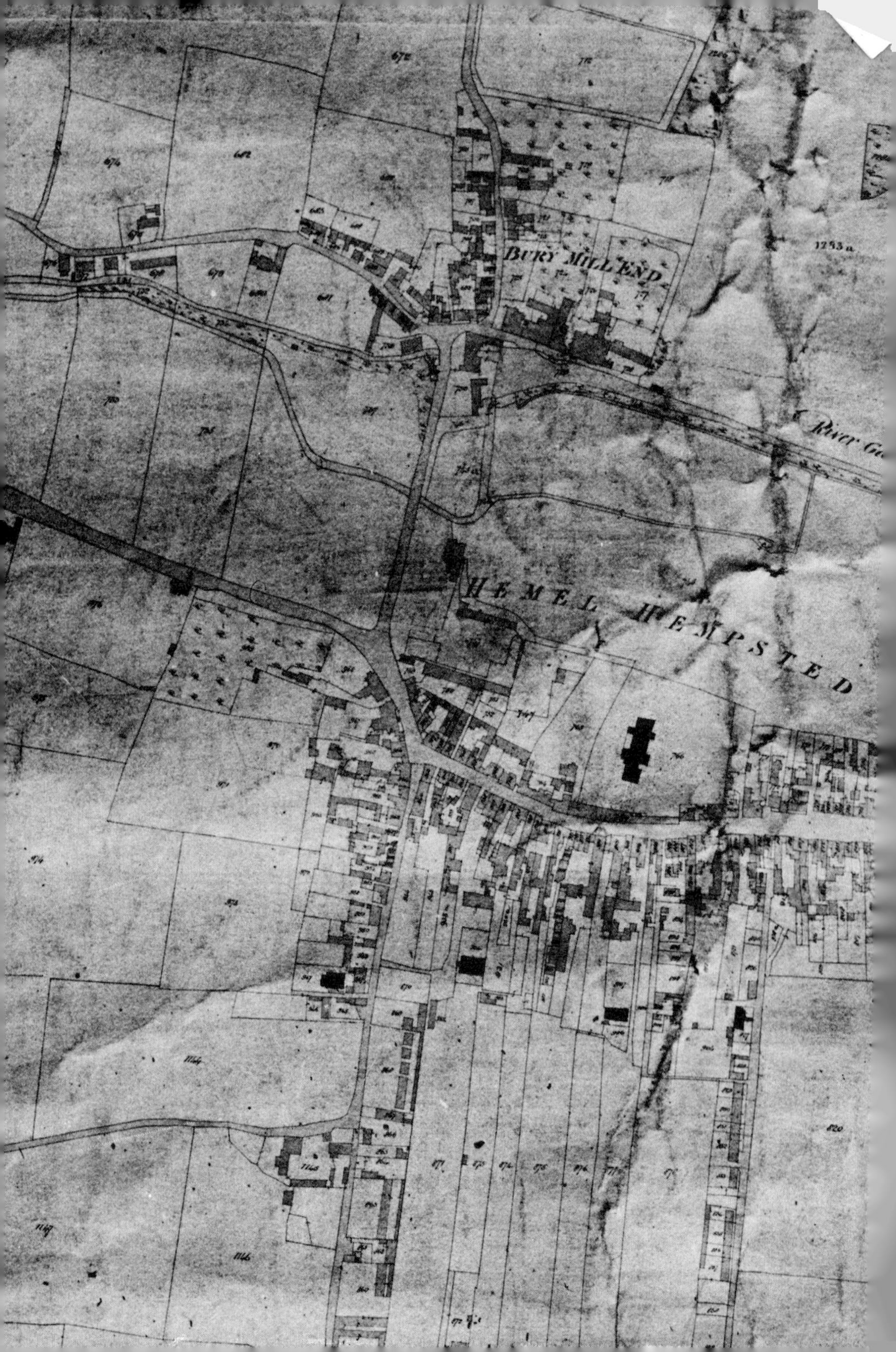
BURY MILL END
HEMEL HEMPSTED